ALL · IN · ONE

PgMP® Program Management Professional

EXAM GUIDE

Joseph Phillips

New York • Chicago • San Francisco • Lisbon
London • Madrid • Mexico City • Milan • New Delhi
San Juan • Seoul • Singapore • Sydney • Toronto

The McGraw·Hill Companies

Cataloging-in-Publication Data is on file with the Library of Congress

McGraw-Hill books are available at special quantity discounts to use as premiums and sales promotions, or for use in corporate training programs. To contact a special sales representative, please visit the Contact Us page at www.mhprofessional.com.

PgMP® Program Management Professional All-in-One Exam Guide

1234567890 FGR FGR 0198

ISBN: Book p/n 978-0-07-154929-5 and CD p/n 978-0-07-154930-1
of set 978-0-07-154927-1
MHID: Book p/n 0-07-154929-3 and CD p/n 0-07-154930-7
of set 0-07-154927-7

Sponsoring Editor Megg Morin	**Proofreader** Carolyn Welch
Editorial Supervisor Jody McKenzie	**Indexer** Claire Splan
Project Editor Carolyn Welch	**Production Supervisor** George Anderson
Acquisitions Coordinator Carly Stapleton	**Composition** Apollo Publishing Services
Technical Editor Julie Wiebell	**Art Director, Cover** Jeff Weeks
Copy Editor Bob Campbell	**Cover Designer** Patty Lee

For my brother Steve Phillips, a great friend and mentor.
If it weren't for Steve's encouragement to write when I was a little guy
I'd probably be selling t-shirts on the beach by now.
Thanks, Steve!

ABOUT THE AUTHOR

Joseph Phillips, PgMP, PMP, Project+, is the Director of Education for Project Seminars. He has managed and consulted on projects for industries, including technical, pharmaceutical, manufacturing, and architectural, among others. Phillips has served as a project management consultant for organizations creating project offices, maturity models, and best-practice standardization.

As a leader in adult education, Phillips has taught organizations how to successfully implement project management methodologies, information technology project management, risk management, and other courses. He has taught for Columbia University, University of Chicago, and Indiana University, among others. He is a certified technical trainer and has taught over 10,000 professionals. Phillips has contributed as an author or editor to more than 30 books on technology, careers, and project management.

Phillips is a member of the Project Management Institute (PMI) and is active in local project-management chapters. He has spoken on management, management certifications, and management methodologies at numerous trade shows, PMI chapter meetings, and employee conferences around the world. When not writing, teaching, or consulting, Phillips can be found behind a camera or on the working end of a fly rod. You can contact him through www.projectseminars.com.

About the Technical Editor

Julie Wiebell, MBA, PMP, CSM, is a project management consultant and part-time university instructor working on her Ph.D. in Applied Management and Decision Sciences with a specialization in Information Systems Management. Her project management experience spans more than 12 years working with private, public, nonprofit, Fortune 100, and IT consulting firms. She is also an active member of the Project Management Institute (PMI), including her local East Tennessee Chapter, and served as Secretary of the PMI Central Ohio Chapter Board of Directors from 2005-2006.

CONTENTS AT A GLANCE

CONTENTS

ACKNOWLEDGMENTS

Books, like programs and projects, are never done alone. I owe many thanks to my friends who have helped me write another book. I give a huge thank you to Megg Morin for her guidance, patience, wisdom, and encouragement. I must also thank Carolyn Welch for her expediency, goodwill, and reliability in her role as project manager. I give a tremendous thank you to my friend and confidant Julie Wiebell for her diligence, hard work, and technical editing abilities. She's done good work keeping me on track and accurate throughout all of the chapters herein. Carly Stapleton and Jennifer Housh both deserve whopping kudos for their support, encouragement, and organization—thanks!

I must also thank my friends Don "Coon Lee" Kunhle for being my running buddy, Greg Kirkland my golfing buddy, and Rick Gordon my sales guru. Fred and Carin McBroom are wonderful people who would love to have you to dinner. Martha Thieme, my neighbor and pal, thanks for the dinners, walks, and nightcaps. Reverend Courtney Richards deserves my many thanks for her laughter, ability to listen before speaking, and all-around encouragement. Thanks to Mike and Kelly Favory for our ongoing friendship, laughter, and companionship. David King, well, you're just getting thanked because I've known you since I was eight. And for my good friend and incredible artist Greg Huebner thanks for the great cigars, conversations, and wisdom (and no, you won't find a particular phrase that you always recommend in this book either). For my brothers Steve, Mark, Sam, and Ben thank you for your friendship and encouragement, and yes, this book will be your Christmas present. Finally, I offer my sincere gratitude to my readers and participants in my seminars. Thank you for allowing me to do what I love.

PART I

Program Management Framework

Earning the Program Management Professional (PgMP) Certification

In this chapter, you will
- Learn the qualifications for the Program Management Professional certification
- Verify your program management experience
- Complete your PgMP application
- Review the PgMP exam details
- Learn the Project Management Institute (PMI) rules for certification

The Project Management Institute has released its new certification, the Program Management Professional (PgMP) certification. This certification is to designate those professionals that qualify through their experience, program management knowledge, and reviews by professional peers as certified program managers. PgMPs are professionals whose day-to-day activities are beyond project management. These people dive into the world of program management and complete organizational vision, objectives, and big, fat accomplishments. Congratulations on your choice to pursue this certification!

As a certified program manager, you've demonstrated your ability to lead, manage, and direct programs. One of the primary goals of the certification is to display the certified program managers within your performing organization and in the international program and project management community. In other words, PgMPs are elite and will stand out from the crowd. Not everyone can be a program manager, and not every program manager will qualify as a PgMP. It's not an easy process to earn this PMI designation, but if it were easy, everyone would do it.

This book will do these things for you:

- Detail the PgMP exam objectives
- Explore the inner workings of program management
- Focus on the PgMP exam objectives

3

- Teach you how programs move through life cycles
- Review how programs and projects work together
- Tell you how to pass the PgMP exam, not just take the exam
- Offer "roadmaps" for each chapter
- Offer 620 practice exam questions (fun!)
- Not be boring (I'll do my best.)

This first chapter details how you, the PgMP candidate, can qualify for the PgMP certification process and all the hoops you'll have to jump through to get your certification. Of course, our pals at the Project Management Institute (PMI) can do whatever they want—and they often do. While the information regarding the exam particulars are correct at the time of this writing, I strongly encourage you to check with PMI's web site regarding exam particulars as you begin to prepare to pass your exam.

Qualifying for the PgMP Certification

Whoo-wee! There are a lot of things a PgMP candidate has to do in order to obtain this PMI certification. As Figure 1-1 depicts, you must take several steps to achieve this elite PMI certification. On one hand, the process to obtain the PgMP certification looks daunting and overwhelming, but on the other hand it's a good thing the certification is tough to get. A difficult-to-achieve certification keeps the market from being flooded with "certified" program managers and makes your certification even more valuable. Hmm—there's that old supply and demand rule creeping in.

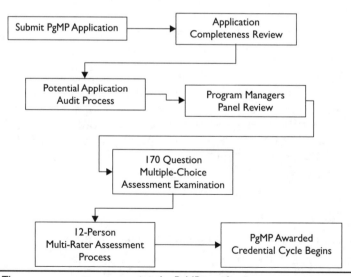

Figure 1-1   There are many steps to earning the PgMP certification.

In this early stage of preparing for your exam, take a moment and visit PMI's web site. You can, and should, download PMI's PgMP Credential Handbook through their web site: www.pmi.org. The handbook details all of the latest exam specifics, it's free, and it provides a sample PgMP testing score report. As with any program, it's imperative to have a vision of where your efforts are leading you.

The second thing you should do—well, at least consider doing—is to purchase a copy of PMI's fascinating book *The Standard for Program Management* (Project Management Institute, 2006). This whopper of a book (all of 104 pages cover-to-cover) is one of the study recommendations from PMI as your prep for your exam. Not to be overly critical, but I've read toaster manuals that were more interesting. You should also have a copy of the third edition of the *Guide to the Project Management Body of Knowledge* (Project Management Institute, 2004), also known as the PMBOK (pronounced Pim-bach).

I'll do my best in this odyssey to keep things factual, exact, and exam-targeted. From time to time, however, I'll reference these books, so you may want to have them handy for a quick reference. On the other hand, I won't get mad at you if you don't want to purchase another book but instead invest your dollars in beef jerky and grape sodas.

Identifying the Program Management Professional Candidate

You're probably assuming that because you manage programs and are reading this book you qualify as a PgMP candidate. Chances are you do, but let's keep in accord with our PMI pals. A PgMP candidate is a professional program manager who can, with little to no supervision, orchestrate multiple projects toward common organizational visions, goals, and business objectives. A PgMP candidate understands the program, the interaction of projects and their deliverables, and the required actions to move the program and its projects toward operational transfer.

As a program manager, you launch projects, write project charters, and assign project managers to your initiated projects. You rely on the project managers to plan, execute, monitor and control, and close each project as part of your program component. Each project is integrated with constituent projects that together serve the vision of the program. Program managers and project managers work toward a common goal and work to share, balance, and negotiate resources throughout the program and for the betterment of the program and its objectives.

Finally, PgMP candidates are competent as project managers and business leaders, and they are responsive to government requirements. PgMP candidates have advanced business skills in finance, international cultural sensitivity, communicating, negotiating, leading, directing, resolving conflicts, and integrating these attributes throughout the program's projects.

Basically, a PgMP candidate is a professional that's been steeped in the business world, understands the nuances of different cultures, knows how projects operate in different environments, is a quick study, and is responsive as projects ebb and flow. While this exam preparation book will show you the mechanics of program management, I think we all can agree that experience equates to a different type of knowledge. As Aristotle said, "What we learn to do, we learn by doing."

Screening for PgMP Qualifications

Alright, you know by now that not everyone can just waltz in and qualify for the PgMP certification. Let's take a look at the big picture of certification to identify just who can do the certification waltz. The first step, so to speak, in the certification process is to complete the lengthy and detailed PgMP certification application online through PMI's web site.

Once your application has been submitted, PMI will review it to check that it is complete. This process takes up to five business days if you submit your application online. PMI wants to make certain that your application includes all of the required experience and education documentation before the application moves deeper into the certification process. Do yourself a favor: double-check your application before submitting it.

Assuming that you have double-checked your application and it's complete and tidy, the application will move into the initial competence evaluation process. At this stage, a panel of program managers will review your application, your work experience, and your documented education. PMI may—Gulp!—choose your application for an audit. The audit process requires you and your referenced managers for your work experience to sign off on the deliverables and programs you said that you led. It's not fun.

Once your application makes it through the initial competence gauntlet, I mean review, you'll be approved to take the PgMP examination. That's the focus of this book—all of the terms, theories, philosophies, and stuff you'll need to know in order to pass the PgMP exam on your first attempt. Once you have received your *authorization to test* letter from PMI, you'll have one year to take the exam. I'm also sure you'll be thrilled to note that your status in the process moves from "applicant" to "candidate." That makes me all tingly just thinking about it.

Once you pass the grueling electronic examination, you're a PgMP, right? Nope. Next you'll have to submit yourself to a Multi-Rater Assessment review. PMI lovingly calls this step the MRA. This final evaluation is not unlike a 360-degree performance review. Here's the fun part, really: you get to choose the twelve participants that will assess your abilities as a program manager. PMI will send the participants of your selection a link to a web-based form where they'll have three weeks to complete the evaluation. The evaluation has 70 questions the participants will have to answer ranking from zero to five, with five being the strongest choice. Of the twelve participants, note that they can't all be your rugby mates from the local pub. You'll have to choose the following combination of reviews for your MRA:

- One supervisor
- Four peers (yeah, rugby!)
- Four direct reports
- Three professional references

Once you have successfully passed all three stages of the certification process, you'll be awarded the awesome Program Management Professional certification. Now the world will know that you are one tough hombre—well, at least when it comes to program management. As of this writing, it's still a mystery whether you'll receive a lapel pin or just a certificate suitable for framing.

Once you're certified as a PgMP, you'll have to maintain your certification by earning continuing certification credits. The Continuing Certification Requirements (CCR) program requires that the PgMP earns 60 Professional Development Units (PDUs) within the three-year certification cycle to maintain her certification status. If you're also a Project Management Professional (PMP), PMI will align the certification dates for both credentials and allow you to maintain both certifications at just 60 PDUs rather than 120 PDUs.

Verifying Your Program Management Professional Eligibility

When you apply to pass the PgMP examination, you'll have to document your months and hours of experience for the examination. Should your application get selected for an audit, you'll have to provide documentation in the form of transcripts and letters of verification that support your program management experience claims.

As part of the PgMP application process, you'll document your work through PMI's Program Management Experience Verification forms. Here's a catch, though: you'll have to document your project and program management experience and the deliverables your projects and programs have created. For every project and program you worked on you'll have to provide a contact, which will be used should you be selected for an audit. And in case you're wondering what'll happen if you're a PMP applying for this certification—you have to reenter your project management work experience on the PgMP application. Nothing is taken for granted.

There are two paths to qualify for the program management certification. Basically, it's with a degree or without a degree. With a Bachelor's degree, the global equivalent, or a higher degree you'll need all of the following within the last 15 years:

- Four years of project management work experience totaling 6,000 hours
- Four years of program management work experience totaling 6,000 hours

With only a high school diploma, Associate's degree, or the global equivalent you'll need all of the following within the last 15 years:

- Four years of project management work experience totaling 6,000 hours
- Seven years of program management work experience totaling 10,500 hours

Here is a bonus: If you've earned a bachelor's degree or better from a university accredited by PMI's fancy Global Accreditation Center for Project Management, you'll get 1,500 hours toward your program management experience hours. With this in your corner, for the math challenged, you'll only need 4,500 hours of program experience. You can check a list of PMI-accredited universities through PMI's web site.

Verifying Your Months of Program Management Experience

As you might expect, you'll need to verify the months you worked on each project and for each program. When you're doing the math for the number of months you've worked on projects, you must count unique, non-overlapping months of project management and program management experience. As Figure 1-2 demonstrates, Program A and Program B overlap each other for three months. In PMI's calculation, this isn't six months of program management experience, but only three months of program management experience. Program C, however, stands alone and that counts for three months of program management experience.

You are allowed, however, to include any program that may have started prior to the 15-year time limit, but work that was completed outside of the 15-year window is dismissed. In other words, you may only count unique, non-overlapping months of work experience within the 15-year window.

Documenting Your Hours of Experience

The second qualifier to apply for the PgMP examination is to document your number of hours of project and program management experience over the past 15 years. You remember everything you've done over the past 15 years, right? Well, specifically, you have to document your program and project management deliverables. For project management you'll have to account for 6,000 hours of experience in the following domains:

- Initiating the project
- Planning the project
- Executing the project
- Monitoring and controlling the project
- Closing the project

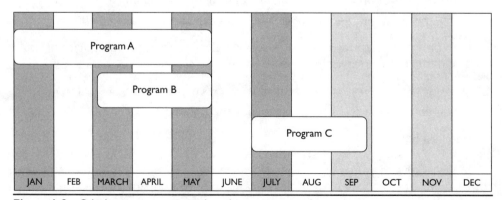

Figure 1-2 Calculate your experience based on unique months.

There is no requirement for a set number of hours in each of the domains, just some experience in each project management domain. You'll also need to document your hours of work experience in the six program management domains:

- Defining the program
- Initiating the program
- Planning the program
- Executing the program
- Controlling the program
- Closing the program

Just as with your project management experience, there's no special distribution of work experience in each domain—just some work experience is required. For example, if your experience includes program management experience across three programs, you don't need to have experience in all six domains for all three programs—just some total experience in all six domains.

Summing Your Experience

Get out your Big Chief Writing Pad and sharpen those number two pencils—you're now a writer! You'll be presented with questions during the application process about your experiences on the programs you have managed for your clients and organizations. The program management questions you will have to answer are somewhat generic, so you will have to reference the exact programs you documented and that you're currently using as a reference to answer PMI's queries about your experience. And don't worry; you don't have to write to the length of *War and Peace*; you're limited to 1,000 characters per question. So choose your words carefully—you do want to be concise and accurate. The responses you provide will be evaluated and will lead to the approval of the PMI program panel. I recommend you craft your responses in Microsoft Word and then copy and paste your responses into the PgMP application form rather than write your response from scratch and click Submit. I'm sure that as a program manager, you know the old adage: measure twice and cut once. And just in case you're wondering what 1,000 characters looks like, examine this paragraph. There are exactly 1,000 characters in this paragraph.

So who reads your responses? A panel of program managers will assess your experience and responses to these assessment questions. More on this in a moment.

Completing the PgMP Exam Application

You can complete the PgMP application online, or you can complete the application by paper and mail it in. You choose. Your choice, however, may determine how soon PMI responds. If you complete the application online, the preferred method, you'll receive a response requesting payment for the application within five business days of receipt.

If you oppose computers, technology, and the advancement of mankind and elect to complete the application through the paper format, your application may take up to 14 business days to be processed. If your application is submitted by a corporation, it may take up to 20 business days for PMI to respond.

Paying for the Application

PMI will respond to your application with a payment notification request. They want their money! The fees for the certification process are determined by the exam delivery method—either paper-based or the more common electronics-based. Basically, if you live within 300 kilometers (186.5 miles) of a Prometric computer–based testing center, you have to take the computer-based test. Here's the breakdown of the exam fees:

- Computer-based testing for PMI members in the U.S.: $1,500
- Computer-based testing for PMI members in Europe: €1,250
- Paper-based testing for PMI members in the U.S.: $1,200
- Paper-based testing for PMI members in Europe: €1,000

If you're not a PMI member, which is just silly, tack on an additional $300 in the U.S. or €250 elsewhere to your exam testing fees. It'll cost you $129 to join PMI plus a few dollars more if you elect to join your local PMI chapter—which is a good thing. As a PMI member, you get some goodies like magazine subscriptions, access to an electronic copy of the PMBOK, and more. You can ponder joining the PMI community through their web site. If you're a student or a retired person, you are eligible for a discount when you join PMI. PMI also has Special Interest Groups (SIGs) that you may want to consider joining—these cost extra, of course.

Getting a Refund

So you've coughed up some serious loot to apply to put yourself through the PgMP process. Let's say that you don't, according to PMI, qualify for the actual examination. What happens to your cash? Good news and bad news: you get some of it back, depending on how far along you are in the certification process.

For starters, you'll be refunded $700 if you fail the initial review of your application or if your application is selected for an audit and you don't pass. That's right, you've just lost $800 of your $1,500 just to submit an application, and you've nothing to show for it. Call me old-fashioned, but I think that sucks.

Next, let's say that you pass the application review and audit, and you're given the green light for sitting the PgMP exam. As you know, you have one year from the go-ahead by PMI to schedule and pass your PgMP exam. If you procrastinate, win the lottery, or just decide to heck with the exam, you can get a $700 refund as well. The catch is that you must request your refund at least one month prior to when your exam eligibility expires. If you ask for your refund within a month of your exam eligibility expiration, well, Ted Knight in the movie *Caddyshack* said it best, "You'll get nothing and like it."

Finally, if you pass the exam review, pass the PgMP exam, but decide you really don't want to participate in the Multi-Rater Assessment (MRA) process, you may ask for a refund of $350. You have to ask for the refund at least one month prior to when the eligibility period of the MRA assessment process is set to expire. Just to be perfectly clear on this point, you get to choose your MRA pool of people. Don't you think most people, after running the PMI marathon of completing the application, perhaps completing an audit, and passing the PgMP exam, would just go ahead and complete the MRA process? That's a rhetorical question. I suppose the lesson to be learned here is this: don't wait to choose your MRA pool, so you don't run out of time and have to forfeit $1,150.

Completing a PMI Audit Process

When you submit your application to PMI, you're basically agreeing that you'll participate in the application audit. Not every single application is audited, but every single application is susceptible to being audited. You won't know if your application is selected for audit until after you've paid for the examination process. It's kind of a surprise: you submit your application, PMI asks to be paid, and then—Wham-bam-thank-you ma'am—you're being audited.

You'll receive an e-mail announcing your luck and how you'll participate in the audit experience. You will have to provide copies of your diploma, autographs of your program and project supervisors, and other proof that all you wrote on your application is accurate. Until you comply and PMI agrees, you won't be able to continue on to the PgMP examination.

If you don't complete the audit, for whatever reason, or if you complete the audit process but it's considered a failure, PMI will allow a $700 refund of your application fee.

Submitting to the Review Panel

Once your application has been submitted and approved, and once you've paid the process fee, your application is then reviewed by a group of program managers. The program managers that participate in the review process have been identified by PMI as subject matter experts in the world of program management.

The program management panel is looking to verify that the PgMP applicant has truly met the requirements and is eligible for the project management certification. They want to see evidence that the program manager has worked with little supervision, coordinated the efforts of multiple projects toward a common goal, and served in ongoing operations toward a common organizational objective.

Should the applicant's experience not meet the expected standards of the program management review panel, a PMI Credential Associate will contact the applicant to bear the bad news. At this point, the applicant and the Credential Associate will discuss the application's shortcomings and how the applicant can provide additional information to move the credentialing process forward. Should the applicant fail the panel review, he or she can receive a $700 refund.

 NOTE The primary panel review process centers on the responses to the questions the applicant is asked during the application completion process. It will behoove you to provide full and concise answers to the questions during the initial application before the cheery Credential Associate contacts you.

PMI promises that each PgMP applicant's identity will remain anonymous during the panel review process to ensure a fair and unbiased assessment of each application.

Taking the Exam

Once you've successfully completed the panel review, you'll receive an e-mail from PMI that you're now eligible to take the multiple choice exam. You'll have one year from the date of this initial notification to actually schedule and complete the examination. Don't let a year fritter away—I've met PMP candidates that have procrastinated their way out of a certification, and I'm sure it'll happen with the PgMP folks, too. In Appendix C, I offer some practical advice to help you move past exam jitters and advice to help you focus on passing the exam.

Next you'll receive an official e-mail from PMI called the authorization to test letter. This e-mail will send you off to the Prometric testing web site, where you'll choose an exam site, schedule to pass your exam, and read all the testing center rules. You can visit www.prometric.com/pmi right now to get a glimpse of what to expect. If you're a PMP, you're already familiar with the warm and cozy testing environment—and the complimentary earplugs. Yes, earplugs—who wants to listen to Faulkner bang on his keyboard in the testing booth next to you?

Fair warning: these testing sites fill up quickly, so get out and schedule your exam as soon as possible. I've seen some exam candidates that have had to wait months to schedule a seat or travel to take an exam sooner rather than later. This is especially true if you wait to schedule your exam and your one-year eligibility period is dangerously close to expiring. In other words, don't wait to try to schedule your exam when you only have three days left in your eligibility period.

Reviewing the Exam Details

The heart of the certification process is your passing the PgMP exam. That's also the heart of this book. I'm not writing specifically on how to do program management bigger and better than ever before. My focus is simple: I want you to pass the exam on the first attempt. While the remainder of this book will delve into the specific process, inputs, and outputs of project management, let's start with a hard look at what you'll be tested on.

Examining the Exam

The PgMP examination has 170 multiple-choice questions—of which 20 questions are considered pretest questions. These pretest questions are sprinkled throughout your exam and do not count toward, or for that matter against, your exam score. These pretest questions are thrown into the pool to test their validity for future PgMP exams; in other words, you're a guinea pig for PMI. You won't know if you're answering a real, live test question or one of these phony questions, so you'll have to answer each exam question with the same effort and care.

For each test question, you'll choose one answer, and any question that's left unanswered is considered wrong. Lesson learned? Never leave a test item blank. Even if you don't know the answer, choose something and move on. You can mark test questions for review, move backward and forward in the software, and change your answers if you really want to. I strongly encourage people to never change their answers unless they have incredibly strong reasons to do so. Your first instinct is usually correct.

Once you enter the testing center and the exam process begins, you'll have 15 minutes to complete a tutorial on how to use the exam software. It's pretty easy business, but taking the tutorial ensures that you know how to use the mouse, select an answer, view an exam exhibit, and navigate through the software. Frankly, if you've ever played solitaire on your computer, you can use the exam software—it's not that difficult. However, take the tutorial. The tutorial is a free 15-minute window you can use to dump out all of your notes, formulas, and other important facts onto your scratch paper.

Once the tutorial session ends, you're into your four hours of exam time. The 15-minute tutorial does not eat into the time allotted for actual testing. You can stretch, take breaks, walk around, even do some tai chi if you want, but you cannot pause the timer once the exam begins. If you run out of time, any unanswered questions are considered wrong—so use your time wisely.

Having said that, in my experience teaching project management and program management boot camps I have seen most folks rush through their questions and fail to use their testing time wisely. I constantly remind participants, and now I remind you, that you do not get extra credits for getting done early. Take your time—you paid for all four hours of exam time, so use it all to your advantage. I recommend that you pace yourself at an easy minute per question; you'll still have over an hour for rest room visits and tai chi.

Mastering the Exam Domains

The PgMP examination has been written and tested by program management experts and is based on the generally accepted guidelines of program management, project management, and periodicals. PMI also reports that the exam questions are monitored through psychometric analysis. Ooh—doesn't that sound scary? It's just a fancy way of saying that the exam items and answers are reviewed in beta and live format for their accuracy, usefulness, and percentage of accurate and incorrect responses by testing candidates. It's all about the statistics of a question being answered incorrectly or correctly often enough.

The 170 exam questions are chunked into the following domains and percentages of the PgMP exam:

Domain	Percentage	Approximate Number of Questions
Defining the program	14%	24
Initiating the program	12%	20
Planning the program	20%	34
Executing the program	25%	42
Controlling the program	21%	36
Closing the program	8%	14

Obviously you're going to pick your study battles wisely. Each of these domains is composed of program management processes. I'll be referencing these domains and the processes that support them throughout the remainder of the book.

Reviewing the Exam Results

Once your four hours of test time are up—or you click the "end exam" button in the testing software—your score will calculated. It's the longest minute of your life while your exam questions are tabulated and your exam score is displayed. You'll also receive an embossed printed score report that will also indicate pass or fail status. You can also access your test score results through PMI's web-based certification system in about a week after your exam is over.

The passing score for the exam is coupled with the Multi-Rater Assessment (MRA) review, which I'll discuss next. You'll have to earn at least a 325 total to pass the PgMP certification process. You will receive a score report for the multiple-choice 170-question assessment exam and another for the MRA. You'll receive a PgMP score report where you'll see your proficiency level in each of the six program management domains ranked from below proficient to proficient.

Retaking the PgMP Examination

You can, if needed, take the PgMP assessment exam up to three times within the one-year period from your authorization to test letter. This is another reason why you want to be cautious with your timing of scheduling your first PgMP exam attempt. If you wait to schedule your exam toward the end of your one-year window and don't pass the exam, you may miss the opportunity to retake the exam, because you're out of time. That's right—you have one year to pass the exam from the date of test authorization, not one year just to schedule it.

Imagine that a friend of yours, not you of course, fails the exam three consecutive times within his one-year time period. Your friend now will have to wait a year before he can start the entire certification process over. The same is true if your friend never takes the exam at all within his one-year eligibility period. If he snoozes, he loses.

There are fees associated with the reexamination process:

- Computer-based testing for a PMI member is $500 or €420
- Computer-based testing for a non-PMI member is $600 or €500
- Paper-based testing for a PMI member is $400 or €335
- Paper-based testing for a non-PMI member is $500 or €420

Your goal, of course, is to focus on passing the examination the first time and to avoid thinking about having to take the exam more than once. I've put these fees here just so that you can tell your colleagues who weren't as wise as you and who didn't purchase this book.

Considering Special Exam Conditions

The folks at PMI are reasonable people. A PgMP candidate may request that the exam process be modified due to handicaps, disabilities, or other conditions that could impair a candidate's ability to complete the exam as normally offered. During the online exam application, candidates are given an opportunity to document their needs. If a candidate is using the paper-based application, the form allows candidates to document their requests therein. In either instance, requests for special accommodations must include supporting medical or other documentation to validate the request.

Adhering to the Security Rules

When you enter the Prometric testing center, you'll be provided with two pencils, a non-programmable calculator, and six sheets of scratch paper. You can use these to help calculate exam questions, deduce questions, and draw pictures of your favorite project manager. All of these materials, however, must be returned to the exam proctor at the testing center. You are not allowed to keep any of the scratch paper once your exam is over. In other words, you can't smuggle any of the questions and answers out of the testing center.

If you've never been in a Prometric testing center, it's nothing to really worry about. The centers in which I've taken exams present a friendly, professional, and typically calm and quiet environment. My testing centers were just a big room with half-sized cubicles. In each cubicle there is a computer where the electronics-based PgMP exam has been installed. Once you've checked into the center, an exam proctor will explain the rules and escort you to your assigned testing cubicle.

Learning from Others

Every time I have passed an exam at a Prometric facility I've been offered either headphones or ear plugs. Both are to silence out any minimal noise from your fellow testers—neither are for listening to music. You aren't allowed to bring anything into the testing center with you. This includes purses, coats, cell phones, jackets, drinks, MP3 players—nothing. I recommend that you dress in layers rather than bringing your wool parka along with you. The testing center will assign you a locker to stash your belongings in, but you cannot open the locker until you're all done with the examination.

Most people, when they're in the center, are well behaved and focused on passing their exam. Any obnoxious behavior will result in a Prometric proctor immediately booting the culprit from the facility. Any PgMP candidates expelled from the testing center for a disruption will forfeit all of their monies for the exam, will have their exam score canceled, and may be subject to PMI refusing a reexamination opportunity.

I took my PMP examination in Chicago. During my test a man near me completely flipped out. He slammed the keyboard on the desk a few times, said a few choice words I can't print here, and generally made a ruckus of the testing center. A proctor zipped into the room and tried her best to usher the irate man out. Apparently, as I learned later, he missed passing his exam by one point. The point of my experience? I wear the earplugs.

As you might expect, no visitors can join you in the testing center. While this may seem obvious, it's a subtle way of saying, "Don't even think about bringing your three-year-old child to the exam with you." Can you imagine that while you're sweating the inner workings of a question centering on earned value management, little Suzie is roaming the aisles of the testing center? Not gonna happen.

Another PMI security rule is that your exam score is only for you—no one else. Your examination score will remain private. Unless someone gets a court order and PMI is lawfully required to release your exam score, no one will know that you did or did not score 100 percent on the exam. You can, if you really want, contact PMI and give them written permission to release your exam score to a specific party.

Keep in mind that while the exam is simply a pass or fail examination, your status as a PgMP (or a holder of any other PMI credentials) is publicly available through the PMI registry of certified project managers and program managers. You can view and search this registry whenever you like through PMI's web site.

Identifying Yourself to the Testing Center

Have you ever heard the story about the really smart college student that would "rent" his brain out to other college kids and take exams for them? That possibility won't happen for PgMP candidates. (Don't e-mail me and ask—I won't even try to do it. Usually.)

When you check into the testing center, you'll have to provide two pieces of identification. The first must be a government-issued identification that includes both your photo and your signature. Should your government-issued ID not include both a photo and a signature, your second form of ID must provide whichever is missing from the government-issued identification.

Here's a big warning: your identification must exactly match the name on your authorization to test letter. Always use your full name as it appears on your identification for all forms when communicating with PMI. So, if your identification lists your name as Gaylord Gordon, but you've been going by Rick, your PMI authorization to test letter and your identification won't match and you won't be allowed into the testing center.

You can use the following as your first form of identification, assuming the ID is valid:

- Driver's license
- Passport
- Military ID card
- National identification card

Any of the following can be used as your secondary form of identification, again assuming its validity:

- Employee ID card
- Credit card with signature
- Bank (ATM) card

If, for whatever reason, you cannot provide the required identification and you are refused entry to the examination, you'll have to submit an application to retake the examination. This means, of course, that you will also have to pay the reexamination fee. Obviously it's in your best interest, Gaylord, to be thorough and accurate in identifying yourself to PMI and Prometric from the start.

Canceling Your Examination

Let's say you got wrapped up in a huge program and just haven't had the time to commit to study for your exam. Or you ate some bad sushi and are seeing things you ate in eighth grade. Or a demand from work won't let you escape a meeting. Any of these unfortunate events will cause you to have to cancel your PgMP examination.

In order to cancel your exam and reschedule to pass it at a later date, you must contact Prometric at the phone number in your PMI authorization to test letter. You must make this cancellation by noon two days prior to when your exam is slated to start. If your exam is to begin on a Monday and you need to cancel, you must call Prometric by Thursday noon. You can, if your sick-sushi self will allow, cancel your exam online through Prometric's web site.

NOTE   I love the Internet as much as the next guy, but for an exam cancellation I recommend a phone call so that you've got a verbal confirmation of the cancellation.

Should you be one of those folks who are taking the paper-based examination rather than the computer-based exam and you need to cancel, you have more stringent rules. You have to cancel your paper-based exam 35 calendar days from the exam start date. You may make this cancellation by e-mailing PMI at pbtexams@pmi.org and explaining your situation. In your explanation and cancellation you must include your

- Full name
- PMI ID number
- Group ID number
- Testing location

You can retrieve all of this information through the paper-based examination sponsor or through www.prometric.com/pmi.

Candidates that do not cancel their exams in the PMI timelines or don't show for their schedule examination lose their testing fee and will have to reapply to take the exam at a later date. All of these rules apply even if you want to reschedule your exam for a closer or later time. Once you're in the designated cancellation window, you're pretty much stuck.

There are, however, extenuating circumstances that may warrant an exception to the rules: a medical emergency, a death in the family, an accident of some dreadful sort. All of these instances, and probably others, need to be documented through an accident report, death certificate (am I the only one thinking of the character George in the television comedy series *Seinfeld*?), or a medical statement verifying your claim. Along with your documentation you'll need to resubmit a reexamination form—all within 72 hours of the scheduled exam date.

I like PMI, really I do, but if I've just been rear-ended on my way to my grandma's funeral and I get a sudden attack of appendicitis the day before my PgMP exam, am I really going to have time or interest in gathering accident reports, a death certificate, and a statement from Dr. Howard? And then there's the form to complete within the next three days. For these wild scenarios the candidate should contact PMI and provide the required information as soon as possible.

PMI will review each case and make a decision as to the extenuating circumstance and make a judgment as to whether the candidate should be allowed to take the examination. Work-related activities are not considered a valid reason for missing the examination. If you are granted permission to retake the exam by PMI, you'll have one year to complete the retake.

Participating in the Multi-Rater Assessment (MRA)

Once you've passed the multiple-choice PgMP exam—congratulations!—PMI will commence the MRA portion of the certification process. When you complete your initial application to become a PgMP, you'll have to provide the contact information for twelve of your favorite and most loyal colleagues. PMI will contact these folks via e-mail and will link them to a web-based performance evaluation of your abilities as a program manager.

Your twelve colleagues that participate in this review have to consist of

- One supervisor
- Four peers
- Four direct reports
- Three professional references

Ideally, these twelve people have seen you in action as program manager. These raters should be able to gauge your performance and abilities as a program manager and provide accurate feedback on your program management performance. Your raters should be fluent in English, as the MRA is offered only in English.

Once your raters have received the e-mail from PMI asking them to participate, they'll have three weeks to complete their assessment. The MRA questionnaire has 70 statements about program management and you, the PgMP candidate. The rater will rank your performance in relation to each statement from zero to five. Zero means the rater has no basis to judge your performance, while a score of five means you're a superhero in program management.

Reassessing the Multi-Raters

If, for some bizarre reason, you do not pass the Multi-Rater Assessment portion of your competency review, you have to wait one year before you can take the MRA portion of the certification process again. You'll receive a score report of how the MRA raters evaluated you, and PMI encourages you to use this report to better yourself as a program manager.

NOTE Again, I like PMI; I think they're doing a wonderful job certifying folks and promoting the business of program management and project management. But can you imagine how steamed a PgMP candidate would be to jump through all the hoops of this certification only to have their own colleagues cause them to fail? Lesson learned? Convey to your MRA raters the importance and consequence of their assessment of your examination. You don't need a joker fooling around with ones and twos on this assessment.

After the one-year cooling-off period you may restart the MRA process again with the same (ha-ha) reviewers or choose brand new ones. The fee for starting the MRA process again is $500. You have six months to start the MRA process or all of your PgMP certification efforts are dismissed, and you'll have to start the entire PgMP process over again.

Now here's something fun: if you pass the MRA process on the second attempt, you are officially certified as a PgMP. If you don't pass the MRA on the second attempt, however, you'll have to wait another year. After this second one-year cooling-off period, however, you're back to square one: you must start the entire PgMP certification process all over.

Using the MRA as a Development Tool

If a friend of yours fails the PgMP certification exam, she can still take the MRA assessment if she'd like to. The idea, and it's a nice idea, is that your friend can receive a performance review from the twelve colleagues and use their findings to better herself as a program manager.

The gotcha here, though, is if your friend doesn't pass the exam but still moves onto the MRA process, she does not have the option to retake the examination. She's basically bowed out of the certification process and has forfeited all time and monies invested in the certification attempt. Tell your friend to buy this book and then pass that exam!

Abiding by the PMI Certification Policies

I've just a few final words of advice about the PgMP and dealing with PMI. Basically, there is no shortcut around the PMI rules, and you don't want there to be one. One of the primary reasons PMI has made this certification so stringent and so tough to achieve is to keep the value of the certification lofty. If this certification were easy to get, it wouldn't amount to much more than a spark in your self-esteem. This hard-to-earn certification carries prestige, ability, experience, and creditability.

Reviewing Your Exam Score

Once your assessment examination is over—and only if you've failed—you'll have an opportunity to review the report. You'll also have the opportunity to review the score as a result of your Multi-Rater Assessment. In other words, if you pass the PgMP assessment exam and you pass the MRA process, you'll simply be awarded the PgMP and there's nothing more to review. As Figure 1-3 demonstrates, your exam consists of six domains.

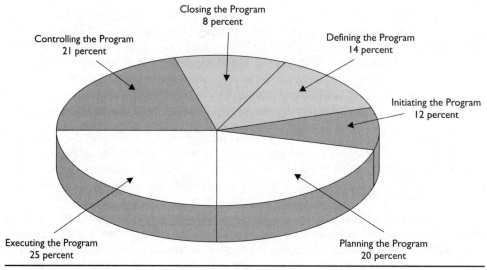

Figure 1-3   The PgMP exam consists of six domains.

Any PgMP candidate that fails the exam or the MRA will only see a proficiency level that equates to the exam score. The report will not show any questions that were answered incorrectly or percentages of questions answered correctly. Any proficiency level lower than the required 325 equates to a failing grade on the PgMP program. Sorry.

Your exam report will include all of the following information:

- Candidate's name
- PMI membership ID
- Your exam registration number
- The testing center where the exam was hosted
- Your score and overall score (you have to beat 325 or your overall score is fail)
- A proficiency rating of below proficient, moderately proficient, or proficient for each of the six domains:
  - Defining the program
  - Initiating the program
  - Planning the program
  - Executing the program
  - Controlling the program
  - Closing the program

The exam score report does not tell you how many questions you answered correctly or incorrectly in each category—just a proficiency rating. You'll receive a copy of the exam report that the Prometric center will emboss with their official seal, and it's yours to keep—suitable for framing.

Appealing a PMI Decision

You can, if you really feel the need to, appeal PMI's decision not to certify you as a program manager. For example, if your application to the PgMP process was declined, or you failed the PgMP certification examination, or your group of multi-raters didn't give you a good review, you can challenge the PMI decision for whatever reason you like.

Of course PMI is the certifying and governing body of their certifications, so they can pretty much do whatever they want with their certifications. If you want to challenge any PMI decision, you'll have to contact the PMI Certification Program Department in writing and plead your case. It's up to PMI's Certification Governance Council to determine if you deserve another shot at the title, Rocky.

Maintaining Your Certification

Once you're certified as a PgMP, you'll have to maintain your certification through the accruement of continuing education hours—more commonly known in the PMI world as Professional Development Units (PDUs). Your certification cycle as a PgMP will last for three years. In order to maintain the certification, you'll need 60 PDUs within your three-year time frame. The requirement to obtain PDUs serves several purposes:

- It ensures ongoing development of program managers.
- It provides ongoing learning opportunities for program managers.
- It standardizes the amount of ongoing education for all PgMPs.
- It gets you involved in the PMI community.

If you're both a PgMP and a PMP, PMI will align both credentials for you and you'll only have to report 60 PDUs total, not 60 for each certification. When you complete your PgMP application, you'll get to choose to keep your existing PMP certification cycle or align everything with your new PgMP certification date. In other words, your PMP and PgMP will end at the same time, and you'll have to maintain both by earning 60 PDUs in the cycle. You'll want to examine your PMP transcript to see how many PDUs you've reported and to determine if it's wiser to complete the current PMP credential cycle or move both certifications together and earn your 60 PDUs over the next three years.

It's not hard to earn PDUs. Join your local PMI chapter, attend their monthly meetings, and go to their classes and events. You can also write articles for trade journals, local chapter newsletters, or project management books (ahem, thank you very much). You can volunteer to help at PMI events, and more. Check out PMI's web site for details on what counts, and doesn't count, toward your PDUs. You'll also use PMI's web site to report the PDUs you've earned.

In addition to earning your 60 PDUs every three years, you have a renewal fee for the PgMP certification in the third year of your certification. If you're a PMI member, the fee is $60; for nonmembers the fee is $150. Cough it up.

Agreeing to the PMI Terms

When you complete your PMI application, you'll have to sign a statement that swears you'll be good and live by the terms and conditions of PMI for the PgMP program.

You'll have to agree that you will keep the contents of the exam confidential and that you won't share any specific question information with anyone.

The agreement between you and PMI requires that any inaccurate information on your application, accidental or not, may lead to further investigation from PMI. Their investigation could result in dismissal from all certification programs.

PMI requires that you report any matters, legal proceedings, lawsuits, settlements, or complaints related to your ability to serve as a PMI PgMP that have already happened at the time of your application. In addition, should any new unpleasantness occur, you're required to report the new actions and conditions to PMI within 60 days of the occurrence. This includes felony criminal charges, convictions, plea agreements, and any other criminal charges relating to acts of dishonesty or unethical behavior.

This agreement confirms that you will participate in any audit by PMI and that PMI may contact the individuals, agencies, and organizations that you reference in your application. Your application and all supporting information you provide to PMI is now their property. Don't expect to receive anything you submit to PMI back; never send them original documents, but crisp clean photocopies only.

You also agree that you will live and abide by the PMI Code of Ethics. You can download a free copy of the six-page Code of Ethics through PMI's web site. The PgMP examination does not test you on the Code of Ethics, but for good measure you should read the code and agree to manage accordingly. I've also included, in Appendix A, a detailed explanation of the Code of Ethics and its mysteries.

Chapter Summary

The process of earning your PgMP certification is not an easy or quick one. The strenuous process to apply for the certification, and the cost, may be enough to filter out applicants who are questionable in their program management experiences. There are a lot of challenges on the road to the PgMP certification:

- Qualify for the examination based on your education and experience.
- Pay for the PgMP certification:
  - Computer-based testing for PMI members in the U.S.: $1,500
  - Computer-based testing for PMI members in Europe: €1,250
  - Paper-based testing for PMI members in the U.S.: $1,200
  - Paper-based testing for PMI members in Europe: €1,000
- Gain approval for your application by a group of PMI-based program managers.
- Potentially have your education and reported program management experience audited.
- Pass the PgMP multiple-choice certification exam.
- Pass the 12-person Multi-Rater Assessment (MRA).
- Maintain your PgMP certification, once you have earned it, by earning 60 PDUs within a three-year certification cycle.

The remainder of this book focuses only on the multiple-choice assessment exam. You're on your own to document your program management experience and education, but I'll help as much as I can with the program management terminology, processes, inputs and outputs, and exam nuances that may trip you up.

The focus of this book is how to pass your PgMP examination, not how to do program management. Certainly the information I'll share herein is based on best practices. The good news is that the PgMP examination and the practice questions I've written in this book are isolated. You only have to worry about politics, feelings, and conditions that are documented in the exam question; don't be tempted to compare how silly things may be in the question compared to the peaceful world your programs operate in (or vice versa). Just answer the question and move on. Pass your PgMP, and then it's back to the real, though imperfect, world.

Key Terms

Application audit   A review of the accuracy of the reported education and program management experience the PgMP applicant has reported to PMI.

Authorization to test letter   A letter from PMI to the PgMP candidate with the Prometric testing center information, instructions for scheduling an examination, and approval of the PgMP candidate's application for certification.

Closing the program   A program management process group that uses select processes, inputs, tools, and techniques to create outputs that lead to the closure of the entire program, program projects, or portions of the program as needed.

Continuing certification requirements   PgMPs are required to earn 60 professional development units (PDUs) per three-year certification cycle.

Controlling the program   A program management process group that uses select processes, inputs, tools, and techniques to create outputs to monitor and control varying aspects of the program and its constituent components.

Defining the program   A program management process group that uses select processes, inputs, tools, and techniques to create outputs to define the goals, vision, and business objectives of the entire program.

Executing the program   A program management process group that uses select processes, inputs, tools, and techniques to create outputs that lead to the execution of the entire program, program projects, or portions of the program as needed.

Initiating the program   A program management process group that uses select processes, inputs, tools, and techniques to create outputs that lead to the initiation of the entire program.

Multi-Rater Assessment (MRA)   An assessment by twelve colleagues of the PgMP candidate. Raters consist of one supervisor, four peers, four direct reports, and three professional references. Raters will assess the PgMP candidate's ability to lead programs.

PgMP multiple-choice assessment exam   A 170-question examination on the skills and concepts of program management. The exam is administered through a Prometric testing center and lasts four hours.

Planning the program   A program management process group that uses select processes, inputs, tools, and techniques to create outputs that lead to the effective planning of the entire program.

PMI Credential Associate   A PMI representative that may contact the PgMP applicant to discuss the candidate's failure to meet the requirements of the PgMP certification process. The PMI Credential Associate and the PgMP applicant may discuss what additional information is needed on the application for the certification process to continue.

Professional Development Unit (PDU)   One hour of PMI-approved continuing education, knowledge base contribution, or program management volunteer work equates to one PDU. Each PgMP is required to earn 60 PDUs per three-year certification cycle.

Program Management Professional (PgMP)   A PMI-certified program manager who has exhibited adequate program management experience and education, passed a multiple-choice examination and a Multi-Rater Assessment, and is in good standing with PMI.

Program management review panel   A collection of PMI-sponsored program managers that will review program management applicants to determine if an applicant should be approved, audited, or declined access to the certification process.

Project Management Institute (PMI)   A global advocate for the profession of project management. PMI is the certifying body for the Certified Associate in Project Management (CAPM), Project Management Professional (PMP), and Program Management Professional (PgMP) certifications. The not-for-profit organization was founded in 1969 and is based in Newton Square, Pennsylvania.

Project Management Professional (PMP)   A project manager who has exhibited educational and project management experience and has passed a 200-question project management assessment exam.

Prometric Testing Center   A professionally monitored and proctored examination facility where PMI, and other organizations, require their certification candidates to take their assessment examinations.

 NOTE   At the end of each chapter I've written 20 questions pertaining to the content of the chapter. I've written the questions to emulate the style and trickiness of the actual examination without revealing any specific examination content. In this first chapter, I've written the 20 questions, though you won't be tested on any of the information I've shared in this chapter. Use these Chapter 1 questions as an opportunity to stretch and use those test-taking parts of your brain that may have been shut off for a while. Finally, on the CD I've included an Excel file called "Exam Scores" that can help you track your strengths, weakness, opportunities, and threats for all of the exam objectives.

Questions

1. You are preparing to pass your PgMP certification exam. In addition to this wonderful book, what PMI publication, specific to program management, can help you prepare for the PgMP certification?

   A. *The Standard for Program Management*

   B. *The Project Management Body of Knowledge*

   C. *The Guide to the Project Management Body of Knowledge*

   D. *Out of the Crisis* by W. Edwards Deming

2. How long does it take for PMI to advance your PgMP application onto the program management review panel to review your responses, experience, and education if you use the web-based application?

   A. 24 hours

   B. 5 days

   C. 6 months

   D. 30 days

3. When does your status move from PgMP applicant to PgMP candidate?

   A. Applicant and candidate are the same thing, so it does not matter

   B. After the Multi-Rater Assessment review

   C. When you receive your authorization to test letter

   D. When you have passed the PgMP multiple-choice examination, but you have not yet completed the MRA process

4. All of the following are required to be involved in the Multi-Rater Assessment process except for which one?

   A. Supervisor

   B. Professional reference

   C. PMI-certified PMP

   D. Direct report

5. If you are certified as a PgMP and are already certified as a PMP, how many Professional Development Units do you have to accrue to maintain both certifications?

   A. 120 for each certification title

   B. 60 for each certification title

   C. 60, as the PMP title will be superseded by the PgMP title

   D. 60 PDUs total—both certifications can share the PDUs

6. Jane is applying for the PgMP certification. Jane has an Associate's degree and many certifications. How many hours of program management experience must Jane have in order to qualify for the PgMP certification process?

   A. 6,000 hours

   B. 10,500 hours

   C. 1,600 hours

   D. 7,000 hours

7. Martha has a Bachelor's degree from a university that is indeed accredited from PMI's Global Accreditation Center for Project Management. How many hours does she earn for this degree toward her PgMP?

   A. 4,500 hours

   B. 1,500 hours

   C. 6,000 hours

   D. None—she must still have the total 7,000 hours of program management experience

8. All of the following are a domain of project management except for which one?

   A. Closing the project

   B. Estimating the project

   C. Monitoring and controlling the project

   D. Initiating the project

9. You are completing the PgMP application and must show your experience in each of the program management domains. How many hours must be reflected in each of the program management domains?

   A. There is no set amount of time that must be spent in each domain.

   B. You are required to have at least 1,500 hours of experience in each domain.

   C. You are required to have at least 1,000 hours of experience in each domain.

   D. You are required to have at least 1,200 hours of experience in each domain.

10. What is the cost of the computer-based PgMP examination for a PMI member?

    A. $329

    B. $1,500

    C. $1,250

    D. $1,200

11. Zoe has applied for the PgMP certification process. Her application was audited by PMI, and it was deemed that she did not have enough program management experience to qualify to move on to the multiple-choice examination. How much of a refund can Zoe expect to receive from PMI?

    A. $1,150

    B. $1,500

C. $700

D. $750

12. You have received from PMI the authorization to test letter. The letter informs you of the testing process, Prometric's telephone number, and other relevant test information. Your boss, Gaylord Gordon, asks you how long you have to pass the exam. What is your answer?

   A. One month from the date of the letter

   B. One year from the date of your application submission

   C. One year from the date of the authorization to test letter

   D. Three years from the date of your application submission

13. How many questions are on the PgMP examination?

   A. 150 questions

   B. 200 questions

   C. 70 questions

   D. 170 questions

14. Howard has entered the Prometric testing center and has just completed the15-minute tutorial on how to use the Prometric testing software for his PgMP certification exam. What is the maximum amount of time that Howard will have to complete all of the exam questions if he wants to reserve a 20-minute window for rest room breaks and tai chi?

   A. 3 hours and 40 minutes

   B. 3 hours and 10 minutes

   C. 2 hours and 40 minutes

   D. 3 hours and 25 minutes

15. Which program management domain equates to the largest percentage of the PgMP examination?

   A. Planning the program

   B. Executing the program

   C. Controlling the program

   D. Defining the program

16. Fred is not happy. He has just failed his PgMP examination. How many more times may Fred take the PgMP examination this year?

   A. None; Fred must wait one year before he can take the examination again.

   B. One; Fred is allowed to take the PgMP two times within one year.

   C. Three; Fred is allowed to take the PgMP three times within one year.

   D. As many as needed; Fred may take the exam as many times as he likes, but he'll have to pay the reexamination fee each time.

17. How much will Fred have to pay for the computer-based version of the PgMP reexamination if he's a PMI member?

    A. $500 for each reexamination

    B. $600 for each reexamination

    C. $400 for each reexamination

    D. $550 for each reexamination

18. All of the following cannot be used as your primary source of identification when checking into the Prometric Testing Center except for which one?

    A. Utility bill

    B. National identification card

    C. Credit card statement

    D. Authorization to test letter from PMI

19. Alice is scheduled to take her PgMP examination next week. To her dismay, a family emergency has happened, and she'll have to fly home to Sheboygan, Wisconsin, and will likely miss her exam. What's the latest time Alice can reschedule her examination without facing a penalty?

    A. 24 hours prior to her scheduled exam start date

    B. 72 hours prior to her scheduled exam start date

    C. By noon two business days prior to her scheduled exam start date

    D. By Thursday the week prior to her scheduled exam start date

20. You've passed the PgMP certification exam, and the last step is the completion of the MRA by your colleagues. PMI has contacted the 12 individuals you've referenced and invited them to complete the 70-question survey. How long do the MRA participants have to complete the survey?

    A. One week

    B. Two weeks

    C. Three weeks

    D. Four weeks

Questions and Answers

1. You are preparing to pass your PgMP certification exam. In addition to this wonderful book, what PMI publication, specific to program management, can help you prepare for the PgMP certification?

    A. *The Standard for Program Management*

    B. *The Project Management Body of Knowledge*

C. *The Guide to the Project Management Body of Knowledge*

D. *Out of the Crisis* by W. Edwards Deming

A. The additional program management book that PMI recommends is *The Standard for Program Management*. B is incorrect, as *The Project Management Body of Knowledge* is more than just one book; it is the sum of all project management articles, books, and experience. C, *The Guide to the Project Management Body of Knowledge* (often just called the PMBOK), is recommended as a study resource, but the question asked for a specific program management book. D is a wonderful book by Dr. Deming, but it is not a program-specific resource.

2. How long does it take for PMI to advance your PgMP application onto the program management review panel to review your responses, experience, and education if you use the web-based application?

   A. 24 hours

   B. 5 days

   C. 6 months

   D. 30 days

B. PMI reports that it will take up to five days to respond to your application, and then they will request payment for the application process. Choices A, C, and D are all incorrect amounts of time.

3. When does your status move from PgMP applicant to PgMP candidate?

   A. Applicant and candidate are the same thing, so it does not matter

   B. After the Multi-Rater Assessment review

   C. When you receive your authorization to test letter

   D. When you have passed the PgMP multiple-choice examination, but you have not yet completed the MRA process

C. Once you've received the authorization to test letter, you'll be titled PgMP candidate rather than PgMP applicant. You'll remain a PgMP candidate until your MRA assessment is complete and you've earned the PgMP, so choices A, B, and D are incorrect.

4. All of the following are required to be involved in the Multi-Rater Assessment process except for which one?

   A. Supervisor

   B. Professional reference

   C. PMI-certified PMP

   D. Direct report

C. You do not need a PMP in order to complete the MRA process. You are required to have a supervisor, professional references, and direct reports as part of the MRA process, so choices A, B, and D are incorrect choices.

5. If you are certified as a PgMP and are already certified as a PMP, how many Professional Development Units do you have to accrue to maintain both certifications?

   A. 120 for each certification title

   B. 60 for each certification title

   C. 60, as the PMP title will be superseded by the PgMP title

   D. 60 PDUs total—both certifications can share the PDUs

   D. If you're a PMP and a PgMP, you may align your credentials and share the 60 PDUs between them. Choices A, B, and C are incorrect.

6. Jane is applying for the PgMP certification. Jane has an Associate's degree and many certifications. How many hours of program management experience must Jane have in order to qualify for the PgMP certification process?

   A. 6,000 hours

   B. 10,500 hours

   C. 1,600 hours

   D. 7,000 hours

   B. Jane is required to have 10,500 hours of program management experience. Choice A, 6,000 hours, is true for PgMP applicants with a Bachelor's degree. C and D are simply bogus answers and are not relevant to the certification process.

7. Martha has a Bachelor's degree from a university that is indeed accredited from PMI's Global Accreditation Center for Project Management. How many hours does she earn for this degree toward her PgMP?

   A. 4,500 hours

   B. 1,500 hours

   C. 6,000 hours

   D. None—she must still have the total 7,000 hours of program management experienced

   B. Martha does earn 1,500 hours of program management credit toward her required hours. A and C are incorrect; Martha, and others, won't earn up to 6,000 hours of credit for their university experiences. Note that D is incorrect, as Martha does earn 1,500 hours of credit, but also it lists the required hours as 7,000, when only 6,000 hours are actually required.

8. All of the following are a domain of project management except for which one?

   A. Closing the project

   B. Estimating the project

   C. Monitoring and controlling the project

   D. Initiating the project

   B. Estimating the project is not a project management domain. A, closing the project, C, monitoring and controlling the project, and D, initiating the project, are legitimate project management domains, so these choices are incorrect.

9. You are completing the PgMP application and must show your experience in each of the program management domains. How many hours must be reflected in each of the program management domains?

   A. There is no set amount of time that must be spent in each domain.

   B. You are required to have at least 1,500 hours of experience in each domain.

   C. You are required to have at least 1,000 hours of experience in each domain.

   D. You are required to have at least 1,200 hours of experience in each domain.

   A. You are not required to have a specific amount of experience in each domain, just some experienced in each. Because of this, choices B, C, and D are all incorrect.

10. What is the cost of the computer-based PgMP examination for a PMI member?

    A. $329

    B. $1,500

    C. $1,250

    D. $1,200

    B. The cost of the PgMP certification is $1,500 per participant. Choices A, C, and D are false values.

11. Zoe has applied for the PgMP certification process. Her application was audited by PMI, and it was deemed that she did not have enough program management experience to qualify to move onto the multiple-choice examination. How much of a refund can Zoe expect to receive from PMI?

    A. $1,150

    B. $1,500

    C. $700

    D. $750

    C. Zoe can expect a $700 refund from PMI. Choices A, B, and D are false values.

12. You have received from PMI the authorization to test letter. The letter informs you of the testing process, Prometric's telephone number, and other relevant test information. Your boss, Gaylord Gordon, asks you how long you have to pass the exam. What is your answer?

    A. One month from the date of the letter

    B. One year from the date of your application submission

    C. One year from the date of the authorization to test letter

    D. Three years from the date of your application submission

    C. You can tell Gaylord that you have one year from the date on the authorization to test letter. Choices A, B, and D are all incorrect time values.

13. How many questions are on the PgMP examination?

    A. 150 questions

    B. 200 questions

    C. 70 questions

    D. 170 questions

    D. There are 170 questions on the PgMP examination. A, 150 questions, is tempting, as 20 of the 170 questions are considered pretest questions and do not count toward your certification. You will not, however, know if you're answering a pretest question or an actual valid question. Choice B is the number of questions on the PMP examination. C, 70 questions, is the number of questions in the MRA process.

14. Howard has entered the Prometric testing center and has just completed the 15-minute tutorial on how to use the Prometric testing software for his PgMP certification exam. What is the maximum amount of time that Howard will have to complete all of the exam questions if he wants to reserve a 20-minute window for rest room breaks and tai chi?

    A. 3 hours and 40 minutes

    B. 3 hours and 10 minutes

    C. 2 hours and 40 minutes

    D. 3 hours and 25 minutes

    A. Howard will have 3 hours and 40 minutes to complete his exam and take 20 minutes in breaks. The total exam time is 4 hours. Choices B, C, and D are all incorrect choices.

15. Which program management domain equates to the largest percentage of the PgMP examination?

    A. Planning the program

    B. Executing the program

    C. Controlling the program

    D. Defining the program

    B. Executing the program accounts for 25 percent of the PgMP examination. Choice A, planning the program, accounts for 20 percent of the PgMP examination. Choice C, controlling the program, accounts for 21 percent of the examination. Finally, D, defining the program, accounts for just 14 percent of the program.

16. Fred is not happy. He has just failed his PgMP examination. How many more times may Fred take the PgMP examination this year?

    A. None; Fred must wait one year before he can take the examination again.

    B. One; Fred is allowed to take the PgMP two times within one year.

    C. Two; Fred is allowed to take the PgMP three times within one year.

    D. As many as needed; Fred may take the exam as many times as he likes, but he'll have to pay the reexamination fee each time.

C. Fred may take the PgMP examination up to three times within one year of his authorization to test letter. A, B, and D are all false statements about the reexamination process.

17. How much will Fred have to pay for the computer-based version of the PgMP reexamination if he's a PMI member?

    A. $500 for each reexamination

    B. $600 for each reexamination

    C. $400 for each reexamination

    D. $550 for each reexamination

A. Fred will have to pay $500 for each additional attempt at the recertification process. Choices B, C, and D are all false amounts for the recertification process.

18. All of the following cannot be used as your primary source of identification when checking into the Prometric testing center except for which one?

    A. Utility bill

    B. National identification card

    C. Credit card statement

    D. Authorization to test letter from PMI

B. A national identification card is a valid form of identification for access to the Prometric testing center. A, a utility bill, and C, a credit card statement, are not valid pieces of identification. Choice D, the authorization to test letter, looks promising, but it is not a valid form of identification for access to the PgMP certification exam.

19. Alice is scheduled to take her PgMP examination next week. To her dismay a family emergency has happened, and she'll have to fly home to Sheboygan, Wisconsin, and will likely miss her exam. What's the latest time Alice can reschedule her examination without facing a penalty?

    A. 24 hours prior to her scheduled exam start date

    B. 72 hours prior to her scheduled exam start date

    C. By noon two business days prior to her scheduled exam start date

    D. By Thursday the week prior to her scheduled exam start date

C. In order for Alice to reschedule her examination, she must reschedule her exam by no later than noon two business days prior to her scheduled exam start date. Choices A, B, and D are all false.

20. You've passed the PgMP certification exam, and the last step is the completion of the MRA by your colleagues. PMI has contacted the 12 individuals you've referenced and invited them to complete the 70-question survey. How long do the MRA participants have to complete the survey?

    A. One week

    B. Two weeks

    C. Three weeks

    D. Four weeks

    C. Your colleagues will have but three weeks to complete the 70-question MRA process. Choices A, B, and D are all incorrect values.

Defining Program Management

In this chapter, you will
- Discover PMI's *Standard for Program Management*
- Explore program management
- Work as a program manager
- Link programs, projects, and portfolios
- Identify the benefits of program management

In your current role as a program manager, you're probably already aware of the basic tenets of program management. You likely have an approach to program management that creates the expected deliverables and benefits for your organization. You likely have an approach to ensure that your project managers and their project team work together to resolve resource conflicts, schedule disruptions, and handle other unpleasant dynamics. You are probably a program management superstar. Good for you!

Every organization is different. Every company uses different processes, different techniques, different inputs, and different outputs. Every program or project has different resources, different managers, and different visions of the benefits that will be created. You know this. Think of all the projects that have fit within the programs you've managed. Does every project manager manage the same? No. Do you work with every client, every resource, or every vendor the same? Of course not. You adapt, adjust, and alter your approach to get the results you expect for the betterment of your program.

On your PgMP examination, however, you won't be tested on how you get your work done, the tricks and techniques you've created, and the organizational process assets that your hard work has created. No, my program management perfectionist, you'll have to learn the way PMI dictates that programs are supposed to work and answer their program management queries the way they think they should be answered. Now, in all fairness, their way and your way are likely in sync much of the time. However, you'll no doubt have those moments when you prep for your PgMP examination when you'll want to scream, "I'd never do it like that!" And that's okay. You don't have to do anything that doesn't work out in the real world—your world. To pass your exam, though, just answer the questions by their rules, according to their world.

My advice? Learn the PMI way. Pass the PMI exam. Earn the PMI credential. And then go on with your life.

Relying on *The Standard for Program Management*

A long time ago I had a boss who told me there are two ways to do anything: the right way and my way—and they're both the same. Yeah, he was a real nice guy. My point being, PMI sometimes reminds me of my old boss. As a program manager you, I hope, realize that there is usually more than just one way to manage a program, organize a project, or execute an activity. On your PgMP examination, however, you'll have to choose the best answer of the four choices for each exam question. So what's the best answer based on?

PMI's book *The Standard for Program Management* is the foundation for the PgMP examination. On the first page of this less-than-fascinating read, the authors share that the book is really an expansion of the popular *A Guide to the Project Management Body of Knowledge* (commonly known as the PMBOK). Your PgMP examination, ergo, is based on these two publications.

Exploring *The Standard for Program Management*

If you're not familiar with this program management book, you're not missing much. I do recommend that you read PMI's program management masterpiece prior to your exam (yawn). Don't worry, it won't take much of your time to read their book—it's barely a hundred pages of content. Here's a brief rundown of what's in their publication—all of which I cover in the remainder of the book you're reading now:

- **Introducing Program Management**   PMI's book begins with the fundamentals of what *The Standard for Program Management* aims to do, defines the relationship of programs and projects, and dives into portfolio management and organizational planning. I cover all of this information—and more—in this chapter.

- **Program Life Cycle and the Organization**   Just as products and projects have life cycles, so do programs. You'll learn about program themes, the varying phases that compose a program, and the management of deliverables, stakeholders, and program governance. I cover these juicy details in Chapter 3.

- **Program Management Processes**   In *The Standard for Program Management* PMI jams all their processes into this one massive chapter. There are tons of processes divided into chunky process groups. Rather than mimic PMI's jam-packed approach, I cover these processes in exam-passing detail in Chapters 4–9. No peeking!

- **Appendixes**   *The Standard for Program Management* has eight appendixes. In case you're wondering, that's five more appendixes than the book has chapters. Three of these appendixes are blah-blah-blah how PMI wrote the PMBOK and who helped. Appendixes D, E, and F are chockablock full of good stuff: program management tools and techniques, program benefits assurance information, and program management controls. Appendix G in their book offers two pages of rather fluffy program management examples. Finally, Appendix H compares and contrasts program management, project management, and PMI's other gem, the Organizational Project Management Maturity Model (sometimes called OPM3). I cover some information from these appendixes throughout the book, but not all of it. Specifically, I only cover the exam-specific information.

And there you have it. That's a quick rundown of *The Standard for Program Management*. In my opinion, PMI has done a good deed of publishing their approach to program management and they've recruited some lofty and wise folks to help them write the standard. It's not a dictatorship, and PMI is wise enough to realize that no organization is going to use the same program management approach, the same program management processes, and the same tools in every program every time. Their goal was to create an initial standard that can evolve, adapt, and offer a baseline for program management. Bully for them!

Exploring the PMBOK Guide

I'd wager dollars to donuts that you, as a program manager, have spent some time of your life as a project manager. Ha! Pay up. In order to be a PgMP, you have to have spent at least four years of your life in project management purgatory. Your role as a project manager has helped you become a program manager, but that doesn't mean you get to ditch all those lessons learned and wisdom from your project management days.

Program managers have to coach, guide, and train their project managers. Program managers must know how projects work and how project processes contribute to the deliverables of the program. While the day-to-day activities of a program manager are not in the management of projects, an understanding of the principles of project management is crucial to effective program management. And you'll be tested on it for your PgMP.

PMI's *A Guide to the Project Management Body of Knowledge*, third edition, is your point of reference for all questions relating to project management. You have to answer these questions, like the rules of program management, the way PMI wants you to answer them—not necessarily how you and your project managers do the work in your programs. Here's a quick tally of what you'll find in the PMBOK and where I cover some of this information through this book you're reading right now:

- **Purpose of the PMBOK**   Chapter 1 in the PMBOK tells you what they're about to tell you. This first chapter reveals the mysteries of how their book is organized and structured. They go on to explain projects, describe project management, and even hint at operations. No real surprise here. I reference projects, project management, and the PMBOK throughout this whole book.

- **Project Life Cycle (PLC)**   The PMBOK's second chapter defines the phases that compose the life cycle of a project, the life cycle of project management, and how the two interact. I discuss the project management life cycle in Chapter 3 of this book.

- **Project Management Process** Projects, like your programs, are composed of a lot of processes. While the focus of this book and your PgMP examination is on the process of program management, you'll need to be familiar with the project management processes. I provide you a cheat sheet of all the project management processes in Chapter 3, as well as a program management processes reference table in Appendix C.

- **Project Integration Management** Project management processes have to work together. Any variation in a project management process has a ripple effect on all the other project management processes.

- **Project Scope Management** The project scope is all of the required work in order to create the deliverables in the project scope statement. I cover scope management in Chapter 6.

- **Project Time Management** The ability of a project manager to deliver his project when he has promised is crucial to the success of a program. I cover the project management processes related to time management in Chapters 6 and 8.

- **Project Cost Management** The more monies that a project spends, the more your program will cost—no math magic here. Program managers and project managers have to work together to estimate, budget, and control project costs. I cover these cost management concepts in Chapters 6, 7, and 8.

- **Project Quality Management** Quality is paramount in each project and is achieved by delivering to the program manager exactly what was promised— nothing more and nothing less. I discuss quality in several chapters, but specifically in Chapter 6.

- **Project Human Resources** The project manager has to lead, manage, and direct the project team, but may also have to discipline team members. Your organization, program office, or program may have rules for human resource management. I discuss these variables in Chapter 6.

- **Project Communications Management** Ninety percent of a project manager's time is spent communicating. Project managers have to know who needs what information, when the information is needed, and in what modality the information is expected. I discuss communications planning for project managers and program managers in Chapters 6 and 8.

- **Project Risk Management** Negative and positive risks have to be identified, documented, analyzed, and then responded to. I discuss the relationship between program risks and project risks in Chapters 6, 7, and 8.

- **Project Procurement Management** Projects that operate within a program have guidelines and procedures for selecting and purchasing from vendors. I discuss project and program management procurement in Chapters 6, 7, 8, and 9. Bring your checkbook.

These twelve topics make up the PMBOK, but the most important program management topics are covered in Chapters 4–12—the project management knowledge areas. In program management there are similar knowledge areas, and their contents often overlap. In each chapter, where it's relevant, I discuss the relationship between a program management knowledge area and the corresponding project management knowledge area. You'll need to know this business in order to pass your PgMP examination.

Introducing Programs

Just so that you and I are, literally, on the same page, I need to define what a program is—and is not. A *program* is a collection of projects managed in a controlled, balanced effort to realize benefits not available by managing each project independent of the others. Programs consist of projects that work in tandem to create a consolidated deliverable that aligns with the strategic vision of the performing organization.

Programs create benefits. This is a common PMI program management theme— and you should learn it, love it, and live it (well, at least until you pass the exam). To quote *The Standard for Program Management*, "A benefit is an outcome of actions and behaviors that provides utility to stakeholders." In other words, a benefit is the result of your work as something that is quantifiable.

 NOTE Don't get stuck on the word utility. It simply means that in which something is useful. It is a term that allows you to quantify the usefulness, purpose, or value of a service, a condition, or even an emotion. You'll see the concept of utility in quality, in customer satisfaction, and most often, in risk management.

I'm sure you've heard the old adage that all companies exist for one reason: to make money. While that purely capitalistic point of view often holds true, many organizations exist for more than the bottom line. Consider not-for-profit entities, government agencies, and colleges and universities. Sure, with all of these there is an element of finance, but it's not always being in the black that counts.

I linger on this because program management, in any environment, must support the strategic vision of the performing organization. Figure 2-1 demonstrates my point. At the highest tier of any organization there's a lofty goal: make money, educate, make the world a better place, or even some combination. The program, at the second tier of an organization, fits under the strategic vision of the parent entity. Because programs consist of projects, the individual projects in turn support the program. The deliverables of each project subserve the rules and objectives of the program. The program subserves the objectives of the parent organization, which in turns aims to satisfy its mission.

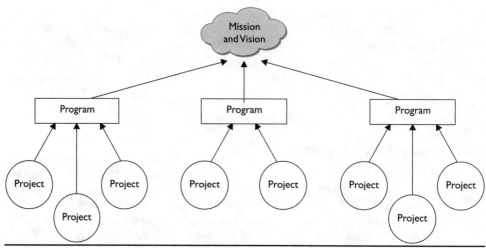

Figure 2-1 Programs support the mission of the organization.

Introducing Program Management

Now that you know that a program is a collection of coordinated projects working together to realize benefits for the performing organization, I'm moving on to the program management goodies. It should come as no surprise that program management is the management of all the coordinated projects within a program. Program management is the effort to coordinate the program's projects to create the anticipated deliverables. Program management is not the actual management of the projects and their day-to-day work; that's the project manager's job, not yours.

Program management centers on three key themes:

- **Benefits management** A benefit is the result of a program; for example, increased revenue, decreased costs, or the reduction of waste. Benefits management is the sum of the planning, tools, and techniques—the overall management of the activities that define, create, maximize, and sustain the benefits created by the program.

- **Stakeholder management** A *stakeholder* is any person, group, or entity that may be affected positively or negatively by the outcome of the program. Technically, this may include passive stakeholders that are interested in your program but aren't directly affected by its outcome. Stakeholder management is the balance of stakeholder identification, communication, leadership, trade-offs, competing objectives, and prioritization of needs and demands.

- **Program governance** All programs must have rules, procedures, and order. Program governance is the enforcement of the rules and procedures an organization follows. It is the policies associated with the program's planning, executing, monitoring and controlling, and closing processes that move the program forward. Program governance is the assurance that all program procedures are followed as planned and expected by the organization, the project managers, and you, the program manager.

These three themes are fundamental to your PgMP examination. I explore the attributes of these themes later in this chapter. You'll learn the processes and activities that allow the program manager to achieve the objectives of each—and you'll learn what to expect on your PgMP exam. For now, just accept that program management consists of benefits management, stakeholder management, and program governance. That's not asking too much.

Identifying Big Bad Programs

According to PMI, programs are collections of projects that work together for benefits that you couldn't realize any other way. Well, that's nice, but what does it mean? Why can't an organization have twenty projects that all help an organization generate more revenue, cut costs, improve customer service, or illustrate any other Business 101 topic you can imagine? How does anyone know if they're really a program manager and not some business demigod managing throngs of project managers?

Ah—benefits. It's all about benefits. The collection of projects that work together toward a common cause, a common goal, and a common purpose with a realization of gained benefits is a program. The very best example I can offer is the creation of a gigantic skyscraper in your home town. Think of all the projects that could exist within the creation of a skyscraper:

- Concept and vision of the building
- Design and architecture of the building
- Mechanical engineering projects
- Structural engineering projects
- Physical creation of the building's structure
- Floor-by-floor design of the skyscraper
- Traffic flow throughout the building
- Landscape architecture for the building
- City planning
- And so much more . . . .

Obviously I'm not an architect, and I'm sure some skyscraper guru out there is rattling off a hundred more projects that contribute to this massive undertaking. My point, however, is that all of these projects are contributing to the final delivery. It is quite feasible to treat the creation of the skyscraper as just one big project and each of the projects just listed as individual subprojects—nothing wrong with that whatsoever.

However, if the performing organization sees this as an opportunity to manage the benefits of these projects, well, that's a different story. Think of how the architects, the structural engineers, the landscape engineers, and even the interior designers can all work together through their projects for the greater good of the program. Think of the time and cost savings they'll realize by working together, through cooperative planning, issue resolution, and a general sense of program community. Programs are about realizing the benefits of cooperating projects rather than the angst and isolating independence of individual projects.

 NOTE Think of the politics that project managers often fall into: resource stockpiling, schedule sandbagging, bloated estimates, and territorial fiefdoms. The goal of program management is break down the "us-against-everyone-else" mentality and coordinate project managers to work together for the common vision and purpose of the organization. When I consult, I find myself reminding project teams, project managers, program managers, and stakeholders of one simple truth: "We are all on the same team."

Managing Large Projects as Programs

It is perfectly acceptable to manage a very large project as a program. The caveat to this acceptability, however, is that large projects operating under the guise of a program must realize collective benefits. Again, it's easy to see this in the skyscraper example. You wouldn't be out of your mind to say that the skyscraper is really just one big ol' project—it'd be tough, but you could do it.

More likely, the major phases and deliverables of the skyscraper are going to be chunked down into manageable projects. The key PMI-ism here is that the management of the benefits of creating the subprojects and creating the skyscraper program would offer gains that you wouldn't ordinarily have otherwise. In other words, what benefits could you and your organization possibly realize by managing the skyscraper creation that you would not realize otherwise?

The advantages of a creating a program are immense, but here are a few headlines:

- Resources, talent, and expert judgment are shared across the program.
- The isolation of project independence is broken down.
- All projects follow the same rules and policies of the program.
- Collective bargaining, shared procurement, and vendor management are unified.
- Risk and issue management is centralized at the program level.
- Information can be more freely shared.
- Communication stems from the program manager for all project managers.

- Stakeholder management follows a common approach.
- Costs and schedule control is managed from a centralized locale.

Programs offer a means to an end. The end, of course, is the realization of an organization's goal, vision, strategy, or mission. Programs and their projects work in unison to satisfy the objectives of the organization. It's the responsibility of the program manager to convey this message to the project managers and the program stakeholders.

Exploring the PMBOK

If you're the program manager, certainly you don't need to know much about project management, right? Well, of course you do! As a PgMP candidate, you've plenty of experience in project management. The rules of project management, for the most part, fold into the complexities of program management. As a program manager, you've got to know how projects are expected to operate, understand the autonomy of your project managers, and know how project managers should work with one another.

For your PgMP exam you'll be tested on how projects and programs work together. In order to answer these questions correctly—the PMI way—you'll need to be familiar with the PMBOK. If you're already a PMP, you've spent hours studying the project management processes, inputs, tools and techniques, and outputs of each project management knowledge area. You won't, however, need to spend an extraneous amount of time in the PMBOK, but you will need to be topically familiar with the concepts and standards the PMBOK does provide.

I've already shared the basic outline of the PMBOK with you, but it's time to dig a little deeper into the PMBOK and how it relates to program management and to you, the program manager. A primary advantage of the PMBOK is that it attempts to establish some common nomenclature for project management. It defines what a project is, what processes a project holds, and the confines of project management versus operations. It's heady stuff.

The policies established within your program serve as enterprise environmental factors for project managers. An *enterprise environmental factor* is the way a project manager is expected to manage her project within the performing organization. Enterprise environmental factors are the rules, expectations, and policies a project manager is expected to operate by.

Your program may also provide, according to the PMBOK, organizational process assets to the project manager. An organizational process asset is any tool, template, application, or guideline your program or organization has created to assist the project manager and internally standardize the management of all projects within the program.

The PMBOK defines nine knowledge areas across five process groups. Within each process group there are a number of processes that move the project forward to the conclusion of a project phase or to the closing of the project. As Table 2-1 depicts, there are 44 project management processes across the five process groups. The number in parentheses represents the number of project management processes you'll find in that process group.

Knowledge Areas	Process Groups				
	Initiating (2)	Planning (21)	Executing (7)	Monitoring and Controlling (12)	Closing (2)
Project Integration Management	Project Charter creation Preliminary Scope Statement	Create the Project Management Plan	Project execution	Monitor and control project work Integrated change control	Close project
Project Scope Management		Scope planning Scope definition WBS creation		Scope verification Scope control	
Project Time Management		Define activities Sequence activities Resource estimating Duration estimating Develop schedule		Schedule control	
Project Cost Management		Cost estimating Cost budgeting		Control costs	
Project Quality Management		Quality planning	Quality assurance	Quality control	
Project Human Resources Management		HR planning	Acquire team Develop team	Manage team	
Project Communications Management		Communication planning	Distribute information	Performance reporting Manage stakeholders	
Project Risk Management		Risk management planning Risk identification Qualitative risk analysis Quantitative risk analysis Risk response planning		Risk monitoring and control	
Project Procurement Management		Plan purchases Plan contracting	Request seller responses Select sellers	Contract administration	Contract closure

Table 2-1 The 44 Project Management Processes

NOTE For your PgMP examination, I'd be familiar with Table 2-1 and these 44 project management processes. I refer to these processes from time to time in the remainder of this book, but for more specific information I highly recommend my *PMP Project Management Professional Study Guide* (McGraw-Hill, 2006). It's superb.

Exploring Real Programs

I like the real world. Sure it's nice to memorize some facts, learn the PMI way, and get some alphabet soup behind your name, but nothing beats what organizations are doing out in the real world with real programs. I'm offering three samples of real-world programs here just for your reference and enjoyment. And because I can.

Massachusetts Public Library Construction Program

The Massachusetts Board of Library Commissioners has created the Massachusetts Public Library Construction Program to help towns in Massachusetts construct new libraries and expand or renovate existing libraries. Their program defines procedures for towns to follow, offering planning guides, workbooks, construction resources, regulations, and guidelines for procurements.

Their program is an excellent example of a program, because it is a collection of common projects working toward a common purpose—to serve the people of Massachusetts. Their program sets the rules and oversees the library projects, but it does not interfere with the day-to-day management of the projects. As of October 2007, this program has provided $278 million in grants for new construction and renovations of existing buildings. Congrats to the Commonwealth.

NASA U.S. Antarctic Meteorite Program

In 1969, Japanese scientists discovered that meteorites that crashed into the romantic sounding "blue ice" of Antarctic were preserved and could be studied. Drawing on their initial findings, the U.S. Antarctic Meteorite Program was created; it involves three U.S. government agencies: the National Science Foundation (NSF), the National Aeronautics and Space Administration (NASA), and the Smithsonian Institution.

The program provides policies and procedures for excavating the meteorites, collecting and analyzing the extraterrestrial objects, and documenting the discoveries. The program aims to learn about the origins of the meteorites to better understand our solar system, and the conditions of the flow of ice in the Antarctic ice sheet. Cool.

Scottsdale, Arizona, Public Art Program

The mission of the Scottsdale Public Art Program is to promote the quality of life in this Arizona city. The program aims to provide public works of arts for its residents and visitors to enjoy and beautify the city. The program provides an art museum without walls to enliven, educate, and inspire. The program's goals range from smaller permanent art projects to the revolving placement of larger public art.

The program, like all good programs, defines the confines of the projects that will operate within its policies, financial constraints, and common vision of the purpose of the artwork. Their collection of artwork as a result of the program is simply amazing. Scottsdale boasts work by internationally recognized artists and up-and-comers. Check it out.

Working as a Program Manager

So what does a program manager do? For starters, the program manager leads project managers to deliver projects that, in turn, support organizational objectives. Program managers go beyond the day-to-day management activities of project managers and influence successes, large and small, of the performing organization. Program managers are leaders and have a significant impact on the organization as a whole.

PMI likes to boast that the PgMP credential will increase your visibility within your organization and in the international community. Just as the requirements to earn the PgMP are high, so too then are the rewards for your efforts and experience as a program manager.

Identifying Program Management Responsibilities

Alright, you've all read the hype about earning the PgMP; now I'm going to dive into the realities of program management. Ready? Program managers don't need hand-holding in order to get work done. They are responsible for the coordinated projects within their programs. Program managers work with the project managers to ensure that their work is done in accordance with the vision of the project—and they find ways to correct problems when they creep into the progress of the program.

Program managers' day-to-day work includes the following:

- Constant monitoring and control to ensure that the projects meet the program scope
- Financial management for the program and its projects
- Abilities to deal with cross-cultural issues

Thus, program managers must be able to do the following:

- Motivate, align, and direct the program stakeholders.
- Provide leadership to the program participants.
- Communicate as needed to the appropriate program stakeholders.
- Influence factors that may affect the project for better or worse.
- Negotiate to reach the best solutions for the program.
- Work with program stakeholders to resolve issues and conflicts.

The program manager needs to keep a constant eye on each project and how the projects work (or should work) in unison to complete the program scope. Program managers focus on the big picture and rely on the performance of the project managers to deliver the details.

Linking Projects and Programs

Programs consist of projects. Projects, in turn, are linked to the program in that their benefits and deliverables contribute to the program scope—of course. Program management, however, is more than just a bunch of old projects working together to create that skyscraper. Program management not only creates a link from the program to the individual projects but also creates links between the projects. Consider the commonalities that a program's projects can share:

- Resource constraints (resources are people, tools, and facilities)
- Risk mitigation activities
- Interdependent project activities (two or more project teams working on one deliverable)
- Shared resources
- Communication and meeting strategies
- Project integration management
- Change control
- Program and project configuration management

 NOTE Cash is a resource for projects, but it's not a resource that is usually shared among projects. Consider that each project in a program has its own budget. Having said that, there are times when monies are shifted from one project to another within a program according to priorities, risks that didn't come true, or cash flow.

The collection of projects is linked together by their common causes—and that's one of the big benefits of a program. Compare the benefits of a program with multiple projects with shared resources to a typical matrix structure with shared resources. In a matrix structure there is often, if not always, a competition for resources. In a project there may be a competition for resources, but the program and the project managers must work together, taking into account priorities, stakeholder demands, and the scheduling of interdependent activities. This is where project management's critical chain management is attractive. Critical chain management considers scheduling in terms of the availability of resources rather than the critical path approach, which makes the assumption that all project resources are always available.

Exploring Portfolio Management

Your organization has a portfolio, and you may not even know it. A *portfolio* is a collection of programs, projects, and even ongoing operations that all have a common purpose: to reach some business objectives. The goal of a portfolio, this collection of organizational business, is to organize all the moving parts of a company. Just because programs, projects, and operations are in a portfolio, doesn't necessarily mean that they are interdependent and directly linked to one another.

Consider Figure 2-2, an IT portfolio. This portfolio consists of a hardware upgrade program, a database project, a datacenter program, and an IT consulting operation. These components of the portfolio are grouped together only because of their base in technology. The projects under the programs are, of course, linked to one another because they support their parent programs. Fascinating.

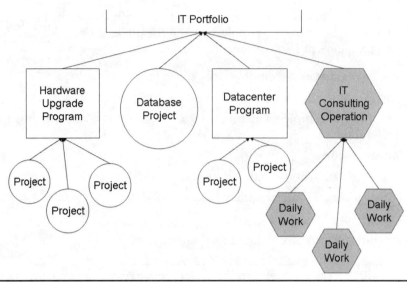

Figure 2-2   Portfolios group common programs, projects, and operations.

Just as a program's projects support the vision of the program, the components of a portfolio must support the vision, or strategic objectives, of the performing organization. If you want to know where a company's priorities exist, just look at its portfolios, the priorities assigned to projects, the cost of labor in each portfolio, and the goals the portfolio aims to achieve. Portfolios show the real intent of any organization.

Launching a Portfolio's Program

Initiating a program within a portfolio is simple, but not always easy. I say that it's simple, because the program directly supports the mission of the portfolio. It's not an easy thing to do, because programs are complex, bulky things that have an immediate need at launch to be completely defined. The definition of the program often moves through rolling wave planning, also known as progressive elaboration. Through iterations of planning and analysis, the scope of the program is defined, the projects within the program are chartered by the program manager, and the portfolio's program is set into motion.

Programs and portfolios interact the most in the initiating and planning phases. Early in the project timeline, as Figure 2-3 demonstrates, the control stems from the portfolio manager for inputs such as schedule planning, budget allocation, goal settings, and constraints. Once the program moves into the phases of execution, monitoring and controlling, and the closing, the control from the portfolio wanes.

Managing a Portfolio's Program

One business advantage of an IT portfolio is leverage and balanced risk within the portfolio. Some components of the portfolio, such as operations, have a relatively low risk, while some projects, such as the database project, could carry a significant amount of

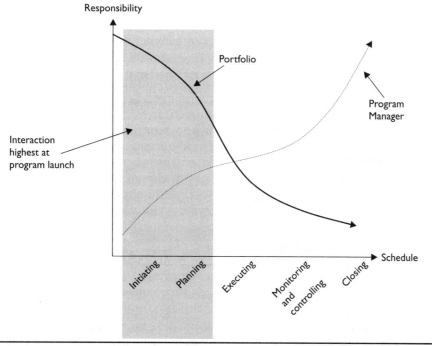

Figure 2-3   Portfolios and programs interact early in the program phases.

risk. The balance of risk is contained within the portfolio through quantitative risk analysis at the organizational level, and the reward for risk acceptance is in proportion to the goals the portfolio is trying to achieve. A portfolio doesn't take on more risk than it can typically offset without some mitigation and intense risk response planning. The risk tolerance of the organization, also known as the risk utility function, determines how much risk the portfolio is willing to accept.

Portfolio managers continue to report to some entity at the portfolio level as the program moves toward its goals, but generally the control is left with the program manager. The management of the portfolio likely comes into play when changes to the program scope are proposed. Then, the program manager and the manager of the portfolio have to consider the impact of the change on several program and project attributes:

- Scope
- Schedule
- Cost
- Quality
- Human resources
- Communication
- Risk
- Procurement

I cover change management in the program in Chapter 10. Changes to the scope of the program may have a ripple effect on all the projects within the program—or they may affect only one project. As every program throughout the world is different, there's no way of saying that change will affect every single project within a program. As a general rule, and for your PgMP certification, know that the impact of a program change that stems from portfolio management requires a study of the change and what its impact will be on each project and on each project's knowledge area. An innocent change can have huge ramifications in the program.

Closing a Portfolio's Program

The end of a program typically does not mean the end of the organization's portfolio. The closure of the program, however, does mean that the program has reached its initiatives and helped the portfolio reach its objectives—hopefully. The closure of a program most likely means the projects within the program were finished and the program manager may complete the closing processes.

Closing the program prompts the program manager and the portfolio's management to issue a certificate of program completion. This document details the deliverables of the program, its projects, and the success or failure of the program's objectives. The program manager creates a program closure report, completes performance reviews of the program's projects, archives the results of the program, and completes the program's lessons learned documentation. I discuss the juicy details of closing a program in Chapter 9.

Exploring Program Management and Project Management

A program consists of projects. Within a program projects come and go. The project gets chartered, the project manager gets selected, and then the project managers, with the program manager's direction, lead their projects to conclusion. The role of the program manager in projects is to coordinate the efforts between projects—not to manage the projects. Program managers work with project managers to solve issues between projects, to track project work, and to eliminate activities that don't add value to the deliverables. Program managers and project managers work toward the same goal—satisfying the program's purpose.

Exploring Project Attributes

A project is a short-term endeavor to create a unique product, service, or condition. A project does not go on, thankfully, forever. Projects require time, resources, and a defined objective—usually just called the project *scope*. Projects are constrained by these three things: schedule, budget, and scope. As Figure 2-4 shows, this is the infamous "Iron Triangle of Project Management."

Figure 2-4
The Iron Triangle of
Project Management
shows the triple
constraints.

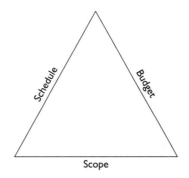

Projects, program-bound or not, move through five process groups:

- **Initiating**   The project is chartered and the project manager is selected.
- **Planning**   This iterative process group creates the project plans and considers the reaction to change.
- **Executing**   The project management plans are executed.
- **Monitoring and Controlling**   The project is monitored and controlled to ensure quality, adherence to the project scope, and tracking of newly identified risks, among other activities.
- **Closing**   The project deliverable has been created, the scope satisfied, and the project is closed accordingly. In some unpleasant instances, the project may be closed because of poor execution, advancements in technology, or a simple lack of need.

In a program, each project is interdependent with other projects. It's feasible, but somewhat unlikely, that only the deliverables of a project may interact with other projects. It is more likely that the program manager and the project managers work together to leverage resources, risk management, schedules, budget, and more to realize all the benefits of coordinating a collective effort for the good of the program and the betterment of each project.

Program managers' primary concern, when it comes to project management, is for the interdependent relationship of projects to run smoothly and on track. A delay or cost overrun in one project can have huge ramifications in other, dependent projects. Project communications up to the program level are mandated by the program manager and by conditions within the project. Communication to the program manager during the execution and monitoring and controlling phases reflects the status, alerts, and risks within a project that may affect the status of other interrelated projects in the program.

Exploring Program Attributes

Because programs are made up of projects, you can expect a fair amount of questions about project management on your PgMP examination. This is key: program managers manage programs; they do not manage the projects within the program. However, having an understanding of PMI-based project management principles ensures that you will recognize the flow of project and program information, who's in charge of what activities, and the processes that move the projects and program toward a successful conclusion.

While project success is measured in how closely the project tracks against its budget, schedule, and scope delivery, program success is measured by its return on investment, benefits gained, and capabilities that the program creates for the performing organization. The abilities of the project managers and the leadership of the program manager directly affect the success or failure of the program.

Project managers focus on the details, while program managers focus on the big picture. This is evident when we compare the planning of both the program and the projects. Project managers and project teams decompose the project work into work packages—the smallest item of the work breakdown structure (WBS). Program managers don't decompose to this level; they create broad, high-level plans that define the project deliverables, but not necessarily the steps to create the deliverables. Program managers think in terms of leadership, vision, and interdependence of projects to create a collective gain.

Exploring Organizational Planning

An *organization* is a collection of people that work together, in theory, to complete some type of work within an enterprise. An enterprise is simply a government agency, a business, or a corporation that was formed to accomplish a mission. Sometimes an organization and an enterprise are the same darn thing. For example, an incorporated company could be an enterprise but may also be considered an organization. Organizational planning, therefore, is planning that determines how the enterprise is divided, and how power is dispersed within the enterprise.

A program within an organization usually aims to satisfy one or more goals of the organization. Its purpose is to simply satisfy organizational goals and strategic objectives. This is a glaring difference between programs within an organization and projects within the same organization. Projects aim to deliver stuff—applications, conditions, and things—or else to create new services. Programs, however, aim to create benefits and capabilities that the organization needs to sustain itself, to grow, to prosper, and to reach its goals. Projects are short-term endeavors within an organization, while programs are likely to hang about for a while.

Organizations always work to ensure that programs, projects, and portfolios are

- Aligned with the goals of the organization
- Invested in the right mix of projects
- Utilizing resources to the maximum potential

Programs can span entire lines of business or be dedicated to just one line of business—it all depends on the strategic objectives and goals of the enterprise. For your PgMP examination, there's no real right or wrong answer as to how an organization is composed and how projects and programs fit within the entity. Who is PMI to say what's right or wrong when it comes to organizational planning? Every entity is different, and what may be right in my company just may not work at all within yours. And that's just fine as long as my program and your programs are working to satisfy the objectives of our separate organizations.

Reaping the Benefits of Program Management

Programs can affect the entire organization for better or for worse. Organizations usually create programs with specific goals in mind: increasing revenue, cutting costs, creating a new organizational benefit, or establishing a new service or condition, to name a few. Organizational strategies use programs to reach goals and realize benefits.

While program managers have to balance stakeholder opinions, competing objectives, resource allocation, and more, the program manager always works for balance in three key themes. Know these and love 'em:

- Benefits management
- Program stakeholder management
- Program governance

From this point forward in this book, I'll always consider how any process, activity, or decision affects these three program management and organizational themes. Are you ready to dive into these objectives a bit deeper? Ready or not, here we go.

Exploring Program Benefits Management

When an organization creates a program, it expects something in return—and not just a hardy handshake. An organization that creates a program is expecting tangible and intangible benefits from the program. An organization must first, at the portfolio level, determine why a program needs to be created, and the goals of the program. Then the program manager creates the projects that will, in turn, create the deliverables that equate to the program benefits.

Program benefits management consists of several key activities. Know program manager responsibilities for your PgMP examination, and you'll be on your way:

- Review the value and organizational impact of the organization's program.
- Work to quantify the specific, measurable, and actual benefits of the program.
- Assign responsibilities within the program to recognize the planned and expected benefits reaped from each program project.
- Identify the interdependencies of projects and the benefits each contributes to the program.
- Complete change analysis for program change requests and understand how the potential changes may help or hinder the ability to reach program objectives.

Benefit management works to quantify and then to realize the expected themes of the program stakeholders. While the organization may have goals for intangible benefits, such as improved customer satisfaction and employee morale, the program manager must work to quantify these subjective themes of program management. Program managers and the committee that leads organizational planning have to be in synch with the benefits planning and analysis of each program. The conclusion of this first step of benefits management leads to in-depth benefits planning. Each project within the program contributes to the benefits realization, which allows the program manager to eventually transfer the gained benefits from the program to the organization through benefits transition.

The benefits realization plan defines the program's expected benefits, is created during the early stages of the program, and defines for the program manager and its stakeholders several key factors:

- Quantified, defined program benefits and how they are to be accomplished
- Mapping of benefits to program outcomes
- Roles and responsibilities for benefits management
- Metrics to quantify and measure the program's benefits
- A communications plan for benefit management
- Specific information on how the program benefits will be transferred into operations

I discuss these activities in the upcoming chapters in more detail, but for now realize the program's benefits are mapped out from the program's launch. Failure to designate what the program should accomplish only sets up the program manager and the portfolio management for failure. While it may seem obvious that the goals and objectives must be specifically defined before a program is launched, this is often an afterthought in the real world for the program manager and the project managers to dwell on while schedules are ignored and budgets are slashed. I often ask in my role as a consultant, "If you don't know what's expected of the program, and of you, the program manager, how can you ever be successful in program management?" It's not different for the PgMP examination.

Managing Program Stakeholders

A program stakeholder, or for that matter a project stakeholder, is an individual or entity that is affected by the outcome of the project or program. A stakeholder, this person or thing, can also help or hinder the program, depending on the stakeholder's opinion and perceived outcome of the program. Positive stakeholders are the fine folks that want your program to succeed. Negative stakeholders, those wet blankets, don't want your program around for another moment.

While it's nice to assume that everyone's a positive stakeholder, it's also nice to assume that the weather is going to be sunny, balmy, and full of rainbows every day. You and I know neither is going to happen often. Negative stakeholders need to be shown, marketed if you will, the positive outcomes of the program and how it helps them, the organization, and even the world beyond the organization.

Key stakeholders in every program include the following:

- **The program director**   This is the executive owner of the program, the person the program manager reports to.
- **Program manager**   This person is responsible for the management of program.
- **Project managers**   These are the managers of the projects that make up the program.
- **Program sponsor**   The champion of the program, this can be an individual, customer, or line of business within the organization. The sponsor, whoever it may be for a program, is responsible for providing the resources (ahem, cash and people) to deliver the expected benefits of the program.
- **Customer**   This entity gets the stuff the program creates.
- **Performing organization**   This is the entity that the program works within.
- **Program team members**   Yes, there is a program team, much as there are project teams. Program team members help the program manager get the program work done. They get coffee and make photocopies. Kidding. They help the program manager complete program processes, communicate with stakeholders, and execute program processes.
- **Project team members**   These are the people on the program's project teams. These are the experts that do the project work.
- **Program Management Office (PMO)**   The program management office is responsible for defining and supporting the program-related governance procedures. The PMO supports the processes and activities within a program.
- **Program Office**   This group supports the program by handling the administrative functions of the program at one central locale.
- **Program governance board**   This fun bunch of folks helps the program manager reach his goals by providing support and resolutions for program risks and issues.
- **Vendors**   Programs' projects need to buy stuff. Rules that affect purchasing within the program will affect the vendors and how the project managers interact with them.
- **Government agencies**   Rules and restrictions from government agencies often affect how the program is operated, depending on the discipline the program centers on. Consider the recent rules of the Occupational Safety and Health Administration (OSHA), the Sarbanes-Oxley Act, and the Health Insurance Portability and Accountability Act (HIPAA).
- **Consumer, environmental, and more**   Depending on the program, there may be stakeholders that are not easily identified but that are concerned and affected by the outcome of the program or projects within the program.

Program stakeholder management is all about communications. I talk more about the communications management plan later in this book, but when it comes to stakeholder management, it's about acknowledging and addressing stakeholder concerns and issues. This includes everything from cultural differences, resistance to the change the program will create, and major issues the program may include. The program manager must meet with and communicate with the stakeholders to discuss and address their concerns to move the program forward. What is the overall goal of stakeholder management? It is to gain acceptance from the program stakeholders.

The stakeholder management plan and the program communications plan identify all the stakeholders and the communication demands that the program warrants. Proper planning identifies which stakeholders will need what information, when they'll need it, and in what modality. It's all about communicating the right message at the right time. Simple enough, right? Of course not. What is said, such as key messages, proactive messages, and direct communication, along with the communications schedule, helps the program manager convert negative stakeholders to positive stakeholders while simultaneously maintaining the pool of existing positive stakeholders.

Managing Program Governance

Growing up, I never liked it much when my brother Sam was left in charge of me. He was a stickler for every conceivable rule my parents had established. Rules, rules, rules. It's no wonder, then, I think of my big (and now much older and grayer) brother Sam whenever I talk about program governance. Program governance, in case you've not guessed by now, is about the enforcement of the rules, policies, and procedures that the program participants must follow.

Unlike Brother Sam, the program governance ensures a consistent framework so that all projects within the program follow the same procedures and expectations to create repeatable, predictable results. This allows for effective decision-making, risk identification and management, and meeting program stakeholder requirements.

Program governance is not an "be-all and end-all" approach. It actually fits within the organization governance and follows the rules of its parents. Figure 2-5 depicts how program management and its governance actually align with the organizational rules and policies—it's not independent of them. In many organizations, though not all organizations, a program board interprets and defines the organizational governance for the program managers. The same board also addresses major issues within the program that the program manager cannot resolve.

The program board accomplishes many things within the program through its governance:

- Program initiation
- Program plan approval
- Program plan changes
- Review of the program's cost, progress, and benefits delivery
- Issue resolution and issue consultation
- Commitment of program resources
- Establishing the program framework
- Ensuring corporate and legal compliance

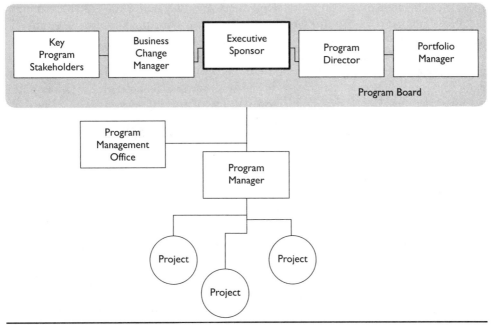

Figure 2-5 The program board oversees program management.

 NOTE Each program may have its own program board, though often program boards consult with all organizational programs. While many program stakeholders participate in the program board, the program sponsor is usually the key decision-maker on the board. You might also know the program board as a governance board or steering committee.

The whole point of program governance is to ensure that the program's projects are working toward the benefits of the program. It allows the program manager to measure and compare the results of the program's projects and their contributions, and equally to work toward the expected benefits of the program. It's also, if not more importantly, about protecting the investments of the performing organization. Program governance allows for consistency within the program and control of the participating, interdependent projects.

Program governance happens throughout the program life cycle by monitoring the adherence to rules and policies at regular intervals and at the completion of phases within the program life cycle. The successful reviews of a program by senior management allow the program to move forward. These reviews also allow program managers to infer corrective and preventive actions to fix problems that have occurred or to add activities to circumvent new problems from creeping into the program.

Chapter Summary

The PgMP examination is based on the not-so-wordy *The Standard for Program Management* and the verbose third edition of the popular *Guide to the Project Management Body of Knowledge*. Both of these books offer insight to the generally accepted practices of program management and project management. And they both read like a toaster manual. While neither book is a thrill, both add significant value to real-world program and project management.

The focus of the PgMP examination is the discipline of program management. Programs create benefits for the performing organization, and their component projects work to create conditions, services, or things that support the strategic objectives of the parent programs. The management and control of the interdependency of projects within a program is an iterative process of program management. The projects within a program work together to help a program accomplish three key themes:

- Benefits management
- Stakeholder management
- Program governance

A program may also provide, according to the PMBOK, organizational process assets to the project manager. An organizational process asset is any tool, template, application, or guideline your program or organization has created to assist the project manager and internally standardize the management of all projects within the program.

Program managers consistently monitor and control the work of the projects to ensure that their deliverables adhere to the expectations of the program scope. Program managers, and the key program stakeholders, are concerned with the scope, schedule, and costs of the program and its constituent projects. Program managers work with the project managers to manage stakeholder concerns and issues, and to resolve issues and differences among the projects.

Programs operate within an organization's portfolio. Recall that a portfolio is a collection of programs, projects, and ongoing operations to satisfy the performing organization's strategic objectives. The collection of items within an organization's portfolio truly shows the intent of a performing organization.

While programs operate within a portfolio and may answer to a program board, project managers and their projects often operate within a program. That's the point of your PgMP certification. Projects move through their phases and process groups to reach a conclusion and satisfaction of their project scope.

The goal of this chapter was to paint a big picture of program management. Keep this final word of advice in mind as you prep to pass your PgMP exam: every organization is different. While the concepts I've painted in this chapter are the generally accepted guidelines for programs, not every organization follows every step I've outlined here. For your PgMP examination, however, pretend that they do.

Key Terms

Benefits management   The sum of the planning, tools, techniques, and overall management of the activities that define, create, maximize, and sustain the benefits created by the program.

Benefits realization plan   Defines the program's expected benefits; created during the early stages of the program, it defines for the program manager and its stakeholders program success factors.

Certificate of program completion   A document that details the deliverables of the program, its projects, and the success or failure of the program's objectives.

Customer   The entity that gets the benefits the program creates.

Guide to the Project Management Body of Knowledge **(PMBOK)**   A PMI publication that defines the generally accepted practices of project management.

Negative stakeholders   People and groups that are simply opposed to the program and don't want the program to proceed.

Performing organization   The entity that the program works within.

Portfolio   A collection of programs, projects, and even ongoing operations that all have a common purpose: to reach some business objectives.

Positive stakeholders   People and groups that are in favor of the success and forward progress of the program.

Program   A collection of projects managed in a controlled, balanced effort to realize benefits not available by managing each project independently. Programs are composed of projects that work in tandem to create a consolidated deliverable that aligns with the strategic vision of the performing organization.

Program director   The executive owner of the program; this is the person the program manager reports to.

Program governance   The enforcement of the rules and procedures of an organization to ensure that they are followed in planning, executing, monitoring and controlling, and closing a program. It affords the assurance that all program procedures are followed as planned and expected by the organization, the project managers, and you, the program manager.

Program governance board   A committee that helps the program manager reach goals by providing support and resolutions for program risks and issues.

Program life cycle   The phases that a program moves through to reach its conclusion.

Program Management Office (PMO)   An office that is responsible for defining and supporting the program-related governance procedures, as well as supporting the processes and activities within a program.

Program management processes   The processes that comprise the program management activities to complete the program life cycle.

Program manager   The person that is responsible for the management of a program.

Program Office   Supports the program by handling the administrative functions of the program at one central locale.

Program sponsor   The champion of the program; this can be an individual, a customer, or a line of business within the performing organization. The sponsor, whoever it may be for a program, is responsible for providing the resources to deliver the expected benefits of the program.

Program team members   Assist the program manager to get the program work done by helping her to communicate with stakeholders, in addition to executing and completing program processes.

Project life cycle   The unique project phases that compose a project.

Project management life cycle   The universal project phases of initiating, planning, executing, monitoring and controlling, and closing.

Project managers   The managers of the projects that make up the program.

Project team members   The people on the program's project teams, the experts that do the project work.

Stakeholder management   A stakeholder is any person, group, or entity that may be affected positively or negatively by the outcome of the program. Technically this may include passive stakeholders that are interested in your program but aren't directly affected by its outcome. Stakeholder management is the balance of stakeholder identification, communication, leadership, trade-offs, competing objectives, and prioritization of needs and demands.

Stakeholder management plan   A program management plan that identifies the program's stakeholders, their roles, and their contributions to the program.

The Standard for Program Management   A PMI publication that defines the generally accepted practices of project management.

Utility   A way in which something is useful. It allows program managers to quantify the usefulness of different attributes of a program and projects.

Questions

1. You are the program manager for your organization. You have eight projects within your program. Who is responsible for the deliverables of each of the projects?

   A. You, the program manager

   B. The project sponsor

   C. The project manager of each project

   D. The project team of each project

2. Which one of the following is not a project management process group?

   A. Initiating

   B. Scheduling

   C. Monitoring and controlling

   D. Closing

3. You are working with one of your aspiring project managers, and she's curious what's so special about a program. Which one of the following is not one of the themes for program management?

   A. Organizational planning

   B. Benefit management

   C. Program governance

   D. Stakeholder management

4. Marty is the program manager for his organization. He's working with the program board to ensure that his program follows the governance as outlined by the board. What is the primary purpose of the program board?

   A. Represents the return on investment of the program

   B. Approves project plans as submitted by the program manager

   C. Provides quality control and scope verification for each project

   D. Provides guidance and decisions regarding program direction

5. Which one of the following is a benefit of creating a program?

   A. The cost of the program is less than a collection of projects.

   B. The schedule to create all the project deliverables is shortened.

   C. Risk and issue management is centralized.

   D. It's easier to communicate among the project teams than with individual projects.

6. You are the program manager for your organization. You are discussing the benefits of program management, and one your negative stakeholders asks why your organization should be investing in a program. Which one of the following program management activities could best answer the negative stakeholder's concerns regarding the investment of the program?

   A. Communication is openly shared among the project participants.

   B. Stakeholder management is centralized.

   C. Two or more projects can work together under the program.

   D. Risk mitigation activities can be shared among the projects.

7. You are working on a new program within your organization's portfolio. Your project is moving through iterations of rolling wave planning to define the program's objectives. Rolling wave planning is also known by what term?

   A. Progressive elaboration

   B. Quantitative risk analysis

   C. Program work decomposition

   D. Iterative planning

8. Your program has just closed. What document should be issued to detail the deliverables of the program, the success and failures of the program's projects, and the completion of the program's objectives?

   A. Final program assessment report

   B. Certificate of program completion

   C. Lessons learned documentation

   D. Program archives report

9. Projects are constrained by three values that are often depicted in the Iron Triangle of Project Management. Which one of the following is not a component of the Iron Triangle of Project Management?

   A. Schedule

   B. Costs

   C. Quality

   D. Scope

10. Which program management theme aims to protect the benefits of the program for the good of the program stakeholders?

    A. Program governance

    B. Benefits measurement

    C. Stakeholder management

    D. Stakeholder communications

11. Benefits management often includes intangible benefits created by the program, such as improved customer satisfaction and employee morale. What program participant is responsible for quantifying these intangible benefits?

    A. Program manager

    B. Program customer

    C. Program sponsor

    D. Business analyst

12. Tom is a program manager for his organization. His program is to create a new customer service datacenter for his company's international operations. Marcy, the Project Director, is concerned with the budget for each of the projects in Tom's program. Fred, the Program Director, is primarily concerned with the communication challenges Tom will face on this international project. Sue, Legal Council, has concerns regarding the Sarbanes-Oxley Act and wants to know how Tom will address these needs on an ongoing process. Diane is the Vice President of Sales for the organization and wants Tom to work with her to maintain current sales and to limit disruptions by his program. To whom does Tom report to in this scenario?

    A. Marcy

    B. Fred

    C. Sue

    D. Diane

13. Which program management plan identifies the program stakeholders?

    A. Program management plan

    B. Stakeholder management plan

    C. Stakeholder identification plan

    D. Communications management plan

14. All programs have rules that must be followed in order to maintain order. The enforcement of the rules is known as which one of the following?

    A. Project governance

    B. Organizational process assets

    C. Program governance

    D. Enterprise environment factors

15. June is the program manager for her organization. She has worked with the key stakeholders, the program team, project managers, and other experts to create the program plan. What entity approves the program plan so that June can begin the program work?

    A. No one; June is responsible for the program plan and its return on investment

    B. The program management office

    C. The program key stakeholders

    D. The program board

16. Which one of the following statements best describes a portfolio?

    A. A portfolio is a collection of projects with a common purpose.

    B. A portfolio is the organization of related projects, programs, and operations.

    C. A portfolio is the sum of the monies invested into programs, projects, and operations for a given time period.

    D. A portfolio is a short-term endeavor to create a unique product, service, or condition.

17. You are the program manager for your organization. Your program is a large construction project near a small lake. Anna, a resident of the city where your program is taking place, is a vocal opponent of your program and its potential impact on the nearby lake. Anna is considered which one of the following?

    A. Stakeholder

    B. Positive stakeholder

    C. Negative stakeholder

    D. Community activist

18. When does the most interaction between programs and portfolios occur in any organization?

    A. They don't; programs are just lumped into portfolios for simple structure

    B. During the program closing phase to prove return on investment

    C. During the program execution phases, as that's when the majority of the program's budget is spent

    D. During the program's initiating and planning phases

19. Which of the following statements best describes a program manager's role concerning projects within a program?

    A. Deflects change in the program so the project managers don't have to worry about change control

    B. Deflects risk in the program to alleviate project risks

    C. Coordinates efforts between projects to solve issues, track project work, and eliminate non–value added activities

    D. Coordinates efforts between project managers to help prioritize project activities

20. When is a project manager assigned to a project?

    A. When the project is chartered

    B. When the project is initiated

    C. When the program is launched

    D. When the program manager deems it necessary

Questions and Answers

1. You are the program manager for your organization. You have eight projects within your program. Who is responsible for the deliverables of each of the projects?

    A. You, the program manager

    B. The project sponsor

    C. The project manager of each project

    D. The project team of each project

    C. It is the responsibility of each project manager to create and deliver the scope of her own project. A, the program manager, is incorrect because the program manager does not get involved with the day-to-day management of each project. B, the project sponsor, is incorrect because the program manager is the project sponsor for program projects. D, the project team, is also incorrect as the project manager is responsible for the actions and deliverables the project team creates.

2. Which one of the following is not a project management process group?

    A. Initiating

    B. Scheduling

    C. Monitoring and controlling

    D. Closing

  B. Scheduling is not a project management process group. A, C, and D are incorrect choices because initiating, monitoring and controlling, and closing are project management process groups.

3. You are working with one of your aspiring project managers, and she's curious what's so special about a program. Which one of the following is not one of the themes for program management?

    A. Organizational planning

    B. Benefit management

    C. Program governance

    D. Stakeholder management

  A. Organizational planning is not a theme of program management. Programs are influenced by organizational planning, but they are not one of the themes of program management. B, C, and D, benefit management, program governance, and stakeholder management, are all program management themes, so these choices are incorrect.

4. Marty is the program manager for his organization. He's working with the program board to ensure that his program follows the governance as outlined by board. What is the primary purpose of the program board?

    A. Represents the return on investment of the program

    B. Approves project plans as submitted by the program manager

    C. Provides quality control and scope verification for each project

    D. Provides guidance and decisions regarding program direction

  D. The program board provides guidance and decisions concerning the program. A, B, and C are all incorrect. A is incorrect because the program manager does this activity. Choice B is incorrect because project managers submit project plans to the program manager, not the program manager to the program board. C, quality control, is an activity the project manager completes on each project.

5. Which one of the following is a benefit of creating a program?

    A. The cost of the program is less than a collection of projects.

    B. The schedule to create all the project deliverables is shortened.

    C. Risk and issue management is centralized.

    D. It's easier to communicate among the project teams than with individual projects.

  C. A program does centralize risk management. A may often be true, but it is not always true. B is a false statement, as the schedule of a program is not always shortened. D is incorrect; while communications may be improved, there's no evidence that communication will always be easier among program project participants.

6. You are the program manager for your organization. You are discussing the benefits of program management, and one your negative stakeholders asks why your organization should be investing in a program. Which one of the following program management activities could best answer the negative stakeholder's concerns regarding the investment of the program?

   A. Communication is openly shared among the project participants.

   B. Stakeholder management is centralized.

   C. Two or more projects can work together under the program.

   D. Risk mitigation activities can be shared among the projects.

   D. Risk mitigation activities can be shared among the projects in the program. The shared risk management activities can reduce the overall cost of the program. A, B, and C are all true statements about the program, but they do not necessarily address the negative stakeholder's financial concern.

7. You are working on a new program within your organization's portfolio. Your project is moving through iterations of rolling wave planning to define the program's objectives. Rolling wave planning is also known by what term?

   A. Progressive elaboration

   B. Quantitative risk analysis

   C. Program work decomposition

   D. Iterative planning

   A. Rolling wave planning is also known as progressive elaboration. Choices B, C, and D are incorrect terms to describe the planning iterations.

8. Your program has just closed. What document should be issued to detail the deliverables of the program, the success and failures of the program's projects, and the completion of the program's objectives?

   A. Final program assessment report

   B. Certificate of program completion

   C. Lessons learned documentation

   D. Program archives report

   B. When a program is complete, the performing organization should issue the certificate of program completion. A, the final program assessment report, is incorrect. C, lessons learned, do happen throughout the program and at the end of the program, but this is not the official program document needed. D is a false statement.

9. Projects are constrained by three values that are often depicted in the Iron Triangle of Project Management. Which one of the following is not a component of the Iron Triangle of Project Management?

   A. Schedule

   B. Costs

   C. Quality

   D. Scope

C. Quality is not one of the three angles in the Iron Triangle. Quality is often placed in the center of the triangle to represent the balance of A, B, and D; schedule, costs, and scope equate to the quality of the project.

10. Which program management theme aims to protect the benefits of the program for the good of the program stakeholders?

   A. Program governance

   B. Benefits measurement

   C. Stakeholder management

   D. Stakeholder communications

   B. Benefits management aims to protect the benefits of the program. A, program governance, is the enforcement of the program's rules and policies. C, stakeholder management, is the identification and communication with the program stakeholders. D, stakeholder communications, is not a program management theme, but it is a crucial program management activity.

11. Benefits management often includes intangible benefits created by the program, such as improved customer satisfaction and employee morale. What program participant is responsible for quantifying these intangible benefits?

   A. Program manager

   B. Program customer

   C. Program sponsor

   D. Business analyst

   A. The program manager must work to quantify the intangible program benefits. A, C, and D are incorrect program participants to quantify the intangible benefits.

12. Tom is a program manager for his organization. His program is to create a new customer service datacenter for his company's international operations. Marcy, the Project Director, is concerned with the budget for each of the projects in Tom's program. Fred, the Program Director, is primarily concerned with the communication challenges Tom will face on this international project. Sue, Legal Council, has concerns regarding the Sarbanes-Oxley Act and wants to know how Tom will address these needs on an ongoing process. Diane is the Vice President of Sales for the organization and wants Tom to work with her to maintain current sales and to limit disruptions by his program. To whom does Tom report to in this scenario?

   A. Marcy

   B. Fred

   C. Sue

   D. Diane

   B. Tom, the program manager, reports to Fred, the program director. Choice A, C, and D are all key stakeholders that Tom will need to communicate and negotiate with. His direct reporting will be to Fred.

13. Which program management plan identifies the program stakeholders?

    A. Program management plan

    B. Stakeholder management plan

    C. Stakeholder identification plan

    D. Communications management plan

    B. The stakeholder management plan identifies the program stakeholders. Choices A and D are true plans, but their purpose is the management of the program and how communications to the program participants will happen. Choice C, the stakeholder identification plan, is a bogus answer.

14. All programs have rules that must be followed in order to maintain order. The enforcement of the rules is known as which one of the following?

    A. Project governance

    B. Organizational process assets

    C. Program governance

    D. Enterprise environment factors

    C. Program governance is the enforcement of the program rules and policies. A, project governance, is superseded by program governance. B, organizational process assets, describes the assets that projects and entities within an organization create—such as software and templates. D, enterprise environmental factors, describes the processes, procedures, and regulations a company must follow, for example, procurement processing and relevant industry regulations.

15. June is the program manager for her organization. She has worked with the key stakeholders, the program team, project managers, and other experts to create the program plan. What entity approves the program plan so that June can begin the program work?

    A. No one; June is responsible for the program plan and its return on investment

    B. The program management office

    C. The program key stakeholders

    D. The program board

    D. The program board approves the program plan. A is incorrect, as June cannot approve her own plan. B and C are incorrect, as the program board is responsible for approving the plan, not the program management office or the key stakeholders.

16. Which one of the following statements best describes a portfolio?

    A. A portfolio is a collection of projects with a common purpose.

    B. A portfolio is the organization of related projects, programs, and operations.

    C. A portfolio is the sum of the monies invested into programs, projects, and operations for a given time period

    D. A portfolio is a short-term endeavor to create a unique product, service, or condition

  B. Portfolios arrange common projects, programs, and operations. A, C, and D are all incorrect descriptions of a portfolio.

17. You are the program manager for your organization. Your program is a large construction project near a small lake. Anna, a resident of the city where your program is taking place, is a vocal opponent of your program and its potential impact on the nearby lake. Anna is considered which one of the following?

    A. Stakeholder

    B. Positive stakeholder

    C. Negative stakeholder

    D. Community activist

  C. Anna is opposed to your program, so she is considered a negative stakeholder. While choice A is tempting, a stakeholder does not fully answer the question. B is incorrect; Anna is opposed to your program, so she is not a positive stakeholder. D is not a program management term—though some may consider Anna a community activist, she's technically a negative stakeholder.

18. When does the most interaction between programs and portfolios occur in any organization?

    A. They don't; programs are just lumped into portfolios for simple structure

    B. During the program closing phase to prove return on investment

    C. During the program execution phases, as that's when the majority of the program's budget is spent

    D. During the program's initiating and planning phases

  D. Programs and portfolios interact the most during the program's initiating and planning phases. Choices A, C, and B are all incorrect.

19. Which of the following statements best describes a program manager's role concerning projects within a program?

    A. Deflects change in the program so that the project managers don't have to worry about change control

    B. Deflects risk in the program to alleviate project risks

    C. Coordinates efforts between projects to solve issues, track project work, and eliminate non–value added activities

    D. Coordinates efforts between project managers to help prioritize project activities

  C. Program managers work to resolve issues, track project work, and eliminate waste. Choice A is untrue, as program managers must readily adapt to change. B is true, as the program manager does work to alleviate risk, but it is not the best choice. D is a false statement.

20. When is a project manager assigned to a project?
    A. When the project is chartered
    B. When the project is initiated
    C. When the program is launched
    D. When the program manager deems it necessary
    A. Project managers are named in the project's charter. Choices B, C, and D are all incorrect choices for project manager assignment.

Introducing the Program Life Cycle

In this chapter, you will

- Explore the program life cycle
- Plan for benefits management
- Plan for stakeholder management
- Plan for program governance
- Explore the program phases

Did you ever run a lemonade stand as a kid? I did. Lemonade stands gave way to mowing lawns, raking leaves, and shoveling snow. Eventually, I sold and traded baseball cards. Ah, yes, I was quite the entrepreneur—and I run my own business still today. I bet you or a program manager colleague of yours has an entrepreneurial streak as well. That's one of the best parts, in my opinion, about being a program manager. It's like running your own business. You get to call the shots, to some extent, and oversee a collection of projects that work together to reach the goals and strategic objectives your organization expects.

Right out of PMI's book, *The Standard for Program Management,* they praise the entrepreneurial zeal it takes to be a program manager. Program managers need more than entrepreneurship; they also require vision, motivation, and sound management processes. That's what this chapter is about—being a great program manager by using those sound business processes.

Technically, this chapter is about the program's life cycle. A life cycle is the, uh, life of a program. A program life cycle includes everything from the genesis of the program, its activities and processes, its deliverables, and its closing. (I could have said death, but that's just too morbid.)

As an experienced project manager, you'll be familiar with many of the themes in this chapter. Programs, as I know you know, are made up of projects. Because the success of a program is dependent on the outcome of the program's projects, you'll receive a refresher of project management terminology mapped to program management. You'll be relieved to know that a program has the same knowledge areas and process groups as a project. You won't be relieved, however, to learn that the individual processes within a program are entirely different than the 44 project management processes.

Finally, before I hop into the meaty stuff, know that a good program manager, a person just like you, doesn't get mixed up in the day-to-day project management. Program managers worry about high-level objectives and depend on project managers to manage and detail the project intricacies. As you move through this chapter, and boy-oh-boy it's a page turner, keep in mind that you're interested in the big picture at the program level, not the minutiae of the projects.

Exploring the Program Management Life Cycle

Programs are big beasts. When you manage a program, you likely don't always look at the whole program, but you see its progression through a series of phases. Each phase allows the program to move on to the next phase, and then the next, and so on until you've reached the end of the program's life cycle—whenever that may be. There's no hard and fast rule about what work makes up a program's life cycle, because work for every program is typically different than that for other programs.

Consider a program in construction versus a program in information technology. The specific work in the phases that compose the construction program would not map very well to an IT program—or vice versa. Now it is completely reasonable, however, that an organization could use the same program model over and over. Let's take the construction project as an example. If the construction organization were to implement the same program for different clients over and over, the phases and projects of the program work would be the same from program to program with adaptations to current situations, risks, and stakeholders.

If you're thinking this model sounds an awfully lot like project management, you're correct. A project also moves through phases until it reaches its end result. The key difference, however, is that programs aim to manage outcomes and benefits, whereas projects are about creating deliverables. Projects create deliverables that may be used immediately by the performing organization, or their deliverables allow other program projects to move forward.

Working with Program Life Cycles

A program life cycle moves through logical phases to reach, typically, ongoing operations or the closure of the program. Within a discipline, such as construction, the phases of the programs are going to be similar from program to program. The nature of a program may shape the phases of the program life cycle. Consider the program governance for each of the following knowledge areas:

- **Scope of the program** The scope of the program defines the benefits of the program.

- **Schedule for program benefit realization** The timeline of the program defines when the project's deliverables may be incorporated into ongoing operations.

- **Budget for the program** The aggregate costs of the projects and the costs of managing the program define the cost baseline.

- **Quality expectations of the program and its projects**   The satisfied quality measured at the end of a program phase allows the program to move on to subsequent phases.

- **Staffing demands**   Consider the availability of skilled labor, consultants, and subject matter experts. A resource shortage may affect the schedule, costs, risks, and other knowledge areas within the program.

- **Communication challenges**   Language barriers, time zone differences, regulatory issues, and stakeholder constraints may affect the phases of a program.

- **Risk management**   Program managers may adjust the phases of a program to account for the amount of risk exposure the program is leveraging in the project.

- **Procurement processes**   Enterprise environmental factors and the rules of the program governance may affect the procurement processes within the program. Consider step funding and cash flow forecasting and their impact on procurement in a program and its phases.

At the end of a program phase the incremental benefits, quality, and program management are reviewed through a phase-gate review. The phase-gate review, sometimes just called a program gate or a gate review, is completed by senior management. The goal of the gate review is to confirm that you, the program manager, are tracking the expected benefits of your program. A gate review is an opportunity for the program manager and senior management to make corrective actions, take preventive actions, or simply allow the program to continue as is.

The gate reviews are often integrated with program funding as Figure 3-1 illustrates. The success of a phase gate review releases funds to move the program to the next phase. This is typically done through step funding (see the steps in the funding?).

Figure 3-1
Step funding provides monies to move the program through its life cycle.

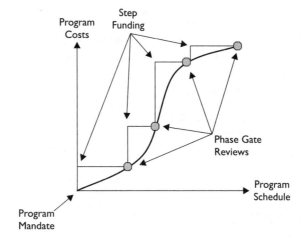

While programs and projects both move through phases, and both may undergo phase reviews, there are three clear differences between programs and projects and their life cycles:

1. Program life cycles often overlap into operations, while projects create the project scope and then are closed.

2. Project deliverables are incorporated into the incremental benefits of the program.

3. Deliverables from multiple projects often need to be integrated with other project deliverables in order for their benefits to be realized.

 NOTE The concept of integrated deliverables to realize the program benefits is subtle. Consider two projects in a program: the deployment of 25,000 computers and the creation of a custom software application for the 25,000 computers. While the deployment of the computers and the creation of the application can happen independently of one another, it doesn't benefit the program until these deliverables are combined for the recipient of the computer and the software.

Projects and their life cycle phases can vary wildly within one program. Consider all the different projects and their respective phases during the creation of a skyscraper. The structural engineering project and its phases are not going to be the same as the phases of the mechanical engineering project. The program manager may, however, define common phase names for all of the projects within the program. The benefit of common, though somewhat generic, nomenclature for each project is the establishment of a standard lexicon and point of reference for all project managers, organizational management, and all the other key stakeholders.

Examining a Program Life Cycle

All of this talk about the differences of program life cycles from program to program and how program life cycles differ from project life cycles probably has you all excited and eager to see how PMI addresses the issue. Right out of their book, *The Standard for Program Management*, PMI identifies a generic program life cycle as seen in Figure 3-2. If I were you, I'd know this generic life cycle for your upcoming PgMP examination. And yeah, that's a big old hint.

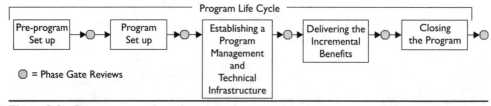

Figure 3-2 Programs move through generic phases to operations.

I'll delve into each of these generic phases later in this chapter, but for now just get acquainted with these phases:

- **Pre-program set up** The program concept is shared, and there's an organizational rally cry for program support and stakeholder buy-in. The program is chartered and the program manager has been identified.

- **Program set up** The program's scope, schedule, activities, costs, and other planning results are generated.

- **Establishing a program management and technical infrastructure** The "bones" of the program are created. The infrastructure defines how the program and its projects will operate.

- **Delivering the incremental benefits** The program's projects are initiated, and the project managers and their project teams go about creating the incremental benefits for the goal of the program.

- **Closing the program** The program moves through its closure and documentation of its successes and failures.

- **Ongoing operations** The realized benefits of the program are incorporated into ongoing operations for the performing organization.

At the end of each program phase there is a gate review, that I mentioned earlier, that allows the program to move onward. The gate review usually also provides a cash infusion to the program through its step funding.

Identifying Program Life Cycle Themes

As you know, there are three themes that span a program's life cycle:

- Benefits management
- Stakeholder management
- Program governance

As a program moves through its phases, the responsibilities of the program manager adjust to manage these three themes based on the conditions the program creates. Program managers are constantly working to maintain balance and react to situations within their programs to realize the expectations of their program customers, senior management, and the project managers within the program.

Enforcing Benefits Management

With all the moving parts of a program, it is imperative that the program manager has created, through the program management technical infrastructure phase, a methodology to realize and track the benefits the program creates. This means that the program manager establishes procedures and process to identify, track, record, and maintain the benefits the program creates.

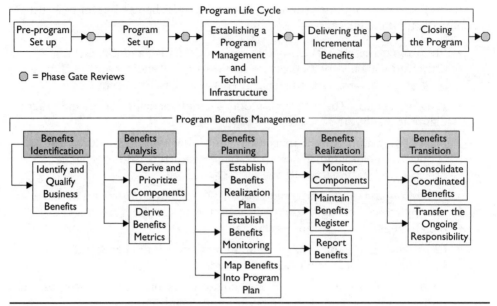

Figure 3-3   Benefit management moves through its own parallel life cycle.

Benefits management also has its own life cycle that runs in parallel to the program as seen in Figure 3-3. As the program moves through its phases, the processes the program manager has identified also evolve, peak, and eventually move into ongoing operations.

Identifying the Program Benefits

When the program is in its pre-program set up phase the program manager, senior management, and the key stakeholders must work together to establish the objectives of the program. Specific to benefits management, this means identifying the business benefits the program will create. When the program is in the pre-program set up phase, recall that its goal is to identify how the program will meet organizational objectives. The identified benefits should be in alignment with the organizational objectives.

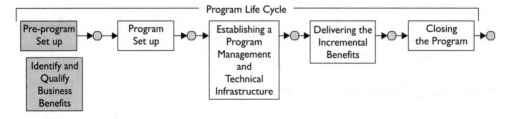

Completing Benefits Analysis

When the program has passed its first gate review and moves into the program set up phase, the program manager has been officially named and the program's charter has been issued. In regard to benefits management, the charter defines the high-level objectives, scope, vision, and the program constraints that have been identified. Based on the charter and any other supporting detail of the program, the program manager must define the specific benefits of the program.

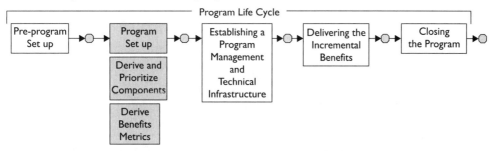

The first benefits management activity is to collect the specific, expected benefits the program is to create for the performing organization from the program charter, senior management, and key stakeholders. Once the benefits have been clearly defined, the program manager works to prioritize the benefit components for project initiation, goal setting, and scope creations.

The second benefits management activity in this phase of the program life cycle is to identify the metrics for success for each of the identified program benefits. In other words, vague, subjective terms like fast, good, and satisfied must have metrics tied to them in order to measure the program's overall success. What's good for the program manager may not be the same level of good the customer envisions.

 NOTE   This is where the old business adage of what gets measured gets done proves true once again.

Planning for Program Benefits

Once the program moves through its second gate, it moves into the "Establishing a Program Management and Technical Infrastructure" phase. The point of this phase is to establish the rules and procedures the program's projects will follow in order to create the benefits the program expects.

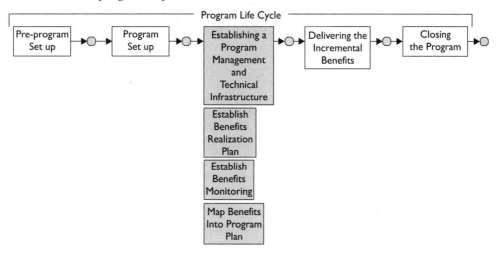

The first benefits management activity in this phase of the program is to create a Benefits Realization Plan. This plan defines how the program and its projects will create the integrated benefits for the program. The plan defines the procedure for benefits realization and the interaction between constituent projects and the program. There is some overlap in this benefits management activity and the program governance activities.

While it'd be nice to assign project managers and go play golf for the duration of the program, you know that's not going to work. That's why the second benefit management activity is the establishment of the benefits monitoring processes. This interaction between the program manager and the project managers measures and qualifies the benefits the program is to create.

The final benefits management planning activity is to map the benefits into the program management plan. This documentation of the benefits includes the qualifiers for success, describes the process of moving the realized benefits into operations, and allows the program to move the benefits into its next phase, Delivering the Incremental Benefits.

Performing Benefits Realization

The program will pass through another gate review, and if deemed worthy, it'll move on to the fourth phase of the program management life cycle: Delivering the Incremental Benefits. This phase of the program management life cycle is about the execution of all the projects within the program. The project managers and their project teams are busy folks now creating the deliverables their project plans call for.

The first benefits management activity the program manager enforces is the monitoring of the program components. The program manager monitors the projects within the program to ensure that each project manager is keeping on task, on scope, on budget, and generally on track in order to create the benefits the program expects. The monitoring and control of the projects by the program manager allow corrective and preventive actions to ensure the project managers create what's expected of them.

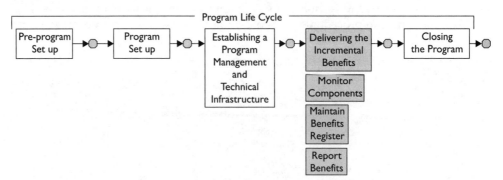

The program manager also creates and maintains a benefits register. This register, most likely electronic, tracks the following benefits characteristics:

- What the benefit is and its constituent components
- What project components are dependent on or contribute to the realized benefit

- Time to create the benefits
- Cost to create the benefits
- Risks and issues surrounding the benefit
- Ancillary benefits tied to the benefit
- All other relevant benefit information

The benefits register allows the program manager to quantify the benefits for the performing organization. It's feasible that the benefits register could trigger profit and loss statements, earned value management scenarios, and overall performance reports. The benefits register certainly becomes part of organizational process assets and may be used in other similar programs and operations.

Simply documenting the benefits in the benefits register won't do. The program manager also relies on the program's communications management plan and reports the benefits to the appropriate stakeholder. While a cursory glance seems to show that benefits reporting is a good and happy thing (it usually is), the delay and cost overruns tied to the realization of the benefit may warrant a variance or exceptions report.

Completing the Benefits Transition Activities

The final phase of the program is to close the program and move the benefits into operations. Closing the program means that the scope of the program has been met or the program was canceled. I'll talk more about program closing and all the work that's tied to it later in this chapter, but for now I want to focus on the benefits transition that moves the realized, documented benefits the projects have created into the ongoing operations of the performing organization.

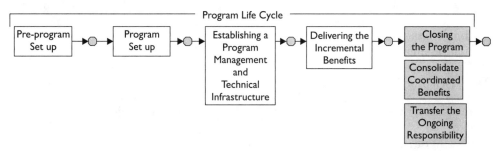

The first activity in this phase is the consolidation of the coordinated benefits. Go back to our skyscraper example. All of the projects in the skyscraper don't do much good on their own; an elevator to nowhere isn't much good. This activity confirms the success of the interrelationships of the projects and their deliverables. This goes beyond my simple elevator example, as this process includes the financial, schedule, resource management, and any other gains the program realized by coordinating the projects in the program.

Once the benefits have been realized, documented, and consolidated, they can be moved into the ongoing operations of the organization. Specifically, this involves the transfer of the responsibility for the benefits the program has created. In most instances the program doesn't cut and run from the program deliverables, but rather it provides an overlap time period from the program closure to the true ongoing operations of the organization. This may be ongoing or initial support and maintenance of the program deliverables or the opportunity to perform quality control, or even the support of a warranty for the deliverables.

Managing the Program Stakeholders

A stakeholder is anyone that has a vested interest in your program. Recall that stakeholders can be the individuals that are affected by your program benefits and the deliverables of your project. Stakeholders can also be organizations such as government agencies and vendors that may influence your project.

Stakeholders can also be positive or negative. Care to guess the difference? It's a pretty straightforward business: the ones that like your program are positive, and the schmucks that hate your program are negative. A central goal of stakeholder management is to market, sell, and create buy-in from all the stakeholders as early as possible in the program. There are lots of ways of accomplishing this process:

- Identify and communicate with the program stakeholders as necessary
- Involve the stakeholders from the pre-program set up phase
- Invite the stakeholders to express the concerns and threats about the program
- Invoke the project manager's communications management plan to communicate with the correct stakeholders in the individual projects
- Iteratively participate in meetings with the program stakeholders

 NOTE I used a bunch of words starting with the letter "I" in the bulleted list. I think it's a good idea for your exam to find patterns and create mnemonics to remember important lists and facts. It helps me—maybe it'll do the same for you.

Program stakeholder management demands a stakeholder management plan. This plan, coupled with a communications management plan, defines all of the program stakeholders—their concerns, positions on the program, and threats they perceive (real or imagined)—as well as how the program manager may communicate with the stakeholders. The point of the stakeholder management plan is to be proactive rather than reactive. In other words, the program manager and the program support staff must anticipate problems and issues that may upset stakeholders and address the issues before the stakeholders learn about them secondhand.

Identifying Program Stakeholders

There are lots of stakeholders in a program—and it's no easy process to identify them. Even changes within the program may cause new stakeholders to be introduced. Changes, in this instance, mean more than expected changes of the program benefit expectations and changes to the project scope; they include changes to vendors, schedules, and laws, along with any other fluctuations in staffing and resources.

Some good news, though: there are always some key stakeholders you'll have on every program. You might as well learn these now and be familiar with these folks for your PgMP exam. Here's a list of your new best friends:

- **Program director**   The big enchilada; this person has the executive ownership of the program.

- **Program manager**   Hey, that's you!

- **Project managers**   These pesky worrywarts hate changes to their project scope, hate changes to their project team, and often hate Monday through Thursday as well.

- **Program sponsor**   Your pal that initiates the program and cheerfully gives you all the resources (cash, materials, equipment, facilities, and people) that you could ever use.

- **Customer**   The person or people that will receive, use, and love the benefits of your program. Okay, they may not love what your program gives them, but just kinda pretend that they do. You'll save on aspirins and ulcers.

- **Performing organization**   No, this is not the Radio City Rockettes. The performing organization is the entity (your company) that sponsors and funds your program.

- **Program team members**   The kind people that fear you and help you get through the program with your sanity. Buy them chocolate, lunches, and martinis every month (and not necessarily in that order).

- **Project team members**   The people who work for your project managers to create the project deliverables that will create the benefits of your program. Buy them chocolate at your discretion.

- **Program management office** (PMO)   If your organization has a PMO, you'll know that it provides structure, rules, templates, software, and direction for your program.

- **Program office**   A centralized office that handles administrative duties centrally for all programs within your organization. (Doesn't that sound nice?)

- **Program governance board**   This group of punchy folks helps you reach your program goals by addressing risks and issues within your program.

- **Suppliers**   Vendors, love 'em or hate 'em, are stakeholders. Make certain they buy you chocolate, lunches, and martinis every month. (Kidding! Don't succumb to ethical compromise over lobsters and blue cheese–stuffed olives.)

- **Government agencies**   Changes to laws and regulations may have an influence on your program.

- **Competitors**   You do have competition, don't you? If your program is a biggie, your competition is likely to keep an eye on your successes and failures.

- **Interested parties**   Not parties like my neighbor George has every weekend, but parties like groups of concerned citizens, consumer groups, and environmental activists.

A big chunk of stakeholder management is to identify these people and determine what their interests, concerns, and perceived threats may be. Document your findings in the stakeholder management plan and communicate accordingly.

Enforcing Program Governance

Program governance is the adherence to the rules, procedures, and infrastructure of the program. Program governance is often enforced by a program steering committee or governance board. The governance board and steering committees review the program's progress, the management of the program's benefits, and the adherence to the infrastructure all program participants agreed to abide by.

In addition to the governance board, the program manager will participate in phase gate reviews at milestones or at the end of a program phase. To be clear, a milestone is a timeless event in the program that signals the program has made progress. Figure 3-4 is an example of a program that has phase gate reviews scheduled at major milestones and at the completion of program phases.

I know you're dying to know what exactly happens in a phase gate review. I'll tell you. The phase gate reviews are an examination of several program characteristics:

- The program's continued alignment with the strategy of the performing organization.

- The program's return on investment (ROI) to date; it's possible there is no ROI, as the program may not realize a profit until the program is completed.

Figure 3-4
Phase gate reviews
can happen at
milestones and
phase completions.

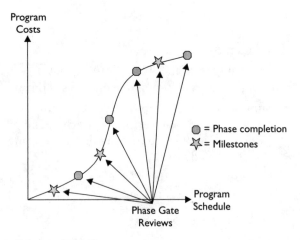

Many programs, such as those in IT, have tiered benefits where an ROI can be realized and cash flow forecasting comes into play.

- The program manager and the governance board examine the response, control, and assessment of threats, issues, and risks.

- The realized and expected benefits are confirmed to still be in alignment with the performing organization's strategic vision.

- The level of risk exposure is measured and considered to still be acceptable, or not acceptable, to the performing organization. Risk identification and analysis is an iterative process within program management and project management. New risks may be identified, and the probability and impact of an identified risk may change in accordance with conditions within the projects and program.

- Finally, the phase gate reviews ensure that good practices are being followed by the program manager and the program management team. Play by the rules.

The whole point of a phase gate review is to confirm that the program manager has met the necessarily criteria to move the program into the next phase of the program. In a sense, phase gate reviews provide a green light to the program manager and ultimately provide a "go or no-go decision" process. I'm certain all your programs are green-lighted and always get the go signal.

Exploring the Program Management Life Cycle

At the start of this chapter, I defined the program management life cycle as the collection of phases that make up the program. A phase, in program management, defines the activities and events that are expected to happen within that time period of the program. The actual work in a program phase can differ from program to program, no doubt about that, but the phases I'm describing in this section, and that you'll need to know for your PgMP certification, are the generally accepted phases that all programs move through.

There are five phases in a program's management life cycle:

- Completing the Pre-Program Set Up Phase
- Completing the Program Set Up Phase
- Establishing Program Management and Technical Infrastructure
- Delivering the Program Benefits
- Closing the Program

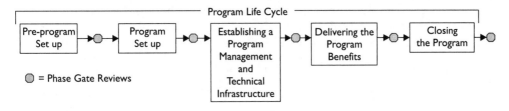

For your PgMP certification exam, learn these phases and their characteristics. Often when I'm teaching a program management course or consulting with an organization, I'll meet program managers that resist the terminology I'm about to share with you regarding phases. These resistant program managers are good people; they have lots of work and responsibility on their plate; and their brains are packed with internal organizational terms, abbreviations, schedules, and more.

Allow me to be frank: in your organization, your job, you can call this stuff whatever the heck you and your boss want to call it. Your terminology doesn't bother me at all, honest! The PgMP exam, however, isn't mapped to your personal program management experience. My desire is for you to pass your exam and to get on with your life. In order for you to do that, you've got to know the PMI way, and this, my friend, is why I'm here to help.

I'm about to step off my PgMP certification soap box, but before I do know this: answer the questions the way PMI expects you to answer them, with their terminology. Once you've passed the exam, you can go about your business out in the "real world." I think you'll discover, however, that regardless of the terminology the attributes of these phases are common with your organization's naming system. As Shakespeare said, "What's in a name? A rose by any other name would smell as sweet."

 NOTE   I bet you didn't think you'd read some Shakespeare in here. My treat for you.

Completing the Pre-Program Set Up Phase

The goal of this first phase of the program life cycle is to create solid support, approval, and morale backing for the program. It's essential for a program to be successful to have the backing of the performing organization. If a program can't gain support of the executive committee, the portfolio management board, or the key stakeholders before the program officially launches, look out for trouble.

In your experiences as a project and program manager, you've probably worked with sponsors, champions, and cheerleaders for your program or projects. The political capital and influence these people can exert for your program lends credibility, buy-in, motivation, and goodwill for the endeavor. You need buy-in and general consensus for your programs.

In addition to the goodwill and support behind your program, there's also likely to be a selection process through a program board, portfolio management group, or executive sponsor. Someone, or some group, has to create a mandate explaining why the program needs to exist within the organization. The mandate, sometimes called a program brief, details the benefits the program will create for the organization and how the benefits will help your organization reach its strategic vision. There are several factors that may contribute to the program selection and initiation:

- Available resources (people, facilities, and funding)
- Initial program estimates

- Program benefits analysis
- Program risks
- Definition of how the program fits into the organization's long-term goals

If you were to compare programs and projects, you'd find that projects are about satisfying a need, creating a unique product or service, or making a new result in any organization. Programs, however, are really about change in an organization. The change comes about through a collection of projects, but the program acts as an organizational change agent to move the organization to a new level of business, to recognize new revenues, or to eliminate waste. With that thought in mind, it's easy to see the value of the pre-program set up phase to clearly establish how the program will map to and reach the strategic objectives through its projects. Also at this time there's some serious thought and discussion as to why there needs to be a program rather than just a project. The organization may consider the following:

- The availability and sharing of resources across the program
- The duration of the proposed program
- Involvement of lines of business and corporate entities in the program
- The nature of the program, which may call for interrelated projects where each project will create project deliverables that will ultimately contribute to the unique set of program deliverables (the output of two independent projects create one usable product or service)

Once the program has been chartered, a high-level program management plan is created. This plan defines why the program has been created, the program objectives, and how the program aligns with the strategic vision of the organization. The plan also defines three program statements:

- **Mission** Why the program exists and the mission it aims to solve
- **Vision** What the organization and the realized benefits will look like once the program is closed
- **Values** How the program will manage trade-offs, competing objectives, and program and organizational decisions as a result of the program

The pre-program set up phase accomplishes several things for you, the program manager, and your organization. First and foremost it defines the strategic value of the program and the business change the program will deliver. The phase also identifies the key decision makers for your program and what their interests and concerns about the program may be. The selection committee will document how the proposed program will bring the organization to its strategic goals and vision through the program's objectives.

In some instances, the pre-program set up phase provides a high-level business case that defines why the program is needed, the feasibility of undertaking the program, and the justification of the organization's resources into the program. Once these hurdles have been cleared and the program is ready to confirm, a program charter is signed by the key stakeholders, and the program manager is officially named.

Completing the Program Set Up Phase

Now that the program has completed its first phase gate review and received "approval in principle," the real work begins. The program manager sets about defining how the program will reach the objectives defined in the pre-program set up phase. The guts of the program set up phase are to create a program management plan to answer the following questions:

- What are the program deliverables?
- When will the deliverables be ready for use?
- What is the program's cost?
- What risks and issues have been identified?
- What program dependencies have been identified?
- What assumptions have been identified and tested?
- What constraints may affect the program?
- What is the plan for the execution of the program?
- How will the program be managed?

These questions are answered by the program manager and the program management team as they complete time and cost estimates, feasibility studies, risk identification, and procurement decisions. The program manager also dissects the program to define what projects will be chartered in order to reach the program objectives. Each project that is identified to be chartered requires a business case that addresses the technical, cost investment, and regulatory concerns for the project.

As you can tell, there's lots of planning to be done in this phase of the program. The results of the planning create several documents and decisions:

- Program scope definition
- Activity definition
- Activity sequencing
- Duration estimates
- Procurement decisions
- Staffing allocation (internal and external acquisition)
- Cost estimating and program budgeting
- Risk management for the program and its projects
- Approval of the program management plan
- Identification of the program management team

In conjunction with these activities, the program manager must continue to foster support for the program through communication with key stakeholders. The stakeholder management plan and the communications management plan will guide the program manager. Updates to these plans happen as new stakeholders may be identi-fied, conditions within the program change, or influences outside of the program, such as regulatory concerns, affect the program.

Establishing Program Management and Technical Infrastructure

This phase of the generic program management life cycle is all about establishing and then enforcing the rules and procedures for the program. The rules of the program are enforced upon the program management team, upon the project managers, and upon the project teams. The rules and procedures ensure that the program manager and by default her project managers are uniform in their approach to the program work.

The program manager may rely on organization-wide tools such as Enterprise Re-source Planning (ERP) software, program and project tracking software, time and ex-pense reporting software, and other tools that can track the moving characteristics of the program. In addition to these tools, the program manager abides by the organiza-tion's enterprise environmental factors, which define the approach and internal pro-cesses of the program, projects, and even operations.

 NOTE   You won't find the term "enterprise environmental factors" in PMI's *The Standard for Program Management* book. I find this especially interesting, as in the third edition of the PMBOK Guide it's mentioned on practically every page. Go figure. If you're not familiar with the term, it simply means the processes of an organization to get things done. A great example of an enterprise environmental factor is an organization's procurement process. How your company buys stuff may be totally different than how my company buys stuff.

The technical infrastructure phase of program management also includes the peo-ple that organize, contribute to, and lead the program. The organizational structure of your program will include

- **Program board**   You've met these people already. They're interested in how your program will help your organization meet its strategic visions. A program board can also be supplemented by the program management office.

- **Program manager**   Of course, the program manager is part of the program structure. Surprise, surprise, surprise.

- **Executive sponsor**   Works with, and sometimes as a part of, the program board to help make program decisions.

- **Program director**   This person owns the program. In most instances, the executive sponsor and the program director are the same person.

- **Program team**   Creates program-level benefits and helps the program manager lead the program.

- **Program office**   Supports the program manager and may influence program governance issues.

These people form the program organization and work with the program manager to move the program and its projects toward delivering the benefits. The structure of the program assists the program manager to lead the project managers and their teams to deliver the program benefits. They'll do this by offering program support, communications, benefits measurement, and issue and risk assessment, as well as by providing facilities and technologies to the program management team.

Delivering the Program Benefits

This phase is like my Uncle Lee: it can go on and on for a long time. The difference between this program phase and my Uncle Lee, however, is that things are getting done. More specifically, the program manager is chartering and initiating projects, plans are being created and executed, and the project deliverables are contributing to the incremental benefits of the program.

This phase is where the essence of the program is being completed, because the projects within the program are creating their deliverables. The larger the scope of the program, the longer and more intense this phase of the program may be. There are several iterative activities the program manager and the program management team do during this phase of the program:

- Initiating the program's projects in a timely manner to meet the program schedule demands
- Monitoring and controlling the program projects through the program governance procedures
- Managing the transition of the "as-is" state of the program to the target state of the program (in other words, getting from the present state to the desired, promised, future state of the program)
- Working with the appointed project managers to ensure that they are adhering to the uniform project management structure the program demands
- Performing project scope verification to ensure that the project deliverables are meeting the business and technical requirements
- Performing scope, time, and cost monitoring and control to ensure that the projects and the program are adhering to the program management plan
- Monitoring, identifying, and documenting environmental changes or issues that may affect the program management plan, the program projects, or the expected benefits of the program
- Working with the project managers to ensure that coordinated efforts and dependencies between the projects are scheduled and performing as expected
- Implementing corrective actions in the program as needed
- Working with interdependent projects to coordinate resource sharing, activity scheduling, and critical chain management
- Evaluating and approving program change requests
- Performing ongoing communications with the program stakeholders
- Performing risk identification, risk documentation, and risk mitigation where necessary

NOTE Risk mitigation is any effort put forth or monies invested in the risk event to reduce or eliminate the probability and/or impact of the risk event. A great, and simple, example of risk mitigation is backing up your computer's data. You've reduced the impact of the risk event of your hardware failing by having a backup of the data. Of course, risk mitigation can be much more complex, like a disaster recovery plan, expedited materials, and resource leveling, in a program.

Because these actions are iterative and a program can be made up of many projects, it will take some savvy, consistency, and leadership to coordinate the efforts of the projects within the program. The program manager's best tool is communication—and that includes the facilitation of communication between project managers. In some larger programs, the program management office will work with the program manager to coordinate the communications and activities of the project teams within the program. When all's said and done, it's the program manager's (or the PMO's) responsibility to identify the intersection and dependencies of projects and to work with the project managers to ensure smooth transactions among the project team.

Closing the Program

Programs don't last forever, though sometimes they may feel like they do. Programs, like their projects, eventually are closed and their benefits are moved on to groups or operations within the performing organization. The point of this phase, in case you missed it, is to close down the program in a logical and orderly fashion and to be certain that the benefits of the program have been transferred to responsible parties within the organization or to the customer.

One of the first activities of program closure is to communicate with the program stakeholders and the program sponsor. The communication, at this point of the program life cycle, is about the program closure and the accomplishments the program made for the organization and the customer. Specifically, the program manager communicates and confirms the status of the program benefits for the customer. The contract of the program may require the program manager or program resources to continue to provide some level of support for the program deliverable.

Once the program has moved into closing, the program manager disbands the program by releasing the program organization: the program management team, administrative support, contracted vendors, and any facilities that have been reserved for the program's usage. The program manager should work to redeploy the human resources and to share the news that facilities are no longer needed by the program. It's not a secret when the program is done.

Part of closing the program is to also document any final lessons learned by the program manager in the organizational database so that the lessons can be utilized by other, similar programs. Bear in mind that lessons learned aren't done just at the end of the program, but throughout the program—though often at the ends of phases and at milestones. Lessons learned often discuss what areas of the program were weak and need improvement, and what the program manager and team did to address the problem.

An important step of closing the program is to discuss any recommended changes to the program that weren't implemented as part of the program but that may be good for the performing organization. In other words, there may have been change requests that for want of time and monies just couldn't be implemented during the current program life cycle. While it won't be a big surprise that the changes were not implemented, the program manager may want the performing organization to implement the changes later through a new program or project.

Finally, the program manager makes certain that all of the program information, records, communications, and supporting details are gathered and archived for future use by the performing organization. This information becomes part of organizational process assets—it's now historical information for other projects and programs the performing organization may launch.

Chapter Summary

Programs are composed of phases. Phases, just like the phases in projects, create a logical progression of events from launch to completion. The completion of a phase results in some definitive deliverable, benefit, or scenario that signals that the program is making progress—the program is moving toward benefits realization and eventually program closure.

At the end of a phase the program passes through a phase gate. Recall that the phase gate is a review of the program's accomplishments in the prior phase and a look forward to what the program will accomplish next. Financing for programs is often released based on the successful pass-through of the phase gate.

One of the main reasons a program is organized into phases, other than the logical progression of the program, is to capture and realize the expected benefits of the program in a timely and orderly manner. Benefits management allows the program manager and the key stakeholders to track, measure, and monitor the program benefits. Program governance ensures that the program manager, the program management team, and the program stakeholders are following the rules and requirements of the program in order to get to the program benefits.

Benefits management is seen throughout all of the phases of the program. In pre-program set up the benefits of the program are identified. In the program set up phase benefits analysis occurs and metrics are defined to measure the benefits of the program. Benefit planning and the establishment of how to monitor the benefits happen in the program management and technical infrastructure phase. You get to realize the benefits from your hard work (and the project team members' hard work) during the phase of incremental benefit delivery. Finally, during the program closure phase the benefits are transitioned into the ongoing responsibility of the performing organization.

Key Terms

Benefits analysis   A program set up process that derives and prioritizes program benefit components and establishes benefit metrics.

Benefits planning   A program management and technical infrastructure phase process that creates a benefits realization plan, establishes benefits monitoring, and maps the expected benefits into the program plan.

Benefits realization   A process found in the course of delivering the incremental benefits program phase. This process includes the monitoring of the program components, the maintenance of the benefits register, and the reporting of the benefits as they come into program fruition.

Benefits transition   A program closure process that consolidates the benefits the program has created and then transfers the realized benefits into ongoing operations.

Closing the program phase   The program moves through its closure and documentation of its success and failures.

Corrective actions   Any effort to rectify problems or issues that are taking the program (or project) off its scope.

Delivering the incremental benefits phase   The program's projects are initiated, and the project managers and their project teams go about creating the incremental benefits for the goal of the program.

Enterprise environmental factors   The policies, procedures, regulations, culture, and conditions that affect the way a program is managed within a performing organization.

Establishing a program management and technical infrastructure phase   Creating the "bones" of the program. The infrastructure defines how the program and its projects will operate.

Lessons learned   Documentation of what was learned about the program's weaknesses, failures, and opportunities to improve overall performance.

Operations   The normal, ongoing, day-to-day functions of an organization.

Phase gate review   The review of the program's adherence to the performing organization's strategic objectives, analysis of any immediate ROI, review of program risks and threats, and confirmation that the program manager and program management team are adhering to the established rules and policies of the program. Phase gate reviews happen at the end of a program phase.

Pre-program set up phase   The program concept is shared, and there's an organization rallying cry for program support and stakeholder buy-in.

Program benefits identification   A pre-program set up phase activity that identifies the expected benefits the program is to create for the performing organization.

Program charter   Identifies the program manager and grants the program management the authority to manage all aspects of the program.

Program director   A key program stakeholder that has the executive ownership of the program.

Program governance   Adherence to the rules, procedures, and infrastructure of the program. Program governance is often enforced by a program steering committee or governance board.

Program governance board   A staff that helps the program manager adhere to the program goals by addressing risks and issues within your program.

Program set up phase   The program is chartered, and the program manager is officially assigned.

Stakeholder management   A program management theme to identify, communicate with, create consensus among, and involve the stakeholders in the program.

Stakeholder management plan   A plan the defines how the program manager will manage the program stakeholders through communications, involvement, and marketing of the program, as well as how she will address perceived stakeholder threats and concerns regarding the program.

Questions

1. You are the program manager for a large manufacturing organization. You have just completed the program set up phase of your program. What event should happen next?
   A. The program moves into establishing a program management and technical infrastructure phase.
   B. The program moves into the delivering the incremental benefits phase.
   C. The program moves into a risk assessment review process.
   D. The program moves through a phase gate review.

2. Stephanie, a project manager of a project in your program, is about to close her project. She has asked you, the program manager, what will happen to the deliverable, a program benefit, of her project if it's not going immediately into operations. What is the most likely response you can give Stephanie?
   A. Her deliverable is considered an incremental benefit and will flow into the benefits of the program.
   B. Her deliverable is considered an incremental benefit and will be held until the program is closed and all the benefits from the program are ready to be moved into operations.
   C. Her project is considered an incremental benefit and will be recorded in the benefits register.
   D. Her project deliverable is considered a tiered deliverable, and her project will serve as an input to another project whose deliverable will flow into operations.

3. In what phase of the program management life cycle is a program chartered?
   A. Pre-program set up phase
   B. Program set up phase
   C. Establishing a program management and technical phase
   D. Delivering the incremental benefits phase

4. The program charter defines all of the following characteristics except for which one?
   A. High-level objectives for the program

B. Program scope

C. Projects that will exist within the program

D. Program constraints

5. You are the program manager of the BHG Program. Your program has moved through its second phase review, and you and the program management team are in the process of identifying how the expected benefits of the program will be realized. What plan should you and your team create in order to define the procedures for benefits realization?

A. Program management plan

B. Benefits realization plan

C. Quality management plan

D. Staffing management plan

6. What will management typically do at the end of a program phase?

A. Fund the program for the next phase.

B. Complete quality control procedures.

C. Complete a phase gate review.

D. Add more projects if the program budget allows them to do so.

7. Which program phase provides a definition of how the program's projects will operate?

A. Program set up

B. Establishing a program management and technical infrastructure

C. Delivering the incremental benefits

D. Pre-program set up

8. When is the program manager identified?

A. During the pre-program set up phase

B. During the program set up phase

C. During the program initiation phase

D. During the project set up phase

9. Mary is the program manager for her organization. She is working with Tom and is explaining that her first duty for the program management set up phase is to identify the program benefits. Which one of the following best describes Mary's responsibility when identifying program benefits?

A. Writing the program charter

B. Defining the project charters

C. Defining the measurable program metrics

D. Defining the project scope of each project in the program

10. Which program management plan defines the procedure for benefits realization and the interaction between constituent projects and the program?

    A. Benefits realization plan

    B. Benefits management plan

    C. Benefits constituency plan

    D. Benefits program integration plan

11. The program manager should create a benefits register for the program. The benefits register tracks all of the following except for which one?

    A. Costs to create the benefits

    B. Ancillary benefits the program may create

    C. The risks of creating the benefits

    D. Time required to create the benefits

12. Your program is to create a new building in your city's downtown. Henry does not want your program to continue and feels that your new building will ruin the character of your city. You can consider Henry what type of stakeholder?

    A. Negative

    B. Positive

    C. Key

    D. Autocratic

13. All of the following are key stakeholders for programs. Which one of the following stakeholders owns the program?

    A. Program sponsor

    B. Program director

    C. Customer

    D. Program manager

14. What entity within a program is responsible for addressing risks and issues within the program?

    A. Government agencies

    B. Program management office

    C. Program governance board

    D. Technical assessment board

15. All of the following are reasons why a program may be initiated except for which one?

    A. Available resources such as people, finances, and facilities

    B. Program risks

    C. Program benefits analysis

    D. Projects within the program

16. You are a program manager for the NHG Company. Your organization would like to launch a new program to create new sales automation software. A document has been created that shares the vision of the new program and how its benefits will help the NHG Company reach its strategic goals. What is this document called?

    A. Program charter

    B. Program benefits mapping

    C. Program brief

    D. Program scope statement

17. The high-level program management plan defines many things about your program and what the program will do for the performing organization. Which one of the following is not defined in the high-level program management plan?

    A. Mission of the program

    B. Vision of the program

    C. Rewards and recognition system of the program

    D. Values of the program

18. Training for project teams is a form of what program and project process?

    A. Corrective action

    B. Team performance assessment

    C. Risk assessment

    D. Preventive action

19. Your program has reached its final conclusion, and you are ready to close the program. All of the following are false statements about closing a program except for which one?

    A. Program information, records, communications, and supporting details are gathered and archived as part of organizational process assets.

    B. Programs do not necessarily end but become part of ongoing operations.

    C. Program managers rarely close programs, because of ongoing benefits management.

    D. Program information, records, communications, and supporting details are gathered and archived as part of enterprise environmental factors.

20. Which program plan defines the program deliverables, the program timeline, and the overall program cost?

    A. The program management plan

    B. The program scope management plan

    C. The program quality management plan

    D. The program integration management plan

Questions and Answers

1. You are the program manager for a large manufacturing organization. You have just completed the program set up phase of your program. What event should happen next?

   A. The program moves into establishing a program management and technical infrastructure phase.

   B. The program moves into the delivering the incremental benefits phase.

   C. The program moves into a risk assessment review process.

   D. The program moves through a phase gate review.

   D. The program will move through a phase gate review at the end of each phase. A is incorrect, as the program will always pass through a phase gate review before advancing to any new phases. B is incorrect, as delivering the incremental benefits phase is the fourth phase of a program, not the second. C is an incorrect statement, as phase gate reviews happen with each phase completion.

2. Stephanie, a project manager of a project in your program, is about to close her project. She has asked you, the program manager, what will happen to the deliverable, a program benefit, of her project if it's not going immediately into operations. What is the most likely response you can give Stephanie?

   A. Her deliverable is considered an incremental benefit and will flow into the benefits of the program.

   B. Her deliverable is considered an incremental benefit and will be held until the program is closed and all the benefits from the program are ready to be moved into operations.

   C. Her project is considered an incremental benefit and will be recorded in the benefits register.

   D. Her project deliverable is considered a tiered deliverable, and her project will serve as an input to another project whose deliverable will flow into operations.

   A. The deliverable of Stephanie's project, like all projects within your program, is considered an incremental benefit and is folded into the program benefits. B is incorrect, as many programs may use the benefits of a project as soon as they become available. All projects don't have to be completed to begin using the benefits of a project. C is technically correct, but it is not the best answer of the choices. D is incorrect, as there is not enough information provided to know if this is the best choice.

3. In what phase of the program management life cycle is a program chartered?

   A. Pre-program set up phase

    B. Program set up phase

    C. Establishing a program management and technical phase

    D. Delivering the incremental benefits phase

    A. Programs are chartered during the pre-program set up phase. Choices B, C, and D are incorrect choices, because the programs are not chartered in these phases.

4. The program charter defines all of the following characteristics except for which one?

    A. High-level objectives for the program

    B. Program scope

    C. Projects that will work within the program

    D. Program constraints

    C. The charter does not define the projects that the program will include. It does include the high-level objectives, the program scope, and the program constraints, so choices A, B, and D are not valid answers for this question.

5. You are the program manager of the BHG Program. Your program has moved through its second phase review, and you and the program management team are in the process of identifying how the expected benefits of the program will be realized. What plan should you and your team create in order define the procedures for benefits realization?

    A. Program management plan

    B. Benefits realization plan

    C. Quality management plan

    D. Staffing management plan

    B. The benefits realization plan is the plan the program manager is seeking in the scenario. Choice A, the program management plan, is the overall program plan and defines communication and program stakeholder management. Choices C and D are not valid program management plans.

6. What will management typically do at the end of a program phase?

    A. Fund the program for the next phase.

    B. Complete quality control procedures.

    C. Complete a phase gate review.

    D. Add more projects if the program budget allows them to do so.

    C. Programs always pass through a phase gate review at the end of each program phase. Choice A, the funding of the next phase, is often, but not always, true of programs. B and D are not valid choices for the program at the end of a program phase.

7. Which program phase provides a definition of how the program's projects will operate?

   A. Program set up

   B. Establishing a program management and technical infrastructure

   C. Delivering the incremental benefits

   D. Pre-program set up

   B. The establishing a program management and technical infrastructure phase defines how the projects within the program will operate. A, the program set up, establishes the program—not the projects within the program. C, the delivering of the incremental benefits, is a result of the program's projects. D, pre-program set up phase, is about fostering support and selection of the program.

8. When is the program manager identified?

   A. During the pre-program set up phase

   B. During the program set up phase

   C. During the program initiation phase

   D. During the project set up phase

   A. The charter is created during the pre-program set up phase, and this is where the program manager is identified. The program manager is not identified during the other phases of the projects, so choices B, C, and D are invalid choices.

9. Mary is the program manager for her organization. She is working with Tom and is explaining that her first duty for the program management set up phase is to identify the program benefits. Which one of the following best describes Mary's responsibility when identifying program benefits?

   A. Writing the program charter

   B. Defining the project charters

   C. Defining the measurable program metrics

   D. Defining the project scope of each project in the program

   C. Mary needs to define the measurable program metrics so that the program's success and objectives can be measured. A is incorrect, as the program charter is not written by Mary (or Tom). B is incorrect, as the chartering of the projects is not done during the program benefits identification. D, defining the project scope, is an incorrect answer, as this activity is not completed during benefits identification.

10. Which program management plan defines the procedure for benefits realization and the interaction between constituent projects and the program?

    A. Benefits realization plan

B. Benefits management plan

C. Benefits constituency plan

D. Benefits program integration plan

A. The benefits realization plan defines how the program will achieve the benefits it aims to realize. Program benefits are gained by the delivering of the project scopes. Choices B, C, and D are all incorrect program management plans for this answer.

11. The program manager should create a benefits register for the program. The benefits register tracks all of the following except for which one?

A. Costs to create the benefits

B. Ancillary benefits the program may create

C. The risks of creating the benefits

D. Time required to create the benefits

C. The benefits register does not track the risks of creating the program benefits. It does, however, track the costs, ancillary benefits, and time requirements of the benefit creation. Choices A, B, and D are incorrect.

12. Your program is to create a new building in your city's downtown. Henry does not want your program to continue and feels that your new building will ruin the character of your city. You can consider Henry what type of stakeholder?

A. Negative

B. Positive

C. Key

D. Autocratic

A. A negative stakeholder, such as Henry, is a person or entity that does not want your program to move forward. B, a positive stakeholder, is someone or an entity that does want your program to move forward. C is incorrect, as key stakeholders are crucial stakeholders to your program's existence; these can be either positive or negative. D is incorrect, as autocratic is a leadership style where the program manager makes all the program decisions.

13. All of the following are key stakeholders for programs. Which one of the following stakeholders owns the program?

A. Program sponsor

B. Program director

C. Customer

D. Program manager

B. The program director owns the program, while choices A, C, and D describe key program stakeholders.

14. What entity within a program is responsible for addressing risks and issues within the program?

    A. Government agencies

    B. Program management office

    C. Program governance board

    D. Technical assessment board

    C. The program governance board addresses risks and issues within the program. A, government agencies, may be considered program stakeholders. B, the program management office, supports the program manager through organizational process assets, guidance, and direction, but not to the extent of risk and issues like choice C. D is also incorrect, as the technical assessment board evaluates change within programs and projects.

15. All of the following are reasons why a program may be initiated except for which one?

    A. Available resources such as people, finances, and facilities

    B. Program risks

    C. Program benefits analysis

    D. Projects within the program

    D. Projects are initiated after the program is charted, so this is the correct answer for the questions. Choices A, B, and C all describe reasons why a program can be initiated, so they are inaccurate choices for the question.

16. You are a program manager for the NHG Company. Your organization would like to launch a new program to create new sales automation software. A document has been created that shares the vision of the new program and how its benefits will help the NHG Company reach its strategic goals. What is this document called?

    A. Program charter

    B. Program benefits mapping

    C. Program brief

    D. Program scope statement

    C. The program brief, also called the program mandate, is the document that defines the benefits and vision of the program. Choices A, B, and D do not describe the benefits and goals of a proposed program. Note that the question states that the program has not been created yet, so the scope statement and the program charter are inaccurate choices.

17. The high-level program management plan defines many things about your program and what the program will do for the performing organization. Which one of the following is not defined in the high-level program management plan?

    A. Mission of the program

B. Vision of the program

C. Rewards and recognition system of the program

D. Values of the program

C. The high-level program management plan does not define the rewards and recognition system of the program. It does define the mission, vision, and values of the program, so choices A, B, and D are incorrect.

18. Training for project teams is a form of what program and project process?

A. Corrective action

B. Team development

C. Risk assessment

D. Preventive action

D. Training program and project team members is an excellent example of preventive action. A, corrective action, happens after the mistake has happened and the management team works to correct the problem. B, team development, is true if all of the program team members are involved in the training. C, risk assessment, is not accomplished through training. Training could be an example of risk prevention, but that was not an option.

19. Your program has reached its final conclusion, and you are ready to close the program. All of the following are false statements about closing a program except for which one?

A. Program information, records, communications, and supporting details are gathered and archived as part of organizational process assets.

B. Programs do not necessarily end, but become part of ongoing operations.

C. Program managers rarely close programs because of ongoing benefits management.

D. Program information, records, communications, and supporting details are gathered and archived as part of enterprise environmental factors.

A. Program information, records, communications, and supporting details are gathered and archived as part of organizational process assets. B, C, and D are all inaccurate statements, so these choices are wrong.

20. Which program plan defines the program deliverables, the program timeline, and the overall program cost?

A. The program management plan

B. The program scope management plan

C. The program quality management plan

D. The program integration management plan

A. The best choice is the program management plan. B, C, and D are not accurate program management plans, so these choices are incorrect.

PART II

Program Management Processes

Welcome to Part II of this book. I hope you've had an intermission, got some popcorn, a box of Junior Mints, and a frosty beverage. This second half of the book focuses on the program management processes that you'll need to know for your examination. It's more fun than pulling a cat backward.

In this part, you'll learn about
- Program management processes
- Program management initiating processes
- Program management planning processes
- Program management executing processes
- Program management monitoring and controlling processes
- Program management closing processes

Exploring Program Management

A process is a set of actions that rely on inputs and create outputs in order to move your program toward the benefits you, the program manager, have promised to your organization. The pressure is on.

This chapter is all about the components of a program and how the moving parts of the program all work together. Or, I should say, how all the moving parts of the program should be working together. I think you and I know that how things are supposed to work in a program is often very different from how they actually do work within a program.

For your PgMP examination, however, you'll be tested on the processes and how they are supposed to work within a program. Keep in mind, dear reader, that my goal is for you to pass the PgMP examination. While I want you to be a good program manager and to have realistic expectations of program management, that's not the primary goal of this book. Answer the questions on your PgMP examination according to the PMI way, not your way out there in your world.

Yeah, you read that correctly. I'm realistic enough to know that you have more than four choices for every program management scenario that creeps into play. On your examination, however, you're pretty much toast if you don't answer the questions the PMI way. This chapter is about the big picture of program management themes and program management process groups. In the next five chapters, I elaborate on the nitty-gritty of each program management process group. Keep that in mind as you move through the chapter; it'll give you something to look forward to.

In this chapter, you will learn
- Program management life cycle themes
- The program management process groups
- All about the program management processes
- How the program management processes interact

Exploring the Program Management Life Cycle Themes

Here's a rhetorical question: why should any entity ever want to manage a program? Why not just create a bunch of projects and get out of the way of all the project managers? You know the answer to this. A program is created so that an organization may realize benefits that the organization could not have realized any other way than by creating and managing a program. A program helps the entity coordinate a collection of similar projects all working together to create the program benefits.

This first chunk of this chapter is about the program life cycle. Recall that the program life cycle is the life of the program, from its conception to its conclusion, as Figure 4-1 illustrates. Programs, like projects, move through a logical progression of phases to reach the conclusion of benefits which are folded, eventually, into operations. It's not a mystery as to what happens at the end of the program: the organization gains the benefits of the program life cycle. And you have a celebratory dinner (I hope).

While programs do move through a life cycle, they also are built to please three themes throughout their existence:

- Benefits management
- Stakeholder management
- Program governance

Yes, I realize that I've talked about these three themes a bunch already, but let's touch base on these once again. These three topics of program management are the crux of why you're a program manager. And you'll want to answer those PMI exam questions in the light of managing these three components as well. Here goes.

Managing the Program Benefits

You and I agree, I hope, that the point of creating a program is for the performing organization to realize benefits that it would not realize any other way. Actually, it doesn't matter whether or not you and I agree on this point: it's the point PMI makes in their book *The Standard for Program Management*. Organizations create programs to realize benefits that they wouldn't have any other way.

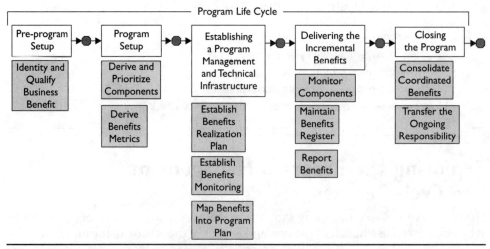

Figure 4-1   Programs move through logical phases.

For your PgMP examination you'll need to know the logic behind program creation and the hopes of realizing new benefits for the performing organization. While it's easy and dreamy to chat about benefits management, let's look at the activities, the work, that go into benefits management:

- Assessment of each perceived benefits value for the performing organization
- Quantification of the impact of benefits for the performing organization
- Documentation of the interdependencies of benefits between projects within the program
- Assignment of roles and responsibilities for the realization of the benefits
- Identification of the specific people accountable for the program's benefits

These activities are launched by the program manager and the team—though their impact is most evident within the program's projects. For example, the scope definition process of a project can be correlated to the program's assignment of roles and responsibilities for the success and realization of the program's benefits. In other words, the processes of the program's projects result in the realization of the program's benefits.

Recall that the program manager delegates the authority, autonomy, and responsibility of the program's projects to the project manager—but she's still responsible for managing the benefits these projects will create as a collective group. The program can't just chat up benefits management and expect the project managers to deliver (okay, the program manager can do this, but her program won't be very successful). It's the program manager's job to hold to the high-level objectives and vision for the program.

 NOTE While the program manager must coordinate the activities among the projects to realize the benefits of the program, it's safe to say that this doesn't mean the program manager will be coordinating the activities within the project—that's the project manager's job. Stay out of the way when it comes to the day-to-day project activities.

The benefits realization plan is the authority for a program's benefits management. This plan, created during the program initiation, defines how the program manager and the project managers will work together to create the benefits for the organization. The benefits realization plan has several components:

- The definition and identification of the relationships between program benefits and how the benefits will come into fruition
- Alignment of the identified benefits with the performing organization's strategic objectives
- When the benefits will be created and delivered for the organization
- How the benefits will be measured and by what metric they'll be measured
- The responsible party for creating and delivering the program benefits
- How the identified benefits will come into existence

When the program is initiated, a business case for the program's existence is created. Within this business case, the expectations of the program benefits are identified. It's this business case that the benefits realization plan is based upon. This is a classic case of progressive elaboration. The business case is written, and from this case the benefits are identified and evolved into the benefits realization plan. Next up, and I discuss it more later, the benefits realization plan is elaborated into the program management plan.

The program management plan, which I delve into in Chapter 6, documents and communicates how the program will create the benefits, includes the necessary steps to get to the benefits, and serves as the baseline for tracking benefits realization.

Managing the Program Stakeholders

Recall that a stakeholder is any person or entity whose interest may be affected by the outcome of your program. There are positive and negative stakeholders, and how you manage them depends on their political position, their perception of your program and its deliverables, your program performance, and a myriad of other factors. While this point may be obvious, to identify the stakeholders internal to an organization the program manager must also work to identify and manage stakeholders that may be external to the organization. Consider government agencies, customers, the community, vendors, and even the media.

As a reminder, here's a quick recap of a program's most common stakeholders:

- **Program director**   The executive owner of your program

- **Program manager**   You!

- **Project manager**   The folks you, the program manager, manage. Project managers manage the projects that comprise your program.

- **Program sponsor**   The person or group that champions the project; the program sponsor provides the resources so that the program manager can deliver the goods.

- **Customer**   The recipient of the program deliverables

- **Performing organization**   A real nice PMI way of saying the organization that's performing the work of the program

- **Program team members**   Your program team that completes program activities (not the same as project team members)

- **Project team members**   The team that completes activities on the program's projects

- **Program management office (PMO)**   The centralized organization that defines and manages the program governance procedures and program processes, and that provides program templates and forms

- **Program office**   A centralized program-support entity that provides administrative support for the program managers

- **Program governance board**   A jolly group of folks that ensures that the program goals are being achieved, makes certain that risks are being anticipated and planned for, and provides support for program issue resolution

- **Vendors**   Suppliers that deliver goods and services to the program

- **Government regulatory agencies**   The program manager identifies and manages these stakeholders, depending on which country the program work is occurring in, the discipline the program entails, and any new policies or laws that may affect the program work

- **Competition and customers**   Yep, even the competitors and customers are considered stakeholders (they are interested in the outcome of your program)

- **Consumer and environmental groups**   These entities can also be considered stakeholders if their interests are affected, or perceived to be affected, by the outcome of your program

The types of stakeholders, their interest in the program, and their positive or negative stance toward the program can shift as the program moves toward its completion. Stakeholders may come and go, depending on the program work that's happening at any given time in the program. It's essential to constantly identify changes to internal and external stakeholders. When new stakeholders are introduced to the program, the program management team must work to identify the program stakeholders, including their concerns, perceived threats, and stance toward the program.

Creating a Stakeholder Management Plan

To manage program stakeholders, the program manager communicates. You just cannot do stakeholder management without communicating with the program stakeholders. They want to know what's happening in the program, and they expect you, the program manager, to tell 'em. In order to manage stakeholders, you'll need to create a stakeholder management plan.

NOTE   The stakeholder management plan may include another plan, called the program communications management plan. The program communications management plan could also be a separate program plan, but the goal is the same: to communicate program information to the program stakeholders as needed.

The stakeholder management plan defines the stakeholder expectations, their concerns, and how and when communication is needed. The stakeholder management plan defines the following:

- **Program stakeholders**   Positive and negative stakeholders are identified; their concerns, perceived threats, and interests are documented. Obviously, this information will help the program manager communicate the right information to the right stakeholders at the right time.

- **Communications management approach**   This stakeholder management plan defines who needs what information, when the information is needed, and in what modality the communication is expected. The program management team aims to define the communication expectations so that they may deliver on the expectations—but that's the key—they actually have to execute this plan to do effective communications management.

- **Change management system**   Changes within a program are expected; the program manager must define the change control processes and how the change control processes will interact with program stakeholders. This means, again, communicating changes as they are proposed, as they happen, and (as the case may be) when proposed changes are declined.

The stakeholder management plan is part of the overall program management plan, but it is updated as needed. Changes to the stakeholder management plan should be baselined by version numbers, dates, or some other unique identifier. The stakeholder management plan is addressed throughout the entire program life cycle—from initiation all the way to program closure.

Adhering to Program Governance

Rules. Program governance is all about the rules the program manager and the program team must follow. Program governance defines the boundaries and expectations of how the program manager and the program team will manage the program, how they will work on the program, and the procedures they'll use to accomplish program expectations.

It's the program board that establishes the rules and procedures the program manager is expected to follow. It's fair to say that program governance operates externally to the program—or you could say program governance is enforced on the program manager and the program management team. Yep—it's someone else establishing the rules and constraints that the program manager is to follow. The program manager adheres to program governance by following the program management processes.

 NOTE   Because program governance is external to the program management processes, it covers the entire program from launch to completion. This means it spans the entire program life cycle.

While I'm stressing the ideas of rules and procedures here, and that's accurate for your exam, keep in mind that program governance and program management processes work together. In the big picture, as in Figure 4-2, the mission, vision, and strategy of an organization are in the best interest of the company—and the program. I think you'll be hard-pressed to find a program that may be in conflict of the organization's mission and vision.

Figure 4-2
Programs must
support the vision
and mission of the
organization.

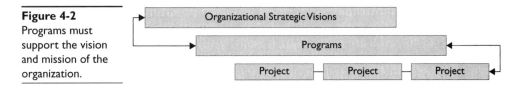

Most accessible to the program manager, however, is the strategy of the organization. Strategy defines the tactics and procedures an organization takes to deliver and support the higher vision and mission of an organization. You've experienced this, I'm sure. Organizations often change tactics but rarely change their mission and vision. Organizations drop tactics as new trends, marketplace opportunities, or signs of customer reluctance come about. Organizational mission and vision rarely change.

Programs are part of portfolio management—a tactical management approach. Programs support the vision and mission of the organization. Program governance, then, is an established approach to keep the program in alignment with the organization tactics to support the higher tiers of mission and vision. Program governance does this through three main themes:

- A program governance board to address program risks and issues
- A program framework for repeatable program processes that support the program's objectives
- Established and documented program processes for efficient decision-making on changes, activities, risks, issues, and stakeholder management

For your PgMP examination, keep in mind that program governance is usually the task of a program governance board that oversees the program. The program manager can usually operate freely in the program—as long as he stays within the confines that the program governance board has established.

Exploring Program Management Process Groups

Programs move through phases. Across those phases, you'll find some terribly exciting process groups. Okay, they are not really all that terrible or exciting—but they are groups of processes. If you've earned your PMP, you're familiar already with the concept of process groups. If you've not gone down the PMP path or you need a refresher, check out Figure 4-3.

According to *The Guide to the Project Management Body of Knowledge* (PMBOK), a process is a set of interrelated actions and activities performed to achieve a specific set of products, results, or services. In program management, that holds true as well. You'll need to know that there are five process groups that span the program life cycle. Each process group has a collection of processes that requires some input, generates some activity, and then creates some output. I dive into all of the specifics of each process group in Chapters 5–9, but I cover the basics of each process group here.

Figure 4-3
Project management consists of five process groups.

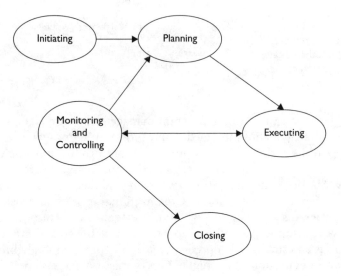

Exploring PMI and Management Processes

When it comes to PMI, a process is basically any management activity that brings about a result. In project management, there are 44 distinct processes that move the project from initiation all the way to closing. In program management, there are 39 processes. As I've taught management seminars for the past several years for organizations around the globe, I've learned one distinct commonality: organizations use different nomenclatures for common processes while the intent and philosophy of the processes remain consistent.

Some organizations call their quality control process "user acceptability testing," and other entities call that same activity "piloting" their deliverable. Out in the day-to-day world, it doesn't really matter what terminology you and your colleagues want to assign to these processes. I'm a huge advocate of not getting bogged down in the terms, but getting the program and its projects done.

Having said that, however, I must add that PMI is doing, and has been doing, something admirable: they are creating a common lexicon for our program and project management industry. When you consider all of the terms, abbreviations, acrostics, and other mumbo-jumbo organizations assign to the program and project processes, it's no wonder confusion can surround project and program management.

I stubbornly use and have adapted the terminology PMI uses in its literature in my management writing and lectures. I encourage you to do the same. You and I have an incredible opportunity to propagate a common management lexicon for our businesses and careers. While you do need to use the PMI verbiage to pass your PgMP exam, the opportunity that we have as a management community to establish a common lexicon for our processes and procedures is immense.

Exploring the Initiating Process Group

The initiating process group is the start of the program. The reason a program is initiated will vary from organization to organization: cutting costs, increasing revenue, or as a public service. The specifics of why a program is initiated are of no consequence for your PgMP examination. What is important, however, is that you know all program initiatives are based on one of three common themes:

- Result of an organization's strategic plan

- Result of an organization's desire to satisfy a portfolio initiative

- Result of an external customer

While it's nice to think of the initiating process group as the official launch of the program work, it's really not. Most likely there's already been a bunch of work in regard to program initiation. Consider all of the program characteristics that have to be addressed before a program can be initiated:

- Development of concepts for both products and services the program will create

- Requirements gathering and scope identification

- Analysis of feasible timelines to complete the program

- Definition of the program deliverables and their impact on the organization

- Analysis of the program costs in relation to the perceived benefits

Of course, to answer the early program questions and to frame the program, it's going to take some funds, time, and resources. Someone, usually the program director, has to have the authority to assign time and resources to these early activities to determine the validity of the proposed program, its solutions, and the direction that will best support the organization's vision and mission.

There are only three processes that make up this first program process group, as Figure 4-4 demonstrates:

- **Initiate the program** This process helps the key stakeholders define the program scope, the program benefits, and the link between the program and the organization's mission and vision.

Figure 4-4
Program initiating
has three processes.

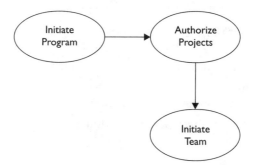

- **Authorize program projects** This is a special process in that it can happen at any time throughout the program except for the program closure. This process allows program projects to be launched.

- **Initiate the program team** This process allows the program manager to acquire and assign program management team personnel to the program to ensure that the program work is planned and executed as required.

That's it for the initiating process group. Well, that's it for now. You'll learn all the details about these three processes in Chapter 5. For starters, just know that the initiating process group allows the program and the component projects to get started and provides the initial staffing for the program management team.

Exploring the Planning Process Group

The purpose of planning anything is to determine how to reach a desired end result; it's no different in program management planning. The processes you'll encounter in the planning process group guide the program management team to the right decisions about the desired direction of the program and determine the actions required to reach the desired program objectives.

Planning is not a one-time activity but rather an iterative process throughout the program. The program manager, the program management team, and other key stakeholders may revisit the planning activities as often as needed throughout the program. As new issues, change requests, and risks are encountered over the life of the program, the first approach to responding to these conditions is to fall back on planning.

 NOTE Planning ends only when the program moves into the closing process group.

The point of planning is to assemble the program management plan. I say assemble, because the program management plan is rarely, if ever, one giant plan, but instead a collection of subsidiary plans. Figure 4-5 depicts the 14 program management processes that the program management plan addresses. The program management plan defines many things for the program manager and the key stakeholders:

- Defines the organization of the program and its projects.

- Provides a program work breakdown structure (PWBS) that visualizes the program deliverables and the work required to satisfy the program scope.

- Identifies internal and external resources to satisfy the program scope.

- Defines the program scope, the required technologies, the program risks, and the costs for delivery of the program requirements.

- Establishes the program schedule and identifies the milestones of the program life cycle.

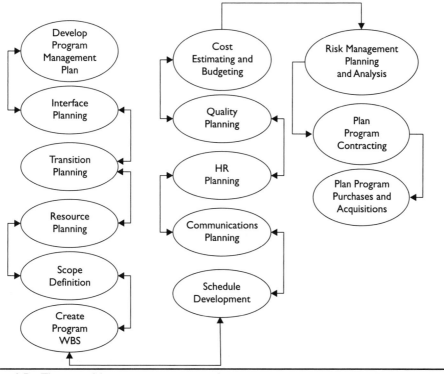

Figure 4-5   There are 14 program management planning processes.

- Provides a program budget and monetary plan to invest the organization's funds in the program on a timeline based on milestones and program deliverables.

- Provides a quality assurance policy for the program.

- Includes readily identified metrics and systems to measure the program performance, benefits delivery, benefits realization, and program sustainment.

- Provides a stakeholder communication management plan.

- Incorporates a risk management approach.

- Includes procedures for all aspects of procurement management.

The program management plan will move through rounds of planning, sometimes called *progressive elaboration*. As changes are expected within a program, approved changes move through an integration management process. This means that the approved program changes are fleshed into the scope, into the program work breakdown structure, and into the corresponding plan where needed. Each program change is considered on its own merits, its benefits, and how the proposed change may affect each area of the program.

Executing Process Group

When you get right down to it, all of the planning doesn't mean squat if the program isn't executed. Plans are great, are mandatory, and direct the project—but it's the execution that gets the thing done. This process group is about doing. The executing process group executes the program management plan and its subsidiary plans to do the work that will get the program from here to that dreamy, desired future state. Figure 4-6 shows the seven program executing processes.

While the focus of the process group is about getting the program work done right the first time, there's also a correlating management focus. The executing processes support the program plans and aim to accomplish benefits management, stakeholder management, and program governance.

It's during this process group that the program team is officially assembled and developed. The program manager works with the program management team, project managers, and internal and external resources to deliver on the promises made in the program management plan. Many, if not all, of these folks are going to be involved in the planning process, so they should already have a good grasp on what activities they'll be doing in the program—and a clear understanding of what expectations for delivery are placed upon them.

NOTE When it comes to the executing process group, it's all about executing the program management plans. Any plan you've created now is executed. It's not rocket science and it's not brain surgery, but it is, I suppose, a bit of rocket surgery.

As you may suspect, the execution of the program management plan means that time and monies will be actually committed to program deliverables in the form of project budgets, staffing, and a schedule of the work. Correct! It's in this process group that the program management team manages the costs, assures the quality of the program deliverables, and maintains the program schedule. One of the processes in this

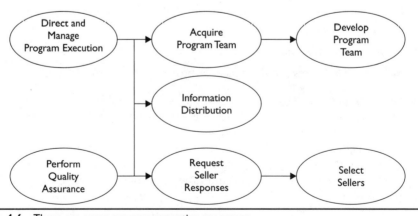

Figure 4-6 There are seven program executing processes.

group is information distribution; specifically, the program manager distributes information regarding overall and specific program status for time, cost, and quality to the appropriate stakeholders.

It's also in the executing process group that the program manager, often with guidance from a purchasing officer or subject matter expert, will initiate the select seller response process. This is the execution of the procurement management plan. The procurement executing procedures, for your PgMP exam, have two related processes: request the seller responses and select the sellers. I get into the specific activities of program procurement in Chapter 7, but know for your exam that selecting the program vendors is an execution process, not a planning process. That's an exam gotcha!

Monitoring and Controlling the Program

While it'd be nice to assume that all of your program management team members and project managers are out there working away for you, the program manager, and that they're doing their work as you've asked them to do, it's not a very good assumption. Plans and promises are nice—but it's the monitoring and controlling of those plans that ensure that project and program management team members are doing their duties.

To take it one step farther, it's not just about the team and project managers doing their work—but also ensuring the quality of the work and the thoroughness of the adherence to the program policies, as well as providing an opportunity to discover strengths, weaknesses, opportunities, and threats (SWOT) within the program. If all this business sounds an awfully lot like the program governance activities, it's because that's essentially what's happening. The stakeholders in the program must follow the rules of the program governance. The monitoring and controlling program process group has 12 iterative processes, as shown in Figure 4-7.

 NOTE There are a dozen executing processes to consider, but integrated change control is one of the most important processes to know for your PgMP exam.

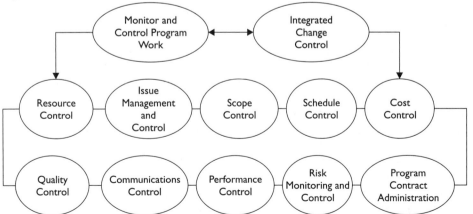

Figure 4-7 There are 12 program monitoring and controlling processes.

One of the most time-consuming activities in this process group centers on change: integrated change control. When changes are proposed in the program, the change is evaluated to consider its value, its benefits, and why the change may be needed. Consider the four primary reasons for change in any program:

- Value-added change
- Errors or omissions resolution
- Risk response
- External change, such as a new law

Each change is evaluated when it is proposed, often through a program change control board, and passes through integrated change control. The integrated change control process entertains the change by considering the impact the proposed change may have on each of the following knowledge areas:

- Program scope
- Program schedule
- Program cost
- Program quality
- Program staffing
- Program communications
- Program risks
- Program procurement

If a change is approved, and changes often are, the change and its ramifications are fleshed back into the program management plan and the appropriate actions are taken to distribute the change down to the component projects within the program. Of course as changes are considered, the program may shift back to the planning processes to determine if the changes are warranted and whether they should be approved or dismissed.

Closing the Program

The final program process group is the closing process group. This process group represents the formal acceptance of the program's benefits and deliverables and moves the deliverables into operations. As you can see in Figure 4-8, there are but three closing processes. At the heart of closing the program is administrative closure—the official and documented closure of the program. When a program manager talks about closing the program, he's usually speaking of administrative closure. Administrative closure is the shutdown of the program and the documentation that accompanies the program.

You, the program manager, can't close the program until all of the component projects have been closed as well. When a project manager has completed the project scope, the project customer completes scope verification. In a program, the customer is often the program manager or a member of the program management team. Scope verification is the official project process of confirming that the project scope has been completed and there's a sign-off of the project deliverables.

Figure 4-8
There are
three program
management
closing processes.

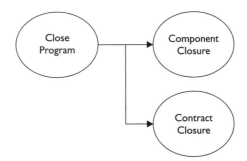

Component project closure also allows the project resources, such as people, tools, and facilities, to be released and reallocated within the program. In some instances a program's project may be canceled (consider the leap in technology or the reduction in program scope). In these instances, the project must still move through scope verification and project closure. These two processes verify the project deliverables and allow the project manager, or a member of the program management team, to document the project's success or failure in the project's lessons learned documentation.

The program's closing process group also includes the contract closure process. It's safe to say that most projects and programs use vendors to reach their expected deliverables for the program. When a vendor has completed its obligations to the program, the contract for the vendor is closed according to the terms of the contract.

 NOTE On your PgMP examination, always, always, follow the terms of the contract. The terms of the contract supersede every other agreement or understanding between the client and the vendor. This is true not only for the PgMP examination, but also for the real world. The terms of the contract are what matter.

All of the contract documentation should be kept as part of the contract file. The contract file is often called for when an internal financial audit of the procurement process takes place. The financial audit is an activity where the organization confirms the vendor lived up to the terms of the agreement and that the vendor also abided by the terms of the contractual obligation.

Finally, it's essential for the program manager to keep accurate and exact records of the entire procurement experience from start to closure. This is important for historical information. In the case of claims between the vendor and the client, the documentation of the agreement will be needed in case of litigation. A reliable knowledge management system and an orderly contract file are mandatory.

Chapter Summary

Good books and programs have themes. With some books, you know what their theme is before you even pick them up—like this one; with other books, like Ayn Rand's *The Fountainhead*, you've got to dig in and just read the thing. When it comes to program management, you always know what the themes are:

- Benefits management

- Stakeholder management
- Program governance

These three themes are consistent throughout the entire program. None of these are completed and tossed away. Benefits management is all about organizing the projects that create the program benefits, and being accountable for the benefits the program promises to create. Stakeholder management centers on solid communication with positive and negative stakeholders to establish a working relationship with the program stakeholders. Program governance defines the rules and procedures for consistency in management and implementation in the program.

A good program manager, such as you, works with these themes through the five process groups of program management:

- **Initiating the program**   The program is launched, and the program's projects are authorized.

- **Planning the program**   The program's intention and direction are planned, documented, and communicated.

- **Executing the program**   Once the program is planned, it's time for the program management team to execute the program plan.

- **Monitoring and controlling the program**   As the program moves forward, a consistent monitoring of the program deliverables, benefits, and program projects must happen. Errors, variances, and issues are managed, documented, corrected, and acted upon in this process group.

- **Closing the program**   Ah, yes, program closure. The formal acceptance of the program deliverables takes place, and the component projects are closed. Program and component project resources are relinquished.

Through these five process groups, the program manager moves the program from a current state to the desired future state. The next five chapters explore each of these process groups in detail. And I promise I won't mention Ayn Rand in the remainder of the book.

Key Terms

Change management system   The change control processes and the change control process interactions with program stakeholders.

Closing process group   The final program management process group that officially closes the program's component projects, releases the organizational resources, and also closes the program contracts.

Consumer and environmental groups   These entities can also be considered stakeholders if their interests are affected, or perceived to be affected, by the outcome of your program.

Executing process group   The collection of the program management execution processes that puts the decisions made in the program management planning process group into action.

Government regulatory agencies   The program manager identifies and manages this stakeholder according to which country the program work is occurring in, the discipline the program entails, and any new policies or laws that may affect the program work.

Initiating process group   The result of an organizational strategic decision to launch the program, initiate component projects, and create the program management team.

Monitoring and controlling process group   The program management processes used to manage changes to the program scope, control the project work, and address all levels of change, consistency, and expectations in all facets of the program.

Negative stakeholder   A stakeholder that does not want your program to exist or to reach its objectives.

Performing organization   The organization that's performing the work of the program.

Planning process group   The collection of iterative planning processes that guide the program manager and stakeholders through the decision-making activities for the project's direction.

Positive stakeholder   A stakeholder that is in favor of your program existing and accomplishing its objectives.

Program communications management plan   Defines the communication demands and expectations for the program stakeholders.

Program customer   The recipient of the program deliverables.

Program director   The executive owner of your program.

Program governance board   A group that ensures that the program goals are being achieved and risks are being anticipated and planned for. The board also provides support for program issue resolution.

Program life cycle   The series of phases within a program used to govern the program, manage the program benefits, coordinate the component projects, and collectively manage risks and issues within the program.

Program management office (PMO)   The centralized organization that defines and manages the program governance procedures and program processes, and that provides program templates and forms.

Program management plan   Documents and communicates how the program will create the benefits and what actions are needed to realize the benefits. It serves as the baseline for tracking benefits realization.

Program sponsor   The person or group that champions the project; the program sponsor provides the resources so that the program manager can deliver the goods.

Stakeholder management plan   A plan that defines the program stakeholders, their expectations, communications management, and the change management system.

Questions

1. Sally is working with Jane, the COO of the NBG Company. Sally is explaining to Jane why NBG should launch a program rather than a series of projects. All of the following are accurate reasons that Sally could include in her discussion except for which one?

    A. NBG could realize benefits through a program that they likely wouldn't realize through a series of projects.

    B. NBG can complete the program more quickly and cost-effectively than it could a collection of individually managed projects.

    C. NBG can implement a program to coordinate the collection of projects that will work together to create the program benefits.

    D. NBG can create a uniform approach for all of the projects within the program.

2. Which one of the following is not a program management theme?

    A. Cost savings and revenue increase

    B. Benefits management

    C. Stakeholder management

    D. Program governance

3. You are the program manager for a program to create a skyscraper in your city. Although your skyscraper was approved and your program is moving forward, some of the local politicians are still wary of your program. They don't like your program and would like to see it fail. You could consider these politicians as what type of stakeholder?

    A. Positive stakeholder

    B. Negative stakeholder

    C. Program governance board

    D. Program customer, as they'll be overseeing approval for your program completion

4. Which stakeholder in an organization assigns responsibility to the project manager of a project within a program?

    A. Program director

    B. Program customer

    C. Program sponsor

    D. Program manager

5. You are the program manager of a large manufacturing program. One of the component projects is the THG Project. This project has a project budget of $2 million and is slated to last eight months. This one project represents a third of the program's schedule and nearly half of the program's budget. Considering the size of the program and the budget, who is responsible for the day-to-day activities of the THG Project?

A. Program manager

B. Program management team

C. Project manager

D. Project customer

6. There are many different plans the program manager must create during the program. Which program plan defines how the program manager and the project managers will work together for the benefits of the program?

A. Benefits mapping plan

B. Benefits realization plan

C. Stakeholder management plan

D. Procurement management plan

7. What document is created when the program is initiated that defines the program benefits?

A. Benefits mapping plan

B. Benefits realization plan

C. Program business case

D. Program statement of work

8. Which program management plan defines the expectations of the program stakeholders?

A. Program communications management plan

B. Stakeholder management plan

C. Benefits management plan

D. Program management plan

9. You are the program manager for the JHN Program. Your program will span several countries, and you'll have to adhere to the laws and customs of each country your program will operate within. What entity, in this example, will establish the rules and procedures your program will follow within your organization?

A. The project management team

B. The local government of each country where the program will exist

C. The program management team

D. The program board

10. All of the following are program process groups except for which one?

A. Program risk management

B. Program initiating

C. Program closing

D. Program monitoring and controlling

11. Your boss, Marty, has asked when the planning for your program will end. What's the correct answer to give Marty?

    A. Planning will end once the program begins executing the program plans.

    B. Planning will end once the program begins to realize the benefits as planned for.

    C. Planning will end once the program moves into the closing process group activities.

    D. Planning never ends.

12. What program management plan document helps the program manager and the program stakeholders visualize the program deliverables?

    A. The program charter

    B. The program scope

    C. The program management plan

    D. The program work breakdown structure

13. Your program is moving through rounds of planning. These iterations of program planning are also known by what term?

    A. Deming's quality management circle

    B. Progressive elaboration

    C. Planning cycles

    D. Planning refinements

14. In which process group does the program management team maintain the program schedule?

    A. Planning process group

    B. Execution process group

    C. Monitoring and controlling process group

    D. Closing process group

15. There are four reasons a change may be introduced into a program. Which one of the following is not a legitimate example of why change may occur in a program?

    A. A new vendor is selected for the program

    B. A value-added change is introduced to the program

    C. As a response to a program risk

    D. As a result of an error or program omission

16. Every program change must pass through which process to determine the proposed change on the program knowledge areas?

A. Integrated change control

B. Configuration management

C. Change control system

D. Scope definition planning

17. You are the program manager of the JHG Program, and you believe that your program is complete. Stacy Ellison, the program director, refuses to agree that the program is closed. What must be true for the program to be considered completed so that the program director can sign off on the program? Choose the best answer:

A. All of the program monies must have been spent.

B. All of the program schedule must have been consumed.

C. All of the program component projects must be closed.

D. All of the program risk management activities must be done.

18. You have determined that a project in your program must be canceled. Which one of the following is not a valid reason for canceling a project?

A. The technology the project will deliver has been surpassed with a newer technology.

B. The project is not performing well on scope and budget, so the project is terminated.

C. The program has experienced a change to its scope that eliminates the need for the project's deliverable.

D. The project manager leaves the performing organization.

19. When can a project manager release the project resources?

A. When the program manager demands that the project manager do so

B. When the project scope is completed

C. When the project has been officially closed

D. When the project resource is no longer believed to be needed

20. You are the program manager for the JHY Program. You are working with several different vendors throughout the program, and you need to quickly reference contract information for one of your vendors. Where can you find the contract information?

A. Centralized procurement

B. Decentralized procurement

C. Contract records management system

D. Contract file

Questions and Answers

1. Sally is working with Jane, the COO of the NBG Company. Sally is explaining to Jane why NBG should launch a program rather than a series of projects. All of the following are accurate reasons that Sally could include in her discussion except for which one?

   A. NBG could realize outcomes through a program that they likely wouldn't realize through a series of projects.

   B. NBG can complete the program more quickly and cost-effectively than it could a collection of individually managed projects.

   C. NBG can implement a program to coordinate the collection of projects that will work together to create the program benefits.

   D. NBG can create a uniform approach for all of the projects within the program.

   B. A program does not necessarily guarantee a faster and more cost-effective solution than a series of projects, so this statement is not an example of why creating a program is good for the NBG Company. Choices A, C, and D are all incorrect choices for this question, because these choices are reasons why the NBG Company should consider a program.

2. Which one of the following is not a program management theme?

   A. Cost savings and revenue increase

   B. Benefits management

   C. Stakeholder management

   D. Program governance

   A. Cost savings and revenue increase are goals of many programs, but it is not one of the three program management themes. Choices B, C, and D are the three program management themes: benefits management, stakeholder management, and program governance.

3. You are the program manager for a program to create a skyscraper in your city. Although your skyscraper was approved and your program is moving forward, some of the local politicians are still wary of your program. They don't like your program and would like to see it fail. You could consider these politicians as what type of stakeholder?

   A. Positive stakeholder

   B. Negative stakeholder

   C. Program governance board

   D. Program customer, as they'll be overseeing approval for your program completion

   B. A negative stakeholder is any stakeholder that does not want your program to succeed. A, positive stakeholder, would describe a stakeholder that does want your program to succeed. C, the program governance board, is usually considered a positive stakeholder, as they have an interest in the success of the program. D is incorrect, as the question doesn't say the politicians are the program customers and will grant approval of the program completion.

4. Which stakeholder in an organization assigns responsibility to the project manager of a project within a program?

    A. Program director

    B. Program customer

    C. Program sponsor

    D. Program manager

    D. The program manager assigns authority to the project managers through the project charters she'll grant and sign. A, B, and C are all incorrect choices, as these people do not assign authority to the project managers through the program.

5. You are the program manager of a large manufacturing program. One of the component projects is the THG Project. This project has a project budget of $2 million and is slated to last eight months. This one project represents a third of the program's schedule and nearly half of the program's budget. Considering the size of the program and the budget, who is responsible for the day-to-day activities of the THG Project?

    A. Program manager

    B. Program management team

    C. Project manager

    D. Project customer

    C. The project manager is responsible for the day-to-day activities of the project. A and B, the program manager and the program management team, both need to stay out of the project manager's way when it comes to the day-to-day management of the project. D, the project customer, does not manage the day-to-day activities of the project.

6. There are many different plans the program manager must create during the program. Which program plan defines how the program manager and the project managers will work together for the benefits of the program?

    A. Benefits mapping plan

    B. Benefits realization plan

    C. Stakeholder management plan

    D. Procurement management plan

    B. The benefits realization plan defines how the program manager and the project managers will work together to realize the program benefits. A, the benefits mapping plan, is not a legitimate program plan. C, the stakeholder management plan, defines how the program management team will communicate with and manage the program stakeholders, not the program benefits. D, the procurement management plan, defines the procurement process and the management of the vendors.

7. What document is created when the program is initiated that defines the program benefits?

   A. Benefits mapping plan

   B. Benefits realization plan

   C. Program business case

   D. Program statement of work

C. The expected benefits are defined in the business case on which the program is based. A is a distracter and is not a valid choice. B, the benefits realization plan, comes after the program business case. D, the program statement of work, is not a valid choice for this question.

8. Which program management plan defines the expectations of the program stakeholders?

   A. Program communications management plan

   B. Stakeholder management plan

   C. Benefits management plan

   D. Program management plan

B. The stakeholder management plan defines how the stakeholders will be managed and communicated with. A, the program communications management plan, is sometimes included in the stakeholder management plan. C, the benefits realization plan, defines how the expected program benefits will come into existence. D, the program management plan, is a collection of subsidiary program management plans and does not directly answer the question as completely as choice B.

9. You are the program manager for the JHN Program. Your program will span several countries, and you'll have to adhere to the laws and customs of each country your program will operate within. What entity, in this example, will establish the rules and procedures your program will follow within your organization?

   A. The project management team

   B. The local government of each country where the program will exist

   C. The program management team

   D. The program board

D. Regardless of the countries the program will span, the program board defines the rules and procedures the program is expected to follow. A, B, and C are all incorrect choices, as these entities do not define the program rules.

10. All of the following are program process groups except for which one?

    A. Program risk management

    B. Program initiating

    C. Program closing

    D. Program monitoring and controlling

A. Program risk management is not one of the five process groups, so this choice is correct. B, C, and D are three of the five program management process groups. The five program process groups in logical order are program initiating, program planning, program executing, program monitoring and controlling, and program closing.

11. Your boss, Marty, has asked when the planning for your program will end. What's the correct answer to give Marty?

   A. Planning will end once the program begins executing the program plans.

   B. Planning will end once the program begins to realize the benefits as planned for.

   C. Planning will end once the program moves into the closing process group activities.

   D. Planning never ends.

   C. Planning ends only when the program moves into the closing process group. Choices A and B are incorrect, because planning includes iterative activities regardless of the benefits that have been realized or the execution of the program. D is also incorrect, as planning does, thankfully, end when the program moves into closing.

12. What program management plan document helps the program manager and the program stakeholders visualize the program deliverables?

   A. The program charter

   B. The program scope

   C. The program management plan

   D. The program work breakdown structure

   D. The program work breakdown structure illustrates the decomposition of the program deliverables. A, the program charter, is the document that grants the program manager authority over the project. B, the program scope, defines the benefits the program aims to create, while C, the program management plan, is a collection of subsidiary plans for the program.

13. Your program is moving through rounds of planning. These iterations of program planning are also known by what term?

   A. Deming's quality management circle

   B. Progressive elaboration

   C. Planning cycles

   D. Planning refinements

   B. Progressive elaboration is an activity that allows for steady incremental steps of planning. A, Deming's quality management circle, defines Deming's Plan—Do—Check—Act cycle of quality management. C, planning cycles, is not an accurate definition of progressive elaboration. D, planning refinements, is a term that is sometimes used in project management to define updates to the project scope; it is not a valid program management term.

14. In which process group does the program management team maintain the program schedule?

    A. Planning process group

    B. Execution process group

    C. Monitoring and controlling process group

    D. Closing process group

    B. The execution process group is where the program management team will maintain the scope, budget, and quality of the program. Choices A, C, and D all describe process groups that do not answer the question.

15. There are four reasons a change may be introduced into a program. Which one of the following is not a legitimate example of why change may occur in a program?

    A. A new vendor is selected for the program

    B. A value-added change is introduced to the program

    C. As a response to a program risk

    D. As a result of an error or program omission

    A. The addition of a vendor should not trigger a change to the program scope. B, C, and D are all valid reasons that a program change may occur. The final legitimate change, which is not one of the answer choices, is that an external event such as a new law or regulation may affect the program.

16. Every program change must pass through which process to determine the proposed change on the program knowledge areas?

    A. Integrated change control

    B. Configuration management

    C. Change control system

    D. Scope definition planning

    A. Integrated change control considers the impact of the change on each knowledge area within the program. B, configuration management, is concerned only with the documentation, control, and tracking of changes to the features and functions of the program deliverables. C, the change control system, is the whole system of change control management and is not the specific change management activity the question calls for. D, scope definition planning, is the activity of defining the program scope.

17. You are the program manager of the JHG Program, and you believe that your program is complete. Stacy Ellison, the program director, refuses to agree that the program is closed. What must be true for the program to be considered

completed so that the program director can sign off on the program? Choose the best answer:

A. All of the program monies must have been spent.

B. All of the program schedule must have been consumed.

C. All of the program component projects must be closed.

D. All of the program risk management activities must be done.

C. The program cannot be considered done until all of the program component projects have been closed. A is incorrect, because the elimination of the program funds does not necessarily mean the program is complete. B is incorrect, as the program may finish ahead or behind the targeted project completion milestone. D is incorrect. While the program risks management activities may be completed, there are still other processes that may need to be completed for the program to be considered done.

18. You have determined that a project in your program must be canceled. Which one of the following is not a valid reason for canceling a project?

A. The technology the project will deliver has been surpassed with a newer technology.

B. The project is not performing well on scope and budget, so the project is terminated.

C. The program has experienced a change to its scope that eliminates the need for the project's deliverable.

D. The project manager leaves the performing organization.

D. Should a project manager leave the performing organization, this does not constitute a reason to cancel the project. If the project was chartered, it was most likely chartered for reasons other than the existence of a particular project manager. A, B, and C are all valid reasons a project may be canceled.

19. When can a project manager release the project resources? Choose the best answer:

A. When the program manager demands that the project manager do so

B. When the project scope is completed

C. When the project has been officially closed

D. When the project resource is no longer believed to be needed

C. When the project is officially closed, the project manager may release the project resources to be allocated elsewhere in the organization. A is not a valid PMI-type answer; if the resources were assigned to a project, they were assigned for a particular reason. B, while tempting, is not the best answer for the question. Choice D is demonstrative of poor planning rather than the relinquishment of a resource based on a project condition. C is the best choice.

20. You are the program manager for the JHY Program. You are working with several different vendors throughout the program, and you need to quickly reference contract information for one of your vendors. Where can you find the contract information?

   A. Centralized procurement

   B. Decentralized procurement

   C. Contract records management system

   D. Contract file

   D. The contract file is the centralized location of the contract records, procurement documentation, and relevant program procurement information. A and B describe an organization's approach to procurement management, while C describes a "dummy" term for the program's record file.

Initiating the Program

5

In this chapter, you will

- Examine program selection approaches
- Learn how to initiate a program
- See how projects are authorized
- Initiate the program team
- Determine initiating program process inputs and outputs

In order to have a program, there has to be, of course, a demand from someone to create one. When you get down to it, it's not that someone is just demanding that a program be created, but more likely that someone is demanding a new service; a new business objective; or a change for the better in the circumstances of a business, a community, or an organization.

Programs generally get created not on a whim but as a result of some serious preprogram planning and thinking. Programs fit into the strategic plan of the organization—they're created to support the vision and mission of the organization. Programs also fit within the portfolio of the organization and aim to satisfy a specific set of objectives by delivering the benefits of the program to support the goals of the organization's portfolio.

Many programs, however, come about as a result of what the customer wants. When you consider all of the disciplines that provide services to customers, it's easy to see that programs could be launched to provide what the customer asks for. Consider information technology providers, architects, manufacturers, construction companies, and more. The desire of a customer can spur an organization's need to launch a new program to satisfy that desire.

Whatever the driving force behind why a program is initiated, a considerable amount of planning, thinking, and analysis is invested in the proposed program. The performing organization, that is, the organization that'll be doing the work, has to frame the scope of the proposed program; develop the program concepts and expected benefits the program can bring about; and plan the schedule, costs, and demands for resources to deliver the program. All of this planning and thinking isn't free—time and monies are going to be invested in the research for a program. Those are sunk costs just to entertain the program's possibility of being initiated.

In this chapter, I'll focus on the three processes of initiating a program, as Figure 5-1 depicts. While there may be just three processes, that doesn't mean that this is a fast and

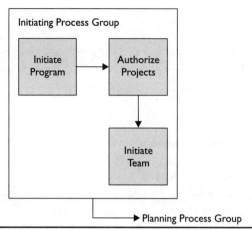

Figure 5-1   There are three initiating processes in program management.

speedy process group. It could take months, even years, to complete the research that signals the time to initiate the program. For your exam, however, keep in mind that the three processes in this chapter are chronological and authorize the program in the organization.

Initiating the Program

Organizations have programs to realize benefits from an orchestrated effort of projects rather than managing a bunch of individual projects. You've got that bit of nutty fun. I'm really talking about an organizational vision. When an organization considers the launch of a program, it's really envisioning the results of the program. The management of the organization is looking into the future to see the benefits the program can bring them, their customers, and their community.

This vision that management may have about the future of their organization and how the potential program may help them reach it is probably pretty fuzzy at the program launch. The vision of the future state may have some exact details, but there's likely some unknown circumstances and conditions that can only be known through additional analysis, thought, and research. These fuzzy questions about the program's direction, scope, and intent are answered by the initiate program process.

The initiate program process provides several things for the organization:

- Defines the program scope
- Defines the program benefits
- Authorizes the program to exist within the organization
- Links the program to the ongoing work and strategic objectives

In order to complete the initiate program process, a schedule and resources will need to be allotted to the pre-program activities. Since the program has not been officially created, the performing organization will have to establish what resources are available to consult and research the program potential. Specifically, the pre-program research must determine the odds that the program will reach time, cost, and scope objectives.

Often the pre-program research is simply called the good old feasibility study. You might also see feasibility studies referred to as concept development. The feasibility study helps the performing organization determine the rough order of magnitude estimate for the cost and schedule, and it frames the program scope. A rough order of magnitude estimate, sometimes just called a ROM estimate, can have a wild swing and an acceptable range of variance; for example, $20 million +100% to –50%. As you can guess, the ROM isn't a very reliable estimate, but it paints a picture of what the program could cost. As the program moves into program planning, a more definitive estimate will be created and the range of variance will grow much, much tighter.

NOTE The feasibility study is usually done prior to the program initiation, though the culture of the program and organization can support launching a program first and then doing the feasibility study.

Performing Program Initiation

One of the first tasks associated with the initiate program process is the classification of program work and the related projects. The organization may begin to organize projects around the deliverables the projects create, the type of work the projects center on, or any logical group of project criteria. My point is that the organization can begin to identify the projects the program will oversee—typically in terms of the expected benefits the projects will deliver to the program and the organization.

There are many different approaches to classifying the program's projects:

- By obvious chronological order
- According to logical program phases
- Based on the technology used in the projects
- Based on the availability of resources, scheduling, or some other logical grouping

The classification of the program's projects can help with the initiate program process to begin drafting the preliminary program scope statement. The preliminary scope statement in this early stage of the program is likely to be broad and susceptible to progressive elaboration. The purpose of the preliminary program scope statement is to frame the major objectives that the program aims to deliver. It identifies the major goals and benefits of the program.

Once the preliminary program scope statement has been created, the program stakeholders must formally accept the program scope. Formal acceptance of the preliminary program scope statement means that the program stakeholders sign off on the scope. Their acceptance of the preliminary program scope statement is a confirmation that the program is needed to realize and support the organization's strategic benefits.

Examining Process Inputs

Every process in a program relies on certain inputs in order to do the activities the process requires. Inputs vary, depending on the process the program is completing at any given time. The activities of completing a program process create outputs that allow the program to move forward. Fascinating, I know. If you reference the PMBOK or *The Standard for Program Management,* you'll see that every process has inputs and outputs. You'll need to be familiar with these for your PgMP certification.

As you move through the remainder of this book, I'll provide nifty little charts like Figure 5-2 that show the inputs to the process. Later, I'll show the corresponding outputs of a process. And since I am such a swell guy, I have included on the CD a Power-Point presentation that has all of these figures in a slideshow for your quick review. The show is called "Inputs and Outputs."

 NOTE   Send me an e-mail and thank me for the slideshow: pgmp@projectseminars.com. I'm kidding. If you do find the slideshow and this book useful, I'd love to hear from you—especially once you knock out the PgMP exam. This is just a quick pep talk. Keep going—you can do it!

Examining Program Initiating Inputs

Now that you know that every process in a program relies on inputs, let's have a look at the first process and all the inputs you'll need to complete the process work. Figure 5-3 illustrates the four inputs to the initiate program process. Many of these process inputs are created external to the program manager's role, but that's not to say that the person that'll be the program manager isn't involved in these input creations, she very well may be.

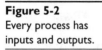

Figure 5-2
Every process has inputs and outputs.

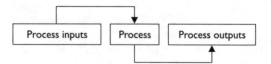

Figure 5-3
There are four
initiate program
inputs.

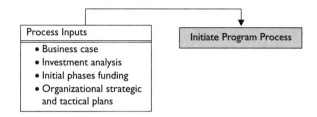

Process Inputs

• Business case
• Investment analysis
• Initial phases funding
• Organizational strategic
  and tactical plans

Initiate Program Process

You'll need a business case—no, not a briefcase, a business case. The business case defines the program, it shows how the program fits into the organization's strategic plan, and it defines the need for the program to be initiated and to exist in the organization. Basically, the business case supports the program's initiation.

Someone within the organization will need to complete the investment analysis. The investment analysis looks at the forecast return on investment of the program. The investment analysis is looking for the return on investment, the break-even point, sometimes called the management horizon, and the cost-to-benefits analysis. The sidebar in this chapter defines three of the most common investment analysis tools.

Linked to the investment analysis, the organization will need to identify the amount of funds that will be allotted to funding for the early phases of the program. In order for the program to begin moving, some funds will be assigned to the program with a cash flow forecasting analysis tied to the program. Figure 5-4 is an example of step funding where the early funds can carry the program through the initial phases and to a specified milestone. Cash flow forecasting is the prediction that by the time the program reaches the first milestone, additional funds will be available to invest in the program to move onto the second phase and so on.

Figure 5-4
Step funding allows
for cash flow
forecasting.

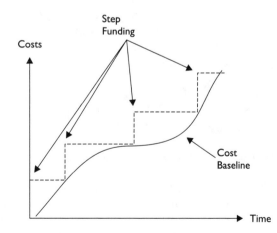

Considering the Time Value of Money

My dad's a great guy, but he likes to remind me how a dollar today isn't worth a dollar back in his day. He still reminisces about the good old days when soda pops were a nickel and movie tickets were a dime. I'm sure I'll be doing the same thing to my son when I'm a bald old man (I know, not far from now). This is an example of the time value of money. There are a couple of nifty formulas that show us how the value of money shrinks or grows over time. This is part of the investment analysis an organization may do when it considers launching a program. Have a look at this math magic.

Future Value of money is a formula that calculates how much a present amount of money may be worth at some point off in the future. Here's the formula: Future Value = Present Value $(1 + \text{interest rate})^n$. Note that n is the power of the time periods. Here's an example where the time period is 5 years, the interest rate is 6 percent, and the present value is $100,000:

1. Future Value = $100,000(1 + 0.06)^5$
2. Future Value = $100,000(1.338226)$
3. Future Value = $133,822.60

This means that the program better be worth more than $133,822.60 in 5 years or financially it's not a good decision. In other words, the company could stick the $100,000 in the bank for 5 years and equal $133,822.60 if it earned just 6 percent.

If you can calculate the future value of money, you can also calculate the present value of some future amount of money. This is useful when a program is predicted to be worth some dollar amount in the future. In this instance you'll divide instead of multiply. Here's the formula:

Present Value = Future Value$/(1 + \text{interest rate})^n$, where n still represents the time periods for the program. I'm going to do a big one; let's pretend a program promises to be worth 19 million dollars in 8 years and the rate of return is 6 percent. The present value formula would read:

1. Present Value = $19,000,000/(1.06)^8$
2. Present Value = $19,000,000/1.593848$
3. Present Value = $11,920,835.61$

This means 19 million in 8 years is only worth nearly 12 million today, assuming a rate of return of 6 percent. And this means that your program better not need more than $11,920, 835.61 to be completed, or it's not a good financial investment. Of course, not all programs are selected purely for financial reasons—there could be laws, regulations, or other benefits that require the program to be initiated.

The final formula to consider is the Net Present Value (NPV). Because programs often have tiered deliverables, the organization may realize benefits from the component projects before the entire program is completed. In these instances, the organization can use the NPV approach to account for the deliverables it will receive each year of the program. Here's how it works:

1. Find the return on investment for each time period of the program.

2. Find the Present Value for each time period using the present value formula.

3. Calculate the sum of all of the Present Value findings.

4. Subtract the organization's investment from the sum of the Present Values.

5. If the NPV is greater than 1, the program is good; less than 1, not so good.

You won't find these formulas in PMI's *The Standard for Program Management*, but you will find them in the PMBOK. Your PgMP exam is based on *The Standard for Program Management* and the PMBOK, so be somewhat familiar with these formulas.

The final input to the initiate program process consists of the organizational strategic and tactical plans. Recall that all programs must support the strategy of the performing organization, so these organizational plans are referenced to ensure that the program is in alignment with the strategic goals of the performing organization.

Examining Initiating Outputs

Once the initiate program process has been enacted, the program is moving, and certain documents are required to allow the program to logically move toward the planning process group. Figure 5-5 represents the eight outputs of the initiate program process. The first output that you need to concern yourself with is the documentation for the program contract or the statement of work (SOW) for the program.

If an organization is completing a program for another entity, for instance, an architectural firm is creating a building for someone else, then a contract is needed. The contractual agreement details the requirements and responsibilities of both parties in order to complete the program. A statement of work defines all of the details of the

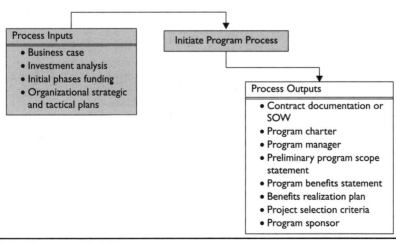

Figure 5-5   There are eight initiate program outputs.

program and is sent to the prospective vendors from the client. The SOW allows the vendors to understand the client's request and create a quote, bid, or proposal based on the SOW details.

For your exam, when a client-vendor relationship exists, the SOW is a precursor to a contract. When the program is being completed internally by an organization and different resources and lines of business will be contributing to the program, a SOW serves in lieu of a contract. In either instance, the SOW typically defines the following:

- The expectations of the program
- Program requirements for technologies, personnel, and even competency levels
- Where the program work will occur
- The anticipated program schedule and deadlines for program benefit delivery, the component project completion dates, and the final program deadline
- Standards and regulations that may affect the program (standards are guidelines and are sometimes optional; regulations are often laws and can be viewed as program requirements)
- Criteria and metrics for program performance and acceptance

Once the contract or SOW has been agreed upon, the program can now be officially chartered by an entity within the organization such as the organizational executive committee, the steering committee, or the portfolio management body. The charter links the program to the organization's ongoing work and strategic plan while also providing a vision statement for the program to achieve. The charter authorizes the program to exist within the organization and identifies the program manager.

The next document that is created is the preliminary program scope statement. This document frames the program and defines the high-level deliverables and objectives for the program. This document will, as the program moves forward, go through rounds of analysis and planning and will eventually become the official program scope statement—but not yet. For now, in initiating, it's just a big, dreamy vision of where the program should end up.

 NOTE The preliminary program scope statement is an excellent example of progressive elaboration. The preliminary program scope statement will move through iterations of details and planning until the program management team arrives at the program scope statement.

The initiate program process also creates the program benefits statement. This document defines all of the good that will come out of the program. It defines the benefits the organization can expect as a result of completing the program and helps the program manager adhere to the benefits management theme of the program.

Within the program there will be component projects. These component projects will be contributing to the benefits of the program and will need to be selected, chartered, and then managed by project managers. Before the program can charter a project, however, there must be a guideline on how projects will be selected and initiated. This guideline is the program's project selection criteria. Because most programs only have so much capital to invest in projects, there must be some selection criteria to filter out projects or to organize component projects for maximum return on investment. Common project selection criteria methods include the following:

- Benefit measurement methods
  - Historical information
  - Scoring models
  - Benefit/cost ratios
  - Project payback period
  - Discounted cash flow
- Constrained optimization methods
  - Linear programming
  - Nonlinear programming
  - Integer algorithms
  - Dynamic programming
  - Multiobjective programming

A fluid document that also comes as an output of the initiate program process is the completion of the benefits realization plan. This plan defines how the program will achieve the benefits it promises to the stakeholders. When it comes to allowing the program to be chartered and financed, the benefits realization plan is key. This plan defines each program benefit, how the benefit will come into operations, and the metrics by which the program benefits will be measured.

Examining Authorize Project Inputs

The second process in the program initiating process group is the authorize projects process. This process allows the component projects to be chartered within the program. The authorize projects process can happen anytime in a program except when the program is moving through the closing activities. Figure 5-6 defines the three inputs to the authorize projects process.

In order to begin authorizing component projects, the program manager will rely on the program scope statement. This makes sense, as every single project within the program is to support and satisfy some part of the program scope. The program scope pretty much follows the program manager and the program management team around, since everything they do has to support the program scope. If a project doesn't directly support the program scope by contributing to the benefits of the program, there's no reason for the project to be authorized.

Figure 5-6
There are three inputs to authorizing a project.

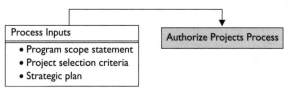

In order to be certain that the component project does indeed support the program scope, the program management team will use four directives for every component project:

- Develop a project business case that shows how the project will support the program scope. The project business case leads to the project schedule, resource allocation, and budget for the project.

- Assign a project manager to the component project. Kinda need a project manager in order to have a project.

- Communicate project information to the project and program stakeholders as needed on a regular basis.

- Enforce the program governance to track and monitor the project benefits and how the project actually contributes to the program benefits.

One of the outputs from the initiate program process was the project selection criteria. That output is needed now. The project selection criterion that was defined as a result of the initiate program process is used as an input to project selection and authorization. The organization's strategic plan may also be used as an input to the authorize projects process, as each project should be, ultimately, in alignment with the organization's strategic plan.

Defining the Authorize Projects Outputs

The authorize projects output defines several things, as Figure 5-7 depicts. One of the most important outputs of the authorize projects process is the program reporting requirements. When you consider all of the project managers, project team members, vendors, and other stakeholders, it's easy to see the amount of communication that can occur within a program. It's essential for the program management team to define who reports to whom in the project hierarchy—and to define what type of communication is expected and when.

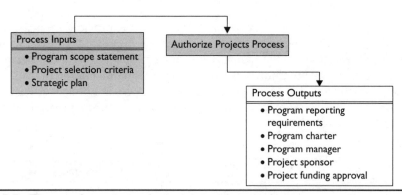

Figure 5-7   There are five project authorization process outputs.

Every new project that is defined within the program will need an accompanying project charter. A *project charter* is the document that formally authorizes the project. It defines several key pieces of project information:

- Requirements for acceptance of the project deliverable
- Business needs of the project and how the project fits into the program
- The project purpose (likely through the project business case)
- Project manager and the project manager's authority level
- Milestone schedule
- Stakeholder influences
- Functional organizations and related stakeholders
- Project assumptions
- Project constraints
- Business case
- Summary project budget

Every project within the program must be chartered, and each charter should address all of these components. A well-written charter defines the project goals, how the project fits into the program, and the expectations of the project manager. A poorly written charter is ambiguous, uses subjective terms, such as good, fast, or happy, and doesn't define achievable objectives for the project manager.

When a project is chartered, there may be a shuffle in the resources among the projects. The program manager may evaluate the projects and work with the project managers to move project resources from one project to another according to demand, priority, or the disciplines the projects focus on. If you've worked with project managers, you know that project managers don't like the idea of anyone taking away their resources—whether they need those resources now or not. The program manager should be prepared for confrontations and may need to rely on program governance and human resource practices to resolve the project confrontations.

 NOTE Remember that resources are people, things, and monies. Additional projects may mean the program manager shifts tools, equipment, facilities, people, and even funds from one project to another. Territorial project managers won't be happy with this decision, so expect to compromise.

The program manager may very well be the project sponsor, but the program governance may direct the chartering and sponsoring decisions for component projects. Whoever charters the component project must be someone within the organization that has the authority to assign resources and finances to the chartered project.

Finally, all projects require three things: schedule, budget, and scope. You probably know these as the triple constraints of project management. The idea is that the project manager must balance all of these to create an equilateral triangle. If any one side of the triangle is out of whack, for example, too much scope and not enough time, the project is likely to fail. Of all these, in my experience, the project budget seems to be the most important issue for organizations. It's also one of the primary outputs of the initiating project process.

Gathering the Program Team Process Inputs

For a program to move forward, it'll require some people to make that happen. The people I am talking about here are the program management team members. I've mentioned them a few times already—they're the folks that do the program work to manage, coordinate, communicate, and facilitate the program management processes. The program manager can't do everything.

The members of the program team are more than just administrative staff; these are experts that contribute to program decisions, ensure that the correct resources are available, and help achieve the program requirements. These people may come from within the organization, be hired as new employees to work on the program, or include contractors and vendors.

There are just two inputs to the initiate program team process, as Figure 5-8 depicts:

- **Recruitment practices**   This input describes how your organization allows the program manager to recruit new program management team members. This is sometimes called part of your organization's enterprise environmental factors. For some organizations, the program manager won't have much say over how the program team is assembled—he'll just inherit the program team. Other organizations, however, may allow the program manager complete autonomy to choose her program team however she likes.

- **Staffing pool description**   The staffing pool description depicts the talent, competencies, interest, availability, and cost of the resources that may be able to participate on the program management team. Ideally, an organization has a centralized database to query the staffing pool of needed characteristics and competencies and what the availability of these resources may be.

These two process inputs may be considered organizational constraints, as the program manager is restricted by the recruitment practices and the available resources. You also have to question the accuracy of the staffing pool description and how recently the pool information was updated. A constraint, to be clear, is anything that restricts the project or program manager's options.

Examining the Outputs of the Initiate Team Process

There are three logical outputs of the initiate team process, as Figure 5-9 depicts. Once the program management team has been assembled, the program manager can begin assigning activities to the core program team. The program team gets to work, as does

Figure 5-8
There are two inputs to the initiate program team process.

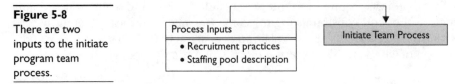

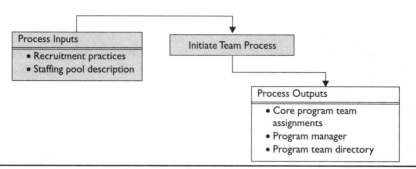

Figure 5-9   There are three outputs of the initiate team process.

the program manager. Just as the program management team gets their assignments, so too does the program manager.

The final output of this process, and your last one to know for this chapter, is the program team directory. The program team directory is the reference of all the program team members, their contact information, and general roles and responsibilities for the program. It's important that all program team members have access to this directory in order to successfully communicate. (I know, I know, it's Captain Obvious here.) The point I'm making is that the simple things are often the things that get glossed over and then become risks and bite the program management team later. For your exam, and out there in your world, make certain the program directory is created and kept current.

Chapter Summary

I've heard some program managers say that management isn't very creative. They see programs as a series of phases, consisting of processes that result in things, services, or conditions. I beg to differ. Programs are all about being creative. Programs are opportunities to create new things, new experiences, and new benefits. No two programs are ever identical. While the method to create these new things may be static, the application of the processes is a unique experience.

Programs get initiated because there's a desire to reach some dreamy, desired future state. There's a vision that the organization's executive committee or a customer of the organization wants to achieve. The program is the method to get from here, the launch of the program, to there, the completion of the program and the creation of the benefits the program creates.

Once a program is initiated, then the project charters can authorize the projects. A project, according to the PMBOK, is a short-term endeavor to create a unique product or service. Projects in a program are considered component projects, and they contribute to the overall benefits the program aims to realize. Just as the program's charter authorizes the program, the project charter authorizes the project. The project charter is signed by the project sponsor, which may often be the program manager.

The final process in the initiating process group is the initiate team process. This process allows the organization to assemble the program management team. This team will work with the program manager to ensure that the proper resources are available to satisfy the program requirements. The team can consist of people from the performing organization, be built from vendors and contractors, or be a combination of both.

This first process group authorizes the program. The program manager's authority is assigned as a result of the program charter. Recall that the program charter authorizes the program and lets the program manager get to work on the program. While the charter launches the program, there may be, or more likely there has been, a ton of work that has already gone into the program selection, feasibility study, and business case for the program to move into reality.

Key Terms

Authorize projects process　The initiating process that allows the project manager to authorize component projects within the program. This process may be done at any time during the program except during the closing phase of the program.

Benefit measurement methods　Approaches to measure, compare, and contrast the expected benefits of projects that may be chartered and included in a program.

Benefits realization plan　This plan defines how the program will achieve the benefits it promises to the stakeholders.

Constrained optimization　A project selection method that uses mathematical models to determine the best, worst, and/or most likely outcome of a proposed project.

Feasibility study　The pre-program research that helps the performing organization to determine the likelihood of a program reaching certain objectives such as time, cost, scope, and quality.

Future Value of money (FV)　Calculates how much a present amount of money may be worth at some point in the future. The formula is: Future Value = Present Value $(1 + \text{interest rate})^n$, where n is the number of time periods.

Initiate team process　An initiating process group process that allows the program team to be assembled, duties to be assigned, and the program work to begin.

Net Present Value (NPV)　A formula that considers the present value of each predicted return on investment for a program that may have tiered deliverables and intermediate returns on the program's investment over a series of years.

Preliminary program scope statement　The initial program scope statement, which includes the high-level objectives for the program.

Present Value of money (PV)　Determines how much a future amount of money is worth today. The formula is: Present Value = Future Value$/(1 + \text{interest rate})^n$, where n represents the time periods.

Program benefits statement　This document defines all of the good that will come out of the program. It defines the benefits the organization can expect as a result of completing the program and helps the program manager adhere to the benefits management theme of the program.

Program business case   Defines how the program may fit into the organization's strategic plan, and it defines the need for the program to be initiated and to exist in the organization.

Program initiating process group   The first of five process groups, this authorizes the program, authorizes the component projects, and initiates the program management team.

Program team directory   A document that defines all of the contact information, roles, and responsibilities for all of the program team members.

Project business case   A document that defines how the component project will support the program scope.

Project charter   The document that authorizes the project to exist within the program. This document also identifies the project manager and his level of authority in the project. The project charter is signed by the project sponsor.

Rough order of magnitude estimate   An early project estimate that provides a "rough estimate" of what the program may cost to complete.

Staffing pool description   Depicts the talent, competencies, interest, availability, and cost of the resources that may be able to participate on the program management team.

Statement of Work (SOW)   Defines all of the details of the program and is sent to the prospective vendors from the client. The SOW allows the vendors to understand the request of the client and to create a quote, bid, or proposal based on the SOW.

Questions

1. The initiate program process provides all of the following for the organization except for which one?
   A. Defines the program scope.
   B. Defines the project benefits.
   C. Authorizes the program to exist within the organization.
   D. Links the program to the ongoing work and strategic objectives of the organization.

2. You work for the NJG Consulting Agency. You and your colleagues are completing the analysis of a potential program to create new manufacturing software. This analysis has taken eight months to complete, and you've been leading the work with seven of your colleagues. You would like to be the program manager, if the program gets initiated by your customer. This is an example of which one of the following?
   A. Feasibility study creation
   B. Sunk costs
   C. Conflict of program interest
   D. Proposal creation

3. Marcy has created a rough order of magnitude estimate for her organization. They are considering investing in a new program. Which one of the following best describes a ROM estimate?

   A. $12 million, +10% to –5%

   B. $12 million, +20% to –10%

   C. $12 million, +100% to –50%

   D. $12 million, +50% to –10%

4. What document will the program stakeholders sign off on to show their acceptance of the program scope?

   A. Project charter

   B. Program charter

   C. Program benefits realization plan

   D. Program preliminary scope statement

5. Justin is working on a document for his organization's executive committee. The document will define a proposed program, demonstrate how the proposed program will fit into the organization's strategic plan, and define why the proposed program should be initiated. What document is Justin creating?

   A. Program business case

   B. Program scope statement

   C. Program feasibility study

   D. Program proposal

6. What is the method of funding that provides finances for the program to reach predetermined milestones, cash flow forecasting, and staged estimates?

   A. Phase gate estimating

   B. Step funding

   C. Stepped cashing

   D. Milestone funding

7. You are the program manager for your organization. You have completed the pre-program research and believe that your program will be worth $950,000 in four years. Your program sponsor is curious what your program would be worth in today's dollars. You considered the rate of return at 6 percent. What is the Present Value for your program?

   A. $752,488

   B. $1,199,353

   C. $4,028,000

   D. $798,319

8. Your program needs $4,250,000 to complete. Your program is likely to last for seven years. Your manager, Gary, wants to know the future value of the program investment if the rate of return could be 6 percent. What is the Future Value for the program investment?

   A. $2,826,493

   B. $6,390,429

   C. $572,776

   D. $31,535,000

9. Which program document includes objectives and high-level deliverables of the program?

   A. Program charter

   B. Program preliminary scope statement

   C. Program business case

   D. Program feasibility study

10. Which time value of money calculation allows you to calculate the present value for a program that has tiered deliverables?

   A. Present Value

   B. Net Present Value

   C. Future Value

   D. Constrained optimization

11. Your organization is participating in a proposal creation for the NHG Corporation. The program is to create a new warehouse for their organization. In this instance, your organization is the vendor and the NHG Corporation is the client. What document will you use to determine the expectations of the program you are creating a proposal for?

   A. Charter

   B. Contract

   C. Statement of work

   D. Preliminary scope statement

12. All of the following are examples of constrained optimization except for which one?

   A. Linear programming

   B. Dynamic algorithms

   C. Benefit-cost ratios

   D. Nonlinear programming

13. You are a program manager for your organization. Your program will include seventeen projects over the life of the program. You may create a component project at any time in a program except for during which process group?

    A. Initiating

    B. Planning

    C. Monitoring and controlling

    D. Closing

14. Which document will serve as an input to the authorize projects process?

    A. Program charter

    B. Project charter

    C. Program scope statement

    D. Program benefits statement

15. Martin is the program director for his organization. He has been working with his program management team to determine which projects should be chartered and how the component projects should be organized. He has asked his program team to create a document that will show how the projects will support the program scope. What document is Martin asking the program team to create?

    A. Feasibility study

    B. Preliminary project scope statement

    C. Business case

    D. Project return on investment analysis

16. In order to authorize a project in a program, what document must be created?

    A. Project scope statement

    B. Project preliminary scope statement

    C. Project charter

    D. Project benefits analysis documentation

17. You have chartered a new project in your program. This new project requires that you move some of the resources from the HJGY Project to the JHY Project. This allotment of resources from one project to another has caused Nancy, the project manager of the HJGY Project, to become frustrated with the change. All of the following are examples of resources that you, the program manager, may move from one project to another except for which one?

    A. People

    B. Schedule

    C. Monies

    D. Equipment

18. You are recruiting program team members for your program. Your organization's rules and policies do not allow you, the program manager, to solicit people from the staffing pool directly to join your program team. This is an example of what?

    A. Human resources best practices

    B. Constraint

    C. Organizational process assets

    D. Staffing pool description

19. Virginia needs to speak with Elizabeth regarding a program issue. Elizabeth is located in another state than Virginia's. What document could Virginia use to quickly locate and communicate with Elizabeth?

    A. Communications matrix

    B. Communications management plan

    C. Program team directory

    D. Program management plan

20. You and people from your organization have worked together to create the program benefits statement. All of the following are not defined in the program benefits statement except for which one?

    A. Program schedule and milestone

    B. Program anticipated budget for the initial phase

    C. Program business case

    D. Organizational benefits of doing the program

Questions and Answers

1. The initiate program process provides all of the following for the organization except for which one?

    A. Defines the program scope.

    B. Defines the project benefits.

    C. Authorizes the program to exist within the organization.

    D. Links the program to the ongoing work and strategic objectives of the organization.

    B. The initiate program process does not define the project benefits. The program benefits are defined in the program's program benefits statement. A, the program scope, is defined later in the program planning process group. C describes the program charter, while D describes the program's feasibility study.

2. You work for the NJG Consulting Agency. You and your colleagues are completing the analysis of a potential program to create new manufacturing software. This analysis has taken eight months to complete, and you've been leading the work with seven of your colleagues. You would like to be the program manager, if the program gets initiated by your customer. This is an example of which one of the following?

    A. Feasibility study creation

    B. Sunk costs

    C. Conflict of program interest

    D. Proposal creation

    A. The pre-program analysis and research is simply called the feasibility study creation. B, sunk costs, describes the monies that have already been invested in the program and that may not be recovered. C is a distracter and is not a valid choice. D, while tempting, is not the best answer for this question, as the question truly describes the feasibility study creation, not the proposal creation.

3. Marcy has created a rough order of magnitude estimate for her organization. They are considering investing in a new program. Which one of the following best describes a ROM estimate?

    A. $12 million, +10% to −5%

    B. $12 million, +20% to −10%

    C. $12 million, +100% to −50%

    D. $12 million, +50% to −10%

    C. $12 million, +100 to −50%, is the best example of a rough order of magnitude estimate. Early in the program this is the first estimate that is created, but it is generally unreliable. As the program moves into the planning process group, a budget estimate and a definitive estimate will be correct with a much tighter and acceptable range of variance. Choices A, B, and D are all incorrect choices.

4. What document will the program stakeholders sign off on to show their acceptance of the program scope?

    A. Project charter

    B. Program charter

    C. Program benefits realization plan

    D. Program preliminary scope statement

    D. The program stakeholders must sign off on the program preliminary scope statement to show solidarity and agreement of the program's intent. A, the project charter, authorizes component projects, and the project sponsor signs this document. B, the program charter, authorizes the program to exist within the organization and precedes the preliminary program scope statement. C, the program benefits realization plan, is created after the scope statement.

5. Justin is working on a document for his organization's executive committee. The document will define a proposed program, demonstrate how the proposed program will fit into the organization's strategic plan, and define why the proposed program should be initiated. What document is Justin creating?

   A. Program business case

   B. Program scope statement

   C. Program feasibility study

   D. Program proposal

   A. Justin is creating the program business case, as it does link the program to the organization's strategic plan. B, the program scope statement, defines all of the program work the program is expected to create. C, the program feasibility study, helps determine if the program should be initiated or not. D, the program proposal, is a distracter and is not a valid choice for this question.

6. What is the method of funding that provides finances for the program to reach predetermined milestones, cash flow forecasting, and staged estimates?

   A. Phase gate estimating

   B. Step funding

   C. Stepped cashing

   D. Milestone funding

   B. Step funding is the intermittent financing to allow the program to reach predetermined program milestones. As the program reaches each milestone, additional funds are infused into the program to allow it to reach its next milestone. A, C, and D are all incorrect choices for this question.

7. You are the program manager for your organization. You have completed the pre-program research and believe that your program will be worth $950,000 in four years. Your program sponsor is curious what your program would be worth in today's dollars. You considered the rate of return at 6 percent. What is the Present Value for your program?

   A. $752,488

   B. $1,199,353

   C. $4,028,000

   D. $798,319

   A. The formula needed for this question is Present Value = Future Value $/(1$ + interest rate$)^n$. In this instance the formula would be $\$950{,}000/(1.06)^4$. Choices B, C, and D are all incorrect calculations for this formula.

$$PV = FV/ (1 + .06)^4$$
$$PV = 950{,}000 /(1.06)^4$$
$$PV = 950{,}000/ (1.26247)$$
$$PV = \$752{,}488$$

8. Your program needs $4,250,000 to complete. Your program is likely to last for seven years. Your manager, Gary, wants to know the future value of the program investment if the rate of return could be 6 percent. What is the Future Value for the program investment?

   A. $2,826,493

   B. $6,390,429

   C. $572,776

   D. $31,535,000

   B. In order to see what the present amount of money is worth in seven years you'd use the formula Future Value = $4,250,000(1.06)^7. Choices A, C, and D are all incorrect formulas for this question.

9. Which program document includes objectives and high-level deliverables of the program?

   A. Program charter

   B. Program preliminary scope statement

   C. Program business case

   D. Program feasibility study

   B. Only the program preliminary scope statement defines the objectives and high-level deliverables of the program. Choices A, C, and D are all incorrect choices, as these documents do not define the program objectives and deliverables.

10. Which time value of money calculation allows you to calculate the present value for a program that has tiered deliverables?

   A. Present Value

   B. Net Present Value

   C. Future Value

   D. Constrained optimization

   B. Net Present Value allows the program manager to calculate the present value of all of the years where the program will have some return on investment. A, Present Value, only considers the end result of the program, not each individual year's return. C, Future Value, considers the present amount of money, typically the program investment, and finds its value for some future date. D, constrained optimization, describes mathematical models, such as linear programming, to determine the likelihood of the program success.

11. Your organization is participating in a proposal creation for the NHG Corporation. The program is to create a new warehouse for their organization. In this instance your organization is the vendor and the NHG Corporation is the client. What document will you use to determine the expectations of the program you are creating a proposal for?

   A. Charter

   B. Contract

C. Statement of work

D. Preliminary scope statement

C. Before you can create a proposal for your client, you'll need the statement of work. The statement of work defines all of the expectations and program conditions. The SOW comes from the client to the vendor—usually along with a request for a proposal. A, the program charter, authorizes the program. B, the contract, comes after the SOW and proposal and is the legally binding agreement between two or more parties in the program. D, the preliminary scope statement, does happen during the program initiating process group, but it does not come until after the program's contract and charter have been created.

12. All of the following are examples of constrained optimization except for which one?

A. Linear programming

B. Dynamic algorithms

C. Benefit-cost ratios

D. Nonlinear programming

C. Benefit-cost ratios describe the benefits to costs for a program. It is an example of benefits comparison. A, B, and D are all examples of constrained optimization.

13. You are a program manager for your organization. Your program will include seventeen projects over the life of the program. You may create a component project at any time in a program except for during what time of the program?

A. Initiating

B. Planning

C. Monitoring and controlling

D. Closing

D. You can create and charter a component project at any time throughout the program except when the program has entered the close program process group. Choices A, B, and C are all project processes groups.

14. Which document will serve as an input to the authorize projects process?

A. Program charter

B. Project charter

C. Program scope statement

D. Program benefits statement

C. The only document of the four that serves as input to the authorization of the program's projects is the program scope statement. A, the program charter, is not an input to the authorize projects process. B, the project charter, is an outcome of the authorize projects process. D, the project benefits statement, is not an input to the authorize charter process.

15. Martin is the program director for his organization. He has been working with his program management team to determine which projects should be chartered and how the component projects should be organized. He has asked his program team to create a document that will show how the projects will support the program scope. What document is Martin asking the program team to create?

   A. Feasibility study

   B. Preliminary project scope statement

   C. Business case

   D. Project return on investment analysis

   C. The business case is the document Martin wants his program team to create, as it is the only program document that demonstrates how a project will support the program scope. A, the feasibility study, is a program document that shows how the program will benefit the organization and adhere to the organization's strategic plan. B is not what Martin is asking the team to create in this instance, as his focus is on the program, not the component project. D, return on investment analysis, happens at the program level and not necessarily for the individual projects.

16. In order to authorize a project in a program, what document must be created?

   A. Project scope statement

   B. Project preliminary scope statement

   C. Project charter

   D. Project benefits analysis documentation

   C. The project charter authorizes the project. A, the project scope statement, defines all of the project work, project expectations, and objectives and is created after the project charter. B, the project preliminary scope statement, does not authorize the project. D, the project benefits analysis documentation, is not a valid choice for the question, as it does not authorize the project.

17. You have chartered a new project in your program. This new project requires that you move some of the resources from the HJGY Project to the JHY Project. This allotment of resources from one project to another has caused Nancy, the project manager of the HJGY Project, to become frustrated with the change. All of the following are examples of resources that you, the program manager, may move from one project to another except for which one?

   A. People

   B. Schedule

   C. Monies

   D. Equipment

B. The schedule is not a resource, but a time management approach. A, people, C, monies, and D, equipment, are all examples of resources that can be moved from one project to another—even if project managers such as Nancy don't appreciate it. Sorry, Nancy.

18. You are recruiting program team members for your program. Your organization's rules and policies do not allow you, the program manager, to solicit people from the staffing pool directly to join your program team. This is an example of what?

    A. Human resources best practices

    B. Constraint

    C. Organizational process assets

    D. Staffing pool description

    B. A constraint is anything that limits the program manager's options. In this instance, the rules and policies limit what the program manager may do to recruit the program team. A, C, and D are not constraints on the program manager but program components.

19. Virginia needs to speak with Elizabeth regarding a program issue. Elizabeth is located in another state than Virginia's. What document could Virginia use to quickly locate and communicate with Elizabeth?

    A. Communications matrix

    B. Communications management plan

    C. Program team directory

    D. Program management plan

    C. This is simply the program team directory that Virginia could use to locate Elizabeth. A, a communications matrix, is a table that shows the interaction of two or more stakeholders. B, the communications management plan, defines when and how stakeholders may communicate with each other. D, the program management plan, is a collection of subsidiary plans and is not the best choice for this question.

20. You and people from your organization have worked together to create the program benefits statement. All of the following are not defined in the program benefits statement except for which one?

    A. Program schedule and milestone

    B. Program anticipated budget for the initial phase

    C. Program business case

    D. Organizational benefits of doing the program

    D. Organizational benefits of doing the program are exactly what is defined in the benefits statement for your program. Choices A, B, and C are not defined in the program benefits statement.

Working with Planning Processes

6

In this chapter, you will
- Develop the program management plan
- Plan for program interfaces
- Plan for program transitions
- Plan for program resources
- Define the program scope
- Develop the program schedule and budget
- Plan for quality
- Plan for procurement and risk

If you were going to build a new house for yourself and your family, you probably wouldn't just get your trusty shovel, hammer, and saw and then get to work building the thing. You'd consider all of the things you'd like the house to be: the bedrooms, kitchen, living areas, even the swimming pool out back and the bowling alley in the basement. You'd capture all of the elements of the new home that you can see in your mind's eye and get them out on paper. You'd also probably consult with an architect or two, a designer, and other experts who know all about building homes.

Yep, you'd do some serious planning, consulting, and thinking before the first scoop of dirt was dug. In program management you can, and are expected to, apply the same cautious and sensible planning. In my seminars I often remind folks that projects fail at the beginning—it's no different for programs. A lack of adequate, serious, and thorough planning only results in a program that's full of errors, headaches, and lawsuits. It's always better to plan to do the work right the first time—and by always I mean every single time. The costly nature of programs demands due diligence by the program manager for adequate planning.

For your PgMP examination you can expect a bunch of questions for program planning. You'll be expected to realize what needs to be planned, who participates in the planning, and the inputs and outputs of each planning activities. The whole goal of planning is to define what you and your program management team will do to complete the goals and objectives of the program.

Developing the Program Management Plan

Every program has a plan that provides structure to the program and offers guidance to the projects within the program. The program management plan is the foundation of the direction the program will follow. Specifically, this big, fat plan explains the program scope, shows how the program scope will satisfy the program's objectives and mission, and provides details on what things and conditions will be evident to signal that the program is, thankfully, completed. Figure 6-1 captures all of the inputs and outputs of this process.

Planning is a program management process that doesn't end until the program has reached its closing phase. Throughout the program the program manager and stakeholders will revisit the planning processes described in this chapter as needed. Planning is an iterative activity that requires time to do—and to do properly. Balanced with planning is executing the program plans—it doesn't do anyone, especially you, the program manager, any good at all if there's a lot of planning and very little doing. Programs are, after all, about creating something—and executing is how the things get created. My point is simple: in order to execute, in order to create, you and your team must first plan on what needs to be created and the activities required to create it.

Examining the Program Management Plan

The program management plan isn't just one big plan, but rather a collection of subsidiary plans. Each plan defines a chunk of the program, addresses a particular program management knowledge area, and defines the tactics the program manager and the project managers will use to reach the end result of the program. I'll be delving into the specifics of the program management plan contents in this chapter, but for now know that a program management plan includes the following:

- Details on how the program is organized
- The program work breakdown structure (PWBS)
- Internal and external resource requirements
- Scope, technology, risks, and program costs
- The program schedule
- The program budget
- Quality expectations and how the program will ascertain the expected quality
- Systems to measure and track program benefits realization and sustainment

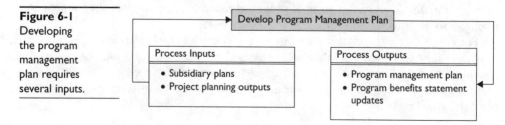

Figure 6-1
Developing the program management plan requires several inputs.

- Internal and external communication requirements
- The risk management approach
- The procurement management plan, which defines all the organization's procurement processes for the program
- The relationship of the program to the supporting program projects

While the program management plan aims to provide a structure and framework for the program from its launch, the program will likely pass through iterations, refinements, and updates. The program manager, ahem, you, should expect the program management plan to be flexible, susceptible to change, and a fluid document. A program manager that expects the program management plan to be exact on the first pass isn't, I'm afraid, being very realistic. The program plan will pass through many changes—it's not a museum piece, but rather a work in progress. The program management plan is an excellent example of progressive elaboration. As more information becomes available to the program manager, more details can be incorporated into the program management plan.

Updating the Program Management Plan

There are several program milestones that signal that additional planning is needed and that the program management plan is likely to change. These common program events likely mean the program management team will need to update the program management plan to reflect the changes.

New Project Initiation

Programs are made up of projects. As new projects are initiated, the program management plan may need to be updated to reflect how each new project will answer the demands of the program, provide the details of the project scope, specify the newly assigned project manager, and refer to each project's plan.

Project Closure

When a project in a program is closed, that usually means the program is moving toward satisfying the program requirements. The program plan should be updated to reflect the project status, include its final performance evaluation, and reference the project's archives. I bet you noticed that I said closing a project is usually a sign of the program moving forward; sometimes, however, it's not that at all. It's possible for a program to have to close a project that's not performing well or a project that's no longer needed in the program scope. In either case, the program plan should be updated to reflect the project's closure and its impact on the program's success.

Organizational Information

Programs are susceptible to issues with their fiscal health, so the performing organization's fiscal year and budget planning processes are reflected, and updated when needed, in the program management plan.

Unplanned Events

Nobody knows what's going to happen five days from now. When unplanned events happen in a program's life, it's time to whip out the red pen and update the program management plan. Consider program-altering events like mergers and acquisitions, corporate downsizing, and other organizational changes.

Risk Results

A *risk* is an uncertain event or condition that can have a positive or negative effect on the program. When the results of a risk event affect the program's ability to continue as originally planned, it's time to update the program management plan to reflect the risk event and the new direction of the program as a result of the risk.

Change in a program is inevitable and even expected. The program management team should quickly go to the program issues and work to incorporate the change into the program plan through planning, research, and consultation. Ignoring the change to the program, like most things in life, doesn't make it go away.

Develop the Program Management Plan

As you know, the program management plan is the collection of subsidiary plans. These subsidiary plans don't just magically appear—of course not—they're the result of hard work, research, and strategic planning. The program management team will work with the project managers, program stakeholders, and subject matter experts to create the subsidiary plans. Each subsidiary plan defines how the program processes related to that program domain can be managed. Here's a quick run-down of all the program management subsidiary plans:

- **Benefits management plan**   This plan defines the definition, creation, and management of the benefits the program will create.

- **Communications management plan**   This plan identifies the program stakeholders, provides the program information they'll need to participate in the program, and defines the expected modality of the communication.

- **Cost management plan**   As you might guess, this plan defines how the program's cost will be defined, committed, and maintained.

- **Contracts management plan**   Every program has procurement needs, and this plan defines the details of the contracts that will be managed.

- **Procurement management plan**   This plan defines the program's procurement management process. It'll define the procurement process, bidder selection, and vendor management. The procurement management plan will reference the contracts management plan as needed.

- **Interface management plan**   A program interface describes the relationship between people, departments, and organizations. This program management plan defines these relationships within, and beyond, the organization, including departments, lines of business, and other open programs.

- **Scope management plan**   This program management plan defines the program scope and how the program scope will be controlled. The plan defines the program management scope change control system, and the process program change requests that must follow to be incorporated into the program plan.

- **Quality management plan**   Quality is a conformance to requirements and a fitness for use. This plan defines how the quality objectives will be met within the project, including the adherence to quality assurance programs, quality control at the project level, and the expected reactions when quality inspections don't meet the defined expectations.

- **Resource management plan**   Resources aren't just people, they're materials, facilities, and equipment. This plan defines how resources will be obtained, managed, and allocated throughout the program. This plan also defines how the resources will be tracked across the program's projects to ensure that resources are not over-allocated and are being used as efficiently as possible.

- **Risk response plan**   Risk identification is an ongoing, iterative activity, and this plan addresses the responses to the identified risk events. The program management team will identify the risk owner, the person closest to the risk event. This person will monitor the risk trigger, which is a sign or condition that the risk may be coming into fruition. The risk response plan defines how the risk owner should react if the risk event passes the risk threshold and the event comes into play.

- **Schedule management plan**   This program management plan defines, well, the schedule. It also defines how changes to the schedule may be allowed, fleshed into the program, and then executed.

- **Staffing management plan**   This program management plan defines the needed resources for the program and how the program will obtain those resources. This program plan also defines how the staff may be brought on to and released from the program.

These subsidiary plans are the result of other planning processes. I'll be covering each of the planning processes through the remainder of this chapter, so you'll have an excellent picture of how the program management plan comes into being.

Planning for Program Interfaces

The interface planning process identifies, documents, and confirms the relationships within a program, with other programs within an organization, and even outside of the organization, such as government, media, or community interfaces. A careful study of the program will reveal where programs need to communicate, interact, or affect other programs and entities. It's the responsibility of this program plan to confirm these relationships and then create a way to manage the interfaces these program relationships demand. Figure 6-2 captures all of the inputs and outputs of this process.

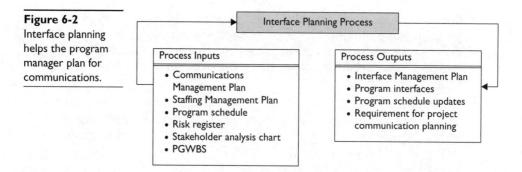

Figure 6-2
Interface planning helps the program manager plan for communications.

As a general rule, the larger the program, the more interfaces you'll find. Many programs will use an integrated team approach among all of the programs that'll interact through their own respective life cycles. This integrated team may address internal program interfaces for each program, but mainly they'll identify and address the interfaces among the programs, government agencies, vendors, and other program stakeholders that will be involved with the program.

Referencing Program Plans

When multiple programs have to coordinate activities, resources, and deliverables, you can bet there will be competing objectives, struggles for resources, and a fight for program power. Each performing organization will have to determine which program's objectives take priority and let their deliverables drive decisions within the program.

One approach that program managers may rely on is the Delphi Technique. It's a tool that uses rounds of anonymous surveys to build a consensus on issues, risks, and objectives within a program. (Although it's named after the Oracle at Delphi, the most important oracle in Greek mythology, you don't have to worship Apollo.) Sorry, there's no magic formula for which deliverables and program objectives are of highest priority. Ask any program manager which program is the most important, and they'll all tell you the same thing: the one they're currently working on. The Delphi Technique is an approach that can build consensus among the program managers.

When a group of program managers has to work together because of their program interfaces, they're primarily interested in communicating among the programs and ensuring the program resources are available as their schedules demand. This means you, the program manager, will bring three chunky parts of your program management plan to the interface planning sessions:

Communications Management Plan

This document identifies who needs what information, when they need the information, and the expected modality of the information to be communicated. Based on the needs of the program interfaces, each program management plan will be updated to reflect any new communication needs among the programs and program interfaces. The communications management plan will likely be updated to reflect three things:

- Newly identified communication requirements as a result of program interfaces

- Creation, or confirmation, of communication channels among the program
- Identification of decision-making channels among the program interfaces

Communication is an essential part of working within your program and with other program managers, so it's imperative to identify, document, and follow the communication channels and decisions among all of the involved programs and interfaces. When you consider the non-collocated nature of most programs, it's easy to see why communication demands are so high.

Staffing Management Plan

This plan identifies the programs' demand for program staff and how the needed staff will be brought on to and released from the program. It's crucial for the program manager to consider the demand and, in some cases, competition for shared staff among the programs and the projects within a program, as well as the availability of those resources. Careful planning among the program teams is needed to ensure that available staff is not over-allocated and that reasonable expectations for staff usage are agreed upon among the program interfaces.

It's not uncommon for program managers to horde or stockpile resources within a program to ensure that they'll have the needed resources at their disposal. I'm sure you've encountered other program managers that do this somewhat unethical practice. While the stockpiling of resources ensures that program managers may have the staff they need when and as they please, other interdependent programs may suffer from not having access to the needed staff.

The staffing management plan is also needed to review the organizational structure and interfaces within an organization and to identify the topology of the program and its projects.

Program Schedule

The program schedules of all the participating programs are reviewed to see milestone delivery dates, the execution of the program work, and the expected dates for program benefits. The interaction of programs may create updates for each program based on contributions from each participating program. Consider the interaction of programs, their deliverables that allow other programs to move forward, and the benefit fulfillment among programs.

Updating the Risk Register

Here's a fun part about program management planning—it's iterative. You'll need to complete risk management planning within your program and with your program interfaces, but I've not had a chance to delve into the steps and practices for effective risk management planning. So out there in the real world, at some point, you'll have to create a risk register after all of the risk planning, but in this section of the chapter you've not learned about risk management planning. It's the chicken or the egg, the cart before the horse, but certainly not pearls before swine. My point being that I'll discuss risk management planning in detail coming up, but for now you'll need an output of the process—the risk register.

The risk register is a collection and documentation for risks within the program. It details several things about each risk:

- What the risk event is
- The risk's probability of occurring
- The risk's impact on the program's finances and schedule
- Who the risk owner is and that person's responsibilities regarding the risk event
- Trends among risks
- What the current status of the risk event may be

The risk register is involved with interface planning, because risks among the programs need to be identified, documented, and responded to. I'll detail the risk management planning process coming up.

Creating a Stakeholder Analysis Chart

An input the program manager can use as part of interface planning is a stakeholder analysis chart. This chart can capture each stakeholder and that stakeholder's position and influence on decisions and outcomes of the project. There are a lot of different approaches to creating a stakeholder analysis chart, but all share a common goal: capture the stakeholders and their stances on program decisions and direction. Each stakeholder analysis chart can be directed toward a program goal or objective. Table 6-1 is a generic example of a stakeholder analysis chart.

The stakeholder analysis chart can be used in a bunch of different scenarios and with a lot of different legends. Consider all the ways you can use this tool:

- Assessment of program contribution
- Risk perspective from each key stakeholder
- Influence of each stakeholder on varying objectives within the program
- Consensus building and program team buy-in

You can pretty much use the chart to capture any characteristic of a group of stakeholders within your program. You can use this chart whenever you need to capture program stakeholder stances on issues within the program.

Examining the Results of Interface Planning

Interface planning is part of the planning process group, so that means it's an iterative process that the program manager may revisit as often as needed. Whenever new program stakeholders, new interactions with vendors, or new interdependencies among programs are identified, it's a sign that additional interface planning is needed.

The primary output of the interface planning process is the interface management plan. This document defines all of the program interfaces, their program influence, and how the program management team will work to manage and maintain the program

| Stakeholders | Role | Program Objective | | | |
		Influence	Attitude	Priorities	Actions
Nancy	Network engineer	High	Positive Ownership of routing	Control of network configuration	Create network topology and IP addressing scheme
Don	Web developer	Moderate	Neutral	ASP development	Identify customer demands for web development
Linda	Electrical engineer	Low	Positive	Date of program work and access to facilities	Confirm resource availability Confirm vendor management solution
Susan	Training manager	Moderate	Negative	Live classroom training, limited web-based training	Work for agreeable solution to web-based training
Martha	Project manager	High	Positive	Control of her project for the web and network integration program	Date move requirements, web-based training bandwidth, control of project change control system

Table 6-1   A Stakeholder Analysis Chart Defines Each Stakeholder and That Stakeholder's Attributes

interfaces. The interface management plan clearly identifies all of the program interfaces and defines an action for the program management team for an interface—usually communication on the program status and performance.

Based on the contributions and requirements of the program interfaces, the program schedule may need to be updated. The program schedule updates may need to pass through a schedule change control board to explain the accommodations of the factors that demand the schedule change. For example, a government audit, inspection, or new law may contribute to the demand for a change to the program schedule.

At the heart of program interface planning is communications management. Effective communications is essential to maintain the interfaces. The program manager will need to contribute to the interface communication and may also expect inbound communications from program stakeholders, project managers, other program managers, government agencies, and public entities such as vendors, media, and customers. Communication is paramount to this process.

Planning for Program Transition

The two happiest days in a program manager's life are the day a program begins and the day the program ends. This planning process defines the activities the program management team will need to complete in order to transfer the program deliverables onto the ongoing operations of the organization. The program transition hands off the program benefits to the recipients of the program and ensures that all of the hard work, investments, and planning to complete the program are transferred and the benefits are truly realized and sustained. Figure 6-3 shows the inputs and outputs of program transition planning.

Creating the Transition Plan

There'd be few things sadder for you if you and your team worked to create a wonderful program, delivered on the promised benefits, and then transferred your deliverables only to witness the program's benefits being squandered. The transition plan relies on three inputs from your early program planning:

- **Program scope statement**   Recall that this document defines the scope of the program and its promises to deliver objectives to the program stakeholders. This is an input, because the program manager needs to complete the program according to scope before the program can be transitioned into organizational operations.

- **Program schedule**   Most programs have tiers of deliverables and benefits rather than just one big package at the end of the program. The program schedule is needed, as it defines when benefits will be expected to be transitioned into usable benefits for the organization.

- **Stakeholder analysis chart**   This chart is used to identify and quantify expectation of the program stakeholders. It's referenced here to ensure the program stakeholders are communicated with and their concerns addressed regarding the transfer of benefits.

The program transition plan aims to ensure the program deliverables and benefits are fully realized and used by the organization. Specifically the transition plan defines how the following components will transfer into operations:

- Program documentation
- Training and materials of the program's product

Figure 6-3
There are three inputs and two outputs for program transition planning.

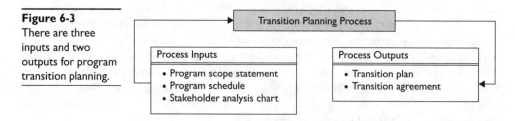

Transition Planning Process

Process Inputs
• Program scope statement
• Program schedule
• Stakeholder analysis chart

Process Outputs
• Transition plan
• Transition agreement

- Supporting systems
- Facilities to maintain the program's deliverables
- Program personnel (shifted from program employees to organizational resources)

It's important for the program manager to identify the appropriate stakeholders and their expectations to receive the benefits of the program. It's up to the program manager to ensure that the recipients of the program realize what they'll be receiving from the program and when the benefits will be heading into operations. The recipients of the program deliverables may be overwhelmed when they realize the responsibility they'll be receiving from the program—along with the associated responsibilities to maintain the program deliverables.

Creating the Transition Agreement

A deal is a deal. When the program is initiated and launched, it shouldn't, and usually isn't, a mystery as to who will receive and be responsible for the outputs of the program. Often a program is the result of a contractual agreement between two or more parties, so the contract puts all of the agreements in writing and is a legally binding agreement. The contract for the program is binding, not just for the program manager's performing organization and its promise to deliver, but also for the recipients of the program's deliverables and their promise to accept the deliverables.

In other instances, the program is not a contractual relationship at all, but an internal agreement between lines of business within a single entity. The transition agreement is needed in this scenario as well, because both internal parties need to recognize their responsibilities and relationship to one another during the program and, obviously, during the transfer of deliverables.

In either scenario keep in mind that program deliverables are often stages throughout the program schedule, and communication to the recipients is paramount. The program management team should work with the recipients to keep them abreast of program benefits they'll be delivering. This communication ensures that the receiving party understands the deliverable is headed their way, and they can prepare their resources and activities to accept the benefits the program has created.

Determining Program Resources

A resource isn't just a person. A resource can be a piece of equipment, like a backhoe; a facility, like a warehouse; and materials, like wood and steel; even software and hardware. Programs and projects will obviously need resources—people and things—in order to complete the program scope. One of the early planning processes is to identify all of the resources the program will need in order to be successful. Figure 6-4 shows the inputs and outputs for resource planning.

When it comes to human resources, top priority should be given to the identification and fulfillment of the resources that are critical to the program, but that the pro-

Figure 6-4
Resource planning creates the resource management plan.

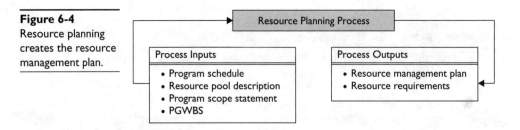

gram doesn't currently have. In other words, if a program has an imminent need for a licensed architect, and there's no licensed architect available in the organization, the program manager better get busy finding one. Use resources like subject matter experts, operational teams, and networking to find the needed resource before the program stalls because of the deficiency.

Creating the Resource Management Plan

The program's resource management plan defines the demand for resources, when the resources will be needed, and how the program will go obtain the needed resources. This plan will either directly define or reference the enterprise environmental factors for procuring resources, obtaining staff, and managing vendors.

I think it's safe to say that most programs rely on vendors at some point to fulfill resource requirements. Vendors can provide materials, services, facilities, and people to help the program reach its objectives. When the program deals with a vendor, however, it's essential to document the exact requirements of the relationship in a contract, a statement of work (SOW), and the program scope statement.

If the organization has done work similar to the current program, there's no need to create a new resource management plan; historical information can serve as a template to adapt the current program needs to.

NOTE   PMI and the real world like to use templates. You might think of a template as a shell-like document where you fill in the blanks specific to your program. PMI, however, considers similar program files that you adapt to your program as a template. Either way the message is clear: you aren't reinventing the wheel. Use historical information to make your program run smoother.

Defining the Resource Requirements

When it comes to staffing as a resource the program manager needs to examine the resource pool to determine what competencies are available for the program. If common resources are shared among the projects within the organization the program manager must examine the utilization of the staff to determine if they're being over-allocated. Over-allocation of resources results in several detrimental things:

- Bottlenecks arise in the program as projects are stalled waiting for needed resources to become available.

- Team and staffing morale declines as resources are overwhelmed with their project workloads.

- Quality may suffer as over-allocated resources rush to complete project assignments.

- Time and monies are wasted as rushed work results in poor quality and corrective actions are applied to the defect.

- Program and project risks increase, reflecting the demand for a limited amount of resources.

- Customer satisfaction may wane if a needed resource is lacking and the program stalls in the resource procurement.

- Unexpected costs for vendor-driven solutions may impact the program's budget.

The resource management plan aims to combat the negatives associated with lacking resources. This program plan may use resource histograms as in Figure 6-5 to determine where resources are being utilized or over-allocated. The resource histogram depicts the utilized resources and determines if any are over-allocated.

In some instances the program manager may elect to level resources according to a heuristic such as no more than 50 hours of labor per week per resource. This approach, called resource-leveling heuristics, will likely cause the program schedule to increase. While the amount of labor may be the same, it will take more calendar days for the resources to complete the assigned activities, because they're limited on the number of hours per time period.

Figure 6-5
A resource histogram shows resource utilization.

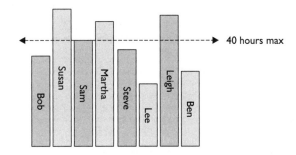

40 hours max

Defining the Program Scope

The program scope defines all of the required work—and only the required work—in order to satisfy the program's objectives. Keep in mind that when I'm talking work in this sense, I mean it as a noun—such as the work of Jackson Pollack (paint dribbles) or the works of Mozart (once a composer, now a decomposer). The work in a program defines all of the things the program will create; the program manager and the recipients of the program must be in agreement as to what the program will create. Figure 6-6 shows the inputs and outputs for scope definition.

Just as the program defines what work will be included, it also defines what work will be excluded. In other words, a program may agree to include the design and construction of a skyscraper, but the program scope statement clearly defines that the program won't be responsible for any of the landscaping on or around the skyscraper. The scope statement defines the boundaries of the program.

The program scope moves through rounds of planning—it's not a one-and-done activity. The program scope definition is an excellent example of progressive elaboration. The scope starts very broad and as more details become available, more facts can be added to the scope statement. At some point, usually when the stakeholders are all in consensus as to the content of the scope, they all sign off on the scope statement and the program can move deeper into the planning process.

 NOTE You know that change is expected within a program, but that doesn't mean that change can happen all the time in wild, random events. The program scope aims to protect itself and will serve as the basis for all future program events and decisions. The whole program is all about satisfying the requirements of the program scope.

Relying on the Program Initiation

Here's something funny: you won't need a program scope statement until you have a program. All right, you caught me again—it's not that funny, but consider my material here, folks—this is program management, not exactly the mother load of comic material. But think about it—customers, management, and even the program team often rush to requirements and benefits of a program before the program has even been authorized. I'm not saying that's a bad thing, but for your PgMP examination those early planning discussions are just fluff if there's no program to map those deliverables to.

So in order to have a program scope statement, you'll need a program. In order to have a program, you'll need the program charter. Recall that the charter is an output of

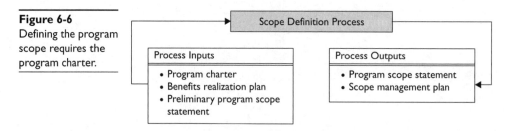

Figure 6-6
Defining the program scope requires the program charter.

Scope Definition Process

Process Inputs
- Program charter
- Benefits realization plan
- Preliminary program scope statement

Process Outputs
- Program scope statement
- Scope management plan

the initiation program process. While the charter authorizes the program, it also links the program to the organization's vision statement. It paints a picture to the desired future state that the program will create for the organization. The program charter is the foundation for the scope definition process.

The goals of a program are always defined in the program charter as it authorizes and launches the program. All constituent projects within the program are authorized as a result of the program charter—and all projects within the program should share the common vision of where the program is heading.

In addition to needing the program charter, you'll also rely on the preliminary program statement. This is another output of the program initiation process (discussed in Chapter 5). This document defines the concept of the program, identifies the program's major objectives, and establishes goals and benefits for the program. Basically the program management team will take the preliminary scope statement, in its broad, rough framework, and build on the early vision of the program. Now that more details have become available, a developed program scope statement can be created.

The final input for the scope definition is the program's benefits realization plan. This plan defines all of the benefits of the program and explains how the program will achieve those benefits. As the program moves through rounds of planning, more factors, decisions, and supporting detail will become available, so the benefits realization plan may be shallow and conceptual initially but will become more viable in the course of program research and planning.

Examining Scope Definition Outputs

There are but two outputs of your hard work in the scope definition process:

- Program scope statement
- Program scope management plan

The program scope statement serves as the baseline for all future program decisions. This means defects in the program, errors, corrective action, quality control, change requests, and just about any other process or program activity you can think of will be implemented in order to satisfy the program scope statement. That's the whole point of the program—define what the program will create and then go create it. You'll rely on the program scope statement throughout the program. It is used for several program management processes:

- Transition planning
- Resource planning
- Creating the program work breakdown structure
- Quality planning
- Communications planning
- Planning program purchases and acquisitions
- Integrated change control
- Scope control

You can safely say that a poorly developed program scope statement will have a negative impact on the rest of the program. The program scope statement is what all future program decisions should be measured against. If the program scope changes, then the program scope statement must be updated to reflect the agreed-upon changes.

The second output of the scope definition process is the scope management plan. This plan defines how the program scope will be created, monitored, controlled, updated, and protected from change. The scope management plan also defines how the program's work breakdown structure will be created. This subsidiary plan documents all of the rules for managing the program scope once it's been agreed upon by the program's key stakeholders.

Creating the Program Work Breakdown Structure

If you've completed your Project Management Professional examination, you're already familiar with the concept of a work breakdown structure (WBS) and how it serves as a centerpiece in the PMI project methodology. In program management you're dealing with a program work breakdown structure (PWBS). The concept is pretty much the same as a project's WBS; the PWBS is a hierarchical decomposition of the program scope. It breaks down the program scope statement into the individual deliverables the program promises to deliver.

To begin creating the PWBS, you'll need the scope management plan. This plan defines how you'll manage the program scope. It's needed here, as the scope management plan should also define how the decomposition of the program scope will commence. It'll define guidelines for the PWBS creation and to what extent the program scope should be decomposed. Figure 6-7 captures the inputs and outputs for the PWBS creation.

If you're using the scope management plan, you might as well use the program scope statement. It's actually a key input to the creation of the PWBS, as the program scope statement is what you and the program team will be decomposing to visualize the elements the program will deliver. The PWBS should reflect the deliverables of the program scope statement. When the program's all done, you should be able to use the PWBS almost like a checklist to show where the promised deliverables are and how they were delivered.

Finally, you'll need the benefits realization plan as an input to the PWBS creation. This plan defines the benefits the program will create and how the program will achieve those benefits. It's used as an input here, because you'll want to be certain the deliverables of the program scope are in correlation to the expected benefits the plan proposes to create.

Figure 6-7
The PWBS is a work breakdown structure for the entire program.

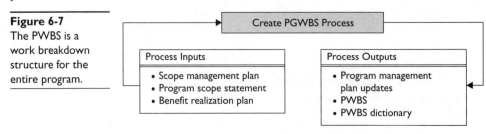

Creating the Program Work Breakdown Structure

This is the heart of the process—creating the PWBS. The PWBS defines and visualizes the technical objectives, the end items, the end results, and the end deliverables the program will ultimately create. It takes the program scope statement and breaks it down into the smallest manageable item—the program packages.

The PWBS does decompose the deliverables of the project; however, take caution. The PWBS doesn't decompose the scope deep into each project's WBS. Generally the PWBS only decomposes the program scope into one or two levels into each project's WBS. You can safely say that the PWBS should be decomposed as far as the program manager's immediate control over the deliverables exists.

At a minimum, the PWBS should include

- Program plans
- Program procedures
- Standards and processes
- Major milestone
- Program management deliverables
- Program office support deliverables
- Public communications
- All non-project work that's included in the program

The PWBS is the program's mechanism for developing and controlling the program scope, the program schedule, earned value management, and program monitoring and controlling processes. While the PWBS does encompass the constituent projects, it does not replace the demand for each project to have its own project work breakdown structure.

A companion document to the PWBS is the PWBS dictionary. Just as its name hints, this dictionary defines the program packages in the PWBS. The dictionary establishes a common nomenclature for program deliverables and helps communicate needs and expectations within the program. Having a common lexicon and understanding of the program deliverables can help the program management team better manage the program. Entries in the PWBS should be completely defined by all of their characteristics and any other relevant information the program management team may want to document about the WBS program packages.

Updating the Program Management Plan

I'm guessing that you know by now that planning is an iterative process. You'll do it over and over and over until you finally shift into closing the program. Throughout planning you'll want to aim for consistency among three primary program documents:

- The program work breakdown structure
- The program work breakdown structure dictionary
- The program management plan

These three documents will serve as a cornerstone to your program, and consistency from document to document will ensure accuracy and reduce the possibility of confusion among project managers and program team members. Here's the basic scoop: when changes enter into the program, there will be a ripple effect throughout all of the program's documentation.

When a change is approved, the program scope will be updated, which in turn means the PWBS needs to be updated, and then the PWBS dictionary, and then out to the program management plan. I'll discuss the entire change management process in Chapter 8, but for now just realize that a change to the program scope means that several documents will have to be updated to reflect the approved change.

Developing the Program Schedule

In order to calculate how long the program will last, the program manager needs to understand the duration of program activities, the anticipated duration of the program's projects, and the amount of effort available to apply the program activities. Developing the program schedule includes several program activities:

- Identification of program components
- Order of execution and interactions of the program components
- Time estimates to complete the program activities
- Documentation of the program milestones and their expected completion dates
- Documentation of the schedule variances and outcomes (an ongoing process)

Because of all the moving parts of a program, schedule development is one of the trickiest areas of program management. The program manager needs to have a clear understanding of how the program and project estimates were created initially. Figure 6-8 has all of the inputs and outputs for this process. It is one thing to rely on historical information to predict the current program duration, but quite another to use a dartboard and a roulette wheel to predict program length.

Considering the Duration Estimating Inputs

Two questions you'll have to answer as a program manager: "How much will this cost?" and "How long will it take to complete?" In order to complete the duration estimating

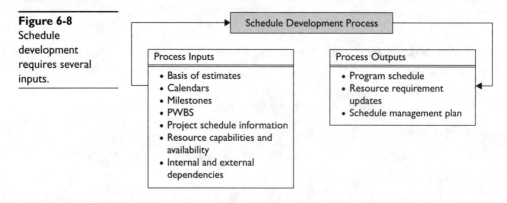

Figure 6-8
Schedule development requires several inputs.

Schedule Development Process

Process Inputs
- Basis of estimates
- Calendars
- Milestones
- PWBS
- Project schedule information
- Resource capabilities and availability
- Internal and external dependencies

Process Outputs
- Program schedule
- Resource requirement updates
- Schedule management plan

process, you'll need several pieces of information as inputs to provide accurate duration estimates.

The basis of estimates is needed to predict the program duration. As I mentioned, historical information is great, but it's not always available. The duration estimates might be based on simulations, expert judgment, or pilot testing of activities. Whatever the case, there needs to be a documentation of how the program and project duration estimates were created so that the program manager can plan accordingly.

There are two calendars for the program manager to consider. The first is the resource calendar, which shows the availability of program resources. Obviously, this calendar shows when program staff members are available, but also when project team members are available to complete assignments. This is important, as project team members may be on multiple projects within the program and coordination of resources is imperative. The resource calendar shows people and their vacation days, but also the availability of resources such as materials, equipment, and facilities.

The second calendar is the project calendar. The project calendar defines when the project work is expected to take place. It considers common holidays for the project team, scheduled pauses in the project, and considerations for coordination among projects within the program. Regularly scheduled events, such as staff meetings and risk assessment meetings, are included in the project calendar.

When the program is initiated, milestones for the program are identified. These milestones and their decomposition in the PWBS are needed to create the program schedule. Milestones show the completion of the things that equate to progress in the program duration. The PWBS is needed because these are the things, specifically the program packages, that will contribute to milestone completion.

Most of the work to be completed within a program is composed of effort-driven activities. This simply means that the more effort is applied to an activity, the faster the activity can be completed. For example, consider an activity to paint 1,000 rooms in a new hotel. It might take a crew of eight painters four weeks to paint the rooms. You could reason that the greater the amount of effort, the faster the work could be completed; that's an effort-driven activity.

The Law of Diminishing Returns, however, comes back to bite you on effort-driven activities. You can't always exponentially add more labor to reduce the amount of time it will take to complete an activity. Consider the painters and the hotel. If 16 painters could finish the work in two weeks, could 32 painters finish the work in one week? And would 64 painters complete the work in just a few days? You can't continually add labor to complete work instantaneously—it works on paper, but not with a paintbrush.

The second part of the Law of Diminishing Returns is that there's only so much yield in relation to your efforts. This means that eventually you're going to be paying more in labor than what the profit, your yield, for the workers will be. While there may only be 1,000 rooms to paint, all of the painters want to get paid for their efforts.

This scenario contributes to the consideration of the competencies and availability of the resources you'll need in the program. The program manager always has to consider if the needed resources are available, their abilities to complete the work in a reasonable time, and their abilities to complete the work with the quality level expected.

When you're creating your program schedule, you also have to consider the activities that are considered of fixed duration. These are tasks that will take a set amount of time regardless of the number of laborers you assign to the task. For example, a manufacturing device can create 1,000 units per hour. If you add more operators to the piece of equipment, it will still only be able to create 1,000 units per hour. The activities in your schedule that are of fixed duration have a correlation between your time estimates and the actual completion of the program.

Your final considerations for the program schedule are internal and external dependencies within your program. Vendors, laws, inspectors, even approval and payments from customers are all examples of external dependencies. External dependencies are any contributions to your program that are out of the program manager's control. External dependencies can become risks if they don't deliver to the program as expected.

Internal dependencies can become risks to the program as well. Internal dependencies are contributions to the program's forward progress from the constituent projects, management decisions, other programs, and internal stakeholder decisions. Internal and external dependencies can also be considered one of the following:

- **Mandatory dependencies** The program activities must happen in this particular order; there's no other way of scheduling the program work. For example, the concrete must cure before the framing of the building can begin. A mandatory dependency is also known as hard logic.

- **Discretionary dependencies** The program activities don't have to happen in a particular, set order. For example, you might normally paint the walls and then install the carpet, but you could install the carpet first and then paint the walls if you wanted to. Discretionary dependencies are also known as soft logic.

All of these inputs will contribute to schedule development process. The goal of the process, as its name implies, is to create a program schedule to predict when the program work, and the project work, should take place in order to complete the program as quickly as reasonable.

Creating the Program Schedule

The program schedule is the planned timeline for when the program work will be completed. As you know, the program is composed of lots of projects. This means that in order to create an accurate program schedule, there must be accurate project schedules. The project schedule for each project ideally uses the approach in time estimating, network diagramming, and resource estimating to determine its completion dates. There's a logical approach to calculating project duration estimates:

1. Project scope is considered and approved for each constituent project in the program.

2. Project scope is decomposed into the project's work breakdown structure.

3. An activity list for each WBS is generated.

4. The required resources for each activity are considered to determine the duration of the project tasks.

5. The activities are sequenced in the order in which they are to be completed; this is the creation of the network diagram for each project.

6. Approved changes to the project scope will cause the WBS, activity list, and network diagrams to be updated to reflect the approved changes.

 NOTE Program projects require an analysis of the critical path, the longest path to project completion, while programs are more concerned about the completion of the program milestones. For your PgMP examination, you may be challenged to calculate a project's float, critical path, or both. I've included on the CD a video that explains the concept of the critical path and how to calculate float. Enjoy!

The duration of each project will contribute to the earliest possible date the program can be completed. The program schedule is not only dependent on the completion of the projects within the program, but also on the completion of non-project program activity, such as risk assessment, communication demands, issue management, and closing the program, among other activities.

The schedule development process usually generates the schedule management plan. This plan defines how the schedule will be created, monitored, and controlled throughout the program life cycle. The schedule management plan will become part of the program management plan.

Compressing the Program Schedule

The schedule development process may go through rounds of estimating, planning, and negotiating with the program stakeholders, the project managers, and the performing organization. Through the rounds of schedule development there may be a demand to compress the schedule duration. There are two primary schedule compression approaches:

- **Crashing** Labor is added to the project work in an attempt to complete the project work faster. This approach assumes that the activities are effort driven. While the method is fairly predictable and reliable, it often adds costs to the program or project that is being crashed, because someone is paying for the labor the program uses.

- **Fast tracking** This approach allows complete phases of a program or a project to overlap. You've probably seen this if you've ever seen a large construction project like a sports arena being built. Half of the arena may have concrete poured and the framing has begun while the other half of the field is still muddy and raw. That's fast tracking—allowing phases of the program to overlap to decrease the duration. While effective in many programs, fast tracking can increase risk if there are mistakes in the early phases while subsequent phases have already started.

Updates to the program scope will demand an update to the program work breakdown structure and the program schedule, and they will likely cause changes within the constituent projects that will be creating the program deliverables. Updates to the resource requirements will also have to be documented if changes to the schedule demand additional resources or limit the usage of certain resources due to collective bargaining agreements or availability.

PART II

Creating a Program Estimate and Budget

Have you ever noticed that it's usually easier to get more time than money? While there appears to be an endless amount of time, funds are always limited. Of course, the reality is that programs have deadlines, and time isn't always the easiest thing to get more of. Money, on the other side of the coin, has no illusion as to how much an organization wants to invest into a program.

Cost estimating is the process of aggregating the costs of the program to determine how much the program should cost. The estimate is a prediction of where the project costs will end. You rarely know how much a program costs until you're done. It's all swami predictions and expert judgment. For each estimate there's some range of variance that's a window of opportunity for the program costs to shift for more or less of the actual costs. Figure 6-9 shows all of the program budget creation inputs and outputs.

Cost budgeting is the process of creating budgets for the entire program, including the constituent projects, non-project activities that are still required to complete the program, and considerations for budget constraints. Budget constraints are usually caps for programs the organization has created based on fiscal constraints, funding limitations, or expert judgment.

Preparing the Program Budget

The program budget is based on the cost estimates and the degree of confidence in the estimates that have been created. The program estimates are based on the cost estimates of the projects and other facets of the program work. The aggregation of the project costs, for example, will help the program manager predict what the entire program will cost. This is a bunch of work for the program manager: management and customers want an accurate estimate of how much it'll cost to create the program, which means several things:

- The program scope has to be decomposed to the PWBS.
- The program projects have to be defined and estimated for costs.
- The program resources have to be estimated for cost (consider labor, facilities, and materials).
- Consideration for the program's contingency reserve to offset risk events has to be planned.
- Documentation of how you arrived at the cost estimate also has to exist (sorry, you can't just make it all up).

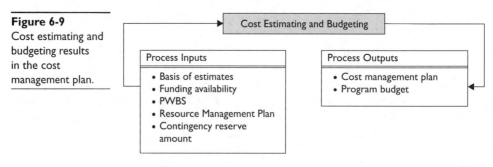

Figure 6-9
Cost estimating and budgeting results in the cost management plan.

While all of this is fine and good on paper, there will be rounds of negotiation, give and take, and the prioritization of objectives based on the availability of funds to invest in the program. The project cost estimates will also be based on different degrees of accuracy, depending on how deep into the program schedule you may be. There are generally three types of estimates for the programs and for projects:

- **Rough order of magnitude estimate**   This estimate's your ball park estimate. It's not very reliable, and you can create one of these with a limited amount of information. Usually this estimate is created with the charter or the preliminary scope statement. The range of variance for this unreliable estimate is –25% to +75% of the predicted costs.

- **Budget estimate**   This estimate type is somewhat reliable, because it usually comes around once the scope statement has been fully developed and approved. If you're working with similar programs, you can use a top-down approach by comparing the costs of the similar program to predict what the current program is likely to cost. The range of variance on this estimate type is –10% to +25% of the predicted costs.

- **Definitive estimate**   This is the most accurate estimate type but also the longest to create, because you must have the PWBS created to account for the costs of each program package. The definitive estimate is sometimes called the bottom-up estimate, because you're starting at the bottom of the PWBS and calculating the costs of each program package and working your way up through the PWBS. The range of variance for this estimate type is –5% to +10% of the predicted costs.

While the constituent projects within your program can use these estimate types and approaches, some of your projects may not have their WBS created to provide you a definitive estimate. One approach to combat this is to use a rough order of magnitude estimate for the entire program, but a definitive estimate for the most immediate delivery phase of the project as in Figure 6-10. This approach is called *phased gate estimating*, where the completion of a program phase is very accurate, while the cost of the whole program becomes more precise as the program moves closer to completion.

Figure 6-10
Step funding funds
the program
according to phases
of completion.

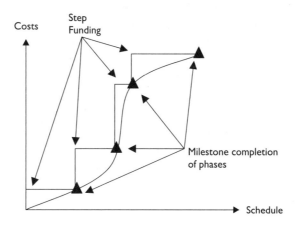

NOTE There's another perfectly acceptable cost estimating method called parametric modeling, or sometimes just a parametric estimate. It's when you have a parameter to multiply costs by, such as cost per metric ton, cost per server license, or even cost per hour. The parametric estimate is a very reliable estimate approach, as the more you use, the more you pay.

Creating the Program Budget

The first result of the cost estimating and budget process is the *cost management plan*. This plan defines how the costs for the program will be managed and controlled. It also defines how the estimate of the program was created and the supporting details of the program estimate. As the program advances, the plan may need to be updated based on several things; these are the most common reasons for an increase in costs:

- Scope changes will usually increase the cost of the program. Scope changes are typically additions to the program, and the cost for the approved change should also be approved—it's not a mistake when a value-added change is incorporated into the program. The program's cost baseline should be updated to reflect the cost of the approved change.

- Errors and omissions can cause the cost of a program to increase or decrease. Failure to accurately capture the cost of the PWBS won't be good for the organization—or the program manager. With this change a variance report, sometimes called an exception report, is warranted to explain the error in the program estimate.

- External changes to cost arise, such as inflation, supply and demand, or fluctuations in the marketplace (consider shipping and travel).

- Defect repair is a waste of time and money. When there are mistakes in the program, usually at the project level, the costs of the mistakes obviously drive costs up. Defect repair is the process of correcting the mistake, but also learning from the mistake so as not to repeat it.

- Flawed estimates can drive the actual costs of the program. Flawed estimates at the project level roll into a flawed estimate at the program level. The program management team must review the individual estimates for each project to test the validity of the estimates and examine their supporting detail.

The cost management plan will document, communicate, and direct the response to an increase to program costs. When an increase in costs is likely to occur, the program manager must go immediately to the problem and find a solution. Solutions may be offsetting the expense by trimming the scope, looking for positive risk events that can save program costs, or even asking for additional funding. When the program manager approaches management with a problem, she should always go with a proposed solution to the problem.

Planning for Program Quality

Quality is a conformance to program requirements and a fitness for use of the product or service the program is creating. Quality is achieved by satisfying the program objectives. Just as your project managers estimate the time and cost of each of their projects, the sum of the quality of their project deliverables, the benefits of the program, contribute to the overall quality of the program deliverables.

When the program manager and his team work together to plan for quality, their goal is to determine what the quality expectations of the program deliverable will be. That is, what will it take to complete the program vision exactly as the customer sees it, considering the constraints such as time and cost. Quality planning really begins with the identification of the quality standards for the program, and then the program management team determines how to adhere to those standards. Figure 6-11 shows the inputs and outputs for quality planning.

An organization may subscribe to a quality assurance program, a six sigma program, or even an ISO 9000 series program where the rules and practices of these quality assurance and quality adherence programs are considered during the quality planning processes. Your organization may not subscribe to one of these management-driven programs, and that's fine, but they probably have a quality policy that will influence your quality planning.

 NOTE   ISO is the abbreviation for the **International Organization for Standardization**. It's called ISO because it's from the Greek iso, meaning uniform. An ISO program means that an organization always follows the same internal processes to achieve the same result. It's not a quality improvement program but a quality adherence program. The ISO 9000 series is for manufacturers, while the ISO 10,000 series is a certification for environmental concerns.

Quality is a management-driven approach and is considered to be planned into the program rather than inspected into the program. You've probably heard of quality assurance (QA) and quality control (QC). QA is a prevention-driven approach where the work is to be performed correctly the first time. QC is an inspection-driven approach where the quality inspectors aim to prove the existence of quality and to keep mistakes out of the customers' hands. Your quality approach will influence all of the projects, how they adhere to the quality assurance program, and the quality control activities within their projects.

Figure 6-11
Quality planning aims to prevent mistakes in the program.

Quality Planning Process

Process Inputs	Process Outputs
• Environmental factors and legislation • Product description • Program scope estimate	• Operational definitions • Program cost of quality • Checklists • Quality improvement plan • Quality management plan • Quality metrics

Preparing for Quality

There are three factors the program management team has to consider when planning for program quality:

- **Environmental factors and legislation**   Consideration of the impact of the program on the environment where the program is taking place is of great importance. The environment of the program can be the physical land, water tables, wildlife, and ecosystems the program may interrupt. The environmental factors also include the culture, issues of attitude, resistance to the program, and the political aspects of the program. The environment is composed of the physical and cultural characteristics surrounding the program.

  The legislation factor considers the laws, requirements, and demands for regulatory compliance of the program. Consider the OSHA requirements for a construction program versus the HIPAA requirements for a health care program. The program manager must identify the laws and regulations that the program is required to adhere to, or there will likely be fines, penalties, delays in the program advancements, and even worse, danger for the program and project team members.

- **Program scope statement**   Quality is achieved by satisfying the program scope statement. The details of the program scope statement serve as an input to the program, because the program management team planning is based on completing the expectations of the program scope.

- **Product description**   The product is the expected benefits of the program. It is the end result of what the program scope will be delivering to the program customers. This document is considered for quality, because it is the parent to the program scope statement. It truly reflects what the program customer expects to receive from the program.

These inputs to quality all demand one thing: communication. You, the program manager, have to complete stakeholder analysis, work with business analysts, and rely on your subject matter experts to confirm that you and the customer are in agreement on what the program will deliver. If there is a discrepancy in the understanding of the product scope, then there will be errors in capturing the program scope. And from here it's a domino effect: the PWBS is wrong, the projects are wrong, and their deliverables will be wrong, and pandemonium ensues.

Examining the Results of Quality Planning

Quality planning results in a quality management plan for the program. This plan defines the quality expectations of the program, the quality requirements for the constituent projects, and the methodology the program will use for quality assurance. The quality management plan also defines the expectations of each project within the program and how the projects will report on quality, adhere to the organization's quality assurance (QA) program, and document their quality efforts.

Besides the quality management plan, there are five other outputs of quality planning you should recognize for your PgMP examination:

- **Operational definitions** These clearly define the terminology and glossary the program will use to describe the program packages, lingo that's unique to the program discipline (such as information technology, construction, and manufacturing), the forms and procedures the organization relies on, and the common lexicon for the program.

- **Program cost of quality** The cost of quality is the amount of funds the program will need to spend in order to achieve the expected level of quality: for example, training, buying the right equipment and materials, safety procedures, and subject matter experts. A failure to provide for the cost of quality results in waste, loss of sales and customer satisfaction, poor team morale, and even loss of life or limb.

NOTE The cost of quality is sometimes called the cost of conformance to quality. Poor quality also has a cost, and it's called the cost of nonconformance to quality. Don't let those terms throw you loopy on the exam.

- **Quality checklists** No surprises here. Checklists are great for repeatable tasks, such as installing 1,000 doors in a building; having each installer following the same checklist ensures that each door, or repeatable task, is completed the exact same way. Checklists are also ideal for activities with safety issues, such as working with electricity.

- **Quality improvement objectives and plan** While the program's primary concern with quality is on technical performance, there's also a process improvement plan that aims to improve the processes the program will follow. As the program advances there will be opportunities to improve bottlenecks, workflow, communication, and overall performance. This plan aims to remove non-value-added activity and streamline stagnant, failing program processes.

- **Quality metrics** Give me a good network. I want fast delivery. Make my customers happy. Those are all subjective, unreliable metrics for quality. What's good, fast, and happy to you may not be the same for me. Quality metrics ties a quantifiable, measurable characteristic to program performance.

You can't achieve quality if you don't know what it is. Once the quality has been defined by the program management team and the program stakeholders are in agreement on what the quality goal is, then the team and the projects can go about achieving expectations. Quality is an esoteric concept; consensus must be gained among the stakeholders on what quality is for the current program, for the current projects in the program, and ultimately for the program's final deliverables.

Planning for Program Human Resources Management

Your program needs people. This process is the planning and documentation of the roles, responsibilities, and reporting structures your program will require. Depending on the size of your program, you may identify individuals, groups of people, or some of both that will fulfill the requirements of your program. In some instances your program may inherit a program team, project teams, and even vendor-based contractors that will support your program. Figure 6-12 demonstrates the inputs and outputs of human resource planning.

The PgMP examination operates under the requirement that you'll first have to plan the program roles by identifying the need for resources, and then you'll define the responsibilities the resources will be assigned to. You'll also have to consider the possibility that some of your roles will require the hiring of new employees that will serve on your program. Your staffing requirements and program management team will help determine your resource demand.

Considering Human Resource Planning Inputs

Human resource planning is an iterative process, as it is part of the planning phase of a program. When more detail becomes available in the program, when changes enter the program scope, or when human resources leave the program or organization, additional human resource planning is required. Initially, however, your concern is to identify what resources the program requires and how you'll satisfy that requirement.

There are five inputs to the human resources planning process:

- **Core program team assignment** Your core program team assignments will be determined by the discipline of the program, your organization's environmental factors, the lines of business your program affects, and management influence over your program. Gaps in the program team assignment to actual organizational resources are an opportunity to hire, procure, or recruit program management team members.

- **Program interfaces** There are five program interfaces you'll have to consider when planning for human resources:

  - **Organizational** This interface includes the departments, disciplines, and lines of business your program will interact with.

  - **Technical** These are the technical disciplines and experts your program will require; those the program's projects will require; and the coordination between the program, the organization, and the projects.

Figure 6-12
The staffing management plan is the primary output of this process.

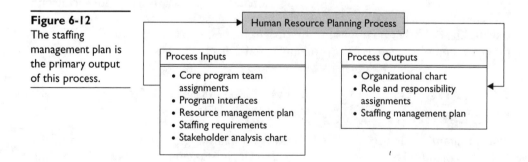

Human Resource Planning Process

Process Inputs	Process Outputs
• Core program team assignments • Program interfaces • Resource management plan • Staffing requirements • Stakeholder analysis chart	• Organizational chart • Role and responsibility assignments • Staffing management plan

- **Interpersonal**   This interface describes the working relationship, the trust, and the respect the people in your program have for one another. It's the social and working relationships among your program participants.

- **Political**   Ah, yes, politics. Politics is the undocumented, but known, undercurrents within an organization that affect decisions, program and project selection, and alliances among the program participants.

- **Logistical**   The time zones, physical difference, language barriers, travel requirements, and international considerations: these are all logistical factors that have to be resolved in the program.

- **Resource management plan**   This program management subsidiary plan identifies the needed resources for the program. In particular, the portion of the plan that serves as an input here covers the requirements for human resources, subject matter experts, and vendors.

- **Staffing requirements**   You can't do everything by yourself. A program manager will need staff to assist in the management of the program, and in some larger program projects there may be staff assigned to or shared among project managers.

- **Stakeholder analysis chart**   This chart captures and documents any number of characteristics about program stakeholders and their influences on the program.

These inputs to human resources planning are pretty bland. As a manager you'll also need to be aware of some common management theories about motivating and leading people. Just be topically aware of these for your examination. They are a snap.

Maslow Hierarchy of Needs

Good old Abraham Maslow—the Charlie Brown of Psychology 101. His theory posits that humans are motivated to perform by our five basic needs:

- **Physiological**   The need for air, water, food, clothing, and shelter (What's this, Abe? No beer?)

- **Safety**   The need to feel safe and secure

- **Social**   The need for love, friendship, and approval from our peers

- **Esteem**   The need for respect, admiration, and approval from those we admire

- **Self-actualization**   The need to fulfill a purpose, personal growth, and knowledge (I'm sure you'll be here at this level once you pass that PgMP examination. Right?)

Herzberg's Motivation-Hygiene Theory

Psychologist Frederick Irving Herzberg created, based on his observations and research, the Motivation-Hygiene Theory, sometimes called the "Two-Factor Theory." Herzberg's theory holds there are two factors you strive for: hygiene agents and motivating agents in your employment. Hygiene agents are the maintenance part of the equation: a paycheck and benefits, job security, safety, relationships with colleagues, and the basic things any employee would expect when they accept a job from an employer. Hygiene agents do not motivate; they're expected as part of the deal of employment. Their absence, however, can de-motivate. If you don't get your paycheck, you're probably not real excited to come in to work on Monday.

Motivating agents are factors that promote performance: achievement, rewards and recognition, growth, responsibility, and opportunity. Motivating agents are things that will motivate employees to excel. Of course you, the program manager, have to know your people and know what motivates them to excel in their performance.

McGregory's Theory X and Y

Douglas McGregor formed this management-perspective theory that paints a negative (X) or a positive (Y) picture of employees. The X perspective believes that employees are lazy, won't work, and have to be micromanaged to get them to do any of their responsibilities. The Y perspective is just the opposite: employees can be self-led, they want to do their assignments, and management can get out of their way.

Ouchi's Theory Z

William Ouchi's Theory Z is sometimes called the Japanese Management Theory, because that's what his theory is based on. Organizations can thrive when managed as Japanese businesses were, with familial environments, participative management, and life-long employment.

Examining the Results of HR Planning

As your human resource planning evolves, your program management team will be able to create an organizational chart. This isn't a chart to get organized in the program, but a chart that demonstrates how your human resources are organized, structured, and managed.

Your program can also be arranged according to an *organizational breakdown structure*. This chart demonstrates how your organization is involved in the program by the resources your program utilizes. This chart can be helpful when you need to identify reporting structures within your organization, to determine where resources are stemming from, and to aid communication.

One of the easiest and most helpful charts is the *responsibility assignment matrix (RAM)*. The RAM is a matrix that usually lists the roles and responsibilities of the program, and the intersection of a role and a responsibility demonstrates some action according to the matrix legend. There are actually several different flavors of RAM charts you should recognize for your examination:

- **Role and responsibility chart**   This matrix, as I just described, demonstrates which role will handle what responsibility.
- **RACI**   This matrix uses the actions of Responsible, Accountable, Consult, and Inform to designate the action required by the role. The actions spell RACI, and this chart is pronounced as "racy."

- **Responsibility assignment matrix**   This generic matrix lists the individuals that will be working on the program, all of the responsibilities that have to be done, and a legend that you can create to represent an action. It's like a RACI, but instead of RACI you can use whatever legend and actions you need to.

The final output of human resource planning is the staffing management plan. This plan defines several things:

- How program team members will be brought on to and released from the program
- How program team members will be disciplined if needed
- How the program will utilize a resource rewards and recognition system
- How the program will use the team members' time
- The training needs for the team members
- Any safety requirements for the program team members
- The program's intent for the usage and management of the resources in the program

Keep in mind that the staffing management plan is a subsidiary plan, and your organization may have a template or standard plan for all programs to adapt. The staffing management plan also defines the ground rules for the organization—and once the ground rules have been established, it's up to the program management team to enforce the rules. There should be no surprises for the program team and the program manager in terms of resource management expectations.

Planning for Program Communications

Communications management is a tricky business. You've got to manage incoming and outgoing communications, create and manage an information retrieval system, judge what information is needed and to whom it's needed—and when. Communications management really comes down to all that is program management. You create plans to communicate. People do their work based on what you've communicated, and then you communicate to other people based on the actions others have done. It's a nonstop process. The bulk of a program manager's job is spent communicating. Figure 6-13 captures all of the process inputs and outputs for program communications planning.

Figure 6-13
This process defines who needs what information and when they need it.

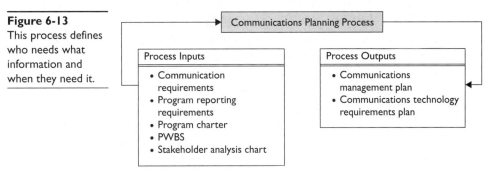

When I teach my fundamentals of project management seminar, we do an exercise where every participant in the room gets their own ball of yarn. Then each person connects their yarn to every other person in the room. Sounds like an easy exercise, right? Before you know it's pure pandemonium. It's tough to tell who's connected to whom, and it's impossible to see any pattern to their group's logic of connecting to others in the room. My point? Each strand of yarn represents all of the communication channels in a project. When it's tough to visually see who you're connected to, it's easy to realize how tough it is to keep track of all the communication requirements.

There's a nifty formula to prove my point (and to save Grandma's knitting yarn). The formula for finding the number of communication channels is $N(N - 1)/2$, where N represents the number of stakeholders. For example, a program may have 140 stakeholders; that'd be $140(139)/2$, which is 9,730 communication channels in this program. The larger the program, the more attention you'll have to pay to communication. The larger the program, the more detail you'll need to provide.

Collecting Communications Planning Inputs

When you begin to analyze the communication demand in your program, you'll need to gather six attributes to determine your communication processes:

- **Communication requirements** I'm going for the big one first. This is the whole point of planning for communications. You, your program team, your project managers and their teams, business analysts, and subject matter experts need to answer four basic questions when it comes to communication requirements gathering. These four questions are at the heart of this program planning process. Answer these successfully, and you'll be on your way.

  - Who needs what information?

  - When do the stakeholders need their information?

  - In what modality will the information be dispersed?

  - Who will relay the information to whom?

- **Program reporting requirements** You'll need to work with management, stakeholders, project managers, the program management, and vendors to determine who needs to report what information and to whom. Consider program aspects such as cost and schedule variance, quality expectations, defect repair, delays, risk, issue management, and any other attribute that may affect the overall program performance.

- **Program charter** The charter has some direction for communications, as it defines the vision and expectations of the program.

- **Program scope statement** The scope statement provides the framework for the program deliverables and communicates the intent of the program.

- **Program work breakdown structure** The PWBS can contribute to communication, as you'll see the need to communicate to project managers, vendors, the program management, and stakeholders based on the deliverable of the program.

- **Stakeholder analysis chart** You can create a stakeholder analysis chart to gauge interest of stakeholders, their concerns and issues, and then address communications of what you've learned.

These six items serve as inputs to communications management planning. When change enters the program, and change will enter the program, you'll have to revisit this process and these inputs to address the changes and to determine the communication affected by the approved changes.

Documenting Communications Management Planning

The results of planning for communication are pretty straightforward. You'll have two program plans that direct how communication is managed and executed in your program. Here are your two communications management plans:

Communications Management Plan

This plan specifically addresses:

- The stakeholders and the information they expect to receive from the program
- The schedule and the conditions that will trigger communications
- The modality of the communication the program will create
- The stakeholders that will contribute communication and the stakeholders that will receive communication in the program

Communications Technology Requirements Plan

This plan addresses the technology the program will use to communicate and the factors that will affect how the program may be able to use the technology:

- **Availability of the technology for the program** Consider cell phone signals, access to web sites and e-mail, and face-to-face communications. Not all communication modalities may be available for all stakeholders.
- **Urgency of the communication** Some communication is fine by e-mail, whereas disasters and large impact risks and issues may demand a phone call or face-to-face meetings. The nature of the message should dictate the best approach for communicating.
- **Program environment** The culture, politics, and sensitive nature of a program will affect how and what is communicated—and to whom. The program environment also addresses the geographical concerns of the program team; consider a co-located versus a virtual team and how communication will be managed for each scenario.
- **Program length** You know that technology changes daily. When you consider the length of your program, current communication devices will probably be superseded by new communication devices. Consider mobile phones today versus a decade ago.

These two plans can be modified to address changes and new events within the program. At the heart of both of these plans is the opportunity to address the demand of communication and the complex nature of programs.

Planning for Program Risks

Risk isn't necessarily a bad thing; it's the impact of the risk event that stings. Risk is an uncertain event or condition that can have a positive or negative effect on the program. I'm sure you have no problem seeing the negative risks: loss of sales, delays, equipment and material failure, hurricanes, fires, and even the loss of life or limb. Positive risks, however, are trickier to see: a discount from a vendor, a flawless, efficient time saver, a by-product that creates a profit.

There are technically two types of risks in a program:

- **Business risks**   These risk events can have a positive or negative effect on the program, depending on their outcome. For example, the capital investment in your program is a business risk. Your program could fail, and the investment could be lost. Or your program could be quite successful, and you generate a ton of profit for the organization. Bravo!

- **Pure risks**   These risk events have only a negative effect on the program. Injured workers, fire, tornados, theft, and acts of God are all examples of pure risks. These you usually try to mitigate and avoid as much as possible. For example, you can provide safety equipment to a crew on a job site but someone could still get injured.

The program risk management planning and analysis process aims to accomplish four things:

- Identify the program risks.

- Perform qualitative analysis on the identified risks to test their validity, probability, and impact on the program.

- Using qualitative analysis, subject some risks to quantitative analysis to determine the true risk exposure, probability, and impact.

- Create a risk response plan to address the risks within the program.

These activities are iterative, so you'll get to do them throughout the program. Risk identification is a crucial program management team activity. The program team should always be on the lookout for new and lurking risks within the program. Whenever a new risk is identified, the risk management planning and analysis process is enacted. Figure 6-14 shows all of the risk management process inputs and outputs.

Examining the Program for Risk

You and your program management team are constantly on the lookout for risks that may impact your program positively or negatively. Early in the program, however, your risk identification process will center on six queries for your program:

- What risks are distributed over multiple projects, and what can we do about them?

Figure 6-14
Risk planning is an
iterative process.

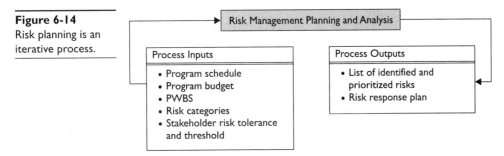

Risk Management Planning and Analysis

Process Inputs

- Program schedule
- Program budget
- PWBS
- Risk categories
- Stakeholder risk tolerance
  and threshold

Process Outputs

- List of identified and
  prioritized risks
- Risk response plan

- What are the root causes of the identified risks?

- What effect will my risk response plan have on the program components and other programs within the organization's portfolio?

- When project managers escalate a risk event, what's the best response to the situation?

- What's the best response for an identified risk event, and how can the response benefit more than one program component?

- What amount of funds needs to be in the risk contingency reserve for the program?

These six questions can guide the program management team through the identification and analysis of the risks within the program. The goal of risk identification and planning in a program is to respond to risks in such a way that several of the component projects benefit from the risk response.

When you're completing the risk identification, planning, and analysis, you'll need several program management plan components to guide this process:

- **Program schedule**   Risk identification takes time, and there needs to be an allotment of program time to accurately review and analyze the program risks. The program schedule is also used to determine the risks that may exist between coordinated projects within the program. Time-based constraints such as deadlines, vendors, busy seasons for the organization, and project schedules are evaluated for risk impact and probability.

- **Program budget**   Risks almost always have a financial impact when they occur. The program budget needs to be reviewed, in addition to the organization's ability to accept the financial risks that may be tied to the program budget. Consider penalties for late delivery, risks surrounding expensive materials and equipment, and positive risks such as vendor discounts for early payment, bulk ordering, and marketplace conditions.

- **Program work breakdown structure**   The decomposition of the program scope can help the program manager identify the risks within the different benefits delivery, interrelationships between projects, vendor involvement, and the program's final deliverable.

- **Risk categories**   The categorization of risks can help the program manager and the program management team complete lateral and associative risk identification based on organizational risk categories. For example, a risk breakdown structure can be created; it's a visualization of the risks within the program, often following the same format as the PWBS.

- **Stakeholder risk tolerance** This input to the risk management and analysis process describes the organization's willingness to accept risk. On a program, however, the risk tolerance level is typically low because of the financial commitment, benefits realization, and priority of the program. Let me defer to project management for one moment: on a low-priority project, such as swapping out all the keyboards in a building, there's likely more willingness to accept a risk in that project than in a high-priority project to move data from all of your servers to brand new servers.

These five inputs will help the program management team identify and analyze the risk events in the program. Remember, and I know you do, risk planning is an ongoing activity. This means whenever there's a change to the product scope, the program scope, it is integrated throughout the program plan. This calls for an iteration of risk analysis.

Completing Risk Analysis and Planning

I guess this heading is a little deceptive, since you only complete risk analysis once the program moves into the final activities of closing. This is because, hint, hint, risk analysis is an iterative process. The first output of this process is a list of identified risks and their priorities for the program. Typically the risk events that are most imminent are the events you're most concerned about. Second to this is the impact of each risk event on the program schedule and budget.

The second output of the risk planning and analysis process is the risk response plan. This plan addresses the positive and negative risks and the methods you've elected to respond to the identified risk events. Of course, the status of the risks can change as conditions within the program may change. When a risk event status is changed, you'll need to review the proposed risk response, and you may have to change the risk response.

There are seven risk responses, three for negative risk events, three for positive risk events, and one that's acceptable for both:

- **Mitigation** This risk response is an attempt to reduce the probability and/or impact of a risk. For example, you may spend $45,000 to reduce the probability of a risk event that could cost your project $95,000 if it were to happen.

- **Transference** This risk response is usually based on a contractual relationship with a vendor. You might transfer the electrical work within your program to a licensed electrical engineering company, because it's too dangerous to complete in-house. The risk doesn't necessarily disappear; electricity is still dangerous, only now someone else is paid to own that risk event. Insurance is another good example of transference.

- **Avoidance** These are any actions that you take to avoid a risk event. You may elect to run two projects consecutively rather than in tandem to avoid the risk between the projects.

- **Enhancement** Sometimes there's a risk that you'd like to have happen, such as a discount from a vendor, a favorable window for weather conditions, or beating a deadline. You can't always guarantee these risks will happen, so you do your best to make them happen.

- **Sharing** Sharing a positive risk happens when two or more entities partner to realize the benefits of a risk they couldn't seize on their own. For example, three construction companies partner to complete a massive sports stadium with their combined talent and effort.

- **Exploitation** This risk response recognizes a risk event that is going to happen, so you exploit the risk event to realize as many gains from the event as possible. Consider selling a by-product of the program, utilization of program staff, and beating a deadline to earn a sizeable bonus.

- **Acceptance** This response is acceptable for both positive and negative risk events. Risks that have a small impact and small probability are often accepted. Larger risks, such as weather, laws and regulations, and stakeholder competing objectives are significant risks that you may just have to accept in your program.

You'll need to know these seven risk responses for your PgMP examination. Your risk response plan will document the risk responses and the conditions surrounding the risks. A risk trigger is often assigned to a risk event; a trigger is a warning sign or condition that a risk event is about to occur. The trigger calls for the appropriate risk response to the pending risk.

Planning for Program Procurement

You're a program manager, and you need to buy stuff. The stuff you need to buy may be materials, services, facilities, labor, and just about anything else your program demands. The program procurement planning process helps you to determine what your program needs to purchase and when to do the purchasing.

What your program needs to purchase is often obvious enough. If you're in construction, you'll need materials and labor. If you're in manufacturing, you'll also need materials and labor. And even in IT, you'll still need materials and labor. The nature of your program, however, will guide you in the services and facilities you'll have to purchase. Think of your most recent program and all the things you had to deal with in order to buy the products and services you needed: vendors, purchasing agents, your organization's procurement rules, subject matter experts, and more characters just to get to the getting part of procurement. Figure 6-15 demonstrates all of the inputs and outputs for this process.

The other half of the proverbial procurement coin is the when. When you'll need the products and services is an important part of the equation. You have to evaluate the program and its capital expenses, the lead time for your organizational policies, and the lead time for the vendor to supply you with the things you need. I've not met too many program managers that can discover a need for a major purchase, whip out the

Figure 6-15
Planning program
purchases requires
several inputs.

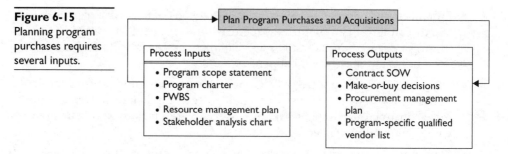

company credit card, and have the product delivered in the afternoon. I'm sure it happens for some lucky souls, but most have to wait, follow rules, plan, schedule, and react to the conditions of the program.

That's what this process is all about: determining how much you need and when you need it. Once you've made that determination, it's time to deal with the contract planning that follows all the excitement of this section. Control yourself! You'll get there in just a moment.

Preparing for Procurement

This is deceptively simple. You need to determine what you need and when you need it. In order to do this complicated task, you'll have to evaluate several project documents:

- **Program scope statement**   The scope your program will create

- **Program charter**   The authorizing document for the program to exist and use resources (Cha-ching!)

- **Program work breakdown structure**   The decomposition of the program scope down to the program packages (The program packages are the real clue to what you'll need to buy.)

- **Resource management plan**   The people and things you'll need to have in your program in order to keep your sanity and complete the program's objectives

- **Stakeholder analysis chart**   Use this chart to capture your stakeholders' opinions, feelings, and direction for the program as a guide to what you'll be purchasing

These five inputs are the foundation for answering procurement questions and needs. Just as I've discussed over and over, changes to the product scope will likely affect these inputs. If these inputs change, you'll likely have to change your procurement planning to buy the right stuff for your program in order to complete the new scope.

Creating the Procurement Planning Outputs

Once you've completed a round of the procurement planning, you'll end up with some nifty results to act on in your program. The results are the solutions you'll have to enter the planning contract phase.

Your first order of business is the creation of the contract statement of work—this document, sometimes just called the SOW, defines what you'd like to purchase from the vendor. The SOW fully describes the requirements for acceptance, quality expectations, delivery requirements, scheduling demands, and just about any other characteristic of the program you want the vendor to adhere to. The nature of the program work, based on the PWBS, really affects what you'll put into the SOW. The details of a SOW in a construction program likely are not the same details you'd add to a SOW for an IT program.

While the SOW deals with vendors, you know that sometimes it's more cost effective to buy than to build. Or you don't have the resources internally. Or you want your staff to focus on the core work, and you want to outsource work that's not core to the program. Or you don't have the time to create whatever it is the vendor can create for you. Or any number of reasons why you'd rather buy than build. And other times it's the opposite, when it's better to build it than to deal with a vendor.

There are, however, instances where it's all just a financial decision whether you should build a thing or buy a thing. Here's a basic approach to determine if you build it or buy it as in Figure 6-16.

Let's say you are considering building a piece of software versus buying it. You've determined that you can build a piece of software for $98,450 internally, and it'll cost you $23,780 per month to support the software. Your favorite vendor tells you that they can build the software for you at the low, low price of $87,650. With the vendor's deal you'll have to pay $25,500 per month for their support. Here's what you'll do:

1. Find the out-of-pocket difference between the buy and the build. In this instance it's $98,450 minus $87,650 for a difference of $10,800.

2. Find the difference in the monthly maintenance fees. Here it's $23,780 minus $25,500 for a difference of $1,720.

3. Divide the out-of-pocket difference by the monthly difference. In this instance, it's $10,800 divided by $1,720 to equal 6.27.

4. Determine how long you're going to use the solution. In this instance if you're going to keep that software around for more than 6.27 months, you should just go ahead and build the software. If that software isn't going to be around more than 6 months, just hire the vendor and enjoy the great deal you've made.

NOTE   For your PgMP examination, and out there in the real world, you won't always make a purchasing decision on price alone. There are lots of other reasons you may build or buy. Always do what's best for the program and your organization.

Figure 6-16
Build or buy charts are based on a purely financial decision.

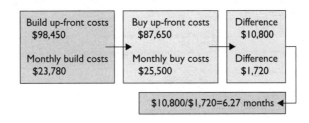

As in most planning processes, you get a plan to guide you through some program activities. The plan for this process is the procurement management plan, which will detail how vendors will be contacted, selected, and then managed once you actually get to the contracting stage. Your program or organization may also rely on a qualified vendor list.

Planning for Program Contracts

Now that the program has completed the procurement planning process, it's ready to determine what contracts are needed, the legal issues of the contracts, and the intricacies of contracts in a program. Generally, program contracts are going to be more cumbersome than a project contract because of the relationships between the performing organization, the vendors, government agencies, and the projects within the program. Figure 6-17 captures all of the inputs and outputs for this process.

Every contract must be for a legal purpose, contain an offer, and include a consideration for the work. The parties involved in the contract must all be in agreement with the terms of the contract and accept the terms by signing the contract. Should a party not live up to the terms, then there are claims, mediation, and most probably, litigation between the parties. Contracts almost always define the locale of where the legal matters will be resolved—such as the court in a particular county and state or which country may have jurisdiction over the legal matters of a contract should claims be escalated to a lawsuit.

Preparing the Contract Inputs

The first thing the program will need to complete the plan program contracting process is the procurement management plan. Recall that this plan, created as a result of the plan program purchases and acquisitions process, defines how vendors will be contacted, selected, and managed.

The next input—and this is a big one—is the determination of what contracts should be used in the program. There are several contract types that you'll need to recognize for your PgMP examination. Depending on the scenario, there are reasons one contract may be better than other contracts. As a general rule, both parties want to be fair while also creating the best deal for their organization. You should be familiar with the contracts listed in Table 6-2.

Figure 6-17
Planning the program contracting results in contracts.

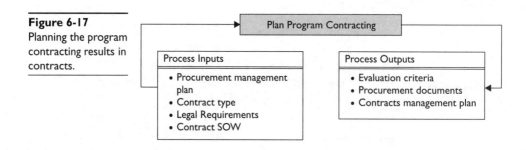

Contract Type	Attribute	Risk Issues
Cost Plus Fixed Fee	Actual costs plus profit margin for seller	Cost overruns represent risk to the buyer.
Cost Plus Percentage of Cost	Actual costs plus profit margin for seller	Cost overruns represent risk to the buyer. This is the most dangerous contract type for the buyer.
Cost Plus Incentive Fee	Actual costs plus profit margin for seller	Cost overruns represent risk to the buyer.
Fixed-Price	Agreed price for contracted product; can include incentives for the seller	Seller assumes risk.
Lump-Sum	Agreed price for contracted product; can include incentives for the seller	Seller assumes risk.
Firm-Fixed-Price	Agreed price for contracted product	Seller assumes risk.
Fixed Price Incentive Fee	Agreed price for contracted product; can include incentives for the seller	Seller assumes risk.
Time and Materials	The vendor bills the client for the time spent on the program and for the materials used as well.	Contracts without "not-to-exceed" clauses can lead to cost overruns.
Unit-Price	Price assigned for a measurable unit of product or time (for example, $130 for engineer's time on the project)	Risk varies with the product. Time represents the biggest risk if the amount needed is not specified in the contract.

Table 6-2   Contract Types

Each contract type has certain legal requirements, terms, and conditions when it may, or may not be, appropriate to use the contract type. Usually the client has the ability to determine which contract type is most appropriate, though clients and vendors may negotiate the contract type and the terms of the contract.

Associated with each piece of contracted work, there should be a contract statement of work. This document defines what the client wants to purchase, the specifications of the contracted work, and the opportunity for the vendor to ask for clarifications of the statement of work. That clarification actually comes in the executing process group, your next chapter, but it's called the bidders conference.

Assembling the Results of Program Contracting

Once the program contracting process has been completed, the performing organization will create three straightforward things:

- **Evaluation criteria**   These are the criteria that will help the program management team determine which vendor they'll actually select. For example, certifications, licenses, experience level, and price may all be evaluation criteria the performing organization may use to determine the best vendor to complete the outsourced program work.

- **Procurement documents**   The collection of the procurement documents is called the procurement package. The specific documents that come out of this process include the contract type, the contract statement of work, the supporting detail, and any organization-specific information regarding purchasing and agreements.

- **Contract management plan**   This plan defines how the performing organization will manage the contracts it has agreed to abide by. This means both the vendor and the client will have to live up to the terms of the contract. The contract management plan is geared more toward ensuring the vendor lives up to its side of the bargain.

These outputs will become inputs to processes in the execution process group. This can be a gotcha moment on your exam: you don't choose your vendors during planning; you choose them during program execution. In planning you'll plan on the procurement management, contract types, and evaluation criteria.

Chapter Summary

Congratulations! You've made it, just about, to the end of one of the toughest areas of preparing for your PgMP examination. Planning is crucial to program management, and it's crucial to your PgMP examination. You'll have to be able to recognize the program processes, their characteristics, and when to use each process.

There were 14 program management processes in this chapter; here's a quick rundown of what you've just read:

- **Developing the program management plan**   This program management process is actually the assembly of all the program subsidiary plans and how you'll manage each area of the program.

- **Interface planning**   This process identifies and documents the relationships the program has to interact with.

- **Transition planning**   This process creates the program transition plan that defines how the program will transfer the program deliverables and benefits from the program team to the organization.

- **Resource planning**   This process plans for the management and acquisition of resources including people, materials, equipment, and facilities.

- **Scope definition**   This complex process is based on the program charter, the preliminary scope statement, and the benefits realization plan. It creates the program scope management plan and the program scope statement.

- **Creating the program WBS**   Guess what this process does. Yep, it defines how the program work breakdown structure will be created. Fascinating.

- **Schedule development**   This process defines the activities to complete the program, their duration, and when the program components will happen.

- **Cost estimating and budgeting**   Cost estimating is the prediction of how much the program should cost based on the cost aggregation at the program level. Cost budgeting creates a program based on the project budgets and program activities.

- **Quality planning**   This process defines the cost of quality, improvement goals, and the quality management plan.

- **Human resource planning**   You'll chart the organization, create role and responsibility charts, and write the staffing management plan through this planning process.

- **Communications planning**   People need to talk to one another within the program. This planning process defines how that'll happen.

- **Risk management planning and analysis**   The risks within a program are identified, documented, qualified, and quantified, and then responses are planned for the risk events.

- **Plan purchases and acquisitions**   You'll have to plan on what to procure and when to procure it, as well as develop procurement strategies.

- **Plan program contracting**   This process creates the evaluation criteria for procurement, contributes to the procurement documents, and creates the contracts management plan.

The overwhelming theme for this chapter, and I hope you picked up on it, is that programs fail at the beginning, not at the end. Planning is an iterative process and, as conditions within the program change, it's time to revisit planning and address each of the 14 processes to see if the change in conditions affects the program's ability to be successful.

Key Terms

Acceptance   This response is acceptable for both positive and negative risk events.

Avoidance   Any actions that you take to avoid a risk event.

Benefits management plan   Defines the definition, creation, and management of the benefits the program will create.

Budget estimate   Usually created when the scope statement has been fully developed and approved. Sometimes called a top-down estimate, because its cost may be based on similar programs to predict what the current program is likely to cost. The range of variance on this estimate type is –10% to +25% of the predicted costs.

Business risks   These risk events can have a positive or negative effect on the program, depending on their outcome.

Communication channel formula $N(N - 1)/2$, where N represents the number of stakeholders.

Communications management plan   Identifies the program stakeholders, provides the program information they'll need to participate in, and defines the expected modality of the communication.

Contract statement of work   Describes the requirements for acceptance, quality expectations, delivery requirements, scheduling demands, and the characteristics of the program you want the vendor to adhere to.

Contract   A legally binding agreement between two or more parties.

Contracts management plan   Defines the details of the contracts that will be utilized.

Cost budgeting   The process of creating budgets for the entire program, including the constituent projects, non-project activities that are still required to complete the program, and considerations for budget constraints.

Cost estimating   The process of aggregating the costs of the program to determine how much the program should cost.

Cost management plan   Defines how the program's cost will be defined, committed, and maintained.

Cost of quality   The amount of funds the program will need to spend in order to achieve the expected level of quality.

Cost Plus Fixed Fee   A contract that defines the actual costs plus a fixed profit margin for a seller.

Cost Plus Incentive Fee   A contract that defines the actual costs plus profit margin for a seller for reaching a predefined goal, such as completing the work early or coming in under budget.

Cost Plus Percentage of Cost   A contract that defines the actual costs plus a percentage profit margin for a seller.

Crashing   Labor is added to the project work in an attempt to complete the project work faster; often adds costs to the program.

Definitive estimate   The most accurate estimate type but also the longest to create, because you must have the PWBS created to account for the costs of each program package. The range of variance for this estimate type is –5% to +10% of the predicted costs.

Delphi Technique   A tool that uses rounds of anonymous surveys to build a consensus on issues, risks, and objectives within a program.

Discretionary dependencies   The program activities don't have to happen in a particular, set order. Discretionary dependencies are also known as soft logic.

Enhance   A positive risk response for a risk you'd like to have happen. Consider vendor discounts, a favorable window for weather conditions, or beating a deadline.

Exploit   A positive risk response used when a probable risk event is exploited to realize as many gains from the event as possible.

Fast tracking   This approach allows complete phases of a program or a project to overlap; often adds program risk.

Firm-Fixed-Price   A contract that defines the agreed price for the contracted product.

Fixed Price Incentive Fee   A contract that defines the agreed price for the contracted product; can include incentives for the seller.

Fixed-Price   A contract that defines the agreed price for the contracted product; can include incentives for the seller.

Herzberg's Motivation-Hygiene Theory   Hygiene factors are expected and do not promote performance, but their absence can de-motivate employees. Motivating agents are factors that promote performance.

Interface management plan   Defines these relationships within, and outside of, the organization, including departments, lines of business, and other open programs.

Law of Diminishing Returns   The limitation of adding labor to reduce the amount of time the work takes to complete; the work itself, the yield, and the profit versus labor constraints restrict the ability to exponentially add labor to reduce the amount of time allotted to the work.

Lump-Sum   A contract that defines the agreed price for the contracted product; can include incentives for the seller.

Mandatory dependencies   The program activities must happen in this particular order; there's no other way of scheduling the program work. A mandatory dependency is also known as hard logic.

Maslow's Hierarchy of Needs   Five needs that humans have: physiological, safety, social, esteem, and self-actualization.

McGregor's X and Y   X management sees the employees as lazy, untrustworthy, and generally incompetent. Y management sees the employees as motivated, competent, and able to self-lead.

Mitigation   This risk response is an attempt to reduce the probability and/or impact of a risk.

Ouchi's Theory Z   The Japanese Management theory. Organizations can thrive like Japanese-managed businesses did with familial environments, participative management, and life-long employment.

Parametric modeling   A parameter is used to calculate costs, such as cost per metric ton, cost per server license, or even cost per hour. Also called a parametric estimate.

Procurement management plan   Defines the program's procurement management process: the procurement process, bidder selection, and vendor management.

Program interface   An entity or person that the program has to interact with.

Program management plan   Not one plan, but a collection of subsidiary plans.

Program packages   The smallest item in the program work breakdown structure.

Program statement   The program scope defines all of the required work—and only the required work—in order to satisfy the program's objectives; serves as the baseline for all future program decisions.

Program work breakdown structure (PWBS)   A hierarchical decomposition of the program scope. It decomposes the program scope statement into the individual deliverables, called program packages, the program promises to deliver.

Project calendar   Defines when the project work is expected to take place.

Pure risks   These risk events have only a negative effect on the program.

Quality assurance (QA)   A management-driven philosophy that plans quality into a program.

Quality control (QC)   An inspection-driven approach that inspects the deliverables to keep mistakes out of the customers' hands.

Quality management plan   Defines how the quality objectives will be met within the project, including the adherence to quality assurance (QA) programs, quality control at the project level, and the expected reactions when quality inspections are less than expected.

Quality   A conformance to requirements and a fitness for use.

RACI   A matrix using the actions of Responsible, Accountable, Consult, and Inform to designate the action required by the role.

Resource calendar   Shows the availability of program resources.

Resource histogram   A bar chart that visualizes the utilization of program resources.

Resource leveling   The compression of the amount of time a resource may be utilized during a given time period; often extends the program schedule.

Resource management plan   Defines how resources will be obtained, managed, and allocated throughout the program. This plan also defines how the resources will be tracked across the program's projects to ensure that resources are not over-allocated and are being used as efficiently as possible.

Resources   The people, materials, facilities, and equipment the program requires to be successful.

Responsibility assignment matrix   A generic matrix that lists the individuals that will be working on the program and all of the responsibilities they have to assume.

Risk owner   The program team member closest to the risk event with the authority to respond to the risk event as planned.

Risk register   The collection and documentation for risks within the program, the risk characteristics, status, probability, likelihood, and potential risk responses.

Risk response plan   Addresses the responses to the identified risk events. The risk response plan defines how the risk owner should react if the risk event passes the risk threshold and the event comes into play.

Risk   An uncertain event or condition that may have a positive or negative effect on the program.

Role and responsibility chart   A matrix to demonstrate which role is responsible for what.

Rough order of magnitude estimate   Usually created with the charter or the preliminary scope statement. The range of variance for this unreliable estimate is –25% to +75% of the predicted costs.

Schedule management plan   Defines, well, the schedule. It also defines how changes to the schedule may be allowed, fleshed into the program, and then executed.

Scope management plan   Defines the program scope and how the program scope will be controlled. The plan defines the program management scope change control system, and the process program change requests that must follow to be incorporated into the program plan.

Share   A positive risk response for two or more entities to realize the benefits of a risk they couldn't seize individually.

Staffing management plan   Defines the needed resources for the program and how the program will obtain those resources. This program plan also defines how the staff may be brought onto and released from the program.

Stakeholder analysis chart   This chart can capture each stakeholder and that stakeholder's position and influence on decisions and outcomes of the project.

Time and Materials   A contract that defines how the vendor will bill the client for the time spent on the program and for the materials; must have a not-to-exceed clause.

Transference   This risk response is usually based on a contractual relationship with a vendor.

Trigger   A warning sign or condition that a risk event is pending.

Questions

1. Which program management subsidiary plan defines the procurement management process for the organization?

   A. Benefits management plan

   B. Interface management plan

   C. Procurement management plan

   D. Contracts management plan

2. Which stakeholder analysis technique can be utilized to build consensus through rounds of anonymous surveys?

   A. The Delphi Technique

   B. The Monte Carlo Simulation

   C. The stakeholder analysis chart

   D. Communications management planning

3. Bob is the program manager of the 420 Program. Where can Bob find details about the program risks, the probability of the risk events, the risk impact, and who the risk owners may be?

   A. Qualitative risk analysis matrix

   B. Quantitative risk analysis matrix

   C. Risk identification process

   D. Risk register

4. The program's transition management plan defines all of the following except for which one?

   A. Training and materials of the program's product

   B. Stakeholder program supporting detail

   C. Facilities to maintain the program's deliverables

   D. Program personnel

5. Which one of the following is an example of a program resource?

   A. An electrical engineer to be utilized at month six in the program

   B. A deadline for the program to be completed by January 30

   C. A demand to not exceed 7.2 million dollars

   D. A risk probability-impact matrix for the program's identified risks

6. Which chart will show the utilization of program resources?

   A. Pareto chart

   B. Resource histogram

   C. Gantt chart

   D. Network diagram

7. You are the program manager for your organization. Management is requiring you to create the most accurate cost estimate for your program. Which one of the following is the most accurate cost estimating approach?

   A. Rough order of magnitude estimate

   B. Budget estimate

   C. Definitive estimate

   D. Hallway estimate

8. Holly is examining the PWBS and wants to see the characteristics of a certain program package. Where can Holly find this information?

   A. PWBS dictionary

   B. PWBS appendix and glossary

   C. Communication management plan

   D. Project management information system

9. Which one of the following scenarios is an example of soft logic?

   A. The hardware must be installed before the software can be installed.

   B. The concrete must be cured before the framing can begin.

   C. Project CFG must be completed before Project NHG may begin.

   D. Project HYT and Project KUY could run together, but for risk's sake they'll run in sequential order.

10. Mary has decided to allow two phases of her program to overlap. This is called what?

    A. Risk acceptance

    B. Fast tracking

    C. Crashing

    D. Lead time

11. Thomas is managing a program to build a skyscraper. He has safety expenses, training to use new materials, and costs to purchase specialized tools to install materials properly. These expenses are all known as which one of the following?

    A. Cost of non-conformance

    B. Cost of quality

    C. Direct costs for the project

    D. Mitigation risk responses

12. Maslow's Hierarchy of Needs defines five levels of needs for all humans. Which one of the following is not one of the five needs?

    A. Psychological

    B. Esteem

    C. Safety

    D. Self-actualization

13. A RACI chart accomplishes what for Jane, the program manager?

    A. Determines how much program schedule compression she can utilize.

    B. Determines when she'll need program resources.

    C. Determines the resource assignments for her program.

    D. Determines the resource roles for her program.

14. A program has 54 stakeholders this week. Next week 21 more stakeholders will join the program. How many more communication channels will the program have next week?

    A. 1,431

    B. 2,775

    C. 210

    D. 1,344

15. Which one of the following is the best definition of a program risk?

    A. A threat to the program

    B. An opportunity for the program

    C. An uncertain event or condition that can positively or negatively affect the program

    D. An unknown event or condition that must be quantified for its impact

16. What is the utility function?

    A. It is a method to quantify the program's risk.

    B. It is a stakeholder's willingness to pay for the program risk.

    C. It is a stakeholder's willingness to accept program risks.

    D. It is a method to create the risk contingency reserve.

17. A portion of your program deals with electrical work. You and your program team have elected to hire a licensed electrical company to deal with all electrical work on the program. This is an example of which risk response?

    A. Mitigation

    B. Transference

    C. Avoidance

    D. Exploit

18. All of the following are examples of positive risk responses except for which one?

    A. Acceptance

    B. Exploit

    C. Enhance

    D. Avoidance

19. You are trying to decide if your program should build or buy a piece of software. You have determined it will cost your program $28,890 to create the software, and it'll cost $11,000 to manage the software each month. A vendor has told you they could create the software for $21,100 and support the software for $9,999 per month. Which is the best decision and why?

    A. You should buy the software if you're keeping the solution longer than 8 months.

B. You should buy the software if you're keeping the solution longer than 18 months.

C. You should build the software if you're keeping the solution longer than 8 months.

D. You should build the software if you're keeping the solution less than 8 months.

20. Which contract type is considered the most dangerous for the customer?

A. Cost plus incentive fee

B. Cost plus percentage of cost

C. Lump sum

D. Time and materials

Questions and Answers

1. Which program management subsidiary plan defines the procurement management process for the organization?

A. Benefits management plan

B. Interface management plan

C. Procurement management plan

D. Contracts management plan

C. The procurement management plan is the subsidiary plan that defines the procurement management process. A, the benefits management plan, defines the definition, creation, and management of the benefits the program will create. B, the interface management plan, describes the relationship between people, departments, and organizations the program has to deal with. D, the contracts management plan, details the type and enforcement of the contract between suppliers and the program.

2. Which stakeholder analysis technique can be utilized to build consensus through rounds of anonymous surveys?

A. The Delphi Technique

B. The Monte Carlo Simulation

C. The stakeholder analysis chart

D. Communications management planning

A. The Delphi Technique uses rounds of anonymous surveys to build consensus on risks and issues within a program. B, the Monte Carlo Simulation, analyzes possible outcomes of events to predict the most likely outcome for all events. C is incorrect, as the stakeholder analysis chart defines stakeholder concerns and priorities. D, the communications management planning process, aims to answer who needs what information, when they need it, the needed modality, and who'll provide the needed information.

3. Bob is the program manager of the 420 Program. Where can Bob find details about the program risks, the probability of the risk events, the risk impact, and who the risk owners may be?

A. Qualitative risk analysis matrix

B. Quantitative risk analysis matrix

C. Risk identification process

D. Risk register

D. The risk register is the document Bob is looking for. A and B qualify and then quantify the risk events. Choice C is the initial process of risk management.

4. The program's transition management plan defines all of the following except for which one?

A. Training and materials of the program's product

B. Stakeholder program supporting detail

C. Facilities to maintain the program's deliverables

D. Program personnel

B. The program transition management plan does not define the stakeholder program supporting detail. It does define choices A, C, and D, so these are all incorrect choices for this answer.

5. Which one of the following is an example of a program resource?

A. An electrical engineer to be utilized at month six in the program

B. A deadline for the program to be completed by January 30

C. A demand to not exceed 7.2 million dollars

D. A risk probability-impact matrix for the program's identified risks

A. A resource is a person, material, or facility the program needs. Choice B and C are examples of program constraints, while choice D is an approach to analysis of the program risks.

6. Which chart will show the utilization of program resources?

A. Pareto chart

B. Resource histogram

C. Gantt chart

D. Network diagram

B. A resource histogram visualizes the utilization of resources within a program. A, the Pareto chart, is a bar chart that shows categories of failure. It's often used with quality control at the project level. B, the Gantt chart, shows scheduled activities across a calendar. D, the network diagram, visualizes the flow of activities from start to completion and is often used at the project level.

7. You are the program manager for your organization. Management is requiring you to create the most accurate cost estimate for your program. Which one of the following is the most accurate cost estimating approach?

   A. Rough order of magnitude estimate

   B. Budget estimate

   C. Definitive estimate

   D. Hallway estimate

   C. The definitive estimate is the most accurate estimate for the program, because it's based on the program work breakdown structure. A, the ROM estimate, is the least reliable estimate. B, the budget estimate, is somewhat reliable, as it's based on the program scope. D, the hallway estimate, is a cute way of referencing the ROM estimate, so it's not very reliable either.

8. Holly is examining the PWBS and wants to see the characteristics of a certain program package. Where can Holly find this information?

   A. PWBS dictionary

   B. PWBS appendix and glossary

   C. Communication management plan

   D. Project management information system

   A. The program work breakdown structure relies on the companion PWBS dictionary to define the characteristics of each program package. B is not a valid term. C, the communications management plan, will not help Holly in this instance. D, the PMIS, is the software that can help manage a project, so this is an incorrect choice for the question.

9. Which one of the following scenarios is an example of soft logic?

   A. The hardware must be installed before the software can be installed.

   B. The concrete must be cured before the framing can begin.

   C. Project CFG must be completed before Project NHG may begin.

   D. Project HYT and Project KUY could run together, but for risk's sake they'll run in sequential order.

   D. The choice to run the two projects sequentially is an example of soft logic. Choices A, B, and C are all examples of hard logic.

10. Mary has decided to allow two phases of her program to overlap. This is called what?

    A. Risk acceptance

    B. Fast tracking

    C. Crashing

    D. Lead time

B. When two phases of a program are allowed to overlap, this is an example of fast tracking. Fast tracking may increase risk, but it's not risk acceptance. C, crashing, would happen if Mary added workers to compress the program schedule. D, lead time, describes two activities, not phases, that are allowed to overlap—usually within a project.

11. Thomas is managing a program to build a skyscraper. He has safety expenses, training to use new materials, and costs to purchase specialized tools to install materials properly. These expenses are all known as which one of the following?

  A. Cost of non-conformance

  B. Cost of quality

  C. Direct costs for the project

  D. Mitigation risk responses

  B. The monies spent to achieve the expected level of quality, including safety, training, and equipment, are all examples of the cost of quality. A is the opposite choice; it's what happens if Thomas doesn't spend these monies. C is incorrect, because these are labeled as program expenses, not project expenses. D is also incorrect, because these are addressing program needs.

12. Maslow's Hierarchy of Needs defines five levels of needs for all humans. Which one of the following is not one of the five needs?

  A. Psychological

  B. Esteem

  C. Safety

  D. Self-actualization

  A. It's not psychological, but physiological needs. Choices B, C, and D are all valid parts of Maslow's theory, so these choices are incorrect choices for this question.

13. A RACI chart accomplishes what for Jane, the program manager?

  A. Determines how much program schedule compression she can utilize.

  B. Determines when she'll need program resources.

  C. Determines the resource assignments for her program.

  D. Determines the resource roles for her program.

  C. A RACI chart determines the resource assignments in the form of responsible, accountable, consult, and inform for the program. A, B, and D are all incorrect choices and do not describe a RACI chart.

14. A program has 54 stakeholders this week. Next week 21 more stakeholders will join the program. How many more communication channels will the program have next week?

  A. 1,431

    B. 2,775

    C. 210

    D. 1,344

D. The question wants to know how many more communication channels will exist next week. The formula N(N − 1)/2 is used here. To solve this question, you'll first find the current communication channels and then next week's communication channels; then find the difference of the two values. The formula is 2,775 − 1,431 channels for 1,344. Choice A is the current number of channels with 54 stakeholders. Choice B is next week's channels with 75 stakeholders. Choice C is 210 communication channels, with only 21 stakeholders. This is a tricky question, so look out for something similar on your exam.

15. Which one of the following is the best definition of a program risk?

    A. A threat to the program

    B. An opportunity for the program

    C. An uncertain event or condition that can positively or negatively affect the program

    D. An unknown event or condition that must be quantified for its impact

C. Risk is an uncertain event or condition that can positively or negatively affect the program—it's not always negative. A and B are incorrect, as risk isn't always a threat or an opportunity. D isn't the best choice, because not every risk is quantified; consider low-level risk events.

16. What is the utility function?

    A. It is a method to quantify the program's risk.

    B. It is a stakeholder's willingness to pay for the program risk.

    C. It is a stakeholder's willingness to accept program risks.

    D. It is a method to create the risk contingency reserve.

C. The utility function describes the organization's willingness to accept risk. Generally the higher the program priority, the lower the organization's willingness to accept risk. A, B, and D are all incorrect descriptions of the utility function.

17. A portion of your program deals with electrical work. You and your program team have elected to hire a licensed electrical company to deal with all electrical work on the program. This is an example of which risk response?

    A. Mitigation

    B. Transference

    C. Avoidance

    D. Exploit

B. Hiring a third party to own a risk is known as transference. A is incorrect, as mitigation is the act of spending money or time to reduce a risk probability and/or impact. C, avoidance, is when extra activities or workarounds are introduced into the program to avoid the risk event. D, exploit, is a positive risk response to take advantage of a positive risk event.

18. All of the following are examples of positive risk responses except for which one?

   A. Acceptance

   B. Exploit

   C. Enhance

   D. Avoidance

   D. Avoidance is the only example of a negative risk response. A, acceptance, is acceptable for both positive and negative risk responses. Choices B and C are examples of positive risk responses.

19. You are trying to decide if your program should build or buy a piece of software. You have determined it will cost your program $28,890 to create the software, and it'll cost $11,000 to manage the software each month. A vendor has told you they could create the software for $21,100 and support the software for $9,999 per month. Which is the best decision and why?

   A. You should buy the software if you're keeping the solution longer than 8 months.

   B. You should buy the software if you're keeping the solution longer than 18 months.

   C. You should build the software if you're keeping the solution longer than 8 months.

   D. You should build the software if you're keeping the solution less than 8 months.

   C. In 8 months your organization would be paying the same amount to build the software if you hired the vendor to create it. The difference of your upfront costs, $7,790, is divided by the difference of your monthly expenses, $1,001. In slightly less than 8 months, your in-house solution would equal the vendor's solution fee. Therefore, if you're keeping the software longer than 8 months you should build it. Choices A, B, and D are all incorrect statements.

20. Which contract type is considered the most dangerous for the customer?

   A. Cost plus incentive fee

   B. Cost plus percentage of cost

   C. Lump sum

   D. Time and materials

   B. The cost plus percentage of costs is the most dangerous for the buyer, because the buyer will have to pay for materials plus a percentage of costs of the materials. If the supplier wastes any of the materials, the buyer will have to buy new materials and pay a percentage of the costs of the new materials even though the vendor is responsible for the waste. A, C, and D are incorrect choices.

Executing the Program

In this chapter, you will
- Direct and manage program execution
- Perform quality assurance
- Acquire the program team
- Develop the program team
- Communicate with stakeholders
- Work with program vendors

While planning is great, it cannot go on forever and forever (something to be thankful for). At some point you and the program team and all the program projects have to go about the business of getting the program work done. All of your plans, your strategic visions, and the customer expectations are coming to life in this section of your program. This is the doing, not the dreaming, thinking, and scheming. If you want the program to get to the end, and I know you do, then you've got to do the work described in your plans to get there.

Executing the program is the juicy part of program management. The program manager, the program management team, and all of the project managers work in orchestration to deliver on the promised deliverables. The program manager oversees everything—like a conductor—and it's her responsibility to ensure that the program stakeholders—from the project teams, program team members, and suppliers to all the program interfaces—are each doing their part to contribute to the program's success.

Directing and Managing Program Execution

Executing the program is taking all of your plans and acting on them. You'll manage and direct the program work, get people onto your program, and have to deal with the program vendors. Acting like a big umbrella over all of this fun is quality assurance. What good does a program that's lacking quality do for anyone? The goal of quality assurance—and I'm certain it's your goal as well—is to do the work right the first time.

While I like to believe that your project teams are made up of adults who can deliver on their promises, work together, and problem-solve, I also know that's not always true. It's up to you, the program manager, to oversee the project managers, resolve inter-project issues, and keep an eye on program and project risks that can threaten the

215

project's success. You don't have time to baby-sit projects, but you do have to make time to oversee the coordination and effective implementation of projects.

Throughout the program, you'll receive change requests. Some will get denied, and some you'll approve (I'll discuss the change control process in detail in the next chapter). The changes to the program scope that do get approved—and you can expect a bunch of them—will have to be incorporated into the program scope, into the project scope, and ultimately into the program and project execution.

When there's a mistake in your program deliverables, you'll fix the mistake; that's what PMI calls a corrective action. Corrective actions move things back into the expectation of the program scope. Sometimes corrective actions are called defect repair. Once you fix the defect, you may also do defect repair validation; that's where your team confirms that the defect repair is valid, good, and acceptable.

Sometimes, and hopefully most of the time, your program team will recognize when there's an opportunity for mistakes to enter the program. In these instances your team will want to apply preventive actions to prevent mistakes from ever entering the program. Training and risk avoidance are two fine examples of preventive actions.

Preparing to Execute the Program

When you leave the planning phase of your program, you'll be armed with a lot of plans that make up the program management plan. It's this plan that will guide you and your program team as you move through the execution processes described in this chapter and out there in your real world. That's not rocket science—your plan directs your actions. Figure 7-1 depicts the inputs and outputs of program execution.

The second input you'll need to execute your program is the program schedule. The program schedule also comes as a result of the program management planning processes and communicates when your program team, your project managers, and the stakeholders should complete their responsibilities in the program. Consider all the things your plan will account for:

- Activities
- Milestones
- Purchases and acquisitions
- Cash flow forecasting

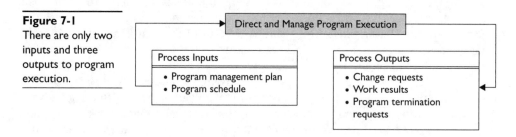

Figure 7-1
There are only two inputs and three outputs to program execution.

Direct and Manage Program Execution

Process Inputs
- Program management plan
- Program schedule

Process Outputs
- Change requests
- Work results
- Program termination requests

- Deadlines
- Performance measurement
- Intent
- Risk events

I'm certain you can think of even more things your program schedule will call for—especially in your area of expertise and in your organization. Here's the great thing about the program schedule and the PgMP examination: it's tough to be tested on very specific schedule items, because each organization, discipline, and program has different concerns to address. Questions on the program schedule will have to be somewhat broad—and that's good news for you.

Examining the Results of Program Execution

The most obvious result of your program execution is work results. Your program is broken down into the program work breakdown structure (PWBS), as described in Chapter 6. The deliverables of your program are built by the work completed by the individual project teams. The aggregate of the project teams will create and compile the things your PWBS calls for, which in turn will equate to the program's product scope to keep the customer happy and your program moving toward its completion date and organizational benefits.

As your program creates things, you can without a doubt expect change requests. The results of program work can result in a change request. Stakeholders have those "aha" moments; this is where the results of your program work cause a stakeholder to have a "value-added change." There's also opportunity to realize an error or omission based on the work your program has done. Whatever the reason, change requests have to be documented and entered into the change control process.

In some instances, the organization may request that a program be terminated. Yikes! There have to be some pretty sizeable reasons that a program should be axed:

- The program deliverables are no longer needed.
- Organizations have merged, and the program is stopped because of the merger.
- The market demand for the program deliverables has waned.
- The program is grossly late.
- The program is considerably over budget.
- The program's deliverables are lacking in quality.
- Laws and regulations.

And this list can go on and on. There are countless reasons a program may be terminated. Whatever the reason the program is closed, lessons are documented, and the organization evaluates why the program was a success up to the termination, or more likely a failure. Not a pleasant day for the program manager.

Performing Quality Assurance

Quality assurance (QA) is a management-driven process to ensure that quality is planned into the deliverables and executed throughout all phases of the program life cycle, and that the execution of the program adheres to the relevant quality standards of the performing organization. You could say that QA is prevention-driven in that you are preventing mistakes from entering the program in the first place. Figure 7-2 shows all of the inputs and outputs of quality assurance.

Quality assurance in program management is not intended to replace the QA activities of the individual programs, but rather to support the QA efforts of the projects. Keep in mind that QA for a program guides and directs the QA activities of each project within the program. Sometimes QA is confused with quality control, but there is a distinct difference: quality assurance is a prevention-driven process to prevent mistakes from entering into the program and its components. Quality control is a project-specific activity that inspects the project work to ensure that the deliverables are of quality and to keep mistakes from entering the customer's hands.

Preparing for Quality Assurance

Each program in the world can create its expectations for quality. Quality, to be specific, is the conformance to requirements and a fitness for use. This means, then, that quality is a very program- and project-specific thing. In order to achieve the expected level of quality in the program, the scope of the program must be fully defined and documented, and the expectations for delivery must be documented and communicated to the program stakeholders.

In other words, in order to achieve program quality you have to know what the program scope calls for. You cannot achieve quality if you don't know what quality is. The first input that you can rely on is a result from the program's planning process group: the quality management plan. Recall that this plan defines what the quality assurance, quality control, and overall quality policy for the program may be.

In addition to the quality management plan you, the program management team, and each project manager must have a clear understanding of how to measure quality. These are the operational definitions of the program: time, cost, scope, metrics, and other measurable components and their acceptance levels, expectations, and goals for improvement.

The work results are the best evidence of quality, or lack of quality if you're a pessimist, within a program. You must have something to deliver, to measure, to prove the

Figure 7-2
Quality is planned into the program, not inspected into the program.

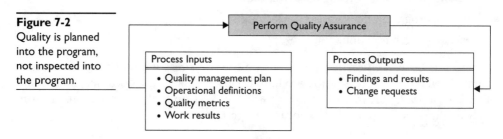

existence of quality. There's a fine line between inspecting the work results, which is quality control, and agreeing that the results of the work show the existence of quality.

Examining the QA Results

Just as work results act as an input to quality assurance, because they prove the existence of quality, so too are your findings and results of the program a result of quality assurance. In other words, the existence, the evidence of quality, is a result of QA. If this sounds like circular reasoning, it's not. Basically the assurance of quality results in quality for the program; quality is not an accident, but rather the result of planning, execution, and quality control.

From a project manager's perspective, your QA program is a rule that the project may adhere to. It's the project's quality policy. Quality control is performed within the project, not the program, and it inspects the work results before the customer sees the deliverables. Any mistakes that are encountered prompt the project team to apply corrective actions. Once the deliverables have been deemed of sufficient quality, then the customer performs their inspection through the project management process scope verification.

Sometimes quality assurance can result in a change request. As the program's projects create the program benefits, there may be opportunities for improvement. These improvements can take the form of corrective or preventive action—either way, the goal is to improve the quality of the program deliverables. Remember, change is expected and inevitable within a program.

Acquiring the Program Team

Here's something kind of goofy: you don't get your program team during the planning process group, but rather during the program execution. I know that seems really weird, but remember the program management plan has iterations of planning and executing. So you plan for the program resources you need and then you get to acquire them according to your staffing management plan. Don't let this one trick you on your PgMP examination; it's not worth the headache. Figure 7-3 shows all the things you'll need to get program team resources.

When you go to hire a person to be on your program team, you have to consider an internal resource versus an external resource. You have to consider how long you'll need a particular competency and whether or not that competency level is even available within your organization. Obviously, if you need a particular skill that's not available within your organization, you either have to hire a resource with that skill or contract with a vendor or consultant for that skill.

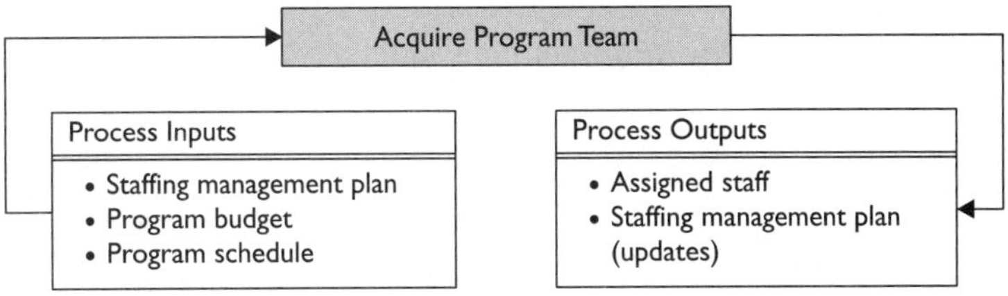

Figure 7-3
Team acquisition is an executing process, not a planning process.

Acquire Program Team

Process Inputs	Process Outputs
• Staffing management plan • Program budget • Program schedule	• Assigned staff • Staffing management plan (updates)

If you hire someone internally, then you've got to consult and negotiate with that resource's manager for their employee to be placed on your program. There are a lot of factors that you have to consider:

- Is the organization available for the duration that your program will need them?
- Who'll do the resources' current operational work when they're doing the work on your program?
- What are the priorities of the organization, and how does that affect placement of a resource on your program?
- How soon do you need the resource?
- Does the person really fit the program needs?
- What are the person's qualifications for the program work?
- How does the program work fit into the person's career path?
- What opportunities does the program offer for the resource?

There are several things to consider as well when hiring a resource from a vendor:

- Which vendor can provide the best resource?
- Who will retain the intellectual property the contracted resource may create?
- How does contracting operate within the organization?
- What is the cost associated with the vendor versus hiring a new employee?
- What is the procurement process of the organization?
- How will the performing organization manage the consultant or contractor?

In either instance the program manager and the program management team need to determine as soon as possible the best route the program should take. Once the decision has been made to hire internally or to procure a resource, action must be taken to ensure that the resource will be in place on the program in time for the program work to be completed. You don't want to discover that the resource you're looking for is in high demand and your program creeps along because you waited to find the correct resource to complete the program work.

Preparing for Team Acquisition

Your primary guide for team acquisition is the staffing management plan that you created during the planning process. Recall that this plan determines several things for your program execution:

- How program team members will be brought onto and released from the program
- How program team members will be disciplined if needed
- How the program will utilize a resource rewards and recognition system
- How the program will use the team members' time

- What the training needs are for the team members

- What the safety requirements may be for the program team members

- What is the program's intent for the usage and management of the resources in the program

The staffing management plan may be updated as needed based on discovery, program work, and program scope changes that require new program resources.

Sure, sure, the staffing management plan is a process input, and it's needed to determine what resources you'll need and when, but you also need to know how much of a budget you can spend on resources. This means, of course, that you'll need the program budget as an input to hire and, ahem, pay for the program resources. This is crucial if you've been forced to procure resources from a vendor. If the cost of the talent you've had to procure is more than you've planned for, uh-oh, you're going to have a cost overrun, and that's not good.

The last input you'll need for this process is the program schedule. This schedule determines when you'll need the program resources. This allows you to communicate with managers in your organization when you'll need their employees to come along and work on your program. This allows management to plan and adapt their work so that you can use their resources as your program warrants.

 NOTE Yeah, I'm writing in a perfect world. You and I know that resources aren't always available when you've communicated with managers that the resource had better, must, be available. For your PgMP examination, put your PMI blinders on, answer their questions their way, pass their exam, and get on back to reality with your PgMP.

The program schedule, coupled with your program budget, allows you to work with the program vendors and their contracted resources for your program. You'll need the schedule to communicate when you'll need the program resources hired from the vendor. You'll need your program budget to spend some moo-lah to hire the resources from the vendors.

Examining the Results of Team Acquisition

I hope this doesn't come as a surprise to you, but you get a staff as a result of staff acquisition. Your program management team, some project managers, experts, and skilled resources that will serve on the program all come about because of the staff acquisition process. This is not to say that the project team members come from this process too—they don't. You're concerned about the high-level resources that will guide, direct, and oversee the big areas of your program.

You might have, if you need to use them, updates to the staffing management plan. Imagine a new resource that you need because of an approved change request, a new discovery within the execution, or an error or omission. Changes to the program staffing management plan, like any plan changes, have to be documented, approved, and then fleshed into execution.

Developing the Program Team

Team development is about getting smarter. It's about helping the program management team develop their individual and their group competencies to be able to better perform on the program. This means education, on-the-job training, and attendance in training classes. If the program team members are lacking in their abilities to complete their program tasks, it's up to the program manager and the performing organization to provide training and educational opportunities to improve their abilities.

Team development isn't all about the program, as Figure 7-4 depicts. Team development is a symbiotic relationship in that the training and education needs for the program should mesh with the program team members' career paths. Ideally, the educational opportunities within the program will help them grow once the program work is completed. There must be some balance between what's good for the program and what's good for the program members.

Like many processes within program management, team development is an ongoing, iterative activity. As deficiencies in competencies are realized, the program manager must address the opportunity to develop the team. Team development isn't just about education needed to complete a program assignment; it also includes grooming program team members to take on bigger roles and responsibilities within the program. Often team development is focused on supporting the program benefits as they transition into operations.

Preparing for Team Development

Team development is a conscious effort to improve the competencies of the program team. This means there's some overlap between executing and planning—specifically the creation and execution of the training plan for the program team. Through any number of assessments, the program management team will develop and act on a training plan to ensure that team development happens to benefit both the program and the individuals.

Sometimes, out there in the real world, you don't get to go and cherry-pick your program team members. Often you inherit a group of folks that may have little to zero interest in your program. Most program managers have this scenario—they wake up one fine day, and there's a group of folks with varying skill levels and abilities that'll serve as the program team. You and this bunch of folks will need to assess skill levels, roles and responsibilities, and the staffing management plan to determine who needs what training and how you'll provide it.

Figure 7-4
You need several things to complete team development.

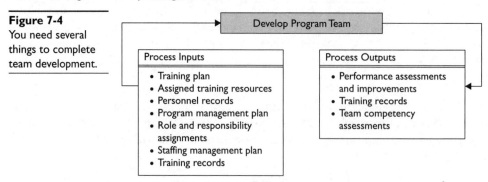

Develop Program Team

Process Inputs
- Training plan
- Assigned training resources
- Personnel records
- Program management plan
- Role and responsibility assignments
- Staffing management plan
- Training records

Process Outputs
- Performance assessments and improvements
- Training records
- Team competency assessments

> ## Turkeys and Team Development
>
> Back when the Internet was the hot new thing, I consulted for a web-based help desk software venture. No one on the program team knew each other, the program manager, or any of the project managers. It was a madhouse—we were churning out code and burning all sorts of billable hours. Finally we had a break in the schedule, and the program manager decided we needed some team development.
>
> This was probably a good idea, considering we barely knew who was doing what—though the checks were clearing and investors were lined around the block. The big idea for team development? Frozen turkey bowling. I kid you not.
>
> We all loaded into a bus, went to a local grocery store at midnight, and bowled with frozen turkeys. It was the most insane thing I've ever done (well, as far as I'm confessing to in this book). We laughed, bonded, got to meet everyone on the program, and enjoyed our break from programming, staffing a help desk, and troubleshooting web servers.
>
> Now here's the bad news. As charming as frozen turkeys, martinis, and bowling pins in aisle 11 are, this experience is not, according to PMI, an example of team building. Team building in the PMI book *A Standard for Program Management* is the process of building individual and group competencies to enhance program performance. So while we were learning about each other, we weren't really becoming smarter in our work. Though you could argue, I suppose, that by learning about one another, we were becoming more proficient, more able to communicate, and more cohesive.
>
> The sad part of this story is that just a few weeks later this company was absorbed by a bigger web giant, and my turkey-slinging teammates and I were released. Some went on to other consulting gigs, some tagged along with the new company, and I went on to program management, consulting, and training. I can hardly pass a frozen turkey without reminiscing about my eight-ten spare pickup in aisle 11.

For your PgMP examination you'll also rely on three other factors as inputs to the develop program team process:

- **Personnel records** This will tell you about each program resource and what their abilities are, their past experience, relative knowledge, and work history. You'll use this information to determine strengths to train others and weaknesses where they'll need development.

- **Training records** If you have a learning management system (sometimes just called an LMS), you should have access to the past training history for each team member. This can help with the development of skills, assignment of resources, and frustration for the program team members. (No one wants to be required to go through training on a topic they've already been trained on.)

- **Program management plan** The program management plan will help you determine what program team members will contribute to different areas of the program—from scope management to procurement management. This plan is an opportunity to identify who needs what level of training and how that level will be ascertained in the different program knowledge areas.

Team development is an ongoing process. While the primary PMI stance is on team development from the perspective of what it contributes to the program, the program manager has to consider how the team works together. There's a natural cycle to team development that begins with the program team forming. Once team members become comfortable with one another, then the team may move through *storming*—where there's some power struggle over issues and decisions. At some point the program team settles into their roles and the power struggles calm—this is *norming*. Finally, the program team goes about the business of getting their work done in their program roles. This final stage is *performing*.

Examining the Results of Team Development

The primary result of team development is improvement for the program and for the individuals on the program team. As the program team completes its work, the program management team should be able to track the improvement in efficiencies, fewer errors, and an overall improvement in project performance.

The program manager has to be realistic on the link between training and performance. While I am a huge proponent of training (it's my primary gig), program managers and organizations should be realistic on training. Classroom training is great and sets a great foundation for success, but the real education comes through experience. The best training, in my biased opinion, is the training that gives individuals the opportunity to experience success and failure with the discipline, software, materials, or knowledge that they'll be responsible for. You can understand how a bicycle operates. You can watch others ride their bike. But until you get on that bike and make it go, you don't know it. It's the same with adult education.

Team development will also prompt the program manager to update the training records for each individual as your organization requires. Documentation of who's completed what training, what their experience based on their training may be, and their efficiencies can help the program as it moves forward. You'll also continue to monitor and evaluate the program management team's assessments and document and address deficiencies in their knowledge.

Distributing Program Information

As a program manager, you know that you've got to talk with people. You can't hide in your office and delegate from behind a brick wall—it's about providing communications, timely and accurate communications, to the appropriate stakeholders, as Figure 7-5 illustrates. Back in planning, you and your team completed stakeholder analysis charts, stakeholder analysis, and answered four questions about communications:

- Who needs what information?
- When is the information needed?
- In what modality is the communication expected?
- Who will provide the information to whom?

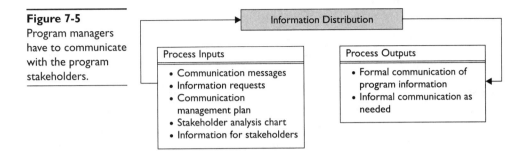

Figure 7-5
Program managers have to communicate with the program stakeholders.

The result of all this communications planning was the communications management plan. It documented the intent, requirements, and expectations of the program manager, the program management team, and the stakeholders in regard to communications. Now you're executing this plan. You're communicating with the program clients, the program sponsors, and the project managers in your program.

The program manager directs and oversees the following communication as defined in the communications management plan:

- Program status
- Project status
- Milestone completion progress
- Program costs
- Program schedule
- Risk analysis
- Change requests to the program scope
- Program change request to the projects affected
- Status of program change requests
- Change request responses and status to the change request originator
- Internal budgetary information
- Government and regulatory filings as required by laws and regulations
- Public announcements

While this list highlights the most common and practical communications, there can be, of course, dozens more types of communications and their requirements. Your organization, for example, may use special forms, reports, and tools to communicate. That's fine—that's part of enterprise environmental factors—the rules of your organization.

NOTE Don't forget that face-to-face communication is the most effective method for communicating in most situations, as you and the other party get to use body language to express and receive messages. Nonverbal communication is 55 percent of communication.

Preparing for Information Distribution

The bulk of the process is based on executing the communications management plan, as it defines who'll need what information and when. For your PgMP examination—and that's the point of this book—you'll need five inputs to information distribution:

Communication Messages This is the information that's being distributed by you and your program team and the inbound communication from your stakeholders that'll prompt you to respond. Consider all the e-mails, phone calls, queries, and sticky notes you receive all the time regarding your program. All those communication messages should be stored, responded to, and documented as part of your information management system.

Information Requests There's some overlap here between communication messages and this input. This input is specific to requesting information on program and project status, change requests, risk analysis and status, and any other program-specific queries. These too will become part of your information management system.

Communications Management Plan You know this one already. It was created back in the planning process group and defines who needs what information, when they'll need it, and in what modality. It's a hoot.

Stakeholder Analysis Charts These capture the program stakeholders—their concerns, perceived threats, stance on program deliverables and benefits, and overall opinions and expectations of your program. These charts can help you communicate the right information to the right people.

Information for Stakeholders This is the very specific response to a stakeholder information request. The information you provide to the stakeholders should be documented and recorded so that you have this as a future reference if needed.

NOTE Paralingual means the tone, pitch, and inflection you use that may affect your communication. Para is from the Greek, meaning beyond, like a parachute or paranormal. It's above the lingual, the words of the conversation. Dad was right; how you say something is often as important as what you say.

These five inputs will help the program manager better communicate throughout the program, not just in terms of the current status of the program.

Reviewing Communication Results

Communication is achieved when knowledge is transferred from one person to another. There's a simple model of communication, as seen in Figure 7-6, which shows information moving from one person to another. I like to use the example of a fax machine as a demonstration.

- **Sender** I want to send a fax to you; I am the sender.
- **Encoder** My fax machine is nifty; it's the encoder.
- **Medium** The phone wires between our fax machines are the medium.

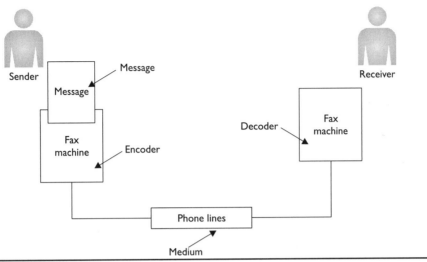

Figure 7-6   The communication model is evident between two fax machines.

- **Decoder**   Your fax machine is pretty cool; it's the decoder.
- **Receiver**   You get my fax! You're the receiver.
- **Noise**   Oops! There's some static on the line, and it disrupts the fax; it's considered noise.
- **Barrier**   Your fax machine is out of paper, and you cannot receive my fax. Anything that prevents communication is a barrier.
- **Acknowledgment**   You receive my fax, and you acknowledge it with a reply. An acknowledgment shows receipt of the message, but not necessarily agreement with the message.

While this model is simple, it demonstrates how communication occurs between two or more parties. This model applies to the two results of information distribution:

- **Formal communication of program information**   You've executed your program communications management plan and have provided information to the program stakeholders.
- **Information communication on an as-needed basis**   You've communicated through e-mails, ad hoc conversations, chat, and quick phone calls. Not every piece of communication is formal.

The execution of your communications management plan is a crucial piece of program management. It's been said that a program manager can't over-communicate. I don't know if I subscribe to the same belief, but I think the philosophy is this: the program manager must constantly be on the lookout for communication opportunities, for communication barriers, and for communication gaps and then work to optimize communications in the program.

Request Seller Responses

Your program will need to buy stuff: materials, services, products, facilities, and other goods. Sellers will provide these things to you at a cost—no surprise there. In order to acquire the things you'll need for your program, you'll have to contact the sellers and communicate with them in order to get them to respond to your requests.

For your PgMP examination this is pretty straightforward business, as you can see in the inputs and outputs of this process in Figure 7-7. This process also sets your program to select a seller in the next, and last, process in the program execution process group. Your work in the planning process will help guide your actions here—you'll need to know what you want to buy before you can actually buy it. Here are the two inputs to this process:

- **Evaluation criteria**   The evaluation criteria define all the rules, qualifications, screening systems, and determinations that help determine which vendor you'll choose to provide the goods and services for your program.

- **Program preferred vendor list**   Your program may have a list of prescreened and qualified vendors that you're allowed to choose from. Your preferred vendor list may be created independent of your organization or in conjunction with your organization's list—it really doesn't matter. The point is, this list has a list of companies that you're allowed to buy from without having to jump through all the hoops of working with a new vendor in your organization.

The results of requesting seller responses are also somewhat straightforward; you have to ask the vendor to provide something so that you can make a decision in the select seller responses. Here are the procurement documents that you'll be creating as a result of this process:

- **Request for information (RFI)**   You need more information about a vendor's services or products, so you ask for more information. This can be anything from a brochure or catalog to a white paper or references about the seller.

- **Request for quote (RFQ)**   You want a price for whatever the seller can provide. You don't need any dream solutions or ideas—just tell me how much. For example, I need a quote for three tons of pea gravel.

- **Request for proposal (RFP)**   This document asks the vendor to create a proposal for your program. An RFP takes your basic vision and allows the vendor to run with it, designing an approach with a lot of features and solutions you may not have thought of. The creation of a web site is a good example. RFPs are a lot of work for vendors.

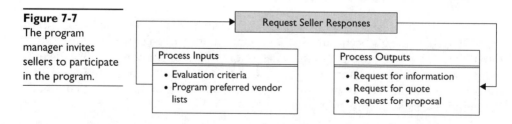

Figure 7-7
The program manager invites sellers to participate in the program.

NOTE   Your organization might use the terminology "invitation for bid (IFB)," and that's fine. A bid and a quote are the same thing: you only want a price, no fancy-schmancy plans or ideas.

Selecting the Program Sellers

Now that the program manager has sent out the requests to the sellers, she'll begin receiving responses from the sellers. These responses will, of course, come back in the form the program manager asked for as depicted in Figure 7-8:

- **Information**   Information as requested in the request for information form
- **Quote**   Just the price in response to the request for quote
- **Proposal**   The dreamy solution in response to the request for proposal form

Armed with this information, the program manager will conduct several activities:

- Review the seller offers.
- Compare and contrast the offers from the different vendors.
- Negotiate the terms for goods and services to be procured.
- Define the roles and responsibilities of both parties in the agreement.
- Define the technical terms and conditions of the work defined in the agreement.
- Define the exact deliverables and the qualifications for acceptance.
- Negotiate and document the final costs of the procured goods and services.

At the program level, the negotiations and seller selections are program-wide. This means terms, conditions, bulk discounts, and pricing cover all of the program components. This agreement should be documented and integrated into the terms of the program contract with the seller. In the next chapter, I'll dive into the contract administration—that's the process of ensuring both parties live up to their agreement in the contract.

Preparing to Select the Sellers

Here's the basic business of selecting a seller (it's not that difficult): sellers want to do business with you as long as the negotiated terms are good for them. You want to do business with them as long as it's good for your program. The evaluation criteria you determined as part of the seller responses are referenced here again to confirm the seller you're considering really does qualify.

Figure 7-8
Seller selection results in several documents for the program.

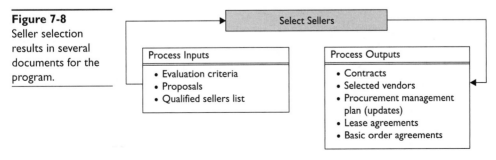

You'll also rely on your qualified sellers list to confirm that the sellers do qualify and that they can work for your organization. If not, you give 'em the boot.

You'll also review the proposals from the sellers to determine if what they've proposed is on target or off the mark. Proposal evaluation is a tricky business. You and the seller may bounce ideas back and forth to adjust the proposal to be more in alignment with what the program deliverables should be. Proposal writing is sometimes difficult for the vendor, because it may mean rounds of analysis, writing, and work and then the vendor may not even get the gig that's being proposed. That's a sad day for the vendor.

Finalizing the Seller Selection Process

Once you select the seller, you get a contract. Recall that a contract is a legally binding agreement between the buyer and the seller and contains an offer, consideration, and acceptance. The person that actually signs the contract for the organizations involved may not be the program manager or the salesperson. This person is sometimes called the delegate of authority—that's the person who has the right to act on behalf of their organization.

You may need to revisit the procurement management plan and update your contract and vendor management sections to reflect the terms of the contract you've agreed to abide by. This can be based on payment terms, performance terms, contractor administration, or any other negotiation of the contract that may affect your management of the vendor.

The contract is an agreement between two or more parties. This can be for goods and services, as I've discussed in this chapter. Or, as I've not mentioned, contracts can define lease agreements for the program. Consider equipment, buildings, vehicles, and other facilities that you might need to lease in order to complete your program.

As a recap, Figure 7-9 demonstrates the entire procurement process. Notice the term *bidders conference* in the graphic? That's a key point in the procurement process that allows the sellers to ask for clarifications about the RFP or RFQ you've sent to them. This graphic, as it happens, is applicable to the entire program and to each of the projects within the program.

Figure 7-9
Buyers and sellers interact throughout the procurement processes.

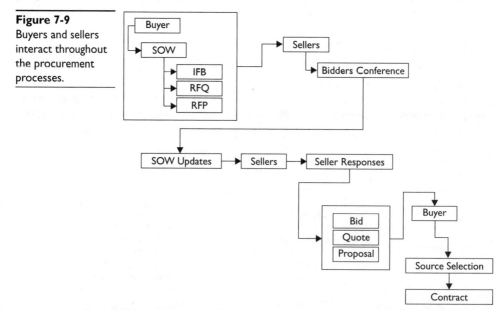

Chapter Summary

The program deliverables and benefits really come about in this execution stage of the program. You and the program management team coordinate the activities of the program, the projects, and inputs from the key stakeholders to move the program forward. Program execution is all about executing the program plans—getting the work done. It's this portion of the program where you'll spend the most time and the most money. It's my kind of action.

In program execution you will also acquire and develop your program team. Recall that team acquisition can come from internal resources, from vendors, or even through hiring new resources to work on your program. Once you've got a program team, you may have to develop its members so that they'll be better able to perform on your program team. In others words, if the program team is lacking in competency, it's part of program execution to train them.

Throughout the program you'll disperse information. The good old formula of $N(N - 1)/2$ defines the number of communication channels where N represents the number of stakeholders in your program. This is more than just program trivia; the formula demonstrates that the more communication channels you'll have in the program, the more you'll have to communicate (well, duh). You'll keep records of your incoming and outgoing communications as part of your information management system.

Serving as a big umbrella for the program and all its components is quality assurance. I know you recall that quality assurance is a management-driven process that aims to do the work right the first time. Its goal is to prevent mistakes from entering the program at all. Quality assurance is a model for the entire program's projects to adhere to. Recall that projects use quality control to ensure that quality exists within the project deliverables and to keep mistakes out of the customers' hands.

The final processes I discussed in this chapter were your favorites—requesting seller responses and selecting program sellers. You use the procurement documents of request for information, request for quote, or request for proposal to invite the vendor to participate in the process. Based on the quotes and proposals, you'll select a vendor, cut a deal, and then hope both parties live up to the deal as defined in the contract.

Program execution can fluctuate, adapt, and adjust according to changes to the program scope. You'll enter program execution from the planning process group. As planning is an iterative process and plans are susceptible to change, it's possible that the program will have to "undo" work and redo work to realize changes the customer demands. In the next chapter I'll focus on monitoring and controlling where the change control system lives. I bet you can't wait.

Keywords

Acknowledgment   A reply affirming receipt of the message, but not necessarily agreement with the message.

Barrier   Anything that prevents communication is a barrier.

Corrective action   Bringing the results of program execution back into alignment with the program scope. It's fixing mistakes and errors.

Decoder   The device that decodes the message into a usable format in the communication model; think of a receiver's fax machine.

Defect repair   An example of corrective action.

Defect repair validation   Confirming that the defect has been repaired and that the result is in alignment with the program scope.

Encoder   The thing that encodes the message to be delivered; think of fax machines, languages, or e-mail systems.

Evaluation criteria   The rules, qualifications, screening systems, and determinations that help determine which vendor you'll choose to provide the goods and services for your program.

Medium   The intermediary network between senders and receivers in the communication model; think of the phone lines between fax machines.

Noise   Any element that may disrupt or distort the communication between the sender and the receiver.

Preventive action   An action to prevent a mistake from entering the program.

Program preferred vendor list   A list of prescreened and qualified vendors that a program manager is allowed to procure from.

Program termination   The program is canceled due to poor performance, change in technology, change in organization demands, cash flow, marketplace considerations, or any number of reasons.

Quality   The conformance to requirements and a fitness for use.

Quality assurance   A management-driven process to prevent mistakes from entering the program's product, deliverables, and benefits.

Quality control   An inspection-driven process to confirm that quality exists within the program's deliverables and to keep mistakes out of the customer's hands.

Receiver   The receiver of a message in the communication model.

Request for information (RFI)   You need more information about a vendor's services or products, so you ask for more information. This can be anything from a brochure or a catalog to a white paper or references about the seller.

Request for proposal (RFP)   This document asks the vendor to create a proposal for your program. An RFP takes your basic vision and allows the vendor to run with it, designing a solution with a lot of features and solutions you may not have thought of. The creation of a web site is a good example. RFPs are a lot of work for vendors.

Request for quote (RFQ)   You want a price for whatever the seller can provide. You don't need any dream solutions or ideas—just tell me how much. For example, I need a quote for three tons of pea gravel.

Sender   The person or entity sending the communication.

Team development   Developing the program team so that members' competency levels are in alignment with the responsibilities they have been tasked with in the program.

Questions

1. Your program team has discovered that 1,250 doors that were installed as part of your skyscraper creation program have been installed to swing out of their rooms rather than into the rooms. You have elected to take the time and monies to fix the problem for these 1,250 doors. This is an example of which one of the following:

   A. Corrective action

   B. Preventive action

   C. Defect repair review

   D. Quality assurance

2. You send your program team through a class to be familiar with new materials your program will be working with. Your goal of the class is to ensure that the program team will understand how the new materials work to decrease mistakes on the program when the materials are used. This training class to prevent mistakes is an example of which one of the following?

   A. Team development

   B. Preventive action

   C. Corrective action

   D. Risk assessment response

3. All of the following are accurate statements about quality assurance except for which one?

   A. Quality assurance aims to prevent mistakes from entering the program.

   B. Quality assurance aims to prevent mistakes from entering the stakeholders' hands.

   C. Quality assurance is a prevention-driven process.

   D. Quality assurance is a management-driven process for the entire program.

4. In which process group does the program team get acquired?

   A. Initiating

   B. Planning

   C. Executing

   D. Monitoring and controlling

5. Henry is ready to acquire the program management team for his program. Which program management plan will guide Henry through the team acquisition process?

   A. Staffing management plan

   B. HR management plan

   C. Procurement management plan

   D. Contract management plan

6. Your program team has never worked with a new type of material your program will call for. Your program team consists of 23 people, most of whom don't know one another. You see this as an opportunity to train the team on the new materials but also to form some bonds and alliances on the program team. This is an example of which one of the following?

   A. Team development

   B. Preventive action

   C. Corrective action

   D. Risk assessment response

7. All of the following are inputs for team development except for which one?

   A. Training plan

   B. Training records

   C. Personnel records

   D. Performance assessment and improvements based on work results

8. Which communication approach is considered to be the preferred method for communicating?

   A. Formal

   B. Written

   C. Face-to-face

   D. Nonverbal

9. What percentage of communicating is nonverbal?

   A. 90 percent

   B. 55 percent

   C. 10 percent

   D. 63 percent

10. You and your program team want to create a chart that will capture stakeholder threats, perceived threats, and needs for program communication. Which chart can best capture this information?

    A. Pareto chart

    B. Ishikawa chart

    C. Stakeholder analysis chart

    D. Communications matrix

11. What aspect of communication affects the message of what's being communicated?

    A. Paralingual aspect

    B. Feedback

C. Eye contact

D. Audience

12. You and a colleague are discussing an issue on the program. Your colleague is deaf, and you're using a sign language interpreter so that you both can communicate with one another. The interpreter is what component of the communication model?

   A. Noise

   B. Medium

   C. Encoder

   D. Decoder

13. Mike and Henry are very angry with one another in their program. Their anger is preventing them from communicating. This is an example of which one of the following?

   A. Barrier

   B. Noise

   C. Medium

   D. Team development issue

14. Michelle needs to buy four new servers for her program. She is only interested in the price the NHG Computer Service Company has for the four servers. What document should Michelle prepare in this instance?

   A. Bid

   B. Request for quote

   C. Request for proposal

   D. Statement of work

15. Which seller response usually takes the most time to prepare?

   A. Request for proposal

   B. Proposal

   C. Bid

   D. Quote

16. What component of the procurement process allows all of the vendors to meet with the buyer for clarifications regarding the statement of work?

   A. SOW updates

   B. Negotiations

   C. Bidders conference

   D. Contract termination

17. Your program is about to procure the services of an electrician. You, the program manager, require that the vendor be licensed to perform electrical work in your state and in a neighboring state. This is an example of which one of the following procurement terms?

    A. Evaluation criteria

    B. Proposal screening

    C. Qualified sellers list

    D. Requirements

18. Which one of the following is not a component of the information distribution process?

    A. Program status information

    B. External filings with the government and regulatory agencies

    C. Public announcements

    D. Team competency assessments

19. Complete the following statement about quality assurance. Regulations are requirements; standards are sometimes seen as _____?

    A. Requirements

    B. Rules

    C. Optional

    D. Laws

20. Which one of the following is not an example of quality assurance?

    A. Adhering to quality policies and standards

    B. Inspecting the project work for mistakes

    C. Preventing mistakes from entering the program

    D. Planning quality into the program

Questions and Answers

1. Your program team has discovered that 1,250 doors that were installed as part of your skyscraper creation program have been installed to swing out of their rooms rather than into the rooms. You have elected to take the time and monies to fix the problem for these 1,250 doors. This is an example of which one of the following:

    A. Corrective action

    B. Preventive action

    C. Defect repair review

    D. Quality assurance

    A. This is an example of corrective action, because you are correcting the problem with the doors. B is incorrect, because the mistake has already entered the program. C, defect repair review, is the next activity that should happen after the doors have been repaired. D, quality assurance, is not the best choice, as this is an example of a mistake entering the program, whereas quality assurance wants to prevent the mistake from entering the program to begin with.

2. You send your program team through a class to be familiar with new materials your program will be working with. Your goal of the class is to ensure that the program team will understand how the new materials work to decrease mistakes on the program when the material is used. This training class to prevent mistakes is an example of which one of the following?

   A. Team development

   B. Preventive action

   C. Corrective action

   D. Risk assessment response

   B. This is clearly an example of preventive action, because you're training the program team to ensure that mistakes do not enter the program. While A, team development is tempting, the question stresses the choice to prevent mistakes from entering the program. C is incorrect, as no mistakes have entered the program as of yet. D is not a valid choice, as not enough information is really provided to understand the risk assessment and if this class is a feasible risk response.

3. All of the following are accurate statements about quality assurance except for which one?

   A. Quality assurance aims to prevent mistakes from entering the program.

   B. Quality assurance aims to prevent mistakes from entering the stakeholders' hands.

   C. Quality assurance is a prevention-driven process.

   D. Quality assurance is a management-driven process for the entire program.

   B. The only choice which does not define quality assurance is choice B. This option defines quality control, which does aim to keep mistakes out of the customer's hands. Choices A, C, and D are all accurate statements about quality assurance, so these choices are incorrect for this question.

4. In which process group does the program team get acquired?

   A. Initiating

   B. Planning

   C. Executing

   D. Monitoring and controlling

   C. The program management team is acquired during program execution. All of the other choices for this question are incorrect.

5. Henry is ready to acquire the program management team for his program. Which program management plan will guide Henry through the team acquisition process?

   A. Staffing management plan

   B. HR management plan

   C. Procurement management plan

   D. Contract management plan

   A. The staffing management plan defines how program team members will be brought onto and released from the program team. In addition, the plan defines how the program team members' time will be utilized on the program. B, the HR management plan, is not a valid plan. C, the procurement management plan, defines the procurement process, not the team acquisition process. D, the contract management plan, defines the administration of contracts between the buyers and sellers within the program.

6. Your program team has never worked with a new type of material your program will call for. Your program team consists of 23 people, most of whom don't know one another. You see this as an opportunity to train the team on the new materials but also to form some bonds and alliances on the program team. This is an example of which one of the following?

   A. Team development

   B. Preventive action

   C. Corrective action

   D. Risk assessment response

   A. In this instance, the goal is to develop the team by educating them on the new materials but also to create some bonds in the team. B is incorrect, as preventive action is focused on preventing mistakes from entering the program. C, corrective action, is also incorrect, as the question does not address errors or rework that need to be completed. This is not an example of a risk assessment response, so D is also incorrect.

7. All of the following are inputs for team development except for which one?

   A. Training plan

   B. Training records

   C. Personnel records

   D. Performance assessment and improvements based on work results

   D. This choice is an output of team development. Choices A, B, and C are all examples of inputs of team development, so these three choices are incorrect for this question.

8. Which communication approach is considered to be the preferred method for communicating?

   A. Formal

B. Written

C. Face-to-face

D. Nonverbal

C. Face-to-face communication is the preferred method, because both parties can rely on nonverbal communications to fully communicate. Choices A, B, and D are all incorrect choices. While these approaches have their place in program management, the preferred, most-effective method is face-to-face.

9. What percentage of communicating is nonverbal?

   A. 90 percent

   B. 55 percent

   C. 10 percent

   D. 63 percent

   B. Fifty-five percent of all communication is nonverbal; this is why telephone calls and e-mails are some of the worst methods to fully convey a message. A, C, and D are all incorrect percentages.

10. You and your program team want to create a chart that will capture stakeholder threats, perceived threats, and needs for program communication. Which chart can best capture this information?

    A. Pareto chart

    B. Ishikawa chart

    C. Stakeholder analysis chart

    D. Communications matrix

    C. A stakeholder analysis chart can capture the program stakeholders, their concerns, perceived threats, stance on program deliverables and benefits, and overall opinions and expectations of your program. These charts can help you communicate the right information to the right people. A, the Pareto chart, is a histogram that illustrates categories of defects or failures within a program. B, the Ishikawa diagram, is a cause-and-effect diagram and is useful for facilitating root cause analysis. D, a communications matrix, depicts which stakeholders will need to communicate with one another.

11. What aspect of communication affects the message of what's being communicated?

    A. Paralingual aspect

    B. Feedback

    C. Eye contact

    D. Audience

    A. Paralingual describes the pitch and tone used to convey the message. The paralingual aspect is how you say the message, not just what's been said. B is the response from the receiver. C and D are not valid choices for this question.

12. You and a colleague are discussing an issue on the program. Your colleague is deaf, and you're using a sign language interpreter so you both can communicate with one another. The interpreter is what component of the communication model?

    A. Noise

    B. Medium

    C. Encoder

    D. Decoder

    B. Medium is the best choice, as the interpreter is moving the message between you and your colleague. Noise is any distraction that affects the message. B and D describe the packaging and unpackaging of the communication message.

13. Mike and Henry are very angry with one another in their program. Their anger is preventing them from communicating. This is an example of which one of the following?

    A. Barrier

    B. Noise

    C. Medium

    D. Team development issue

    A. Anything that prevents communication is a barrier. B, noise, is something external that may disrupt the message. C, medium, is the network between the receiver and sender. D is not the best choice, as this question centers on communicating.

14. Michelle needs to buy four new servers for her program. She is only interested in the price the NHG Computer Service Company has for the four servers. What document should Michelle prepare in this instance?

    A. Bid

    B. Request for quote

    C. Request for proposal

    D. Statement of work

    B. When Michelle, or any program manager, is only interested in a price, then a request for quote is the best option. A, a bid, is the response from the seller to the buyer. C, request for proposal, is a query for the vendor to provide ideas and solutions for the work. D, the statement of work, usually accompanies complex procurement packages and request for proposals.

15. Which seller response usually takes the most time to prepare?

    A. Request for proposal

    B. Proposal

C. Bid

D. Quote

B. The seller response of a proposal usually takes the longest time for the vendor to complete for the buyer, because it includes a custom solution, whereas a bid or quote is a price-driven solution. A is incorrect, as it's the document from the buyer to the seller.

16. What component of the procurement process allows all of the vendors to meet with the buyer for clarifications regarding the statement of work?

   A. SOW updates

   B. Negotiations

   C. Bidders conference

   D. Contract termination

   C. This is an example of a bidders conference. All of the sellers are invited to attend so that all of the bidders have the same information to prepare their quotes or proposals for the program. A is not valid, as a SOW update may result from a bidders conference. Negotiations don't happen at the bidders conference, but usually in vendor selection. D, contract termination, happens after the contract has been awarded.

17. Your program is about to procure the services of an electrician. You, the program manager, require that the vendor be licensed to perform electrical work in your state and in a neighboring state. This is an example of which one of the following procurement terms?

   A. Evaluation criteria

   B. Proposal screening

   C. Qualified sellers list

   D. Requirements

   A. This is an example of evaluation criteria; if the electrician isn't licensed in both states, he doesn't qualify for the program. B, C, and D are all incorrect answers for this answer choice.

18. Which one of the following is not a component of the information distribution process?

   A. Program status information

   B. External filings with the government and regulatory agencies

   C. Public announcements

   D. Team competency assessments

   D. Team competency assessments are an output of team development. While they are communicated in the learning management system and resource pool update, they are not a component of the information distribution process.

Choices A, B, and C are all incorrect, as the program status information, external filings with the government and regulatory agencies, and public announcements are all components of the information distribution process.

19. Complete the following statement about quality assurance. Regulations are requirements; standards are sometimes seen as _____?

    A. Requirements

    B. Rules

    C. Optional

    D. Laws

    C. Regulations are requirements and are never optional; standards are sometimes seen as guidelines and are often considered optional. A, B, and D all describe laws and regulations, which are not optional.

20. Which one of the following is not an example of quality assurance?

    A. Adhering to quality policies and standards

    B. Inspecting the project work for mistakes

    C. Preventing mistakes from entering the program

    D. Planning quality into the program

    B. Inspecting the project work for mistakes is an example of quality control, as it aims to prevent mistakes from reaching the customer. Choices A, C, and D are all examples of quality assurance activities, so these choices are incorrect for this question.

Monitoring and Controlling the Program

In this chapter, you will
- Lead integrated change control
- Control the program resources
- Control program issues
- Control the program scope
- Monitor and control the program schedule and costs
- Perform quality control
- Monitor and control program risks
- Administer the program contracts

Monitoring and controlling the program means that you will ensure that the constituent projects of the program are performing as expected and that you'll be able to react to projects that aren't performing well. You'll work with project managers to gather and compile statistics, reports, and performance reviews of the projects. You'll also work with your program management team to monitor the program packages and how they are performing. Program packages are the non-project activities that are specific to the program progress.

Monitoring and controlling the program has direct ties to the program governance requirements. The program and its projects must continue to adhere to the program governance rules, or there'll be troubles on the program. You can expect to administer corrective actions to the program to get the program work back in alignment with what the governance board expects. In your keen insight as a program manager, you'll also anticipate when you'll need to apply preventive actions so that troubles don't come knocking on your door.

Throughout the program, you'll be monitoring and controlling all aspects of the program's work, resources, schedule, quality, communications, risk, procurement, and more. One of the biggest chunks of monitoring and controlling the program is controlling change throughout the program. Integrated change control ensures that changes to any area of the program are evaluated for their impact on the rest of the program. This is a big, fat chapter, and there are a lot of activities to consider for your PgMP exam. You can expect approximately 42 questions on your PgMP exam on monitoring and controlling.

Performing Integrated Change Control

In program management change is inevitable. It's essential that a program manager has defined a methodology of how changes to a program will be considered, controlled, approved, or declined. The integrated change control process aims to coordinate changes across the entire program. Integrated change control considers changes that are proposed, such as a change to the program scope, and changes that may have already occurred in the program, such as a change due to a new law, regulatory compliance, or a risk impact.

Integrated change control accomplishes several things:

- Facilitates the approval and denial of change requests.
- Escalates change requests according to predefined authority levels to approve or decline the change.
- Captures when changes to the program have already happened.
- Influences factors that may cause program changes.
- Confirms that changes benefit the program and are agreed upon.
- Manages how approved changes are fleshed into the program scope, time, and budget.

The process of integrated change control is completed through analysis of the program change and what impact it may have on the rest of the program. Consider a change to the program scope and its impact on cost, time, risk, resources, and the rest of the program. A simple change can become very complex when all of the ripples of the change are evaluated. Figure 8-1 shows all of the areas of the program that must be considered for a change's impact when dealing with integrated change control.

Consider also that a program change doesn't always begin in the program scope. Changes to the program can also originate from schedule, cost, even contracts—just about anywhere you can imagine in the program. Furthermore, changes to the program don't always play nice. You know there's politics, changes that happen through miscommunications, project managers that don't follow directions, unanticipated risks that lurk in the program, and more. Managing change is a constant battle for the program manager, and integrated change control is the weapon of choice.

Figure 8-1
Integrated change control examines all areas of the program for impact.

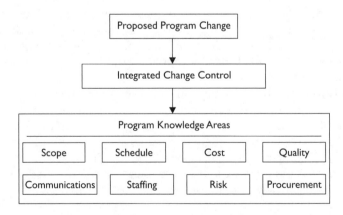

Preparing for Integrated Change Control

Integrated change control won't happen on its own; a concerted effort from the program management team ensures that integrated change control works. Most often integrated change control will begin with a change request. This assumption is true in the perfect world where project managers and program stakeholders actually complete a change request form, but we know that out there in the real world that doesn't always happen. For your exam, however, change requests are documented and verbal change requests are not approved. As Figure 8-2 demonstrates, there are seven inputs and seven outputs to integrated change control.

While it's true that most change requests are documented and focus on changes to the program scope, that's not all that an integrated change request does. Recall that this program process also evaluates the program's and constituent projects' performance. A project within the program that is not performing well is affecting the program performance. You could argue that a poorly performing project is changing the program's ability to deliver the benefits, and that's why integrated change control is concerned with the projects' performance.

The performance of the program and the constituent projects allows the program manager then to react to poor performance. These reactions come in the form of hiccups, tremors, and sleepless nights. Kidding. The program reactions I'm talking about are corrective and preventive actions. Corrective actions are measures taken to fix the problems and to learn not to repeat the problems again. Preventive actions, as the name implies, anticipate problems and prevent the risk, issues, errors, or other bad stuff from ever entering the program.

Examining Integrated Change Control Outputs

The most obvious result of integrated change control is the approval of a change request. Approved change requests have been evaluated, and their impact on the entire program has been considered. When a change request is approved, the change will be incorporated into the program management plan and into the program scope, time, and cost. The PWBS may have to be updated, and the activity list, the program's risk register, and any other parts of the program management plan that are affected by the change will be updated to reflect the approved program change. There are actually seven outputs of the integrated change control process.

Figure 8-2
Integrated change control has seven inputs and seven outputs.

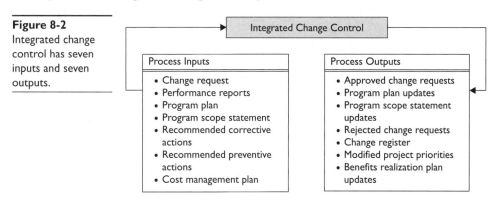

Integrated Change Control

Process Inputs	Process Outputs
• Change request	• Approved change requests
• Performance reports	• Program plan updates
• Program plan	• Program scope statement
• Program scope statement	updates
• Recommended corrective	• Rejected change requests
actions	• Change register
• Recommended preventive	• Modified project priorities
actions	• Benefits realization plan
• Cost management plan	updates

When a change is approved, especially a change to the program scope, the change will trickle down to the program's projects. The change from the program to the project will often reorder the project priorities and cause the project manager and project team to reorder their project scope, project WBS, and activities to deliver on the new benefits the program demands. You can expect some pushback from project managers, but remember, the program owns the projects.

In case you're wondering about those changes that don't get approved, well, they aren't chucked out the window. The rejected change requests are documented in terms of why they weren't approved, and the stakeholder requesting the change is notified of the change request's demise.

Both approved and declined change requests are documented in the change register. The change register is a database of the changes that have been introduced to the program and why the change was incorporated into the program—or why a change request was not approved for the program. When the program reaches its conclusion, this helps as a reminder of why changes were approved or denied. There's no confusion as to why a program benefit exists or was never introduced as a result of a program change request.

Controlling the Program Resources

This monitoring and controlling process, resource control, is all about controlling the program resources and their costs. The program management plan, your favorite plan, defines the resources your program will need to deliver the benefits the program stakeholders expect. Recall that a resource isn't just a person, but also materials, equipment, and facilities.

When it comes to monitoring the human resources of your program, the focus is often on costs and availability. Obviously, the more a person is utilized within the program, the more someone pays for that person's time—either by program, by department, or by project. The accountability of a resource's time in a program often falls under cross-charging, that is, the dissection of labor expense by program, constituent project, or indirect costs shared by the organization.

Considering Resource Control Inputs

As you can see in Figure 8-3, there are seven inputs to resource control. You won't need all seven of these inputs for every instance of controlling the program resources—just rely on the inputs you will need in order to complete the task at hand. Each input is applicable to the situation you're facing; consider how you'd control a resource that was a contractor versus a resource that is a piece of equipment or material. Obviously you wouldn't manage each the same way—or people may think you're a touch nutty.

Programs, especially in the construction and manufacturing industries, often rely on lease agreements for equipment. The lease agreements, which are contracts, will stipulate how long the equipment is to be leased for, the terms for extending or terminating the lease, the payment requirements, and all the related business of leasing the equipments. Other industries, such as IT, may have lease agreements in the form of service contracts, bandwidth, or even storage space on remote servers. My point being,

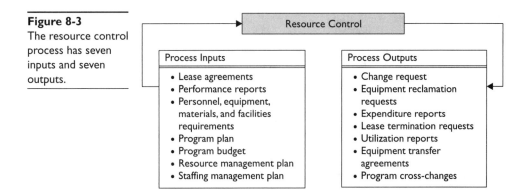

Figure 8-3
The resource control process has seven inputs and seven outputs.

Resource Control

Process Inputs	Process Outputs
• Lease agreements • Performance reports • Personnel, equipment, materials, and facilities requirements • Program plan • Program budget • Resource management plan • Staffing management plan	• Change request • Equipment reclamation requests • Expenditure reports • Lease termination requests • Utilization reports • Equipment transfer agreements • Program cross-changes

there is some overlap with this process input and the program contract administration, which I discuss later in this chapter.

The program manager will also rely on performance reports to see how well human resources are doing—and what their performance is costing the program. Performance reports are usually centered on human resources, but you could do performance reports on equipment such as manufacturing devices, networks, servers—even services such as shipping and travel.

The program management plan and the program budget are inputs to resource control, too. They define what people, equipment, materials, and facilities are required to complete the program. The costs for these resources are linked to the cost monitoring and controlling process I discuss in a few pages. Finally, there are two plans that oversee the program resource utilization:

- **Staffing management plan** Defines when human resources will be brought onto and released from the program, how the resources will be managed and utilized, and their associated costs.

- **Resource management plan** Defines what resources, such as equipment, plants, test beds, data centers, materials, tools, real estate leases, and other non-human resources will be needed, when they'll be needed, and what their costs are.

For your PgMP examination know that a resource isn't always just a human resource. Resources can also be materials and equipment. Both types of resources have a cost factor associated with each, and the determination of who pays for what resource and what the program receives as a result of the payment is defined in the program management plan, the program budget, the resource management plan, or the staffing management plan.

Exploring Resource Control Outputs

Just as there are seven inputs to resource control, there are also seven outputs of this process. Since resource control is an ongoing process, the results of the process will vary, depending on what resource is currently being controlled in the program. As is often the case in program management, resource control can result in a program change request. Change requests are fed back into the integrated change control process.

The cost, utilization, and cross-charges of the resources are all results of controlling the program resources. The costs of all materials, equipment, and human resources have to be accounted for and linked to the work and deliverables the resources have contributed to. When a resource is no longer needed on the program, several things can happen, depending on what the resource is:

- Materials are returned to the vendor, if possible, or sold or used elsewhere in the organization.

- Leases may be terminated if the lease agreement allows early termination.

- Leased equipment and space must be released and returned when they're no longer needed, to avoid additional program costs.

- Resources may be transferred to the receiving entity as part of the program deliverable (considering software and hardware technologies).

- Staff members that are no longer needed in the program must be released from the program and returned to operations or other utilization within the organization.

Sometimes equipment that is in an organization's inventory is set aside just for the program to use. When the program is done with the equipment, it should go back into the organization's inventory so that other programs and entities within the organization can use the equipment. The program may also assign resources to projects within the program and then reclaim the equipment to move to other constituent projects.

Monitoring and Controlling the Program Work

Programs get done by people doing the work that the program requires; nothing unusual about that. The work that the people in the program and in the projects do to complete the program deliverables, however, must be monitored and controlled to ensure that it is done according to design and that program expectations are being met. It doesn't do anyone much good if the program work is completed late, full of mistakes, or over budget.

This process aims to collect, measure, and consolidate information about the program's performance. Once program performance has been evaluated, measured, and inspected for performance trends, then reactions to the measurements are implemented. The goal of monitoring and controlling the program work isn't just information for information's sake; the goal is to improve the overall program performance.

Monitoring and controlling the program work really is about monitoring and controlling the individual projects within the program and how each project is contributing to the program's success or failure. Each project's performance can be measured in terms of any or all of the following:

- Project scope achievement

- Cost and schedule adherence

- Quality goals

- Human resource performance

- Meeting communication expectations
- Risk management practices
- Vendor management

Monitoring and controlling the program work also evaluates the performance of the program deliverables that are not created at the project level, but at the program level. This may include program deliverables such as program plans, program communications, risk management, and process improvement.

Gathering Monitoring and Controlling Work Inputs

There are just four inputs to the monitoring and controlling work process, as seen in Figure 8-4. Because this process is completed throughout the program, the actual content of these inputs will change to reflect the current status of the program and project performance. Performance reports, probably the best barometer of the program and project health, are the most reliable input for this process.

The program management plan is also an input to the process, because it communicates the expectations and requirements for the program and its performance. Think about all the components of the program management plan and how each subsidiary plan defines the strategic objectives of the program. Each of the following components can be measured for program performance and completion of program work:

- Benefits management plan
- Communications management plan
- Cost management plan
- Contracts management plan
- Interface management plan
- Scope management plan
- Procurement management plan
- Quality management plan
- Resource management plan
- Risk response plan
- Schedule management plan
- Staffing management plan

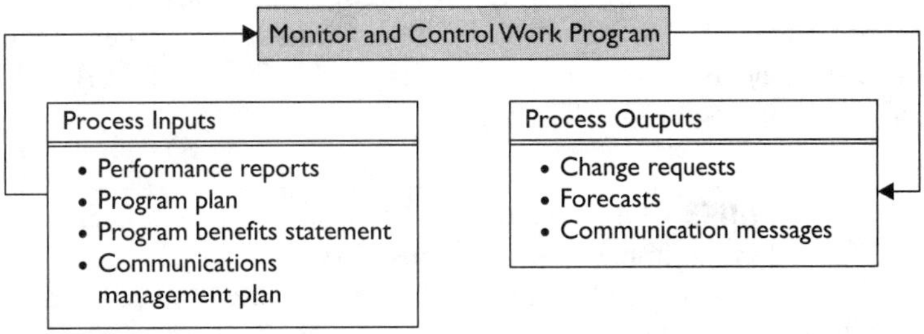

Figure 8-4
The monitor and control the program work process creates three outputs.

Monitor and Control Work Program	
Process Inputs	**Process Outputs**
• Performance reports	• Change requests
• Program plan	• Forecasts
• Program benefits statement	• Communication messages
• Communications management plan	

Each of these plans relate to some program activities and responsibilities for the program management team. The monitor and control program work process can be linked back to each of these subsidiary plans and measure the program work and its ability to meet expectations of these plans.

One of the major themes of program management is benefits management. The program benefits statement is considered an input to this process, because it clearly defines the benefits the program is to create for the program customers. If the work is not done in alignment with the expectations of the benefits statement, then the work is, technically, out of the program scope, and the program is creating things that do not add value to the program customers. Adding features to the program or project scopes to consume the budget is known as gold plating.

Finally, the communications management plan is seen as a direct input to monitoring and controlling the program work. I know I've already mentioned this plan as part of the program management plan, but it's called out specifically here because it defines three things:

- Who needs what information in regard to the program work
- When the information is needed in terms of the program work
- The expected modality in which the information is needed

The communications management plan will define things like reports based on conditions within the program; escalation processes; and how to communicate variances, exceptions, and defects within the program.

Reviewing the Results of Controlling the Program Work

There are but three outputs to this process, as seen in Figure 8-4. Keep in mind that the monitoring and controlling of the program work is an iterative process that will adapt to the conditions within the program. This process is done throughout the life of the program, not just once.

It should not be a surprise to you to see that change requests are one of the outputs of this process. Change requests may come about as a result of controlling the program work based on discoveries for improving the program deliverables and benefits, based on errors and omissions, based on changes in technology within the program, or simply based on program performance. Changes to the program scope don't always have to be adding things to the scope—a poorly performing program may need to trim the program scope to hit a deadline or meet budget expectations.

The second output of this process is program forecasts. Considering what the program has done so far, the program management team may predict how the program performance will continue to go. The obvious forecasts center on time and costs, but forecasts may also be created on the basis of risks, program benefits, resource demand, and other trends within the program.

NOTE One common approach to creating forecasts is based on earned value management (EVM). I discuss EVM later in this chapter; it's a suite of formulas used to predict and display program and project performance.

The final output is the result of communicating. If you communicate, you'll have, well, communication messages. While it's long been said that face-to-face communication is the preferred method of communicating, it's also nice to have evidence of what's been communicated in writing.

Face-to-face communication allows people to take advantage of the nonverbal aspects of a conversation. Nonverbal communication is actually 55 percent of communication; that's why phone calls and e-mails are often considered some of the worst methods for communicating. In today's world, however, program and project teams are virtual teams where team members are dispersed around the globe. Chances are you'll have to rely on collaborative software, e-mail, and the Internet to communicate with your clients, team members, and project managers.

Managing and Controlling Program Issues

Programs always have issues. Issues are topics that direction and determination need to be assigned to. Issue resolution can go in several different directions, and usually there's some turmoil and opposing views on each side of the outcome of the issue. For example, your program can have an issue over which vendor to use based on price, availability, previous experience with the vendor, and so on. Or you can have an issue over which database server you want your program to use. Or you can have an issue with what color paint the program purchases.

Issues are just about anything that has some controversy, program impact, and disagreement surrounding it. Issues can become risks, and this process, issue management and control, is done in tandem with risk management and control. In order to do issue management and control, you have to identify, track, and close issues so that they don't cause delays or incur program costs. You'll resolve issues, according to *The Standard for Program Management*, using one of several approaches:

- Resolving the issue through an issue owner
- Modifying the program requirements
- Modifying the program scope
- Adjusting organizational policies
- Changing stakeholder expectations

 NOTE That last one, changing stakeholder expectations, is my favorite. Try that one out and let me know how it works for you. I guess you could tell the stakeholders that they need to lower their expectations to be more in alignment with what they're experiencing. That's just not nice.

Keep in mind that issue management and control isn't just at the program level, but also for the constituent projects within the program. Ideally your project managers can work to resolve their own issues, but sometimes issues from projects need to be escalated to the program level for resolution. You might experience this when there's an issue that arises between projects, such as competition for resources or expected deliverables, and the project managers can't resolve the issues themselves.

Collecting Inputs for Issue Management

In order to begin issue management and control, you'll need to establish an approach for how issues are identified within the program. You'll do this through the creation of an issues register where all program issues, their characteristics, and possible outcomes are recorded. Each issue should be reviewed by an authoritative body or a person with the experience and expertise to review and close the risk. This person or body is also known as the issue owner.

As you see in Figure 8-5, there are four inputs to this process. Based on the performance of the program and the projects, new issues may be identified—and recorded in the program's issue register. This means, of course, you'll also need work results to see if there are issues, from quality control to defect repair review, in the deliverables and things the program work creates.

Overseeing all of this business is your program management plan; you'll need this plan, because there could be issues arising from the real experiences of the program, as opposed to what the plan called for. A difference between the program plan and the implementation of the program plan can generate an issue. For example, consider a construction program that has created a reasonable schedule to complete the building. The plan is solid, based on historical information, and reliable. During the actual construction, however, the discovery of ruins of a past civilization can cause the project to stop while archeologists perform an analysis of the site. Now you have an issue that wasn't anticipated.

Documenting the Results of Issue Management

As your program moves toward the lovely day of closure, you'll experience rounds and rounds of issue identification and issue resolution. Issue resolution is done on a regular schedule and is really part of your program governance—as it should define the rules for issue identification and issue resolution, along with the process for escalating issues that need to be resolved. Figure 8-5 shows the four outputs of issue management and control.

As you might guess, change requests can come from issue management. If you want to change the program scope to address an issue, then you'll need a documented change request. The change request can be to add things to the program scope or, more likely when an issue is concerned, to take things out of program scope. Changes to the program scope always pass through integrated change control—so the parallel process of

Figure 8-5
Issue management and control is an ongoing process.

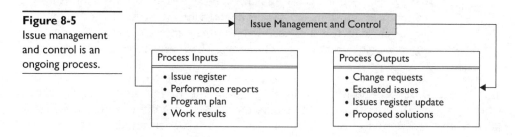

risk monitoring and control is still linked to issue management even when a change to address the issue is created.

Sometimes issues can't be resolved by the program management team and need to be escalated to a reviewing body, key program stakeholders, or even the program customer. Consider issues linked to finances, schedule, and scope. Whenever an issue is identified, it's documented in the issue register, and when the issue is resolved, its resolution is also documented in the register. Of course, there may be multiple proposed resolutions for each issue, and these are documented as well. Someone or some entity, the issue owner, needs to make a decision or the issue will become a program risk.

Controlling the Program Scope

You can bet your bottom dollar that your program will have changes to the program scope, and that'd be a safe bet. Scope change control is all about controlling, tracking, documenting, and approving or declining change requests that will affect the program's product. Of course you won't approve every change request—that'd be just silly—but you will consider every documented scope change request and determine its impact on the program as a whole. This process has six concerns:

- Document and catalog change requests.
- Evaluate each change request for its impact on the program as a whole.
- Determine why the change request has been proposed.
- Communicate the status and ultimately the decision regarding the scope change request.
- Archive the change request, decisions regarding the change request, and any supporting detail for the scope change.
- Incorporate approved change requests into the program management plan.

While this all looks nice and neat here on paper, you know it's just not this easy out there in our real world. It's not unrealistic for the program manager to get bombarded with change requests—that's why it's essential to have a good, solid change management system that captures change requests. The scope change control system should have rules, boundaries, and an established workflow for how change requests are considered, evaluated, and then implemented.

Considering Scope Change Requests

When you're performing the activities in the scope change control process, you'll have, as seen in Figure 8-6, seven inputs to the process. Each of these inputs is considered for its overall impact on the program as a whole. The integration of concerns for each of these inputs will help the program management team, the program manager, or even a change control board understand the value and outcome of each proposed change request.

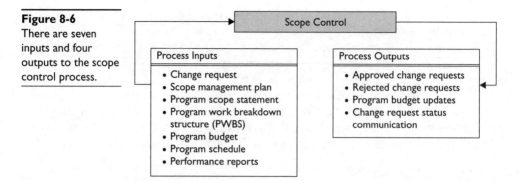

Figure 8-6
There are seven inputs and four outputs to the scope control process.

Scope Control

Process Inputs
- Change request
- Scope management plan
- Program scope statement
- Program work breakdown structure (PWBS)
- Program budget
- Program schedule
- Performance reports

Process Outputs
- Approved change requests
- Rejected change requests
- Program budget updates
- Change request status communication

The scope management plan may be the most important input to this process, because it defines the program scope and the scope change control process. It has defined the rules and procedures for how changes are considered, evaluated, and fleshed into the program scope or rejected. Coupled with the scope management plan the PWBS is an important input, because it helps the reviewers of the change request determine the exact areas of the program that will be affected by the change.

As you may have already guessed, each change request is also evaluated for its financial and time impact on the program. A change request to the program scope may be a genuinely value-added change, but the impact on the program budget and/or the program schedule is too serious to take the change on. Not every change will affect the program budget (consider changing a server or workstation's name sequencing). It's also true, of course, that every change may not affect the program schedule (consider changing materials the program uses).

Finally, performance reports are considered an input to the scope change control process, because the overall health of the program may influence whether or not a new change can be incorporated. A program that's slipping on schedule and bleeding cash won't likely be able to accept scope changes as easily as a healthy, solid program. No surprises here. What may happen, however, is that the sickly program may need to trim the program scope to reduce expenses and stick to a predetermined budget or schedule—that's not fun, but it may happen.

Completing Scope Control

This part's pretty easy. There are, as you can see in Figure 8-6, four outputs of change control. You're going to have approved changes and rejected changes as two of your primary outputs of controlling the program scope. The hard part, I'm afraid, is getting those changes into the scope, the PWBS, and the program actions, and then out into reality. You can also expect some unhappy people when you have to reject their change requests and explain why the change has been rejected.

Some changes (not every change) will require the program budget to be updated. The cost associated with the change needs to be reflected in the program budget—and someone, usually the person making the change request, has to pay for the cost of the approved change. When a scope change is approved, the program's cost baseline may be updated to reflect the new costs incurred by the approved change request.

As the proposed change is evaluated, tested, and pondered over, the requestor of the change may be curious as to what's happening with her change request. This means you or your program management team will have to communicate with the stakeholder as to the change's current status. Status can vary: pending, approved, rejected, closed, or whatever nomenclature your program wants to assign to the process. Change request status is documented and becomes part of the program's historical information.

Controlling the Program Schedule

No one likes a program that's late. The customers don't like it, the project managers don't like, your other stakeholders don't like it—and I know that you don't like it. There are many factors that affect a project's timeliness, and they're different from program to program. Controlling the program schedule is really about controlling the factors that affect the program's ability to deliver on its promises and benefits according to the agreed schedule.

Controlling the program schedule requires that the program manager track the actual start and finish dates of the program activities. The sum of the activities' deliverables will move the program to the plotted milestones, and from here everyone can clearly see whether the program is on schedule, slipping from schedule, or—wonder-of-wonders—ahead of schedule.

Depending on the measurement of the program schedule, the program management plan may need to be updated to react to the schedule status. In my experience as a consultant, it's almost always that the program schedule is dwindling away from the predicted schedule baseline. Sometimes, however, it's a pleasant surprise to adapt to a program that's cruising ahead of schedule. Usually a positive experience on the program schedule is because of a program risk that didn't occur or an opportunity that's allowed a constituent project to leap ahead.

Preparing for Schedule Control

Controlling the program schedule is an ongoing battle. From the day the program starts, all sorts of factors will try to attack your program schedule. Your job as the program manager is to collect and process the information as quickly as possible and then react to the problems and opportunities. Figure 8-7 shows all of the inputs you'll need to complete schedule control.

Performance reports, the program schedule, and the individual project schedules will be the most obvious inputs to controlling the program schedule. Performance reports will show how the program is performing in terms of time to reach the program

Figure 8-7
Schedule control happens in parallel with program execution.

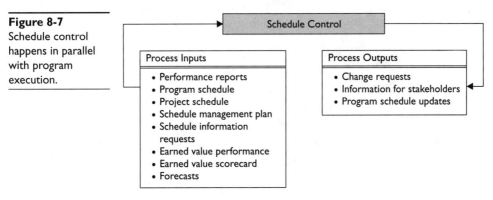

milestones, and from there you can continue as planned, make adjustments to the program schedule, or create changes to the program scope that'll reflect the time issues at hand. Sometimes, and I hope this is the situation you find for all your programs, you'll be able to move ahead in the program rather than adjust the scope because the schedule is slipping.

One thing that usually bites all program managers is Parkinson's Law. Parkinson's Law states that work will expand to fill the amount of time allotted to it. This is most evident on program and project task assignments. If good old Fred is assigned a task, and Fred thinks it'll take 30 hours to complete the work, he may report that it'll take him 40 hours to do the work. Fred is allowing ten hours of fudge time—that's time for errors, if he gets stuck, or the unknowns that he may encounter in his efforts. The trouble is that if Fred doesn't get stuck, doesn't have errors, and completes the work as assigned, it'll still take him 40 hours to complete the work, because he's reported that's how long it'll take him to do the work. It's just like the day before you go on vacation, you can get a gazillion things done, but on your return it takes you all day to do one task.

Parkinson's Law is based on activities that are effort-driven. Effort-driven means that the more effort you apply, the less time the activity may take to complete. For example, if it takes ten painters four days to paint a house, you may be able to double your efforts by adding ten more painters and complete the work in two days. Of course this isn't always true, for a variety of reasons. At the top of the list is the Law of Diminishing Returns.

The Law of Diminishing Returns basically states that as more investment is made, the overall return from that investment diminishes. Figure 8-8 depicts the Law of Diminishing Returns. The investment here is in the labor in relation to the cost of painting the house. You're only going to get so much profit from painting the house, and the more labor you add, the more your costs increase, while your profit decreases.

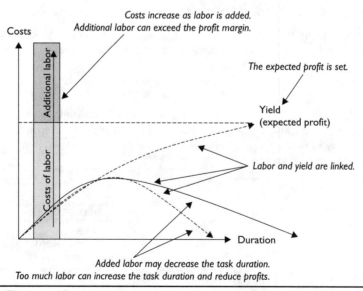

Figure 8-8   The Law of Diminishing Returns affects how much labor can be added.

The other problem with adding more and more labor is that work, regardless of how much labor you add, will always take some amount of time to complete. You can't exponentially add labor to decrease the amount of time it takes to paint the house. In theory you could keep adding painters to get the entire house painted in a few minutes, but in reality that's just not going to work.

Of course sometimes adding labor is worth the extra costs to realize the time gained—this is called *crashing*. Crashing adds labor to decrease the amount of time it takes to complete the work but adds to the cost of the work, because you have to pay for the labor.

The schedule management plan will address how the program schedule is created, what the expectation of the program schedule is, and how the program schedule can be changed. It'll also address any activities that the program management team may do in conjunction with the key program stakeholders—such as conditions for when to trim the program scope, when to add to the program budget to purchase additional labor or equipment that may reduce the program schedule, and how to react when risk affects the program schedule.

The program stakeholders should be interested in how the program's schedule is progressing. Stakeholders will query the status of the program via schedule information requests. Your response will help them plan for cash flow, project scheduling, and anticipation of when the program will be completed. They basically want to know how the program's going and when you'll be done.

Earned value management is a suite of formulas that you'll use to relate costs to the program schedule. The schedule performance index (SPI) and the schedule variance values are the two primary values that'll show how well the program is performing. The lower the SPI, the worse the program is doing. When you look at the schedule variance, you want that number to be as close to zero as possible. A negative number is bad, while a positive number may actually reflect poor estimating for completing the program.

 NOTE If you're not familiar with earned value management, the sidebar on the next page addresses the suite of formulas for both time and cost.

Based on the outcome of your earned value management assessment, you'll be able to create performance reports, an earned value scorecard, and forecasts for how the program is moving along and when it'll likely be completed. The goal of earned value management is to measure and forecast program performance.

Reflecting the Program Schedule

When you measure and evaluate the program schedule in order to control the program schedule, you're going to create data. Drawing on this data, you'll be able to predict if the program is going to finish as planned or if the program schedule needs to be updated to reflect a new likely finish date for the program.

Sometimes, but not always, you'll have to change the program scope in order to meet schedule requirements. If a program is running late and the primary benefits must be completed by a specific date, then the program scope may need to change to complete on time and to focus on the primary requirements of the program. Any changes to the program scope must flow through the program's change control system and program integrated change control.

Your program stakeholders will need to receive regular updates on the program schedule regardless of the program health. You can provide several types of program information for them:

- Performance reports
- Earned value scorecard
- Change requests
- Variance reports
- Exceptions reports
- Status reports

 NOTE A variance report and an exceptions report are the same thing.

Finally, after reviewing the program schedule, the schedule management plan, earned value management, and the conditions within the program, you may have to update the program schedule. Most often when the program schedule is updated, it's for additional time, though sometimes your program may be moving ahead of schedule, so the program end date can be changed to reflect an early completion date. This usually happens when an expected risk didn't come true, so the anticipated delay was avoided. (Hooray!)

Using Earned Value Management

Earned value management is a suite of formulas that can measure program performance. You'll need to be topically aware of these formulas and how to use them for your PgMP examination. Out here in the real world, however, there are a lot of software applications that'll do this business for you and allow you to add variables, fluctuations, and other considerations that you won't have to fool with on the exam.

Earned value management is a method to assign dollar amounts to the work that your program has performed and the work your program was scheduled to perform, as well as to forecast how the remainder of the program is likely to continue given current experiences. Don't get too worked up over these; it's not as complex as some jokers would have you believe.

Earned value (EV) is simply the percentage of the program that is complete times the assigned budget for the program. The assigned budget for the program, called the budget at completion (BAC), is based on what you promised the final cost of the program to be. Here's how the formula looks: Earned Value = %Completed × BAC. So, if your program is 30 percent complete and your budget is $1,500,000, your Earned Value would be 30 percent of $1,500,000, which is $450,000.

Planned value (PV) is the amount the program should be worth according to the calendar. In other words, a program manager has promised that the program would be 40 percent done on June 1. This means that the organization can plan on the program being worth 40 percent of the BAC of $1,500,000 on June 1. In this example, the planned value is 40 percent of $1,500,000, which is $600,000.

Cost variance (CV) is the difference between the earned value of the program and the actual costs of the program. In this example, I said the program was 30 percent complete, which is $450,000 in EV. However, the program had wasted materials, rework, and other expenses to reach the 30 percent mark in the program and they spent $570,000—more than the earned value amount. The cost variance is the earned value amount of $450,000 minus the actual costs of $570,000 for a cost variance of negative $120,000. Uh-oh! This program is losing money!

Schedule variance (SV) is the difference between the earned value and the planned value. In this instance the earned value is $450,000, because the program is 30 percent complete. It's June 1, however, and the program is supposed to be 40 percent complete. This variance is EV – PV, which is $450,000 – $600,000, which is negative $150,000. This program is running late.

The cost performance index (CPI) shows how well the program is performing on its budget. The closer to "1" the value is, the better the program is doing. You'll find this value by dividing the EV by the AC of the program. This time it'll be $450,000/$570,000, which is 0.79 when I round up. This number means that the program is actually losing 21 cents on every dollar it invests in this program. Yikes!

The schedule performance index (SPI) is similar to the CPI formula, but its concern is to assign a value to performance of the schedule. It is simply EV/PV, which is $450,000/$600,000 and equals 0.75. Again, the closer to "1," the better the health of the program; this program is off schedule by 25 percent. Not good.

Given what we've found so far, you can create a new estimate of where the program's final costs are likely to be. The Estimate at Completion formula is the original BAC/CPI; in this instance it's $1,500,000/0.79 and equals an estimate of $1,900,000, rounded up. You are basically accounting for the 21 cents the program is losing on every dollar.

If you know that your program will now need a total $1,900,000, you can also calculate the Estimate to Complete (ETC) formula. The ETC is EAC – AC. In other words, you're trying to find out how much more the program needs to complete. In this instance the EAC of $1,900,000 less the AC of $570,000 means the program will need $1,330,000 more to reach the program's end.

The last formula for now is the Variance at Completion. This one is a snap. It's simply the original BAC minus the EAC you just calculated. In this ugly program the BAC started at $1,500,000 and the EAC was calculated to be $1,900,000, so the VAC for the program will be negative $400,000.

Controlling the Program Costs

When the idea of a program is considered, and when the program itself is being formulated, and when the program is officially launched, and throughout the entire life of the program, there is one constant concern: control the program costs. And that's fair when you consider all of the moving parts, the monies invested in the program, and the monies that may not be invested in other programs and projects in the organizational portfolio. Controlling the program costs is a paramount concern for any program manager.

This program process is really about controlling changes to the program that may adversely affect the program costs. It's also about keeping your eyes on the program budget and the program expenses, along with deriving information from the costs the program incurs. Controlling and monitoring the program costs is an ongoing activity that has branches into procurement, contract administration, and loads of communication.

Examining Cost Control Inputs

There are six inputs to the cost control process, as Figure 8-9 demonstrates. Of all these inputs, the program budget is arguably the most important, because it's often viewed as a cap or not-to-exceed amount for the program deliverables. In all fairness, the program budget may also have a range variance associated with it; for example, the program budget could be $4,000,000 plus or minus 6 percent.

Each project within the program will have its own budget to complete its own project work. The aggregation of the program budget is composed of the expenses of the constituent components within the program. There will be, however, actual costs related to non-work activities within the program that need to be accounted for and monitored. For example, there may be travel expenses, equipment and office leases, consultants, legal fees, permits, and other sundry costs that the program will incur but that aren't necessarily tied to the individual projects within the program.

The cost management plan will dictate how the program costs will be estimated, as you know, from the planning work you did in Chapter 6. The cost management plan will also—and this is the part that's relevant here—define how the costs will be reviewed, tracked, monitored, and then communicated to the program stakeholders. The review of the program costs, typically through earned value, is how the program management team will communicate and react to variances within the program.

Figure 8-9
The cost control has six inputs and four outputs.

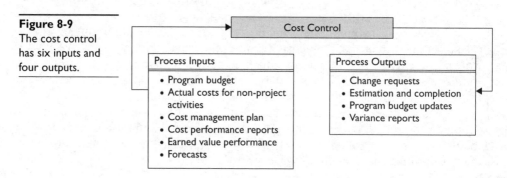

The two most important earned value management formulas dealing with costs are the cost performance index (CPI) and the cost variance equations. The CPI demonstrates how healthy the program is doing on costs, while the cost variance reveals the difference between actual costs and the earned value of the program. You want the CPI value to be as close to 1 as possible and the cost variance to be as close to zero as possible.

Earned value management will allow the program manager to review and assess the program's health and then make a forecast of where the program is heading. There are several earned value management formulas that you can use to predict the program's future success:

- **Estimate at completion**   This formula predicts how much the program is likely to cost when it's all said and done. It's based on the CPI and how much you originally predicted the program would cost to complete.

- **Estimate to complete**   This formula considers the current status of the program and then predicts how much more money your organization will need to sink into the program in order to reach the end.

- **Variance at completion**   This straightforward formula compares how much the program was supposed to cost with how much it'll cost now to complete; it predicts the variance the organization can expect at completion.

You'll need to be aware of the earned value management concepts and formulas for your PgMP certification. If these formulas are new to you, I highly recommend you read the sidebar "Using Earned Value Management" earlier in this chapter.

Reviewing the Cost Control Outputs

Figure 8-9 shows that there are just four outputs of the cost control process. You, the program manager, will be completing cost control throughout the program, so the exact details of these outputs will vary, depending on the conditions within your program. That may seem obvious, but I want to stress a point here: as risk, delays, and the unknown seep into your program, you'll have to react, judge, trim, and consult on what's the best approach to move forward. All that reacting and consulting will also drive program costs—not just the unknown issues that will certainly happen in any program.

Change requests can happen at any time in a program, but change requests tied to cost control have a magical way of getting approved faster than any other change requests in the world. A change request to trim the program scope, to change materials, or to change any deliverable of the program scope to save on program costs must flow through the cost change control system. The reason for the change request and its overall impact on the program must be documented as part of the change.

Often in your program you'll need to create a new cost estimate for the program's completion. There are several things that may affect the program's cost without changing the program scope during the execution of the program, including

- Risks
- A change in program labor

- The cost of materials due to market conditions
- Inflation, economy, supply and demand
- Defects and waste
- Non-value adding activities
- Poor estimates
- New laws and regulations

As these changes to the program costs are approved, or if the program scope is increased, then the program budget will need to be updated to reflect the additions to the program scope, the change in the cost of the program, and the reason the change has occurred. All changes to the program scope, regardless of its reasons, must be documented for future reference.

Should the program be running over budget, the program manager will need to create a variance report. This report should detail what the cost overrun is, why it has happened, the recommended response to the cost overrun, and how the program will avoid the cost overrun in the future.

NOTE Your organization may call a variance report an exceptions report. They are the same thing.

Performing Quality Control

Quality is about fulfilling program requirements. You could accurately reason, then, that quality is achieved by completing the program scope, as it was defined between the program management team and the program stakeholders. Quality is reached when the program scope is reached. From here you could also reason that poor quality is achieved when the deliverables do not sync up with the program scope. The difference between what was created and what was required is a variance in quality.

Quality control is the process of ensuring that the program deliverables are meeting the program requirement. It is an inspection-driven process that requires the program manager, the project managers, experts, and other key stakeholders to inspect the results of the program work to ensure that the results are meeting the demands of the program scope. If not—then it's poor quality and the problem must be addressed.

As you might guess, quality control is performed throughout the program. The goal of quality control is to catch mistakes before they enter the customers' hands. If a mistake is found, then you've got to fix the mistake—of course. Much of today's quality control efforts are based on Deming's quality cycle, as seen in Figure 8-10.

Readying for Quality Control

There are four inputs to quality control, as seen in Figure 8-11. The quality management plan defines how quality will be achieved and how quality will be controlled through inspections and reviews. This plan is a key input to the process in any program because it will define the very specific quality control activities for the program.

Figure 8-10
The quality cycle is based on Deming's Plan-Do-Check-Act cycle.

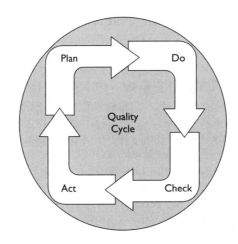

If you think about this, and I'm guessing you are, the quality control activities are different from program to program. Consider the types of inspections you'd complete in a skyscraper program versus the quality control activities you'd do in an information technology program. The philosophies and principles of quality control are universal; the activities associated with the process, however, are unique to each program.

One universal idea is the usage of checklists. Checklists are ideal for activities that are repeated over and over throughout a program. A checklist can ensure that each step of a repeated activity is done exactly the same way over and over throughout the entire program regardless of which person is completing the task. I am assuming that the individual is competent and is following the checklist's instructions each time in order to have the same repeatable results.

So much of quality control is based on inspection. You have to get out there and inspect the deliverables of the projects and the results of the program work. Quality control is an inspection-driven process. In order to inspect, however, you have to have something to inspect—work results. The inspection of the work results should be documented and signed off by the person reviewing the work.

The final input of quality control is performance reports. Performance reports are a great indicator of the health of the program. It's a safe bet that when the program performance is slipping, the program's quality is also slipping. You know what happens: the program is running late, so people rush to complete their work. Their rushed work

Figure 8-11
Quality control is an inspection-driven process.

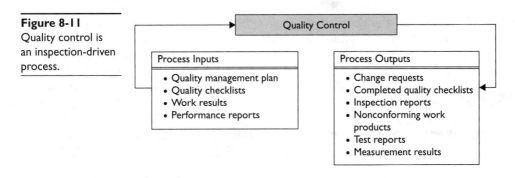

results in more errors, which result in more delays, which start the whole cycle over again. Cost overruns are also an indicator that there could be quality problems, as the variance reports may indicate the need for defect repair.

Examining Quality Control Outputs

There are six outcomes of quality control, as Figure 8-11 demonstrates. The first one you've seen before: change requests can come from just about any process within the program. A change request can be generated from the results of quality control. The requestor may want to change the program scope to reflect a higher demand for quality, trim the scope to meet the quality levels that are being experienced, or change the program scope for any number of ah-ha moments during the quality control inspections.

The checklists that are generated during quality control and the inspection reports that are signed off by the quality control inspectors become part of the program's historical information. The checklists and inspection reports hold people accountable for their work.

Sometimes, and hopefully not often, a program may result in work products that don't conform to the program scope. This means that these deliverables are not of quality and must be dealt with. Usually this will mean someone's got some explaining to do, and resources may have to be assigned to redo the unacceptable work results. No one is happy when the results of the program or project don't conform to the program scope; it's a waste of time and money.

Finally, your program may have test results from your acceptability testing, materials testing, or any other conformance testing that indicates the quality of the deliverables. The testing reports become part of the program's archives and support future decisions in the program and its projects. You'll also have the results of the program measurements for the program deliverables. These measurements will vary from program to program, but most include cost, time, and scope adherence.

Controlling the Program Communications

Programs are big beasts. Consider all of the internal stakeholders for a program: project managers, users of the program's benefits and deliverables, functional managers, project team members, managers in strategic and financial planning, and even more depending on the program. Now consider all the possibilities for external stakeholders: media outlets, government agencies, organizational customers, vendors, buyers, and possibly more.

All of these stakeholders, internal and external, need to hear news, updates, status reports, and other information, depending on which stakeholder you're addressing, about your program. People want to know, need and demand to know, what's happening with your program. You have a lot of communicating to do—a whole bunch. It should come as no surprise, then, that there is an entire program management process dedicated to controlling the program communications. Let's "talk" about it.

Gathering Communication Control Inputs

Before you can start yakking away about your program, you'll need five inputs to control communications, as you can see in Figure 8-12. Since programs are typically flooded with change requests, it makes perfect sense that you'll first collect approved change requests for your program scope. You'll have to communicate to stakeholders about the approved changes and how that'll affect the program's deliverables and benefits.

You'll also rely on your program management's communications management plan. This is the document you created during the program management planning phase. This plan defines how you'll communicate, which is really executing, but you'll use it as an input to communications control to ensure that you're keeping your communication promises. Recall that it answers three questions:

- Who needs what information?
- When is the information needed?
- What modality is the communication expected in?

Sometimes, and sometimes often, management will offer directives for the program, the projects, and other stakeholders involved in the program. These directives will, no doubt, spur some communication actions for the program management team. Of course the content of the directives will determine what's being communicated and how the communication will take place. Basically, when management offers advice, a direction, or a direct order, you're going to talk about it.

Throughout the program, you'll be creating performance reports based on the program's schedule, cost, quality, and scope adherence. These performance reports will serve as an input to the communications control process, because the scores and overall performance of the program may escalate the demand for communications. You'll rely on your stakeholder analysis charts, coupled with the performance reports, to guide your communication efforts to the correct stakeholders and their identified concerns for the program.

Communicating the Program News

Have a look at Figure 8-12 again; there is just one output of the communications control process: the communications management plan. I know that seems a little weird, because the communications management plan is also an input to the communications control process. This is an example of a program's circular reasoning.

One day you probably won't have a communications management plan, so you'll create one. As the program moves forward, you'll reference the communications management plan on how you'll monitor and control communications. Depending on what you're doing in the program, you'll update, rewrite, and adapt the communications

Figure 8-12
The communications control process centers on program communication.

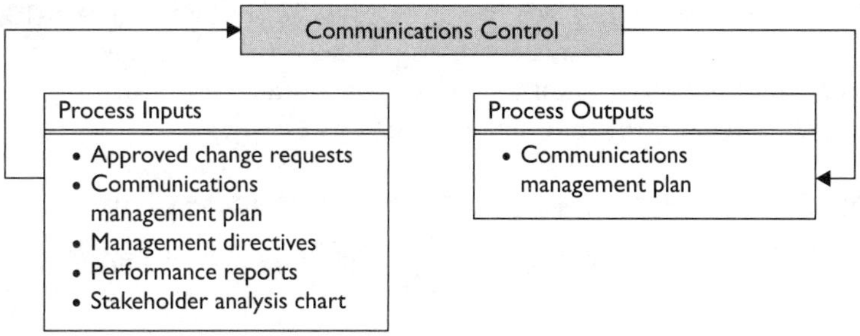

Communications Control

Process Inputs
- Approved change requests
- Communications management plan
- Management directives
- Performance reports
- Stakeholder analysis chart

Process Outputs
- Communications management plan

management plan to reflect new and current expectations. Recall that planning is an iterative process and it's okay to update plans—as long as changes are communicated and approved.

Reporting on the Program Performance

Linked to the communications control process is performance reporting. It should come as no surprise that the program manager will need to keep tabs on the cost, schedule, and quality of the program and complete performance reports to reflect the program's health. Recall that the performance reports are an input to the communications control process—they'll help you determine what types of communications are needed in the program.

Performance reporting is typically automated—consider the reports you probably already create in your project and program management software. At the program level the reports are concerned with the big picture of the program, not the minutiae you'll find at the project level. You can, if you need to, zoom in on key project performances that may have ripple effects to other projects within the program, but you don't have to.

Prepping for Performance Reporting

Think of the most common things you need to measure in a program:

- **Costs**   Accurate cost measurements contribute to the program's performance on the budget.
- **Schedule**   The ability of the program to adapt and react to fluctuations in the program's schedule will determine the program's ability to complete on time.
- **Quality based on work results**   Quality is measured in order to confirm the presence of quality before the customer receives the program deliverables.
- **Variances**   The understanding of why a cost or schedule variance has occurred will help the program prevent the variance from occurring again.
- **Adherence to the program management plan**   The program management team and the constituent projects must follow the program governance, or else chaos creeps into the program.
- **Overall program performance**   It won't be a secret if the program isn't performing well. You and others will know—and it's your responsibility to measure and report where the program is doing well and not-so-well.

Guess what? These are the six inputs, as seen in Figure 8-13, that you'll need to complete the performance reporting. Make sense? You need to measure these six things to reflect how the program is performing and so you can communicate the program's health to the appropriate stakeholders.

Responding to Performance Reporting

Once the program manager has completed the performance reporting, he'll have four outputs of the process, as shown in Figure 8-13. Performance reporting will create some,

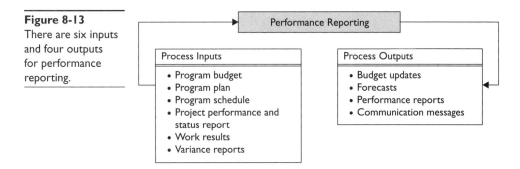

Figure 8-13
There are six inputs and four outputs for performance reporting.

Performance Reporting

Process Inputs	Process Outputs
• Program budget • Program plan • Program schedule • Project performance and status report • Work results • Variance reports	• Budget updates • Forecasts • Performance reports • Communication messages

um, performance reports. These reports will show how well the program is performing and may often offer resolutions for improving program performance.

The biggest challenge is often an update to the program budget due to lacking performance and a request for additional funds. Sometimes there aren't additional funds for the program to receive, so it's a matter of trimming the program scope to reflect the funds that are available to complete the program. While change requests are not a direct output of performance reporting, it may prompt processes such as quality control and issue management, which in turn may call for change requests.

You'll be able to do some forecasting based on your performance reports. You can use earned value management, program simulations, and expert judgment, but often the best predictor is based on what the program's already experienced. You'll want to identify trends and repeatable delays—or gains—and work to attack those or exploit them.

Of course all of this performance reporting and forecasting needs to be shared with your program stakeholders—and that's the last output of this process. You'll create communication messages such as e-mails, memos, reports, web site updates—and whatever else is appropriate for your program to communicate the good or less-than-good news.

Monitoring and Controlling the Program Risk

I know you remember all the fun I talked about in Chapter 6 on risk management planning. This is the twin brother to that conversation—risk monitoring and controlling. This action-packed process is all about ensuring that you and your team are following your risk management plans to conduct several activities:

- Ongoing risk identification
- Tracking identified risks
- Implementing your risk response plans
- Determining the effectiveness of risk responses
- Working with projects to resolve their risks when needed
- Escalating risks that haven't been resolved

Risk monitoring and controlling happens as soon as the program execution begins. Recall that the planning, execution, and monitoring and controlling activities are iterative by nature, and they naturally overlap within a program. As new risks are identified, you'll shove them back to the planning processes, incorporate your plans into execution, and then balance the execution with these monitoring and controlling processes. That's just amazing, I know.

Starting the Risk Control Process

There are five inputs to the risk monitoring and control process, and you've already created these inputs during the planning processes. Keep in mind that as the details of the program change and evolve, so to will the risks and their characteristics. You'll likely be moving from these processes back to planning to update your findings and risk management approach. Figure 8-14 shows all the risk monitoring and control inputs that you'll need to get started.

The risk response plan is the mother of the risk monitoring and controlling activities, because it has identified the program risks and shares what your plan of attack for the risk events may be. As your program is executed in parallel with these processes, this plan dictates the agreed risk responses while this process tracks the effectiveness of each response. You'll want to make certain that your risk responses, mitigation, transference, and even your contingency plans are valid and that they're working.

In tandem with the risk response plan, you'll use the list of risks and their priority levels to address what you're monitoring throughout the project. As the program moves toward each milestone, the priority of current risks will become more important than risks downstream. In other words, a sliding window based on the program's completion will reveal current risks that need to be monitored and controlled.

The last three inputs to monitoring and controlling should be fairly obvious by now. You'll use the program work breakdown structure (PWBS) to help highlight risks in the different parts of the PWBS and to assist you and your program management team to identify any new risks that could be lurking in the shadows or introduced by changes to the scope and the PWBS. You'll rely on performance reports, as a program that's not healthy is probably taking on risks of failure due to schedule, costs, and quality issues.

Finally, you'll rely on the risk register to be the database of program risks and their trends, status, and outcomes. The risk register is a centralized database of program risks and their characteristics. You'll use the risk register, like the list of prioritized risks input,

Figure 8-14
The risk monitoring and controlling process seeks to contain risks.

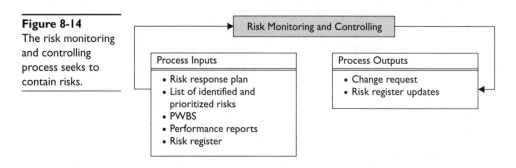

to see current risks within the program, but the risk register should offer more details and characteristics of the risks you've identified in the program.

Completing Risk Monitoring and Control

Figure 8-14 has some good news for you: there are just two outputs to know from risk monitoring and control. The first output is your favorite, I'm sure: change requests. Change requests can be generated from risk monitoring and control based on several factors, including:

- The impact of the risk increases, so a change request is made to change materials, to hire a vendor, or to trim the risk from the program.

- The program has incurred a schedule delay risk, so a change request is created to trim the program scope in order to meet the program's deadline.

- The program has realized a budget risk, so a change request may be created to trim the scope as a way to complete the program with the current amount of funds without asking for more monies.

- Quality risks have been identified, so a change request is generated to lower the quality expectations, change materials, or change services.

- The program's performance is beyond what was expected, so a change request is generated to add more deliverables to the program scope.

The second output of the risk monitoring and controlling process deals with new risks you've identified and the outcome of your planned risk responses. First, you and your program team are to be on the constant lookout for new risks that may enter into the program. When a new risk is identified, the risk register is updated with the risk and its characteristics, impact, and probability. The risk is moved back into the planning processes, where a detailed assessment of the risk can made.

The risk register is also updated to reflect the outcome of your risk responses. You will need to record the validity and accuracy of your risk responses in the risk register to track how well your response worked—and to use this information as part of your lessons-learned activities in the program. Of course, programs sometimes get lucky, and perceived risks don't happen at all—these dodged bullets also need to be recorded in the risk register.

Administering Program Contracts

This process is all about managing the relationship between the buyers in the program and the sellers providing resources to the program. The program manager works to ensure that the sellers are living up to the terms as defined in their contracts—and she also works to ensure that her organization is also keeping up their end of the agreement. For your exam you'll want to note that this process is specifically at the program level; it is not concerned with the individual procurement processes that are likely happening within the individual projects.

This process is a tricky one, because there are so many implications when a program manager monitors contracts. First, a deal is a deal; whatever the contract says and both parties have agreed to is what has to happen in the program. This means that there can be legal implications for both parties if they don't abide by the terms of the contract.

Besides the legal implications of the contract, there are also deadlines, budgets, and political issues that swarm around the contract. Sometimes when I teach, a participant will say that if a seller misses their deadline they'll sue them, or there's cost penalties for the vendor. That may be true, but I am certain everyone in the program would much rather just have the deadline met rather than face a reduction in fees or the nastiness of a lawsuit. If a contract falls through, then there's also the chance of bad publicity surrounding the contract and the program. No one wants that—well, no one other than the attorneys.

Starting Contract Administration

Figure 8-15 shows the six inputs you'll need to start the contract administration process. Of course you've got to have a contract—you'll need something to control. The terms of the contract that both parties have agreed to really override everything else; promises, handshakes, and verbal agreements all disappear when you're reviewing a signed contract.

You'll also have two plans that'll guide this process. The first is the program management plan, as it'll address all issues of the program where a contract may be integrated. Consider the nine knowledge areas and where contracts can come into play:

- Scope
- Time
- Cost
- Quality
- Human resources
- Communications
- Risks
- Procurement

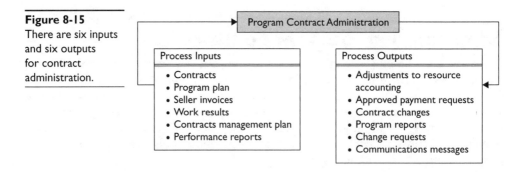

Figure 8-15
There are six inputs and six outputs for contract administration.

Program Contract Administration

Process Inputs	Process Outputs
• Contracts	• Adjustments to resource accounting
• Program plan	• Approved payment requests
• Seller invoices	• Contract changes
• Work results	• Program reports
• Contracts management plan	• Change requests
• Performance reports	• Communications messages

These nine knowledge areas from the program management plan will be used in conjunction with the contracts management plan. Recall that this output from the planning process group details how contracts will be created, how they will be administered, and how both parties will keep their agreements. It also defines the penalties for both parties if they don't adhere to the contract. You may also need the contracts management plan to define how claims will be administered or escalated to legal ramifications.

The seller invoices and the work results are both needed for the contractor to get paid. You'll want to see the evidence of the work completed in full and in accordance with the contract in relation to the invoices the seller will provide. The contract itself should define the payment system for the vendor to follow; for example, a contract may offer a 1 percent discount if the invoice is paid within 10 days; otherwise, it's paid in full within 30 days.

NOTE The discounted rate for early payment is sometimes said as "1 percent net 10, otherwise net 30." It means pay me in 10 days and I'll slice off a bit for early payment. Otherwise, wait and pay me the whole thing. The small discount is good cash flow for the vendor. As a vendor myself I love it, but sometimes the small discount isn't worth the hassle for the vendor, so I'm waiting for the mailman and my check. If you'd like to send me a check, just e-mail me, and we'll figure something out.

The final input to this process is the performance reports you'll create throughout the program. Performance reports traditionally show how well the program is performing, but you can also create them to track how well the vendors are doing their work. Performance reports may be used to assure that the vendor is completing their work according to terms in their contract.

Completing Contract Administration

There are six juicy outputs of contract administration—all of which are neatly displayed in Figure 8-15. The first output is all about the costs of the resources your program consumes. The most common resource is people—and people, the labor in your program, cost money. If your program has contracted labor, it's easy to see that the more labor you use, the more it'll cost your program.

The second resource is the materials, equipment, and facilities your program relies on. This is where wasted materials, idle equipment, and facilities that aren't being utilized can suck a program's budget dry. This output is the clarification, reduction, or relinquishment of resources that aren't being properly utilized.

An input to this process was a seller invoice. Once you've approved the work, you'll also approve the invoice. I hope you do, especially if I'm the vendor wanting to get paid. This process creates an approved payment request, and the vendor and the program move along. No surprises here.

A surprise you may find, however, is the desire to change the contract. Contract changes can be requested because a vendor or seller wants to renegotiate the terms of the contract in relation to conditions in the program, changes to the program scope, the schedule, the cost of materials, or just about anything else the program contract covers—or fails to cover. Changes to the contract can also stem directly from change requests in the program. Contract administration usually relies on a contract change control system, and many contracts define how changes to the contract may come about.

The final two outputs of this process are a snap. First you'll have program reports that measure and document how the program is doing in relation to the vendors involved in the program. These reports can be included with the program's performance report, but they're always included as part of the program's archives.

The final output of this process, and the final output for this chapter, is communication messages. You and your vendor need to talk. It's always ideal to leave a paper trail between the vendor and the program so you've some evidence of conversations that have happened. While I say this, I'll also say that regardless of what communication messages have been created between you and the vendor, the contract always, always, overrides everything else.

Chapter Summary

I bet you're glad to see the end of this chapter! It was jam-packed with all sorts of goodness. Monitoring and controlling is a big, big process group that all begins with the integrated change control. The integrated change control process examines any change that may be introduced to the program and considers the change's impact on the different facets of the program.

From integrated change control you learned about the specific monitoring and controlling processes, starting with resource control. Resources, including people, equipment, materials, and facilities, have to be monitored and controlled—in terms of not just time utilization, but also costs that are associated with each resource. A program manager wants to get the best usage of the resource for the best price of the resource.

Throughout the program you'll encounter issues, so they'll need to be monitored and controlled—as well as documented. Issues are documented in the issue register, and as the issue is escalated and resolved, or the conditions surrounding the issue change, the issue documentation is updated.

Probably the biggest chunk of processes discussed in this chapter was the triple constraints all projects and programs have: scope, schedule, and cost control. Scope control is about protecting the program scope from non-value-added change, while considering and approving relevant changes that are good for the program. Typically when the scope is changed, there's a need for additional time and additional costs, but not always. Both schedule and cost control are concerned with maintaining and improving the performance of the program and with removing non-value-added changes.

Quality control is the process that aims to keep mistakes out of the customers' hands by ensuring that the work is completed according to the demands of the program scope. Quality control is an iterative process, and it is driven by inspection. The results of testing, measurements, inspection reports, and checklists all contribute to historical information for the program.

Two processes that are closely associated are communications control and performance reporting. The first, communications control, aims to manage the flow of communications among the stakeholders of the program and to keep stakeholders abreast of issues and resolutions within the program. The second, performance reporting, is sharing the performance reports, forecasts, budget updates, and other communication messages with the program stakeholders.

A risk is an uncertain event or condition that may help or harm the program. Risk control is the process to ensure that the program is following the risk response and to check the validity of the proposed risk responses. Change requests and updates to the risk register were the two outputs of this process.

Finally, you learned about the program contract administration and all the fun you can have with it. Basically, this process is concerned with the vendor and the buyer both living up to the terms of the contract. Communication messages, change requests, approved invoices, and reporting were a few of the outputs of this process.

For your PgMP examination you must be familiar with the processes I've covered in this chapter. I know, there are a bunch of them. I encourage you to create some flash-cards for the terms and facts as part of your study material, but especially for this chapter, as there are tons of terms and a lot of facts to forget. Keep moving forward—I've got confidence that you can pass your exam.

Key Terms

Communications control   A monitoring and controlling process to manage program communication among the program stakeholders.

Cost control   A monitoring and controlling process to monitor, control, approve, decline, and respond to changes to the program costs.

Effort-driven activities   The more effort that is applied, the less time the activity may take to complete.

Integrated change control   A process to approve and decline program changes by examining all of the areas the change may affect in the program. These areas include scope, time, cost, quality, human resources, communications, risk, and procurement.

Issue   A topic that needs direction and determination to reach a resolution. Issue resolution can go in several different directions, and usually there's some turmoil and opposing views on each side of the proposed outcome of the issue.

Issue management and control   A monitoring and controlling process to facilitate the documentation, management, and resolution of program issues.

Issue owner   The person that is responsible for reaching a decision on an issue.

Parkinson's Law   A law that states that work will expand to fill the amount of time allotted to it.

Perform quality control   A monitoring and controlling process to manage the program quality; it is an inspection-driven process to keep mistakes from reaching the program customers.

Performance reporting   A monitoring and controlling process that works in tandem with the communications control process to report on the health of the program in all areas.

Program change requests   Documented requests to change the program scope.

Program contract administration   A monitoring and controlling process to ensure that the buyers and sellers are both following the terms of the program contracts.

Program resource   A human resource, or else equipment, materials, or facilities that contribute to the program work.

Resource control   A monitoring and controlling process to control the utilization of all program resources, including human resources, materials, facilities, and equipment.

Resource management plan   Defines what resources, such as equipment, plants, test beds, data centers, materials, tools, real estate leases, and other non-human resources will be needed, when they'll be needed, and what their costs are.

Risk monitoring and control   A monitoring and controlling process to ensure that new risks are being identified, existing risks are being monitored, and the planned responses for risk events are monitored for their effectiveness.

Schedule control   A monitoring and controlling process to manage and react to changes in the program schedule.

Scope control   A monitoring and controlling process to control, approve, and decline changes to the program scope.

Staffing management plan   Defines when human resources will be brought onto and released from the program, how the resources will be managed and utilized, and their associated costs.

The Law of Diminishing Returns   As more investment is made, the overall return from that investment diminishes. You cannot exponentially add labor to reduce the duration of a task and maintain the yield (profit) the task represents.

Questions

1. Marcy, the program manager of the BHF Program, has just received notice that a change to the program scope will need to be included in her program. Marcy needs to evaluate the change to see how the change may affect all of the knowledge areas within the program. Which monitoring and controlling process can help Marcy evaluate the change?

   A. Integrated change control

   B. Risk monitoring and controlling

   C. Contract change control

   D. Program contract administration

2. A change has recently been approved for Mike's program. Mike has updated the program scope to reflect the change, but what must be updated next?

   A. Integrated change control

    B. Earned value management

    C. Program contract

    D. Program work breakdown structure

3. Your program management team has encouraged training on a new material your program will be using. They want to offer the training to reduce the possibilities of mistakes in the program when using the new material. The training is an example of what?

    A. Defect repair

    B. Defect validation

    C. Preventive actions

    D. Risk identification

4. All of the following are examples of resources except for which one?

    A. Leased equipment

    B. Materials

    C. People

    D. Schedule

5. Jason is the project manager for a project in the JII Program. He has encouraged his team to add extra features in the software his project is creating for the program. When a project is creating things outside of the program scope that consume the assigned budget, this is known by what term?

    A. Value-added change

    B. Integrated change control

    C. Scope management

    D. Gold plating

6. Why are telephones sometimes considered a poor method of communicating?

    A. Because telephone calls can be disconnected.

    B. Because technology may not always mesh among telephone providers.

    C. Because telephone calls do not allow for ad hoc conversations.

    D. Because telephone calls do not allow for non-verbal communications.

7. All of the following approaches are ideal methods for resolving issues within a program except for which one?

    A. Assigning an issue owner

    B. Modifying the program scope

    C. Changing the program requirements

    D. Adding to the program budget

8. Where are program issues documented?

   A. Issue log

   B. Issue register

   C. Risk register

   D. Issue database

9. Mary, a project manager in your program, has called you, the program manager, and demanded that you add a change to program scope. You agree with Mary that the change request should be entertained. What must Mary do to move forward with her change request?

   A. Add the change request to the scope and complete integrated change control herself.

   B. Document the change request in a change request form.

   C. Add the change to the program scope herself, as she is a project manager.

   D. Create a change request charter justifying the change request.

10. A program is over budget, and its schedule is slipping. Management has demanded a change to the program scope. What type of change could this program consider?

    A. Anything that management demands

    B. A change to reduce the program scope

    C. A change to add additional funds to the program scope

    D. A change to add additional time to the program schedule

11. You are the program manager for the UGF Program. This program has a budget of $47,500,000. The program was supposed to be 55 percent complete at this time, but due to some delays it is only 40 percent complete. The program has also spent $28,300,000 to date. What is the planned value for this program?

    A. $19,000,000

    B. $26,125,000

    C. $28,300,000

    D. There is not enough information to know the planned value

12. You are the program manager for the UGF Program. This program has a budget of $47,500,000. The program was supposed to be 55 percent complete at this time, but due to some delays it is only 40 percent complete. The program has also spent $28,300,000 to date. What is the cost performance index for this program?

    A. 0.67

    B. 0.72

    C. –$9,300,000

    D. $19,000,000

13. You are the program manager for the UGF Program. This program has a budget of $47,500,000. The program was supposed to be 55 percent complete at

this time, but due to some delays it is only 40 percent complete. The program has also spent $28,300,000 to date. What is the estimate to complete for this program?

A. $70,750,000

B. $42,450,000

C. $23,250,000

D. $9,300,000

14. You are the program manager for the UGF Program. This program has a budget of $47,500,000. The program was supposed to be 55 percent complete at this time, but due to some delays it is only 40 percent complete. The program has also spent $28,300,000 to date. What is the schedule performance index for this program?

A. 0.67

B. 0.73

C. –$19,000,000

D. –$7,125,000

15. Management wants to know, given current conditions within the program, what the expected variance at completion for your program will be. Which formula will you use to provide this information?

A. EV/PV

B. BAC/CPI

C. EAC – AC

D. BAC – EAC

16. All of the following are outputs of the schedule control process except for which one?

A. Change requests

B. Information for stakeholders

C. Schedule variances

D. Program schedule updates

17. A program is moving ahead of schedule and the program manager, Jane, is able to return a piece of rented equipment eight months earlier than what was anticipated. This has saved the program $83,000. What should Jane do with the program savings?

A. Keep it in the program as a buffer against unknown risks.

B. Keep it in the program as an opportunity to incur new costs.

C. Return in to the program's organization, since the funds are no longer needed for the equipment.

D. Return it to the program's organization with an opportunity to use the funds should the program need them later.

18. Which one of the following is not an activity of the risk monitoring and controlling process?

    A. Completing quantitative risk analysis

    B. Tracking identified risks

    C. Executing risk response plans

    D. Determining if new risks have developed

19. Which one of the following is an output of the communications control process?

    A. Communications management plan

    B. Performance reports

    C. Stakeholder analysis charts

    D. Approved change requests

20. A vendor has submitted an invoice for the work they have completed in your program. You have reviewed the work results and found them to be accurate. What should you do next in regard to the vendor's invoice?

    A. Consult the program contract process to determine the next steps.

    B. Approve the payment request.

    C. Complete a performance report of the vendor.

    D. Close the vendor's contract, as they have completed the program work.

Questions and Answers

1. Marcy, the program manager of the BHF Program, has just received notice that a change to the program scope will need to be included in her program. Marcy needs to evaluate the change to see how the change may affect all of the knowledge areas within the program. Which monitoring and controlling process can help Marcy evaluate the change?

    A. Integrated change control

    B. Risk monitoring and controlling

    C. Contract change control

    D. Program contract administration

    A. Integrated change control is the best answer, because it does examine all of the knowledge areas to determine how the change affects the program as a whole. B, risk monitoring and controlling, is incorrect, because this is only one of the areas that integrated change control examines. C and D both deal with the procurement knowledge area, so these choices are also incorrect.

2. A change has recently been approved for Mike's program. Mike has updated the program scope to reflect the change, but what must be updated next?

    A. Integrated change control

    B. Earned value management

C. Program contract

D. Program work breakdown structure

D. Once the program scope change has been approved and it has been fleshed into the program scope, the program work breakdown structure is updated next. A, integrated change control, is incorrect, because this would happen before the change has been approved. B and C are not relevant, because you don't have to use earned value management to consider a change request and not all program changes will affect the contracts.

3. Your program management team has encouraged training on a new material your program will be using. They want to offer the training to reduce the possibilities of mistakes in the program when using the new material. The training is an example of what?

A. Defect repair

B. Defect validation

C. Preventive actions

D. Risk identification

C. This is an example of a preventive action, as it wants to stop mistakes with the new material from entering the program. A and B are both incorrect, as these both deal with working with errors that have entered into the program. D, risk identification, is not a valid choice, as this question is looking to prevent mistakes, not identify risks.

4. All of the following are examples of resources except for which one?

A. Leased equipment

B. Materials

C. People

D. Schedule

D. The program schedule is not a resource, so this choice is correct. Choices A, B, and C are all examples of resources, so these choices are wrong for this question.

5. Jason is the project manager for a project in the JII Program. He has encouraged his team to add extra features in the software his project is creating for the program. When a project is creating things outside of the program scope that consume the assigned budget, this is known by what term?

A. Value-added change

B. Integrated change control

C. Scope management

D. Gold plating

D. When a program manager or a project manager adds things to the program scope in order to consume the entire assigned budget, this is an example of gold plating. The remaining funds in the budget should be returned to the organization rather than adding things to the program scope that weren't required. A, value-added change, is incorrect, because the question is dealing with adding unapproved extras and changes to the scope. If it were a value-added change, then it'd be an approved request. Choice B and C are incorrect choices for this answer, because neither choice identifies the unapproved changes to consume the assigned budget.

6. Why are telephones sometimes considered a poor method of communicating?

   A. Because telephone calls can be disconnected.

   B. Because technology may not always mesh among telephone providers.

   C. Because telephone calls do not allow for ad hoc conversations.

   D. Because telephone calls do not allow for non-verbal communications.

   D. Because fifty-five percent of all communication is non-verbal, telephone calls are often considered a poor method of communicating.

7. All of the following approaches are ideal methods for resolving issues within a program except for which one?

   A. Assigning an issue owner

   B. Modifying the program scope

   C. Changing the program requirements

   D. Adding to the program budget

   D. Simply adding funds to the program budget won't resolve a program issue. Choices A, B, and C are all based on PMI's *The Standard for Program Management,* so these choices are incorrect for this question, because these choices are examples of resolving issues.

8. Where are program issues documented?

   A. Issue log

   B. Issue register

   C. Risk register

   D. Issue database

   A. Issues are stored in the issue log. There is not an issue register or issue database, so choices B and D are both incorrect. Choice C is incorrect, because the risk register is for risks only—not program issues. When an issue is deemed a risk, it may be moved to the risk register and managed there.

9. Mary, a project manager in your program, has called you, the program manager, and demanded that you add a change to program scope. You agree with Mary that the change request should be entertained. What must Mary do to move forward with her change request?

A. Add the change request to the scope and complete integrated change control herself.

B. Document the change request in a change request form.

C. Add the change to the program scope herself, as she is a project manager.

D. Create a change request charter justifying the change request.

B. Change requests must be documented to be considered. Choices A and C are both incorrect, as Mary is a project manager and isn't capable of approving changes to the program scope on her own accord. D is incorrect, since there isn't a change request charter form—this is not a valid term.

10. A program is over budget and is slipping on the program schedule. Management has demanded a change to the program scope. What type of change could this program consider?

A. Anything that management demands

B. A change to reduce the program scope

C. A change to add additional funds to the program scope

D. A change to add additional time to the program schedule

B. Often when a program is over budget and behind on schedule, an organization may elect to reduce the program scope to complete the program with the amount of funds and time available. Choices A, C, and D are not valid choices for a program that is over budget and behind schedule.

11. You are the program manager for the UGF Program. This program has a budget of $47,500,000. The program was supposed to be 55 percent complete at this time, but due to some delays it is only 40 percent complete. The program has also spent $28,300,000 to date. What is the planned value for this program?

A. $19,000,000

B. $26,125,000

C. $28,300,000

D. There is not enough information to know the planned value.

B. The planned value is $26,125,000 and is calculated by finding the percent complete of where the program is supposed to be at this point in time. A, $19,000,000, represents the earned value of the program—the actual percentage of the program that is complete. C, $28,300,000, is the actual costs the program has incurred to date. D is incorrect, because there is enough information to find the planned value.

12. You are the program manager for the UGF Program. This program has a budget of $47,500,000. The program was supposed to be 55 percent complete at this time, but due to some delays it is only 40 percent complete. The program has also spent $28,300,000 to date. What is the cost performance index for this program?

   A. 0.67

   B. 0.72

   C. −$9,300,000

   D. $19,000,000

   A. The CPI is 0.67 and is calculated by using the formula EV/AC; in this instance that'd be $19,000,000 divided by $28,300,000. All of the other choices do not reflect the cost performance index, so they are wrong.

13. You are the program manager for the UGF Program. This program has a budget of 47,500,000. The program was supposed to be 55 percent complete at this time, but due to some delays it is only 40 percent complete. The program has also spent $28,300,000 to date. What is the estimate to complete for this program?

   A. $70,750,000

   B. $42,450,000

   C. $23,250,000

   D. $9,300,000

   B. The estimate to complete is how much more money the program needs to complete the program scope given current conditions in the program. The formula is EAC − AC. Choices A, C, and D do not reflect the estimate to complete the program, so these choices are wrong.

14. You are the program manager for the UGF Program. This program has a budget of 47,500,000. The program was supposed to be 55 percent complete at this time, but due to some delays it is only 40 percent complete. The program has also spent $28,300,000 to date. What is the schedule performance index for this program?

   A. 0.67

   B. 0.73

   C. −$19,000,000

   D. −$7,125,000

   B. The schedule performance index is 0.73 and is calculated by using the formula EV/PV. Choices A, C, and D are not accurate calculations.

15. Management wants to know, given current conditions within the program, what the expected variance at completion for your program will be. Which formula will you use to provide this information?

   A. EV/PV

   B. BAC/CPI

C. EAC – AC

D. BAC – EAC

D. Management wants to know what the expected variance for the entire program will be, so choice D is the correct choice. Choice A is the formula for finding the schedule performance index. B is the formula for finding the estimate at completion. C is the formula for finding the estimate to complete.

16. All of the following are outputs of the schedule control process except for which one?

   A. Change requests

   B. Information for stakeholders

   C. Schedule variances

   D. Program schedule updates

   C. A schedule variance will not occur as a result of the schedule control process. Choices A, B, and D all are outputs of the schedule control process.

17. A program is moving ahead of schedule, and the program manager, Jane, is able to return a piece of rented equipment eight months earlier than what was anticipated. This has saved the program $83,000. What should Jane do with the program savings?

   A. Keep it in the program as a buffer against unknown risks.

   B. Keep it in the program as an opportunity to incur new costs.

   C. Return in to the program's organization, since the funds are no longer needed for the equipment.

   D. Return it to the program's organization with an opportunity to use the funds should the program need them later.

   C. Part of cost control is to return unneeded funds to the organization when they are no longer needed, so this is the best choice for the question. Choice A is incorrect, as quantitative analysis is the proper method for creating a contingency reserve. Choice B is incorrect, because the program shouldn't incur new costs unless changes have been approved for the costs and scope. Choice D is also incorrect, as the performing organization would need to justify the needs for additional funding regardless of what's happened in the program prior to the need.

18. Which one of the following is not an activity of the risk monitoring and controlling process?

   A. Completing quantitative risk analysis

   B. Tracking identified risks

   C. Executing risk response plans

   D. Determining if new risks have developed

   A. Quantitative risk analysis is part of risk planning, not monitoring and controlling, so this choice is correct. Choices B, C, and D are all activities that are included with the risk monitoring and controlling process, so these choices are incorrect.

19. Which one of the following is an output of the communications control process?

   A. Communications management plan

   B. Performance reports

   C. Stakeholder analysis charts

   D. Approved change requests

   A. There is only one output of the communications control process, and that is the communications management plan. Choices B, C, and D are all inputs to the process, so these choices are incorrect for this question.

20. A vendor has submitted an invoice for the work they have completed in your program. You have reviewed the work results and found them to be accurate. What should you do next in regard to the vendor's invoice?

   A. Consult the program contract process to determine the next steps.

   B. Approve the payment request.

   C. Complete a performance report of the vendor.

   D. Close the vendor's contract as they have completed the program work.

   B. If the work has been completed and approved, you should approve the payment request. A is incorrect, as this is what the program contract process calls for. C is incorrect, as this may come after the payment unless your contract specifically has this stipulation as a requirement for payment. D is also incorrect, because vendors may have intermittent payments without completing all of their contracted work. Consider a contract that may last for several years.

Closing the Program

In this chapter, you will
- Examine the program deliverable
- Complete the lessons learned documentation
- Administer performance reviews
- Close the program
- Close program components
- Celebrate because the program is done

The two happiest days in a program manager's life are the day the program starts and the day the program ends. The clouds roll back, the sun shines on your face, there's a rainbow off in the distance, and a roaming choir breaks out with Beethoven's "Ode to Joy." It's a brilliant, happy day. Okay, that may be a slight exaggeration, but gosh, closing that program feels pretty darn good. Before you pop the cork on the champagne bottle or cut any ribbons, there are some final activities that you, the program manager, must do.

The closing process group is the formal process of moving the program deliverables and benefits into operations—and getting the program stakeholder to officially sign off on the program and accept all that you've created. Once the deliverables have been passed off, the program and all of its parts are closed, terminated, and finished.

The closing of the program is proof that the deliverables have been accepted, or in some unpleasant scenarios, it provides evidence of the work the program did up until the program was prematurely terminated. Programs can be closed for poor performance on cost, schedule, quality, and a number of other reasons. Once the program is closing, for better or for worse, the documentation of the program is archived as part of your organizational process assets. This documentation is more than just your lessons learned; it includes contracts, legal filings for intellectual property that's been created, and details on preventive maintenance and support of the program's deliverables.

Just as you're thrilled the program is done, so are your program team members and the constituent project team members. When the program is closed down, the human resources are released from the program. Sometimes the release of resources is a sensitive issue, as the resources may also be let go from the organization if there isn't a position or work for them to do post-program. Just as human resources are released from the program, so too are resources such as facilities, equipment, and materials.

Preparing for Program Closure

While most of the attention to closing happens at the grand finale of the program, the truth is that closing really happens throughout the program. You'll close projects, portions of your program, and you'll complete lessons learned, documentation, and archiving as you move along. As you close projects and non-project activities that aren't viable for the program any longer, you'll complete the activities in the closing process group.

The whole goal of closing the program isn't just to be done; the goal of closing the program is to get the sponsor and the customer of the program to formally accept the program deliverables. This formal acceptance comes about by the sponsor and the customer verifying that the deliverables of the program have been met and signing off on closure documents. You'll do this not only for the whole program, but also for the constituent projects within the program.

Preparing to Close the Program

Closing the program is all about getting the customer, and often the program sponsor too, to accept the deliverables of the program. This is the primary input to the close program process; it's tough to close the program when the deliverables are not acceptable. While this is the primary input, there are six outputs of the close program process, as you can see in Figure 9-1. The approved deliverables may not be just for the program. Recall that the closure of a program's project may contribute benefits to the program, so these need to be approved as well in order to close the program.

Lessons learned are a big part of program closure. It's essential to complete lessons learned as the program moves forward, not just as the final closure procedure winds down. Think of how big and juicy some programs are—it'd be tough, if not impossible, to recall all of the things that did or didn't work throughout the program. Lessons learned are considered an input and an output of program closure, because this documentation is cumulative through the program. Once the entire program is closed, all of the lessons learned are archived with the program documentation.

 NOTE I often get asked in my seminars, "Why do I need to write the lessons I've learned if I've already learned them?" You document what you've learned for two reasons: first, others learn from you, and your documentation helps that process. Second, the documentation of what you've learned holds you accountable to the learning for future programs.

Figure 9-1
There are six inputs and six outputs of closing a program.

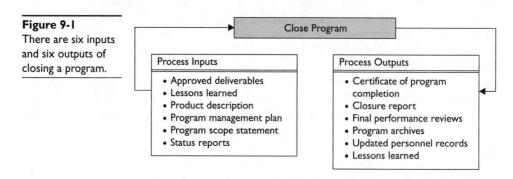

Close Program	
Process Inputs	**Process Outputs**
• Approved deliverables	• Certificate of program
• Lessons learned	completion
• Product description	• Closure report
• Program management plan	• Final performance reviews
• Program scope statement	• Program archives
• Status reports	• Updated personnel records
	• Lessons learned

The product description is an input to the close program process, because the deliverables and benefits of the program and constituent projects should be in support of the product description. Coupled with the product description is its decomposition to the program scope. These two documents are what the customer and the program sponsor are likely to have in mind as they review the deliverables that your program has created. What the program has created had better be in support of the scope and product description or there will be some unhappy people.

The program management plan is also considered an input to the closing process, because this plan defines what each component of the program and its knowledge areas will be accountable for. For example, consider the schedule, the costs, the identified risks, and the quality mechanisms that the program management plan will be able to reference during closing.

The last input to the close program process is the status reports that have been created to date. Since the close program process happens throughout the program, the status reports will reflect the health and performance of the program to date. Consider a program that has delivered its first benefit, but the status reports show the cost performance index as being very low, or the schedule variance to be high. The status reports, timeline, budget, and scope of the program are all considered to determine how the program should move forward.

Examining the Close Program Outputs

When the entire program is closed, the program manager, the program sponsor, and often the program customer will sign the certificate of program closure. This document, the first output of the close program process as seen in Figure 9-1, officially closes the program. This document formalizes the acceptance of the program deliverables and verifies that the program is closed.

In tandem with the certificate of program closure, the program manager will create closure reports that reflect the performance and deliverables of the program. The closure reports may be created throughout the program as projects are closed, as non-project activities are closed, or if the program is terminated early. These reports are archived with the program documentation.

The program manager, sometimes with the program sponsor, should review the performance of the program management team and the project managers as the projects and the program are closed. These reviews track the performance of the projects, that of the program as a whole, and how the individuals on the teams contributed to the project's success or failure. The final performance reviews often contribute to the individual's performance review and may be tied to a rewards and recognitions program in the organization. These reviews contribute to the personnel records of the workers as well.

I've already mentioned lessons learned a bunch—and I hope you've gotten the importance of this documentation for the real world and for passing your PgMP examination. Still, the lessons learned documentation is a key output of the closing process, as it documents what you've learned. As you know by now, lessons learned and all the other documents, contracts, plans, files, and communiqués are all stashed away in the program archives never to be seen again. Just testing! For your PgMP examination you'll use these program archives for ongoing support, maintenance, and future programs that may be similar to this program you've closed.

Closing Program Components

The projects within a program are rarely going to last as long as the program itself. You'll schedule most projects as big chunks of work to create the benefits, the deliverables, for the organization. As projects complete their project scope, you'll confirm that the projects have indeed met their project scopes and that they may close according to plan.

The project closure for a program isn't the same as an independent project closure. The project closure in a program has to verify that the projects have completed their deliverables that other projects may be waiting for—and the program manager has to validate that project closure was led by the project manager and the project was successfully closed. Typically, projects move through five process groups, much like a program:

- Initiating
- Planning
- Executing
- Monitoring and controlling
- Closing

Once a project closes, the project resources can be reallocated back into operations, or more likely, the resources can be moved onto other projects within the program. The idea of moving resources back into the program's projects assumes that a resource can be shifted from one project in the program to another. The idea of realizing project resources also includes materials, equipment, and facilities, not just people.

Prepping to Close a Project

As you can see in Figure 9-2, there are three inputs to the component closure process and five outputs of the process. The first input is cost control for the projects. This makes sense. The project budget is really part of the program budget, and you'll need some accountability for how the project funds were spent to create the things in the project's work breakdown structure. The accumulation of the project budget contributed to the sum of the program budget.

The lessons learned of the project are also created. Now here's a goofy something for you PMPs that are pursuing your PgMP. In *The Project Management Body of Knowledge*, your favorite book in the world outside of this one, lessons learned are technically an executing process in a project. That's right, project management fans, lessons learned are an executing process. Check out the PMBOK, section 4.4.

Figure 9-2
There are three inputs and five outputs of component closure.

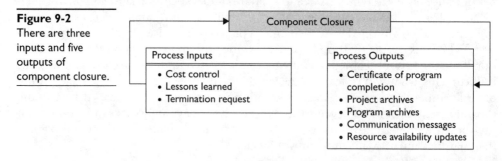

Component Closure

Process Inputs	Process Outputs
• Cost control • Lessons learned • Termination request	• Certificate of program completion • Project archives • Program archives • Communication messages • Resource availability updates

So what does that mean for your PgMP certification? Not much, other than that the lessons learned of a project should be happening throughout the project and then collected at the end of the project closure. The collected project lessons learned are folded into the program's lessons learned and also become part of the program's assets.

The final input to the component closure is the termination request for the constituent component. There will be, from time to time, the desire to kill off a project for various reasons, including these:

- The program or project is behind schedule.
- The program's budget is losing funds.
- The project's quality is poor.
- The program manager has made trade-offs with other projects in the program.
- The project's deliverable is no longer needed.

When a project's deliverable is no longer needed, the project must be terminated. When a project is terminated, the project should still complete scope verification to show what the project has done up to the point that the project was canceled. The project manager should also complete lessons learned and close out the project to reflect the project's work and the organization's investment. The program manager should also complete the lessons for the program and review the project manager's and the project's performance.

Reviewing the Outputs of a Program Component

First off, a program component is usually a project within the program, but not always. A program component could also be non-project activity that happens at the program level but is not duplicated at the project level. For example, you could have a program-centric training program that's not a project but supports the program itself. Or you could have IT support for the entire program, including servers, printers, administrators, and the like. The support isn't a project; it's part of the program.

When you're closing a program component, project or non-project, the intent is identical. You're trying to determine several things:

- Has the component reached its objectives?
- Is this component no longer needed?
- How well has this component performed?
- What activities must happen to dismantle and close the component?
- What will happen to the component resources?

These questions will help the program manager write the closure report and complete the performance reviews for the resources in the program. The closure report specifically answers how well the component performed and contributed to the overall health of the program. The performance reviews should be linked to the personnel records and should require you to update skill sets, work history, and other relevant info that'll be useful for future reference.

Both projects and programs have archives. All of the project information, documentation, plans, communication, and reports should be collected into a centralized project file and then nested into the program archives. This is important, because it will serve as historical information if there's ever an operations-based question that may need to query the specific deliverables and approach of a project within your program.

Project Closing Activities

Program managers are concerned with the activities specific to the program. Projects are within programs, but there's a real distinction between the activities that are unique to the program manager and the activities that should be reserved for the project manager. Now I'll be the first to admit that every organization is different and every organization has its own approach to just how involved the program manager should be in the projects. However, as a general PMI rule, there must be a distinct line between project management and program management.

Closing is one of those gray areas where the project manager and the program manager's activities may overlap just a bit. In program management, there are just three processes unique to closing, the details of this chapter. In project management, however, there are just two processes: closing the project and closing the contracts. Because projects are tucked under the program management umbrella, some programs may elect to centralize all contracting in the program. This means that there's even less control for the project manager to close her contracts. When a project manager closes a project, there are six inputs to closing:

- **Project management plan** Communicates what the project is to do for the program.

- **Contract documentation** Defines what the vendors and sellers are required to do in the project.

- **Enterprise environmental factors** These are the rules and policies that the program governance and the performing organization have established for the project manager.

- **Organizational process assets** These are the forms, software, historical information, templates, and any other tools that will help the project manager close the project.

- **Work performance information** Details on how well the project is performing contribute to the project's closure.

- **Deliverables** The project has to create things for the program and the organization.

These six inputs allow the project manager to close the project, and even a phase of the project, according to plan and in alignment with the rules of the program. The project closure creates four outputs:

- **Administrative closure procedure** This is the documentation, collection, and archiving of all the project communication and reporting.

- **Contract closure procedure** The contract in a project is closed according to the terms of the contract and in alignment with the program governance.
- **Final product, service, or result** When the project's done, there has to be something created for the program; this allows the project and team to be disbanded.
- **Organizational process assets** These are the lessons learned and other contributions to the historical information for the organization.

Closing a program is different than closing a project. The closure of a successful project supports the program moving forward. The program manager and the project manager should communicate and document in the project plan the expectations of each so that there's no confusion as to who does what and when they'll do it. Basically, you want to define the responsibility and roles for project closure to support the goals and rules of the program.

Closing Program Contracts

Closing a program contract can really happen at any point in the program, but it is a specific closing process. This process is about ending a program contract according to the terms of the contract—both the seller and the customer are involved in the process. Both parties want to make certain that the other party has completed its legal obligations and that the program's needs have been met.

Sometimes, and these aren't very happy times, the contract has to be terminated early. There are numerous reasons a contract has to be terminated—quality, poor performance, the contract deliverable is no longer needed. Whatever the reason, the terms of the contract usually provide some detail as to the process and obligations of both parties to terminate the contract early.

Prepping for Contract Closure

I think it's a safe bet to say that in most contracts the vendor delivers as promised, and the organization pays the vendor for their deliverables. Vendors will provide delivery notices to the organization, and that'll lead to, eventually, vendor invoices. Tied to this typical client-vendor relationship in a program is an *acceptance report*. This report confirms that the vendor did indeed provide the things the contract called for. This is the first input to the contract closure process as detailed in Figure 9-3.

You know by now how much PMI (like me!) loves documentation. It's no different with contracts. The contract itself is the primary documentation, but there'll be more—and sometimes a lot more documentation. The statement of work; the request for proposal, bid, or quote; and the vendor's responses; all the way to the contract and the acceptance report—all go into the contract file. In addition, you'll create a contract performance record. These records track how well the vendor has performed on their deliverables, their contributions, and often how their contracted labor helped the program reach its objectives.

Figure 9-3
Contract closure has four inputs and two outputs.

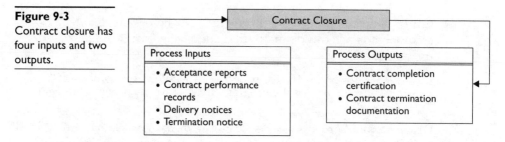

If a contract is completed or if a contract is terminated, both instances require the program manager to inspect the deliverables of the vendor's work and to confirm that the program has received all that it is paying for. In the instance of a terminated contract, the program manager reviews the work that was delivered and reviews the work that was not delivered by the prematurely terminated contract.

Completing Contract Closure

Just as the program and projects have a certificate of completion, so too does the contract. This certificate is evidence that the vendor has completed their obligations to the program and is often linked to the final payment from the organization. Both parties should receive a certificate of completion to show that the contractual obligations have been met.

NOTE   The terms of the contract will override everything else. Whatever handshake promise a vendor provides is overruled by what's in writing. For your PgMP examination know that the contractual agreement is a legally binding agreement between the buyer and the seller.

In those instances when a contract has to be terminated early, it's important to document why the contract has been canceled. This documentation can reflect the vendor performance, communications from the vendor, and claims between the vendor and the performing organization. A claim is a documented disagreement between the vendor and the buyer where one party (and sometimes both) disagrees with the conditions, performance, or payments. The contract should always have an escalation process defined should litigation between the parties arise.

Chapter Summary

When you are closing a program, a contract, or a component of the program, you always confirm and document that it's truly time to close. When you close a component project, for example, the project moves through its own, similar closing processes, but you're confirming that the project truly has met the required scope. When you close a contract, you and the vendor confirm that the contract and deliverables are in sync. And then there's the big cheese: closing the program. When a program is officially and finally closed, the program, the program's customer, and the program sponsor all contribute to the confirmation and agreement of closing the program.

PART II

From time to time a program's component, a program contract, or even an entire program can be terminated earlier than was planned. When a program component, typically a project, is terminated, the reason the project is closed gets documented just as if the project had met its planned conclusion. This mean the project process of scope verification will take place. The same is true for contracts and even for programs: there must be a documented explanation of why the program or contract was terminated early.

Finally, for your PgMP examination, don't be tricked by the closing process. While it's true that there are just three processes in this chapter, it's still an important and sometimes complex portion of a program. According to PMI at the time of publication, the PgMP examination includes approximately 14 questions on the closing processes—that's nearly 8 percent of your exam. Don't shrug off or gloss over these processes—it'll haunt you later if you do.

Key Terms

Certificate of program completion   A document that proves the acceptance of program closure.

Close program process   The formal acceptance of the program's outcome.

Closure report   The final report on the program's health and completion.

Component closure   The program process to close a project within a program or to close a non-project activity within the program.

Contract termination documentation   The formal documentation of why a contract has been terminated before it was originally scheduled to end.

Organizational process assets   The collection of tools, templates, software, and other assets that an organization has to benefit the completion of programs and projects.

Program archives   All of the documentation on the program, contracts, communications, supporting detail, and program projects are archived and become part of organizational process assets.

Project closure   Project activities that close out the project to support the goals of the program.

Resource reallocation   The reassignment of project resources once a project has been closed.

Questions

1. Mary Anne is about to close her program, and she is curious about which stakeholder should be involved in the closure process. Of the following, which stakeholder(s) should be included in the program closure process?

   A. Program steering committee

   B. Program governance board

   C. Program customer

   D. Program stakeholders

2. What must be true before for a program can be closed?

   A. Projects under the program must first be closed.

   B. The program management team must have completed all program processes.

   C. The project resources must be reallocated to the performing organization.

   D. The program customer must complete the contract payment request.

3. All of the following are reviewed during the program's closing process procedures except for which one?

   A. Program scope

   B. Closure documents of the program's constituent projects

   C. Closure documents for the non-project activities

   D. Program budget

4. Which one of the following is an input to the close program process?

   A. Certificate of program completion

   B. Personnel records

   C. Product description

   D. Closure report

5. Martin is closing his program, and he's working with the program sponsor to review the program's deliverables and benefits. Janet, the program sponsor, is very pleased with the program and agrees that the program has met the program scope. What should Martin and the program sponsor do next?

   A. Sign the certificate of program completion.

   B. Complete the program's budget.

   C. Release the program's resources.

   D. Close the constituent projects before closing the program.

6. When does the close program process happen in a program?

   A. Throughout the program as projects and non-project activity are closed

   B. Only when all of the program's deliverables have been approved

   C. As each program is completed, the close program process is started

   D. As the program customer demands

7. What closing process group process facilitates the closure of program projects?

   A. Close program

   B. Scope verification

   C. Component closure

   D. Project closing process group

8. Nancy, a project manager in your program, has just completed her project and is ready to close the project. What roles do you, the program manager, play in Nancy's project closure?

   A. You must facilitate the project closure proceedings, as you're likely the project sponsor.

   B. You must sign off on the project deliverables before Nancy may close the project.

   C. Your program management team must facilitate the close project process.

   D. You will validate and ensure that the project closure has indeed taken place at the project level.

9. Which one of the following is not an input to the component closure process?

   A. Resource availability

   B. Cost control

   C. Lessons learned

   D. Termination request

10. A project within your program is no longer needed, so you have decided to terminate the project. What should happen to the project resources that are no longer needed in the project?

    A. They should be released from the organization.

    B. They should be given a negative review for their poor performance.

    C. They should be reallocated and used where appropriate.

    D. They should be released from the project and assigned to roles according to human resources.

11. You are the program manager of the NOP Program. One of your projects, the ABS Project, has closed. This project required considerable training of several key resources on a new material your organization will now sell. What should you do now that the ABS Project has closed?

    A. Issue a certificate of project completion.

    B. Update the personnel records of the team members on the ABS Project.

    C. Reassign the resources to other program activities.

    D. Complete scope verification of ABS Project.

12. Which one of the following items will not help you complete the contract closure process?

    A. Program WBS

    B. Termination notice

    C. Acceptance reports

    D. Contract performance records

13. A vendor has promised to provide support beyond the closure of the contract. What must you do to ensure that your program receives the support the vendor has promised?

    A. Make certain to remind the vendor of the promised support as the program nears its conclusion.

    B. Withhold payment to the vendor until the promised support has been delivered.

    C. Add the promised support to the program's WBS.

    D. Confirm that the promised support is included in the contract between you and the vendor.

14. What will you need to provide to a vendor when you want to terminate their contract due to poor vendor performance?

    A. Final payment for the vendor's work

    B. Termination notice

    C. Contract documentation

    D. The original proposal the vendor provided

15. You and a vendor are in disagreement about a portion of the program they have been hired to complete. The vendor has issued a claim against your organization, and it appears your program is headed toward a legal battle. What will determine where the lawsuit between you and the vendor is heard?

    A. Where the program is headquartered determines where the lawsuit may take place.

    B. Where the vendor is headquartered determines where the lawsuit may take place.

    C. Whoever files the lawsuit first has precedence as to the locale.

    D. The program's contract will define where the lawsuit may take place.

16. What two things must be documented if you wish to terminate a vendor's contract?

    A. The work that the vendor has performed and the work the vendor has not performed

    B. The contract between your organization and the vendor and the quality of the vendor's work

    C. The contract and the scope verification document

    D. The scope verification document and the termination notice

17. Who must sign off on the program's projects when the projects are completed in the organization?

    A. The project manager

    B. The program stakeholders

    C. The project management team

    D. The program customer

18. The GHB Project in your program has been performing very well. It is on schedule and has no cost variances. You have decided, however, that this project needs to be terminated. Which one of the following is a likely reason why the project should be terminated?

    A. The project manager is not meeting the project scope as planned.

    B. The project resources are not completing their project tasks as assigned.

    C. The program scope has changed.

    D. The program scope has not changed, but the project scope has changed.

19. A project manager reports that he has met all of the requirements of the project scope and is ready to close the project. What must the project manager do with the project customer before he can close the project?

    A. Complete scope verification.

    B. Complete quality control.

    C. Complete quality assurance.

    D. Obtain a termination notice from the program manager.

20. The close program process has six inputs and six outputs. Which output of the close program process is also an input to the close program process?

    A. Approved deliverables

    B. Lessons learned

    C. Personnel records

    D. Program archives

Questions and Answers

1. Mary Anne is about to close her program, and she is curious about which stakeholder should be involved in the closure process. Of the following, which stakeholder(s) should be included in the program closure process?

    A. Program steering committee

    B. Program governance board

    C. Program customer

    D. Program stakeholders

    C. Of the answers listed, only the program customer should be involved in the program closure process. If the program sponsor were a choice (but it's not), that'd be valid as well. A, B, and D are all incorrect choices, because these folks are not involved in the close program process.

2. What must be true before for a program can be closed?

   A. Projects under the program must first be closed.

   B. The program management team must have completed all program processes.

   C. The project resources must be reallocated to the performing organization.

   D. The program customer must complete the contract payment request.

   A. All projects within the program must first be closed before the program may be closed. B is incorrect, because not all processes may be used in every program, and it's not always the program management team that's responsible for completing program processes. C is incorrect, because resources are not always reallocated to the organization. D is incorrect for two reasons: the program may not always have a final payment request, as some programs are completed within an organization. Second, the contract will determine when the payment request is to be made.

3. All of the following are reviewed during the program's closing process procedures except for which one?

   A. Program scope

   B. Closure documents of the program's constituent projects

   C. Closure documents for the non-project activities

   D. Program budget

   D. The program budget is not reviewed as part of the close program process. Choices A, B, and C are incorrect answers, as these are reviewed during the close program processes.

4. Which one of the following is an input to the close program process?

   A. Certificate of program completion

   B. Personnel records

   C. Product description

   D. Closure report

   C. The product description is the only answer that is an input to the close program process. The certificate of program completion, personnel records, and the closure report are actually outputs of the close program process.

5. Martin is closing his program, and he's working with the program sponsor to review the program's deliverables and benefits. Janet, the program sponsor, is very pleased with the program and agrees that the program has met the program scope. What should Martin and the program sponsor do next?

   A. Sign the certificate of program completion.

   B. Complete the program's budget.

   C. Release the program's resources.

   D. Close the constituent projects before closing the program.

A. Janet and Martin can sign the certificate of program completion. Choice B is incorrect, as completing the program's budget is not part of program closure. C is incorrect, as the program resources aren't always people; they may be materials, equipment, and facilities. D is incorrect, as the constituent projects are closed in order for the program scope to be completed.

6. When does the close program process happen in a program?

   A. Throughout the program as projects and non-project activity are closed

   B. Only when all of the program's deliverables have been approved

   C. As each program is completed, the close program process is started

   D. As the program customer demands

   A. The close program process happens throughout the life of a program, not just at the conclusion of the program. B does not answer the question as completely as choice A. C is incorrect, as there is but one program, not programs nested within other programs. D is incorrect, as a demanding customer is not a valid reason to launch the close program processes. Should the program get canceled, however, then the close program processes may be launched.

7. What closing process group process facilitates the closure of program projects?

   A. Close program

   B. Scope verification

   C. Component closure

   D. Project closing process group

   C. When a component project is complete, the component closure process should be started. A is for the program, not the projects within the program. B, scope verification, happens at the project level, not the program level. D is incorrect, as it describes the closing processes that are performed at the project level, not the program level.

8. Nancy, a project manager in your program, has just completed her project and is ready to close the project. What roles do you, the program manager, play in Nancy's project closure?

   A. You must facilitate the project closure proceedings, as you're likely the project sponsor.

   B. You must sign off on the project deliverables before Nancy may close the project.

   C. Your program management team must facilitate the close project process.

   D. You will validate and ensure that the project closure has indeed taken place at the project level.

   D. The only interaction you'll have with closing program components is to ensure that the projects within the program have been closed at the project level. A is incorrect; the project manager facilitates the project closing, not the program manager. B is incorrect, as the program's scope management plan will determine which individual signs off on project deliverables. C is also incorrect, as Nancy, the project manager, completes the project closing processes.

9. Which one of the following is not an input to the component closure process?

    A. Resource availability

    B. Cost control

    C. Lessons learned

    D. Termination request

    A. Resource availability is not an input to the component closure process. Choices B, C, and D are inputs to the component closure process, so these choices are incorrect for this question.

10. A project within your program is no longer needed, so you have decided to terminate the project. What should happen to the project resources that are no longer needed in the project?

    A. They should be released from the organization.

    B. They should be given a negative review for their poor performance.

    C. They should be reallocated and used where appropriate.

    D. They should be released from the project and assigned to roles according to human resources.

    C. Remember, resources are more than just people; materials, equipment, and facilities will also be reallocated as needed. A is incorrect, as not all resources will be released from the organization when a project is terminated. B is incorrect for two reasons: first, a project may be terminated because of changes to the program environment, even when a project is performing well; second, project resources could be materials, equipment, and the like, so their performance is irrelevant. D is also incorrect, as not all resources are people.

11. You are the program manager of the NOP Program. One of your projects, the ABS Project, has closed. This project required considerable training of several key resources on a new material your organization will now sell. What should you do now that ABS Project has closed?

    A. Issue of a certificate of project completion.

    B. Update the personnel records of the team members on the ABS Project.

    C. Reassign the resources to other program activities.

    D. Complete scope verification of ABS Project.

    B. Once a project has closed, especially one with a lot of newly learned skills, the personnel records should be updated. A is incorrect, as this is not a valid program management term. C is incorrect, as the resources may not always be appropriate to reassign to other program activities. D, scope verification, is not correct, because scope verification is a project process, not a program management process.

12. Which one of the following items will not help you complete the contract closure process?

    A. Program WBS

    B. Termination notice

    C. Acceptance reports

    D. Contract performance records

    A. The program WBS is not needed during contract closure. Choices B, C, and D are all incorrect choices, because termination notices, acceptance reports, and contract performance records are all inputs to the contract closure process.

13. A vendor has promised to provide support beyond the closure of the contract. What must you do to ensure that your program receives the support the vendor has promised?

    A. Make certain to remind the vendor of the promised support as the program nears its conclusion.

    B. Withhold payment to the vendor until the promised support has been delivered.

    C. Add the promised support to the program's WBS.

    D. Confirm that the promised support is included in the contract between you and the vendor.

    D. The contract overrides all other promises and agreements. It is paramount to get the entire agreement between the vendor and the buyer in writing, in the contract. Choices A, B, and C are all incorrect, because these do not support the terms of the contract, which will override all other agreements.

14. What will you need to provide to a vendor when you want to terminate their contract due to poor vendor performance?

    A. Final payment for the vendor's work

    B. Termination notice

    C. Contract documentation

    D. The original proposal the vendor provided

    B. According to PMI's *The Standard for Program Management,* the program manager will provide a termination notice to the vendor detailing why the contract is being terminated. Choice A is incorrect, because the vendor may not be receiving any additional monies if the contract is terminated. Choice C and D are incorrect, as these are not inputs to the contract closure process.

15. You and a vendor are in disagreement about a portion of the program they have been hired to complete. The vendor has issued a claim against your organization, and it appears your program is headed toward a legal battle. What will determine where the lawsuit between you and the vendor is heard?

    A. Where the program is headquartered determines where the lawsuit may take place.

    B. Where the vendor is headquartered determines where the lawsuit may take place.

    C. Whoever files the lawsuit first has precedence as to the locale.

    D. The program's contract will define where the lawsuit may take place.

    D. The contract should define where legal claims will take place. Contracts, in the U.S., are backed by the court system. Choices A and B are incorrect, because the headquarters of either party typically has no bearing on where the lawsuit may occur. Choice C is also incorrect, as the contract's terms on legalities would take precedence on the order of legal filings.

16. What two things must be documented if you wish to terminate a vendor's contract?

    A. The work that the vendor has performed and the work the vendor has not performed

    B. The contract between your organization and the vendor and the quality of the vendor's work

    C. The contract and the scope verification document

    D. The scope verification document and the termination notice

    A. When you must terminate a vendor's contract the work that has been performed and the work that has not been performed by the vendor must be documented in order to complete the close contract process. Choices B, C, and D are incorrect, as these choices do not support the contract closure process.

17. Who must sign off on the program's projects when the projects are completed in the organization?

    A. The project manager

    B. The program stakeholders

    C. The project management team

    D. The program customer

    D. The program customer or the program sponsor can sign off on the component projects within a program. A, the project manager, is incorrect, because the project manager does not approve her own project deliverables. B, the program stakeholders, is an incorrect choice, as a program may literally have thousands of stakeholders. C, the program management team, is also an inappropriate choice.

18. The GHB Project in your program has been performing very well. It is on schedule and has no cost variances. You have decided, however, that this project needs to be terminated. Which one of the following is a likely reason the project should be terminated?

    A. The project manager is not meeting the project scope as planned.

    B. The project resources are not completing their project tasks as assigned.

    C. The program scope has changed.

    D. The program scope has not changed, but the project scope has changed.

    C. A well-performing project can still be canceled due to reasons outside of the project's control or influence. Changes at the program level can cause the project to be terminated. A and B are incorrect choices, because the question states that the project is performing well. D is incorrect, as the project scope in a program must be in alignment with program scope.

19. A project manager reports that he has met all of the requirements of the project scope and is ready to close the project. What must the project manager do with the project customer before he can close the project?

    A. Complete scope verification.

    B. Complete quality control.

    C. Complete quality assurance.

    D. Obtain a termination notice from the program manager.

    A. Scope verification leads to formal acceptance in a project, so it must be completed prior to project closing. B, quality control, happens throughout the project and does not involve the project customers. C, quality assurance, is a quality approach to prevent mistakes from entering the project. D is also incorrect, as termination notices are given to close projects and contracts earlier than what was originally planned.

20. The close program process has six inputs and six outputs. Which output of the close program process is also an input to the close program process?

    A. Approved deliverables

    B. Lessons learned

    C. Personnel records

    D. Program archives

    B. Lessons learned is an input and an output of the program close process. Choices A, C, and D are individual inputs and outputs of this process.

PART III

Managing Projects and Programs

In the final part of this book I'll compare and contrast projects and programs. Program managers and project managers must work together, not against one another, for the program and the projects to be successful. The partnership that exists between program managers and project managers helps the organization, the customers, and the program as a whole.

In this part, you'll learn about

- Program management knowledge areas
- Interaction among the program management knowledge areas
- Program schedule, cost, and scope management
- Program and project management relationships
- Project management expectations
- Project management processes
- Project management knowledge areas

Programs can't really exist without projects. Projects, on the other hand, can do just fine without programs. As a program manager, you'll want to know how programs and projects work together and how projects may operate under the program governance. You'll also want to understand the cooperative relationship between programs and projects for your PgMP examination.

Chapter 10 in this part takes a detailed look at the nine knowledge areas that span the entire program. These knowledge areas are integrated; performance and activity in any of the nine knowledge areas affect the performance actions of the other eight knowledge areas. You'll see that the processes in Chapter 10 are cross-referenced with the traditional program management process groups of initiating, planning, executing, monitoring and controlling, and closing.

Programs and projects have very similar process groups and share the same nine knowledge areas as defined in the PMBOK. Chapter 11 in this part will address the project process groups that your project managers will manage to allow a project to move from its initiation to its closing. While program managers aren't involved directly with the management of project processes, they may consult and offer advice on the project management processes you'll learn.

It's important for program managers to have a clear understanding of the activities and actions that project managers are doing without hovering over each project manager. In this part, I'll cover the life cycle of a project and how it works under the auspices of a program. I know you're revved up, so let's get going!

Program Knowledge Areas

In this chapter, you will
- Work with program integration management
- Manage the program scope
- Develop the program schedule
- Manage the program costs
- Ensure quality throughout the program
- Work with the program risk register
- Create and manage program contracts

Throughout this book, you've studied the exam objectives by following the traditional five process groups to get you from program initiation to program closing. This five process group approach is a lovely, logical approach, but it's not the only way to look at a program. Programs are also composed of nine knowledge areas that span the five process groups. Here are the nine knowledge areas you'll encounter on the PgMP examination that are unique to program management:

- Integration management
- Scope management
- Time management
- Cost management
- Quality management
- Human resources management
- Communications management
- Risk management
- Procurement management

If you're thinking that these look awfully like the nine knowledge areas that make up Chapters 4–12 in the PMBOK, you're right! These knowledge areas, which you just might already know from your time as a PMP, are the same knowledge areas for a program. You'll find some differences, however, between the processes that are tucked into these program knowledge areas and the processes in a project knowledge area.

Performing Program Integration Management

Here's the deal: program integration management is just a nice way of saying, "these are the gears of program management." These gears ensure that all of the process groups work together and allow the program to move from its initiation to its conclusion in the closing process group.

Chapters 5–9 took a detailed look at all of the processes, their inputs and outputs, and how these processes work together. Program integration management, and the rest of these knowledge areas, actually span each process group. Have a look at Table 10-1, as it gives an exact look at how the program knowledge areas and processes intersect.

Program integration management is, if you're counting processes, the largest knowledge area. It's the only knowledge area that spans all of the process groups. It's chockablock full of iterative processes, coordinating activities, and a general overview of all the stuff that's going on in the program. Figure 10-1 captures all of the processes for this knowledge area.

Initiating the Program

All programs start with a vision of some lusty future state that the program will create for the organization. The first program process, initiating the program, helps the organization capture and document the program scope and the expected benefits the program should create for the organization.

This initial process also helps the organization link the purpose of the program to the ongoing needs, goals, and vision of the organization. A company that builds skyscrapers isn't likely to start manufacturing bicycles; the program's mission has to fit into the vision and purpose of the organization, and this process helps you, the program manager, work with the stakeholders to make certain that happens.

Figure 10-1
Program integration management has 10 processes.

Program Integration Management
• Initiate program
• Authorize projects
• Develop program management plan
• Direct and manage program execution
• Integrated change control
• Resource control
• Monitor and control program work
• Issue management and control
• Close program
• Component closure

Program Knowledge Areas	Initiating Process Group	Planning Process Group	Executing Process Group	Monitoring and Controlling Process Group	Closing the Process Group
Integration Management	Initiating the program Authorizing projects	Developing the program management plan • Interface planning • Transition planning • Resource planning	Directing and managing program execution	Integrated change control Resource control Monitoring and controlling program work Issue management and control	Closing the program Component closure
Scope Management		Scope definition Creating the PWBS		Scope control	
Time Management		Schedule development		Schedule control	
Cost Management		Cost estimating and budgeting		Cost control	
Quality Management		Quality planning	Performing quality assurance	Performing quality control	
Human Resource Management	Initiating the program team	Human resource planning	Acquiring the program team Developing the program team		
Communications Management		Communications planning	Information distribution	Communications control Performance reporting	
Risk Management		Risk management planning and analysis		Risk monitoring and control	
Procurement Management		Planning program purchases and acquisitions Planning program contracting	Requesting seller responses Selecting sellers	Program contract administration	Contract closure

Table 10-1 Nine knowledge areas span the five process groups.

Once the program stakeholders are in agreement on the program scope, the program can be officially chartered. The program charter is a document created and signed by an organizational steering committee or a portfolio management body. The charter links the program to the ongoing work of the organization and often describes the program vision. The program vision describes the conditions that signal the program is complete and has reached its objectives.

Authorizing Projects

I know you know that programs are composed of projects. Projects are the individual components that help a program reach its cost, schedule, and scope objectives. This process has four activities within program integration management:

- Developing a business case for each project to secure project funding
- Assigning a project manager
- Communicating project information to the appropriate stakeholders
- Implementing a program governance structure to track project progress and benefit delivery

While programs do oversee projects, the program manager does not get wrapped up in the day-to-day business of project management. That's the project manager's job. This isn't to say that the program manager doesn't get involved at all with the program projects, but rather the program manager relies on the project manager to manage the projects without the constant oversight of the program manager.

 NOTE Projects can be initiated at any phase of the program except during the closing phase.

Developing the Program Management Plan

Program integration management moves the program into the planning processes once the program has been chartered. The program management plan process is a bit deceptive in this knowledge area. While it's true that developing the program management plan is a planning process, the specific program plans are unique to each knowledge area. For example, communications planning creates the communications management plan, quality planning creates the quality management plan, and so on. This process actually addresses three specific types of program planning:

- **Interface planning** This planning process identifies and documents all the relationships within the program, external to the program, and between programs within an organizational portfolio. This planning helps to identify all of the coordination, logistics, and communication channels the program must interact with. This process creates the interface management plan.

- **Transition planning**   Programs do not last forever (thankfully). This process aims to define how the program's deliverables will be transferred from the program ownership to the organizational operations. It defines how the program team members will transfer the deliverables to the ongoing activities of maintaining, using, and supporting the program benefits for the organization. The program transfer is a formal, documented, and often contract-based process. This planning process creates the transition plan and the transfer agreement.

- **Resource planning**   This iterative planning process defines all of the people, materials, equipment, facilities, and other program resources needed to satisfy the program scope. Resource planning also defines how the identified resources can best be used across the program for maximum return on program investment. Resource planning creates the resource management plan and a list of all required resources.

The program integration management planning processes are iterative activities. As conditions shift, changes are proposed, and other fluctuations within the program occur, the program manager and the program team will revisit these processes and update each respective plan.

Directing and Executing the Program

In program management, and often in life, nothing ever happens until someone does something. This program integration management process delivers the program's benefits. It is the execution of the program's plan to create the benefits the customer expects. As planning has created the direction for the program, now the program management team, the project managers, and the project team members do their work to deliver on the program's promises.

This process will create three things:

- **Change requests**   All change requests have to be documented before entering their appropriate change control system.

- **Work results**   The execution of the program management plan will result in deliverables, benefits, documentation, and other outputs.

- **Program termination requests**   If a program is not performing well or there are conditions outside of the program's control, such as a law or regulation, the program may be terminated.

It's this process where corrective and preventive actions will be folded into the program work. Recall that corrective actions are sometimes referred to as defect repair, and preventive actions are sometimes the avoidance risk response. Approved changes to the program scope will also be implemented in the executing process.

PART III

Monitoring and Controlling the Program

There are four program integration management processes in the monitor and control program work process group. These four processes have a common thread: control the program according to the program management plan. These four processes are linked to the program management planning processes and the program execution as Figure 10-2 depicts. Planning directs the program, execution builds to the program benefits, and control ensures that the work is done according to plan.

The four program integration management processes are

- **Integrated change control**   A program can expect change throughout its life cycle. When a change is proposed, however, the impact of each change must be examined at every point it may affect the program. This means that each knowledge area is examined to see how the change affects the remainder of the program. Considering a change to the program scope, this process would examine the cost, schedule, quality, human resources, communications, risk, and procurement impacts of the proposed change. If the change is approved, ramifications of the approved change must be incorporated into the other knowledge areas.

- **Resource control**   The budgeting and scheduling of program resources must be controlled throughout the program's life or costs will skyrocket, schedules will slip, quality may be affected, communications will suffer, and there may be contractual issues affected. This process works with the appropriate program management plan and the work results to control and manage the program resources.

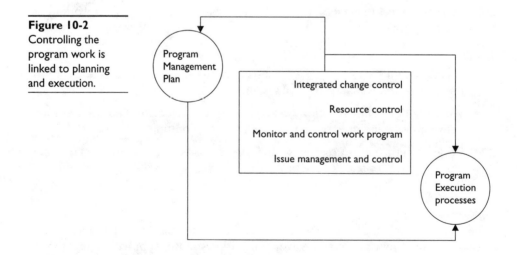

Figure 10-2
Controlling the program work is linked to planning and execution.

- **Monitor and control the program work**   Based on the performance of the program, the program management plan, and communication demands, the program management team ensures that the program work has been done according to design. This process also allows the program manager to forecast the program's health, usually through earned value management, to manage change requests, and to communicate with program stakeholders about the program.

- **Issue management and control**   Part of controlling the program work is to control the issues surrounding the program. This process identifies, tracks, and closes issues through the issue register. It's important for each issue to be assigned to an issue owner, an individual who understands the issue, its potential outcomes and impacts, and who has the authority to resolve the issue or escalate the issue to a higher power. Issues from program projects often fall into this program process when they can't be resolved at the project level.

These four processes are also iterative; as the program moves forward, there will no doubt be changes, issues, resource challenges, and ongoing program work. The key thing to remember about these four processes, in regard to program integration management, is that you'll be considering the effect of these processes on the remaining eight knowledge areas.

Closing Program Projects and the Program

There are two program integration management processes in the program closing process group. The most prevalent process is the component closure process. I say it's the most prevalent, because there are lots of component projects within a program, so this is the program closing process you'll use most often to officially close projects.

This closing process isn't concerned with the project management activities to close a project, but rather the higher-level process to close the project. These program-level activities include

- Validating the project closure with the project manager
- Reallocating project resources within the program, when appropriate and available
- Closing and archiving the project records
- Communicating with the program stakeholders that need to know about the project closure as needed

The second program integration management process that happens in closing is your favorite of all: closing the program. This beefy process is based on the approved deliverables of the program, the program management plan, the fulfillment of the program scope, and the collection of the program status reports.

When the program is officially closed, the program manager, the program sponsor, and usually the program customer all review the program deliverables in comparison to the program scope statement to verify the completeness of the program scope. These three stakeholders will all sign off on the program and issue the certificate of program completion. The program manager will also create a closure report and final performance reviews for the program. All of the lessons learned, contracts, communications, and other program documents are archived.

Managing the Program Scope

This knowledge area is all about fully defining the program scope, decomposing the program scope, and then working to control the program scope. This knowledge area is concerned only with the program work; costs, schedule, risks, and all that jazz aren't a concern here. This knowledge area is very specific to what the customer, the organization, or the program sponsor demands, requires, and needs for the program to be considered a success.

The program scope is tied to the program theme of benefits management. Benefits management begins with the identification of the benefits the program will create for the organization. The analysis of the benefits will help the program management team and the stakeholders prioritize the program components and create a methodology to measure the success of a program reaching the defined benefits.

The benefits realization plan is a key component in program scope management, as it sets the path for how the program will ascertain the expectations of the performing organization. There are just three processes in the program scope management knowledge area as defined in Figure 10-3.

Defining the Program Scope

In addition to the benefits realization plan, the program manager will rely on the program charter to go about creating the program scope statement. This document defines everything the program scope will include as part of the program—and clearly identifies things that fall outside of the program scope. The program scope statement will serve as a guide for all future program decisions, as it defines what the program expects to deliver.

Defining the program scope is a planning process, which means that it's an iterative process. This tricks some people, but not you, I'm sure. The idea of defining the program scope iteratively is sometimes called progressive elaboration by your pals at PMI. Progressive elaboration means that you're starting with a very broad definition, and then through a series of refinements as more detail becomes available your program scope statement can become more and more precise.

Figure 10-3
There are three processes in the scope management knowledge area.

Program Scope Management
• Scope definition
• Create PWBS
• Scope control

You know that changes are going to be approved in a program, and these changes will need to be reflected in the program scope statement. Approved changes will pass through this planning process, as the scope statement will be updated to reflect the new and approved scope changes.

Creating the Program WBS

Creating the program work breakdown structure is the second planning process of the scope management knowledge area. The PWBS is a decomposition of the program scope to reflect all of the specific program deliverables. The PWBS clearly illustrates the results of the program that are also defined in the program scope statement.

Just as changes to the program scope are incorporated into the program scope statement, so too are changes to the program scope statement added to the PWBS. The PWBS includes:

- Program deliverables
- Program plans
- Program standards and processes
- Major milestones
- Program office support deliverables, such as templates and software

The PWBS can be a huge document, as it captures all of the deliverables, results, and end items created by the entire program—including the program's component projects. Anything that's not captured in the PWBS is a clear signal that it's not part of the program scope, so it is considered out of bounds for the program. All of the elements of the PWBS are also defined in the PWBS companion document, the PWBS dictionary.

Controlling the Program Scope

This program scope management process is a monitoring and controlling process—the only one that deals with scope management. Scope control takes a bulldog stance on changes to the program scope: it doesn't want changes that aren't approved, aren't needed, and can't be paid for in time or monies.

This process performs several activities specific to the program scope:

- Documents proposed scope change requests
- Evaluates scope change requests
- Determines the nature of the scope change request
- Facilitates the communication of the scope change request to the appropriate program stakeholders
- Manages the activities to fold the approved changes into the program management plan and its components

> ## Managing Knowledge Areas
>
> If you've read all of the chapters up to this one, you might have noticed that all of the processes in this chapter have already been talked about but in process groups rather than knowledge areas. That's correct! These are the same processes that are plotted out in the five process groups: initiating, planning, executing, monitoring and controlling, and closing. The five process groups describe the logical flow of a program from start to finish. The processes are the activities that create something and allow the program to move forward.
>
> The nine knowledge areas covered in this chapter define the nine things every program manager needs to be thinking about for every decision in the program. The activities and decisions that happen in one area of the program will have a direct influence on the results of the other knowledge areas. For example, a poor job of controlling the program scope will affect the program's schedule, cost, quality, risk, communications, and even procurement and human resources. You'll be hard pressed to find a situation where poor performance in any knowledge area doesn't affect the other knowledge areas.
>
> For your PgMP examination you'll need to recognize the processes and how they move the program forward. Based on my seminars and readers of my other management books, I've found two different types of thinkers. The first batch like to visualize their processes in a sequential order, like a story, to move from initiating to closing. Other readers like to use the knowledge areas to think about related processes, such as quality planning, quality assurance, and quality control.
>
> My advice for you is to find an approach that makes the most sense for you, and stick with it. I don't believe that there's a better way or a wrong way to learn the program management processes you'll need to know for your exam. Just know 'em, pass the PgMP exam, and then get back to your life.

This process will also document and archive change requests that are not approved. This is an important function, as stakeholders may require evidence later in the program's closing as to why their pet scope change request wasn't incorporated into the program. Of course you would have already communicated the denial of the scope change request, but the documentation of the denied change request is an important safety net.

Managing the Program Time

When you consider all of the projects, non-project activities, coordination, and logistics of program management, it can be overwhelming. The program schedule can, at first glance, be a spaghetti bowl of starts and finishes. What's really going on there, however, is a progression of work to reach the program milestones.

This knowledge area has two processes, as Figure 10-4 depicts. Managing the program time starts with the program scope and the estimated amount of time it'll take to complete the program work, when the program milestones should, or must, be met in order to reach the program's completion date. Some programs must be completed by a set deadline, while other programs take a more organic approach and allow the estimate of the program work to determine when the program can reach its natural conclusion.

Figure 10-4
There are two
processes in the
time management
knowledge area.

Program Time Management
• Schedule development
• Schedule control

This knowledge area is integrated with the other program management knowledge areas, because it depends on availability of program resources, the cost of the needed resources, the quality demands of the work, communicating the program schedule, examining the schedule impact of risk events, and the timings of contract completion and contracted labor. Schedule management also considers the time needed for the program management activities, not just the labor to complete the core program work.

Developing the Program Schedule

This first program time management process is the planning process. Developing the program schedule first defines the program components that will need to be created in order to reach the program deliverables and benefits. Once the program components have been identified, there'll be an analysis of the order in which the components should be chartered and launched. This time analysis will also provide the estimated duration for the program components to create their deliverables, the expected milestones, delivery dates, and a summation of when the program will end.

A key input to this time management process is the PWBS. Since it is a decomposition of the program scope, it'll help guide the program management team on what exactly is needed for program completion. Tied to the PWBS is the availability of the needed resources, the resource capabilities, and any internal and external dependencies that may create bottlenecks for the program schedule.

This process creates the program schedule, and it also provides a mechanism to update the program schedule as changes to the program scope or conditions within the program warrant. Schedule changes should also follow the schedule change control system to capture their impact on the other knowledge areas. This process also creates the schedule management plan, which will define how the schedule is managed, controlled, and allowed to be changed.

Controlling the Program Schedule

While it's mandatory to have a program schedule, it won't do much good if the schedule is not actively monitored and controlled. Controlling the program schedule is an ongoing process to track the estimated start and finish dates of program work to the actual start and finish dates. The difference between the actual and estimated dates will expose how the program is slipping behind—or moving ahead of schedule.

This process also works closely with the other program control processes, as they all have an effect on the program schedule. Changes to any of the other knowledge areas can have detrimental or positive effects on the program schedule. While most changes are often seen as having a negative impact on the program schedule, some changes or events can create opportunities for the program to move ahead faster than planned.

Consider a risk event that doesn't happen, such as delays for poor weather, so the program can surge ahead to take advantage of good weather.

Managing the Program Cost

One of the central concerns for any organization launching, or considering whether to launch, a new program is the cost of the program. As part of the program's portfolio, the program is an investment of capital, and the organization logically expects a return on its investment. Programs aren't a hobby.

The investment of the funds into the program is in relation to the cost estimating and budgeting of the program. Once the program is launched and monies are invested in the program, ongoing communication about the program's performance is needed. Parallel to the cost planning and estimating is the cost control process. Figure 10-5 depicts the two cost management processes for this program knowledge area.

This process is integrated into the other knowledge areas, because each knowledge area has some costs associated with it. Consider each of the knowledge areas, the anticipated costs to manage them, and their influence on program costs. The costs for the program are not just the costs to do the program work, but also the costs to manage the program itself.

Estimating and Budgeting the Program

Cost estimating and budgeting is a program planning process that creates a cost aggregation for all of the program components to determine a program estimate. It considers all of the program management activities, all of the program projects, and any non-project activities that need to be financially accounted for. This process relies on the PWBS, the resource management plan, and the supporting detail of the cost estimates to determine the reliability of the program's cost estimate.

The budgeting portion of this process creates budgets for the program, the program's projects, and the non-project activity the program demands. The program budgeting also considers the financial limitations of an organization due to business cycles, fiscal year budget assignments, and limits on financial commitments.

This process also has a direct link to the risk management knowledge area, as it works with risk planning to determine the amount of funds that should be allotted for the risk contingency reserve. As new risks are discovered, they are analyzed for their financial impact on the program, and financial decisions are made to address the risk in terms of its impact, its probability, and the risk event value.

Figure 10-5
There are two processes in the cost management knowledge area.

Program Cost Management
• Cost estimating and budgeting • Cost control

Controlling the Program Costs

This process is the financial watchdog over how the program spends the program budget. It evaluates financial changes to the program budget and identifies variances from the program estimates and the actual costs of the program work. Cost control also identifies trends to predict where and when cost variances are likely to occur in the program so that the program management team may attack and anticipate the cost issues.

While it's easiest to think of cost control as a program process to control costs and prevent cost overruns, it's also an opportunistic process. Cost control requires the program management team to be on the lookout for positive risks, opportunities, and discoveries that can save and earn funds from the program to return to the organization.

Managing the Program Quality

Quality is one of those weird terms that people toss around without really defining what it is. For your PgMP certification, however, quality is the conformance to requirements and a fitness for use. Quality is the ability of the program deliverables to satisfy the stated and implied needs. To put it directly, quality is the completion of the program scope.

This program management knowledge area has three processes, as seen in Figure 10-6. Each of these processes is integrated with the other program management knowledge areas, as poor quality has a direct influence over the program. Imagine the cost and schedule overruns due to poor quality. Imagine the heated communications and risks that could be introduced if quality is poor. And of course quality has a direct bearing on whether the program customer signs off on the program deliverables.

For your PgMP examination know these three processes and how your primary goal of quality is to satisfy the program scope according to the stated needs and objectives in the program scope statement. Quality in the program is also concerned with the management of the program and its control over the program projects.

Planning for Quality

Quality is planned into a program, never inspected in. This is a nifty way to shift the program back into planning as needed so that the project management team can do the program work correctly. It's generally most cost effective and easier on your program schedule to plan how the program will reach the quality expectations the first time rather than inspect and patch the problems during the program execution.

Figure 10-6
There are three program quality management processes.

Program Quality Management
• Quality planning
• Perform quality assurance
• Perform quality control

The idea of planning quality into the program assumes that the program manager, the program sponsor, and the program customer know what it is they'd like the program to accomplish. Vague metrics, such as fast, good, and happy, aren't definitive metrics that the program management team can measure to determine the program's performance. A cornerstone of quality planning is to identify the relevant standards, metrics, and expectations in measurable terms so that the program has set expectations for acceptance.

This program process is responsible for defining the cost of quality; this is the amount of funds that the program will need to spend in order to reach the expected level of quality. For example, training, safety measures, and correct materials and tools are all examples of the cost of quality. If the program cuts corners and the organization does not provide the program team training, provide safety measures, or supply other resources, the program will suffer in quality, loss of life or limb, or rejected deliverables from the customer. The results of poor quality are sometimes called the cost of non-conformance to quality.

Performing Quality Assurance

The second quality management process in this knowledge area is the perform quality assurance process. This process is an iterative process that checks the program to confirm that it is adhering to the quality standards and quality policies as defined in the quality planning process. This process is performed throughout the life of the program—it's not over until the program is over.

The perform quality assurance process examines more than just the program, but also the quality of the projects within the program. The quality within a project should support the parent program's quality policy and adhere to the quality demands that will, in effect, support the program customer's quality demands for the program.

When quality is discovered to be poor, the work will need to be corrected. When the poor quality of the work is corrected, there will also be a defect repair review to confirm that the corrective actions have been properly implemented. Part of defect repair and its review is to learn from the mistake so that the program doesn't suffer from the defect again.

Controlling Program Quality

This final quality management knowledge area process is all about inspecting the work results to confirm that the results do, or do not, meet the expected levels of quality. This inspection-driven process creates several things for the program:

- Completed quality checklists for the program archives
- Work results inspection reports
- Non-conforming work results
- Testing reports
- Measurement results

These outputs allow the program management team to determine if the inspected product meets the quality standards as defined by the quality management plan or if the work is faulty. Faulty work must be corrected before the program can continue.

Managing the Program Human Resources

As a program manager, you've got to manage time, costs, scope, quality, and all the other program management knowledge areas. While each one of those knowledge areas presents its own challenges, perhaps the most challenging is the management of human resources. This knowledge area requires a constant eye on the human factor and the politics, beliefs, values, motivations, and policies that help you manage the people your program relies on to reach its conclusion. There are four processes in this knowledge area, as Figure 10-7 shows.

For your PgMP examination you'll want know how these four processes operate to help your program move forward. One of the best methods is to understand what motivates the individuals working on the program and then create a rewards and recognition system to address their motivating factors. Understanding what motivates people helps you create a system so that you and your program team workers get what's wanted.

Initiating the Program Team

I bet you can guess what this process does. Yep, it gets the needed program resources onto and working on the program. While it sounds easy, it's really a bit more complicated than just assigning some folks to get work. It really involves an analysis of what resources are needed on the program team, determining if the resources are available, and even negotiations to hire the needed resources for the program.

NOTE This process may be supplemented by the upcoming acquire program team process in the execution process group. Some team members may be brought onto the program to help the program launch, and then they're released from the program and replaced by the acquisition of new program team members.

This process happens in conjunction with the initiate program process. The program management team should be in place prior to the program kickoff meeting. This means that all procurement of augmented staff, personnel hiring, and the collection of organizational resources are in place on the core program team. The program manager is also assigned, of course, and leads the program team on their assignments and team responsibilities.

Figure 10-7
Human resource management has four processes.

Program HR Management
• Initiate team
• Human resource planning
• Acquire program team
• Develop program team

Planning for Human Resources

This planning process is responsible for determining the needed program human resources in order to complete the program requirements. This includes identifying and documenting the program's roles and responsibilities and reporting relationships based on the program roles. This documentation of the roles can include both the internal and external roles that the program will rely on to complete the program work.

This process will rely on the identification of the program interfaces, which may include the functional units within the organization, such as the IT and finance departments. The program interfaces should also be identified as the point of contact for the different domains, responsibilities, and reporting structures between the program and the leaders of the program interfaces. A stakeholder analysis chart will help you identify the expectations of the program stakeholders. In addition, a communication matrix may help identify who reports to whom in the program.

This program process also creates the staffing management plan. Recall that this plan determines how program team members will be brought onto and released from the program in terms of conditions, milestones, schedules, and resource availability. As changes within the program occur, this plan will likely need to be updated to reflect the new requirements, schedule, and demand for resources.

Acquiring the Program Team

This execution process addresses the decision to use internal human resources, external human resources, or a blend of both. The decision to use the internal and external resources is based on several program factors:

- Type of resource that is needed
- Availability of the needed resource
- Length of time the resource is needed
- Cost of an external resource
- Timing of the need for the resource

Both internal and external resources present their own challenges for the program. Internal resources require the examination of the resource pool for a resource with the competency and skill set the program requires. If there's an internal resource, there are the negotiations between the program management, the resource, and the resource's functional manager to shift the resource to the program.

External resources have the complications of negotiating for cost and availability, and for incorporating the contracted resource as part of the program team membership. Questions concerning the hiring of a contractor versus a new employee also need to be addressed. It may be more cost-effective to hire a new employee for the program's duration than to procure a contractor. The organization must also consider the advantages of retaining a resource that has the hands-on knowledge of creating a program deliverable to assist in the support of the deliverable once the benefits move into operations.

Developing the Program Team

You want a program team that is competent, confident, and eager to work on the program. This execution process tries to accomplish all of those goals by providing the training, experience, and opportunity for the program team member. Developing the program team is an attempt to address any lack in competence in the program team that may be hindering the program's performance while also addressing benefits for the program team members' career paths. In other words, it's an opportunity to create a win-win for the program and the team member.

Team development is an ongoing process throughout the program. As the team members' roles and positions on the program team begin to diminish because their roles are nearing completion, team development tries to address their future assignments. This means that team development will work with each program team member, the organization, and the program to usher him to new responsibilities in the program, in the organization, or in a supportive role for the program benefits and deliverables.

Managing Program Communications

Talk may be cheap, but it can be expensive in a program when a program manager fails to do it. The program communications management knowledge area is about defining the information that's needed and then providing that information to the appropriate stakeholders at the right time and in the correct format. Communication takes up a large slice of every program manager's time, so it's important to manage this knowledge area with full control.

This knowledge area, which has four processes as shown in Figure 10-8, is integrated into all of the other knowledge areas when you consider the information from each knowledge area that must be communicated to the program stakeholders—both internal and external. The old formula of $N(N - 1)/2$ depicts the number of stakeholders in the program; you can save some time on your calculator and just accept that the larger the program, the more detail and communications you'll have to provide.

As changes in the program happen, and they will, you'll have to communicate on the status of the change, the health of the program, how the change has affected time and cost, and the impact of the change on all the other knowledge areas. As a rule, it's mandatory to document program communications—especially communications that result in promises and decisions. You'll want a paper trail to the supporting details for the decisions that have been made in the program.

Figure 10-8
Communications management has four processes.

Program Communications Management
• Communications planning
• Information distribution
• Communications control
• Performance reporting

Planning the Program Communications

In order to accurately communicate, the program manager will spend time with the stakeholders and the program management team to determine who needs what information, when the information is needed, and in what modality the recipient of the communication is expecting the information. The discoveries of these needs are documented in the communications management plan. This plan provides several things for the program:

- Program status
- Program component status
- Milestone completion progress
- Program costs and schedule updates
- Risk analysis information
- Status of program change requests
- Government and regulatory filings as required by laws and regulations
- Public announcements

Communications planning is an iterative process that may be updated, depending on conditions within the program. As changes to the program happen, the communications management plan may need to be updated to reflect the new communications requirements. Because this process is part of the planning process group, it will happen throughout the program, not just once and be forgotten.

Providing Program Communications

The second communications management process is information distribution. This is an executing process, as you're executing the communications management plan. Information distribution must be completed in a timely and accurate fashion, or the program may suffer ramifications. It's important to follow a regular schedule in the program for status, variance, and milestone completion reports. Information distribution provides communication to three program channels:

- Program clients
- Program sponsor(s)
- Component project managers

These three channels will expect information on the program progress, costs, schedule, risk, and other news concerning the program management knowledge areas. One primary communication is the status and integration of approved change requests to the program scope. This is key: if scope changes are not communicated to the component projects, then time and costs may be wasted, since the project managers will continue to deliver their current project scopes rather than creating the changes your program scope now demands.

Controlling the Program Communication

If you've ever played the game "telephone," you know how wacky and out of control people can interpret and twist information. It's not different in your program. What starts out as a simple communication can turn into a perceived disaster, if the information is not communicated properly. The communications control process works to ensure that communication is properly done according to the communications management plan.

One of the primary inputs to this process, and a common theme throughout this chapter, is change requests. Change requests and their status, impact, and implementation must be communicated through the information distribution process I talked about earlier in this chapter. The communications control is the enforcer of that executing process when it comes to change requests. It ensures that the proper communication is done according to plan, on schedule, and in the correct modality.

You'll also have to work with management directives and communicate that news to the appropriate stakeholders. Of course you'll do this business as professionally and completely as possible; you don't want to disperse information only to be flooded with e-mails and phone calls from stakeholders asking for clarifications and additional information. It's important to clearly communicate; otherwise, interpretations and miscommunications will ensue.

Reporting on the Program Performance

This final program communications management knowledge area process requires the program manager to consolidate program performance information. This means the program manager needs information on how the entire program is doing, including the work results from the project components that contribute to the program benefits. The program manager won't typically go inspect the project work but will rely on the performance reports the project managers are required to submit to the program manager.

This process is also concerned with the program costs and the program budget. You probably remember that performance dealing with costs and schedule can be expressed through earned value management. The cost and schedule variances often lead to variance reports, sometimes called exception reports. The program manager can also use the EVM formulas for the cost performance index and the schedule performance index to show the health of the program.

This process also does some program forecasting as to the final estimated costs, the predicted costs the program will need to complete the program, and what the expected variance of the program will be given the current conditions within the program. Again, EVM will help the program manager capture the estimate at completion (EAC), the estimate to complete (ETC), and the program's variance at completion (VAC). All of this business is captured in performance reports that will eventually become part of the program's archives.

Managing the Program Risks

A risk is an uncertain event or condition that may affect the project in a positive way or, more often, in a negative way. Programs begin with a classic business risk: the investment of monies into a program. There is a risk for the organization that the monies sunk into the program may never be recouped. There's a risk that the program may fail and all of the investment could be lost. The flip side of this risk, however, is the reward that the program will receive by accepting the risk. For any identified risk there should be a reward for accepting the risk; the reward should be in relation to the risk that's been accepted. Of course some risks are worth taking, while other risks are best avoided.

This program management knowledge area has two processes; Figure 10-9 depicts the two risk processes. These risk management processes are iterative throughout the program life cycle. The program manager and the program management team are constantly on the lookout for new risks, risks that may not have been identified yet, and potential solutions for risk events.

These risk processes are revisited whenever there are changes to the program scope, cost, schedule, or contracts. Changes to the these four areas of the program almost always introduce new risks events that must be identified, evaluated, planned for, and then managed. A failure to consistently examine the program for new risks events can quickly lead to the program's demise.

Planning for Program Risks

The risk management planning process documents and defines how the risk management activities for the program and the constituent projects will happen within the program. This process begins with the identification of the program risks, the risks' characteristics, and what the potential responses for the identified risks may be. This process happens over and over throughout the program—so learn to love it.

Once the risks have been identified, they'll move into qualitative analysis. You could say that qualitative analysis "qualifies" the risks for further analysis. This quick base analysis will quickly judge the probability, impact, and overall score for each risk event. Qualitative analysis is not a very reliable approach to scoring risk events, but rather a foundation to determine a consensus on which risk events should go on to additional study and which risks events should just be monitored.

The risk events that are deemed quite serious go onto quantitative analysis, where the goal is to "quantify" the risk events. This approach is much more in-depth than the qualitative analysis and takes much longer to complete. Quantitative analysis usually relies on a risk probability-impact matrix to gauge the risk event value and to build the program's contingency reserve. The contingency reserve is a portion of the program's budget reserved to offset risk events.

Figure 10-9
There are two processes in the risk management knowledge area.

Program Risk Management
• Risk management planning and analysis
• Risk monitoring and control

The final portion of the risk management and planning process is the creation of risk responses. You may recall that there are seven risk responses:

- **Acceptance**   Used for both positive and negative risk events.

- **Avoidance**   Used for negative risk events; the risk is avoided.

- **Mitigation**   Used for negative risk events; the impact and/or probability of the risk event is reduced.

- **Transference**   Used for negative risk events; the risk transferred to a third party, usually for a contracted fee.

- **Sharing**   Used for positive risk events; the event is shared with another party.

- **Enhancing**   Used for positive risk events; the conditions surrounding the positive risk event are enhanced to try to make the positive risk event happen.

- **Exploiting**   Used for positive risk events; the positive risk event is going to happen, so the organization exploits the event for its benefit.

This process is completed throughout the program, including the analysis of inter-project risks. The goal is to identify root causes of risks, spot trends, and address the core issue of risks with the most appropriate risk response. Sometimes risk events within the program components may need to be escalated to the program level to find the best solution or response. The program management team must encourage the component projects to consistently address the risks within their projects.

Monitoring and Controlling Program Risks

This risk management process is obviously a monitoring and controlling process. It is done in tandem with program execution, as that's when risk events are going to peek out of the shadows and attack the program implementation. The program's risk response plan is used as an input to the process, since it will define how the program should respond to risk events that are coming into fruition.

Throughout the program, the PWBS is also a reference for risk monitoring and controlling. As the program completes the deliverables and benefits outlines in the PWBS, the risk monitoring and controlling process can help anticipate and remind the program management team what risks are pending in the program by examining the PWBS. As changes enter the program scope, they'll be reflected in the PWBS; this redundancy will help highlight risk events that may be caused by changes to the program scope.

The overall health of the program will be documented in the communications management process's performance report. Risk management is integrated into performance reporting, as a poorly performing program is a signal that risks of failing are threatening the program. The inverse is true too: a well-performing program is a sign that there may an opportunity to seize positive risks and take advantage of new benefits. Remember, risk itself is not a bad thing—it is the risk event's impact and reward that bring about the positive or negative.

Managing the Program Procurement Processes

This final program management knowledge area deals with procuring the resources your program needs to deliver its benefits. This knowledge area has six program management processes, as Figure 10-10 depicts. You'll invest time planning what to procure, how to procure, and when to procure. You'll also determine the contract types that are the most appropriate for your program.

Once you've created a plan, you'll execute the plan by working with the available sellers for your program. The sellers will participate in this knowledge area by providing responses, negotiating, and bidding on the assignments. In the executing process group, you'll select the seller for your program.

Now that you've got a contract, the vendor gets to work on fulfilling the terms of the contract, and you'll work with the vendor to ensure its living up to its end of the bargain. Once the vendor has completed the work and your program has kept its end of the contract terms, the contract is closed and the vendor is released from the program.

Planning the Program Procurement

Most programs are going to need to purchase things, labor, tools, equipment, and other resources for their program to complete the program scope. There are two planning processes that will help the program manager complete the procurement. The first one is the plan program purchases and acquisitions process. You'll plan for several procurement decisions:

- What to procure
- The schedule for procuring the goods and services
- Developing procurement strategies
- Whether the program should make or buy the goods or services
- How the procured items could better the program

You'll rely on the scope and the PWBS as two primary inputs to help with the purchase planning. When it comes to what labor you should procure, you'll rely on the resource management plan to help you determine the utilization of resources and if you'll need to hire or contract additional labor for the program. The primary output of this process is the procurement management plan.

Figure 10-10
There are six processes in the procurement management knowledge area.

Program Procurement Management
• Plan program purchases and acquisitions
• Plan program contracting
• Request seller responses
• Select sellers
• Program contract administration
• Contract closure

The decisions that are made in the initial plan program purchases and acquisitions process are an input to the plan program contracting process. This planning process uses the procurement management plan, the decisions of what needs to be procured, and the contract statement of work to determine which contract types should be used in the program. The outputs of this planning process will create the contracts management plan.

Working with Sellers

Sellers, sometimes called vendors, are the companies that a program will work with to purchase the needed resources. There are two executing processes you'll use to work with sellers in your program. The first one is to request a seller response. You'll execute this process by contacting the sellers through advertisements, such as public notices in your newspaper's advertising section, by calling sellers you know and inviting them to participate, or by using a preferred vendors list your organization provides.

When you execute the seller response, you'll usually provide a contract statement of work that details the goods or services you want to procure. The contract statement of work, sometimes just called a SOW, details what your program needs and is usually updated based on queries and clarifications when dealing with the vendors. You'll get these queries and clarifications through a bidders conference that you host.

Here's the typical procurement approach:

- You create a contract statement of work detailing what you want to buy.
- You create a request for quote (RFQ), an invitation for bid (IFB), or a request for proposal (RFP).
- You give the SOW and the RFQ, IFB, or RFP to the vendors you'd consider doing business with.
- You host a bidders conference where all of the sellers can attend and ask for clarifications about your SOW and questions about the work you want them to do for you.
- Considering the outcome of the bidders conference, you'll update the SOW and resubmit it to all of the potential sellers so that everyone has the same information to create a bid, quote, or proposal.

NOTE A bid and a quote are the same thing: just a price, no fancy ideas. You'll usually ask for a bid or quote when you know exactly what you want, such as four tons of pea gravel. A proposal, however, provides lots of fancy ideas and suggestions for your program. You'll ask for a proposal when you have a good idea of what you'd like, but you need some guidance, such as designing a new web site.

The sellers will provide their bids, quotes, or proposals as you've asked, and then you'll do the second procurement management executing process: selecting a seller. If you've asked for a bid or quote, price is usually the determining factor, though you may have other concerns, such as date of delivery, warranties, and the like. If you've asked for a proposal, then it's usually much more involved. You'll have to read, evaluate, meet with the sellers, and ponder the suggestions you've received to make a decision on which vendor will win the contract.

The primary output of selecting a seller is the contract for the goods and services the vendors will provide to the program. You may also have updates to the procurement management plan to reflect any adjustments you and the vendor have negotiated, such as terms of payment, delivery methods, and other contract requirements. The contract will be an input to the monitoring and controlling process, program contract administration.

Administering the Program Contract

Here's the scoop with this monitoring and controlling process: both parties have to live up to the terms of the contract. It's easy for the program manager to see how well the vendor is performing, as he can track costs, schedule, quality of work, and other details of what the vendor is providing to the program. What's not so obvious, however, is that the program manager's organization has obligations outlined in the contract as well. Both parties have to abide by the terms of the contract.

As the vendor completes their work, they'll submit invoices for the work they've done. The program management team will inspect the vendor's work and confirm that it's complete or not. If the work is lacking, the seller must redo the work in order to satisfy the contract terms before being paid. When the seller's work is complete, the payment request will be approved, and the vendor is paid.

When change requests are made in the program scope, they may affect the program's sellers. The contracts should define how changes may enter the contract. Some contracts allow changes to be added to the contract via an addendum, while other contracts may require a whole new contract, if the cost of the change exceeds a given amount. Whatever approach is taken, communication with the seller about the change is mandatory, or there'll be confusion, frustration, and possibly claims to settle.

Closing the Program Contracts

Once the seller has completed their obligations to the program, their contract may be closed out. The completion of a contract is verified by the acceptance reports that the vendor has completed the work or provided the goods requested by the program. When the program management team confirms that the acceptance of the work is complete, then the program will issue a contract completion certification.

Sometimes a contract needs to be canceled, because the vendor has not been performing as the program's contract requires. Late deliveries, poor quality in the seller's work, or other performance issues may lead to early contract termination. There may also be times when changes to the program call for a contract to be terminated regardless of the seller's performance. The program will issue the vendor a termination notice explaining why the contract is being terminated. Whether a contract is closed successfully or terminated, the documentation is included in the contract file and becomes part of the historical information.

Chapter Summary

Programs are full of processes, and processes fit into the nine knowledge areas. Each knowledge area has its own theme, and it's a nice way to compartmentalize what the program is currently focusing on. While you can chunk out the program into these nine different knowledge areas, it's important to remember that what activities you do in one knowledge area will affect how accurately the other knowledge areas can be managed. This describes program integration management—all of the moving parts of the program affect one another.

The triple constraints of program management are addressed in scope management, cost management, and schedule management. These three things must be in balance with one another, or the program will suffer. You can't have more scope than you have time or budget. Scope management is the foundation for determining how long the program takes to complete and how much the program benefits will cost to achieve.

Quality is not only affected by the triple constraints, but also by the planning put into the program. A failure to plan for quality will almost certainly result in poor quality for the program's stakeholder. The quality assurance process aims to do the program work right the first time rather rush through the work and hope for the best. Once the work is completed, quality control ensures the existence of quality in the program deliverables.

The next two processes are tightly linked—human resource management and program communications management. The staffing management plan defines how the staff may be brought onto and released from the program. The program manager will need to communicate with the program resources, but also with management, vendors, external contacts, and other program stakeholders.

Program risk management is a knowledge area that can affect the entire program if it's not managed properly. Risk planning includes the identification and analysis of the risk events. Recall that there are two types of risk analysis: qualitative, which is fairly light and subjective, and quantitative, which is the more intense analysis. Once the risks have been analyzed, each risk is given an appropriate response.

The chapter wrapped up with procurement management. Programs almost always need to buy stuff, and the program procurement management knowledge area guides the purchasing. Program managers will work with sellers to negotiate, agree to terms, and then abide by a mutually binding contract. When contracts are complete, there's an issuance of the certificate of completion. Sometimes, and hopefully not too often, contracts can be terminated based on poor performance or an outdated need for the contracted work.

Key Terms

Integrated change control   Programs can expect change throughout their life cycles. When a change is proposed, however, the impact of each change must be examined at every point it may affect the program.

Interface planning   This planning process identifies and documents all the relationships within the program, those external to the program, and relationships between programs within an organizational portfolio.

Knowledge area   A portion of the program management focusing on a specific topic; there are nine program management knowledge areas (program integration management, scope management, time management, cost management, quality management, human resource management, communications management, risk management, and procurement management).

Program communications management   The program management knowledge area responsible for communications planning, information distribution, communications control, and performance reporting.

Program cost management   The program management knowledge area that facilitates the cost estimating and budget for the program and provides for cost control.

Program human resource management   The program management knowledge area that allows the program team to be initiated and acquired and the human resources for the program to be planned. This is also the knowledge area that hosts team development.

Program integration management   The program management knowledge area that provides processes for initiating the program, developing the program plan, executing the plans, providing program control, and closing the program and its components.

Program procurement management   The program management knowledge area that facilitates the planning of purchasing, contracting, working with sellers, performing contract administration, and the control closure.

Program quality management   The program management knowledge area that hosts the quality planning, quality assurance, and quality control–related processes.

Program risk management   The knowledge area responsible for risk management planning and analysis while also supporting risk monitoring and control.

Program scope management   The program management knowledge area that is responsible for defining the program scope, creating the program work breakdown structure (PWBS), and controlling the program scope.

Program termination requests   If a program is not performing well or there are conditions outside of the program's control, such as a law or regulation, the program may be terminated.

Program time management   The program management knowledge area responsible for creating and controlling the program schedule.

Resource planning   This iterative planning process defines all of the people, materials, equipment, facilities, and other program resources needed to satisfy the program scope. Resource planning also defines how the identified resources can best be used across the program for maximum return on program investment.

Transition planning   Programs don't go on forever (thankfully), so this process aims to define how the program's deliverables will be transferred from the program ownership to the organizational operations.

Questions

1. You are the program manager of the HYGH Program. Your program management team has identified the program's risk. Where are these risks documented?

    A. Risk identification forms

    B. Risk log

    C. Risk database

    D. Risk register

2. Which program management knowledge area has processes in each of the program management process groups?

    A. Program integration management

    B. Program risk management

    C. Program quality management

    D. Program human resources management

3. Marcy is the program manager of the HUF Project. Marcy is identifying the people that will support the deliverables once the program is completed. These deliverables, the benefits of the program, will become part of the organization's operation. What is this activity called that Marcy is completing?

    A. Resource planning

    B. Transition planning

    C. Interface planning

    D. Close program process

4. What monitoring and controlling process will examine the impact of all changes to the program scope and how they affect all of the program's knowledge areas?

    A. Program integration management

    B. Integrated change control

    C. Change control system

    D. Issue and management control

5. Henry's program has been performing with many cost and schedule variances. Henry's management has decided to cancel the program. What program management process will facilitate this program cancellation?

    A. Close program

    B. Component closure

    C. Perform quality assurance

    D. Contract closure

6. You are the program manager of the CGR Program. You and your program management team have created the program scope statement, and your program sponsor has signed off on the document. Which document should you create next?

    A. Risk management plan

    B. Program charter

    C. Program work breakdown structure

    D. Program schedule

7. Which risk management knowledge area process activity can help you create the risk contingency reserve?

    A. Qualitative analysis

    B. Quantitative analysis

    C. Risk identification

    D. Risk probability-impact matrix

8. Which program management knowledge area defines the program budget?

    A. Program integration management

    B. Program cost management

    C. Program charter

    D. Initiating process group

9. You are the program manager of HUYY Program. You need to purchase 45 copies of a project management software program for your project managers in the program. Which procurement document could you provide to the sellers if you are only interested in a price for the software?

    A. Quote

    B. RFP

    C. IFB

    D. Charter

10. Complete the following statement: _____ is/are planned into a program, not inspected into a program.

    A. Costs

    B. Quality

    C. Requirements

    D. Scope changes

11. Which earned value management formula can help forecast the program's variance at completion?

    A. EAC

    B. VAC

    C. BAC

    D. CPI

12. Issue management and control is a program integration management process. This process identifies issues and what other related activity?

    A. Promotes issue to risks

    B. Documents issues in the risk register

    C. Documents issues in the issue register

    D. Documents issues in the issue log

13. Your program is performing very well, and you're actually ahead of the planned program schedule. You discover that your program has an extra $225,000 in the program budget that you won't need to meet the program scope. What should you do with the $225,000?

    A. Add features to the program scope to consume the funds.

    B. Return the funds to the organization as part of cost budgeting.

    C. Add the funds to the program's contingency reserve.

    D. Return the funds to the organization as part of cost control.

14. In which knowledge area does the performance reporting process exist?

    A. Program integrated management

    B. Program communications management

    C. Program cost management

    D. Program quality management

15. Your program has 129 stakeholders, but next month the pool of stakeholders will grow to 211. How many more stakeholder communication channels will your program have next month?

    A. 8,256

    B. 22,155

    C. 13,899

    D. 3,321

16. Which risk management knowledge area process activity can help you identify the risks that will need a more in-depth analysis?

    A. Qualitative analysis

    B. Quantitative analysis

    C. Risk identification

    D. Risk probability-impact matrix

17. You have invited all of the sellers to a meeting to discuss the program's contract statement of work. What is this meeting called?

    A. Sellers' conference

    B. Stakeholder kick-off meeting

    C. Bidders conference

    D. Contract risk analysis meeting

18. All of the following are processes in the program human resources management knowledge area except for which one?

    A. Develop program team

    B. Human resource planning

    C. Acquire program team

    D. Performance reporting

19. Your program scope statement has been going through rounds of revisions on its way to its final approved form. These rounds of revisions are also known by what term?

    A. Progressive elaboration

    B. Scope control

    C. Iterative planning

    D. Stage gates

20. Which program management knowledge area allows projects to be authorized within the program?

    A. Program procurement management

    B. Human resources management

    C. Program integration management

    D. Projects are not authorized within programs

Questions and Answers

1. You are the program manager of the HYGH Program. Your program management team has identified the program's risk. Where are these risks documented?

    A. Risk identification forms

B. Risk log

C. Risk database

D. Risk register

D. Risks are recorded in the risk register. While some organizations may use a risk identification form, it is not where the risks are recorded, so A is incorrect. B, the risk log, is not a valid term. C, the risk database, is not a valid program management term.

2. Which program management knowledge area has processes in each of the program management process groups?

A. Program integration management

B. Program risk management

C. Program quality management

D. Program human resources management

A. Only the program integration management knowledge area has processes in all of the process groups.

3. Marcy is the program manager of the HUF Project. Marcy is identifying the people that will support the deliverables once the program is completed. These deliverables, the benefits of the program, will become part of the organization's operation. What is this activity called that Marcy is completing?

A. Resource planning

B. Transition planning

C. Interface planning

D. Close program process

B. Marcy is planning the transition for her program to operations. A, resource planning, identifies the resources needed on a program. C, interface planning, identifies and plans for the relationships between the program, the projects within a program, and other entities the program will interact with. D, close program process, is not a process that addresses operational transfer.

4. What monitoring and controlling process will examine the impact of all changes to the program scope and how they affect all of the program's knowledge areas?

A. Program integration management

B. Integrated change control

C. Change control system

D. Issue and management control

B. The integrated change control process examines the impact of a change on all of the program's knowledge areas. A, program integration management, is the knowledge area that hosts integrated change control. C is incorrect, as there are four change control systems: scope, schedule, cost, and contract. D is not a valid choice, as issues are not the same as changes.

5. Henry's program has been performing with many cost and schedule variances. Henry's management has decided to cancel the program. What program management process will facilitate this program cancellation?

   A. Close program

   B. Component closure

   C. Perform quality assurance

   D. Contract closure

   A. When a program is terminated, the close program process is invoked. B, component closure, is the process used to close program projects. C, perform quality assurance, is incorrect, as this is not a closing process. D, contract closure, is also incorrect, as the question wants the process to terminate the program, not a contract.

6. You are the program manager of the CGR Program. You and your program management team have created the program scope statement, and your program sponsor has signed off on the document. Which document should you create next?

   A. Risk management plan

   B. Program charter

   C. Program work breakdown structure

   D. Program schedule

   C. Once the scope statement has been approved, the next logical choice is to create the program work breakdown structure (PWBS). A, the risk management plan, comes later in the planning processes group, as does D, the program schedule. B, the program charter, actually precedes the scope statement, so this is an incorrect choice.

7. Which risk management knowledge area process activity can help you create the risk contingency reserve?

   A. Qualitative analysis

   B. Quantitative analysis

   C. Risk identification

   D. Risk probability-impact matrix

   B. Quantitative analysis will use a risk-probability impact matrix to help you determine the risk contingency reserve. A, qualitative analysis, is incorrect, as this activity provides only a high-level review of the identified risks. C, risk identification, identifies the risks but does not analyze them. D, a risk probability-impact matrix, can be used in qualitative and quantitative analysis—also, notice the question asked for an activity.

8. Which program management knowledge area defines the program budget?

   A. Program integration management

B. Program cost management

C. Program charter

D. Initiating process group

B. This isn't a trick question—the program cost management knowledge area defines the program budget. A, C, and D do not define the program budget, so these choices are incorrect.

9. You are the program manager of the HUYY Program. You need to purchase 45 copies of project management software program for your project managers in the program. Which procurement document could you provide to the sellers if you are only interested in a price for the software?

  A. Quote

  B. RFP

  C. IFB

  D. Charter

  C. The program manager needs only a price for the software. The only answer that asks the seller for a price is the IFB, the invitation for bid. A is wrong, because a quote is what the seller will provide to the buyer. B is incorrect, as a request for proposal is asking for more than just a price. D, charter, is also wrong, as this is the document that authorizes the program.

10. Complete the following statement: _____ is/are planned into a program, not inspected into a program.

  A. Costs

  B. Quality

  C. Requirements

  D. Scope changes

  B. Quality is planned into a program, not inspected into a program. Choices A, C, and D are all incorrect statements.

11. Which earned value management formula can help forecast the program's variance at completion?

  A. EAC

  B. VAC

  C. BAC

  D. CPI

  B. The variance at completion (VAC) is the only forecasting formula that will predict how the program will end on cost variance. A, the estimate at completion (EAC), predicts how much the total program costs will be, given the current conditions. C, the budget at completion, is not a forecasting formula. D, the cost performance index, tells how well the program is doing on costs and is not a forecasting formula.

12. Issue management and control is a program integration management process. This process identifies issues and what other related activity?

    A. Promotes issue to risks

    B. Documents issues in the risk register

    C. Documents issues in the issue register

    D. Documents issues in the issue log

    C. Issue management includes the activity to document the identified issues in the issue register. A and B are incorrect; risk management planning and analysis would identify and document risks in the risk register. D is incorrect, as there is not an issue log, but an issue register.

13. Your program is performing very well, and you're actually ahead of the planned program schedule. You discover that your program has an extra $225,000 in the program budget that you won't need to meet the program scope. What should you do with the $225,000?

    A. Add features to the program scope to consume the funds.

    B. Return the funds to the organization as part of cost budgeting.

    C. Add the funds to the program's contingency reserve.

    D. Return the funds to the organization as part of cost control.

    D. Part of cost control is to return extra funds back to the organization. Choices A and C are incorrect, as A describes gold plating the program scope, and choice C is not the correct approach for adding funds to the contingency reserve. Choice B is almost correct, except it's not the cost budgeting process to return the funds to the organization.

14. In which knowledge area does the performance reporting process exist?

    A. Program integrated management

    B. Program communications management

    C. Program cost management

    D. Program quality management

    B. Performance reporting only exists in the program communications management process. Choices A, C, and D are all incorrect, as these knowledge areas do not host the performance reporting process.

15. Your program has 129 stakeholders, but next month the pool of stakeholders will grow to 211. How many more stakeholder communication channels will your program have next month?

    A. 8,256

    B. 22,155

    C. 13,899

    D. 3,321

    C. By using the communications formula of $N(N - 1)/2$ for the current and future number of stakeholders and then finding the difference, you'll arrive at choice C. A, B, and D are all incorrect answers for the number of communication channels.

16. Which risk management knowledge area activity can help you identify the risks that will need a more in-depth analysis?

    A. Qualitative analysis

    B. Quantitative analysis

    C. Risk identification

    D. Risk probability-impact matrix

    A. Qualitative analysis is a fast and subjective process to determine which risks should go on to the more in-depth quantitative analysis. Choice B is incorrect, as quantitative analysis is the next round of analysis. C is tempting, but identified risks move through qualitative analysis before moving on to quantitative analysis. D is simply the matrix to create a risk event value.

17. You have invited all of the sellers to a meeting to discuss the program's contract statement of work. What is this meeting called?

    A. Sellers' conference

    B. Stakeholder kick-off meeting

    C. Bidders' conference

    D. Contract risk analysis meeting

    C. When you invite all the bidders to a conference to discuss the contract statement of work, well, that's a bidders conference. Choices A, B, and D are all incorrect terms I made up just to trick you and make you angry. I am sorry.

18. All of the following are processes in the program human resources management knowledge area except for which one?

    A. Develop program team

    B. Human resource planning

    C. Acquire program team

    D. Performance reporting

    D. Performance reporting is hosted by the program communications management knowledge area. Choices A, B, and C are hosted by the program human resources management knowledge area, so these choices are incorrect.

19. Your program scope statement has been going through rounds of revisions on its way to its final approved form. These rounds of revisions are also known by what term?

   A. Progressive elaboration

   B. Scope control

   C. Iterative planning

   D. Stage gates

   A. Progressive elaboration for the program scope describes the series of detail and discovery that is added to the program scope statement to make it complete. Choice B, scope control, describes the activity to prevent unneeded changes to the program scope. Choice C is incorrect; this term isn't valid. Choice D is a term you'll usually find in projects—it describes the stages associated with milestones, step-funding, and estimating.

20. Which program management knowledge area allows projects to be authorized within the program?

   A. Program procurement management

   B. Human resources management

   C. Program integration management

   D. Projects are not authorized within programs

   C. Component projects are authorized within programs, and this process is hosted in the program integration management knowledge area. A and B are incorrect, as these activities are for the program, not the projects within the program. Choice D is incorrect, as projects are authorized inside of programs.

Programs and Projects

In this chapter, you will

- Explore projects within programs
- Initiate a new project
- Create a project management plan
- Execute the project
- Monitor and control the project
- Close out a program's project

A project is a short-term endeavor to create a unique product or service. Projects are unique in that they are finite—they don't go on and on like an organization's operations. Programs, as you know, are collections of projects orchestrated to work together to realize benefits that could not have been realized by managing each project independently of the others.

Within a program, projects are launched and chartered, and then the project manager is expected to manage the project to completion. As a candidate for the PgMP certification you know how projects are supposed to operate and you know how projects can succumb to the old "of mice and men" adage—both often go astray. For your PgMP examination, however, you will need to know how PMI expects your project managers to manage a project within your program.

Like programs, projects are composed of a suite of processes. These processes share the same process groups as a program: initiating, planning, executing, monitoring and controlling, and closing. Projects also have the same nine knowledge areas that you've learned about for programs. What you'll learn that's different between these two entities, however, are the actual processes within the process groups and knowledge areas. That's the primary goal of this chapter: to give you a robust and efficient recap of project management from PMI's point of view.

Initiating a Project

Within your program you'll have to initiate and authorize projects for them to complete the program deliverables and benefits you're expecting. There are some rules, however, as to how projects may be initiated within your program. There is also some specific terminology that applies to program management and not so much to project management—and vice-versa. You'll need to be able to discern program processes from project processes and when it's appropriate to choose one over the other.

As you can see in Figure 11-1, there are just two project management processes in the initiating process group. You will have to complete these two processes for every project that gets initiated in the program—and for any projects that you may happen to be the sponsor of that are outside of your programs.

Projects are often initiated, as a general rule, to increase the revenue of an organization or to reduce the costs of an organization. Within a program, however, projects are initiated to contribute to benefits and deliverables the program promises to create. Projects, regardless of where they live—in a program or independently in an organization, need to support the business mission, fit the strategic vision of the organization, and have a clearly defined objective that spells out what it takes for the project to be successful.

Chartering the Project

A project charter is a magical thing; it gives authority to the project manager. A project charter authorizes the project manager to use the monies, time, and resources as required to complete the objectives of the project. The project charter is supposed to be writing within the program, signed by you—or the program sponsor—and it identifies the lucky soul that will be the project manager.

The project charter provides for several things:

- **Project requirements for satisfaction**   The project charter must clearly define the requirements for the project to be successful. This can be metrics for satisfaction on the product scope; metrics for project performance; and cost, schedule, and scope objectives. The project manager needs goals to plan and aim for.

- **High-level business needs**   The project charter should define how the project will fit into the program. This includes the expected deliverables for the project that will be passed on to the program's benefits, to other projects within the program, or directly to the program customer.

Figure 11-1
Initiating has only two project processes.

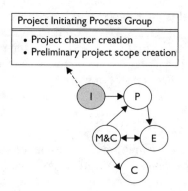

Project Initiating Process Group

- Project charter creation
- Preliminary project scope creation

- **Milestone schedule** A milestone is a timeless event that shows progress within the project. A milestone schedule offers the dates when the project is expected to reach the identified milestones.

- **Stakeholder influence** A stakeholder is anyone that has a vested interest in the project. You can have positive and negative stakeholders that want the project to succeed or to fail. You, the program manager, are a positive stakeholder, as the outcome of the project has a direct bearing on your program.

- **Functional organizations** The project will have to interact with departments, lines of businesses, customers, government agencies, and other organizations that affect how the project will be managed. The project charter needs to define these organizations and what each organization's level of interest and participation may be.

- **Assumptions** An assumption is anything that you believe to be true, but you haven't proved.

- **Constraints** These are anything that limits the project manager's options. Time, cost, and scope requirements are the three most common constraints.

- **Summary budget** The charter should have a summary budget that defines the maximum capital allowed for the project.

All of these things go into the project charter. The charter is then signed by the project sponsor and the project's identified project manager. Charters are rarely edited or changed once they've been approved and set into action. While charters allow the project to be launched within a program and they authorize the project manager, it's important for the program manager to respect some boundaries between the activities of program management and the activities of project management. While there may be some decisions that are deferred to the program manager, it's important to not hover or crowd the project manager. In other words, put some trust in the project manager and stay out of the way.

Creating the Preliminary Project Scope Statement

The *project scope statement* is a document that defines what entire project will create and deliver as part of the project. It defines everything that the project will create for the organization—and sets some boundaries as to what the project won't create. The preliminary scope statement creates an initial foundation for the direction the project will take and offers some direction for the next process group, planning.

The preliminary project scope statement includes all of the following:

- Project objectives
- Project deliverable characteristics
- Acceptance criteria for the project deliverables
- Project boundaries of what's in and out of scope
- Constraints and assumptions

- Initial project risks
- Milestones
- Initial WBS
- Rough order of magnitude cost estimate
- Configuration management requirements
- Approval requirements for project completion

This preliminary project scope will probably undergo some major revisions before it is signed off as the official project scope statement. The project manager will learn new information through stakeholder analysis, testing, and talking with the project stakeholders about their interests, needs, and concerns for the project. This process is an example of progressive elaboration. *Progressive elaboration* is a term to describe the incremental steps by which information contributes to a project or program. In this instance, the preliminary scope starts with a broad painting of how the project should be and then, as information becomes available, it becomes more and more exact. I'll talk more about the project scope statement in one moment.

Working Project Life Cycles

A life cycle is how long something will live. Projects and programs are both temporary things that won't live forever—though it may often seem like they will. Sometimes you might hear someone grumbling on about their project life cycles. *Project life cycles* is a term that gets twisted, mutilated, and overused without the grumbler ever really defining exactly what he is grumbling about. I'm going to get crystal clear for you on this business.

I'll start with the most obvious life cycle: the project management life cycle. This is the logical progression of the five process groups within a project. Projects begin with initiating and then move on to planning. From planning it's on to executing, monitoring and controlling, and then closing. All projects, from IT to construction, move through these five process groups. These are universal to all projects—even if your organization calls them something fancy or different, the philosophy is still the same. Of course, project management philosophy aside, you should know the process groups, as PMI calls them for your PMI exam.

The second life cycle is the project life cycle. This is probably what most grumblers mean when they talk about their project life cycle. A project life cycle describes the unique phases and nature of each individual project. Consider a project in technology and its special phases, terminology, and pocket protectors. Now consider a project in construction with its own special phases, languages, and hardhats. The special nature of the discipline the project is centered on determines the special phases for the project. In other words, every project has its own unique life cycle.

You won't have the same project life cycle in technology as you do in construction, because the discipline and nature of the projects are totally different. What you will have, however, is the same project management life cycle in both projects. Technology and construction, and every other project for that matter, will all move through the five process groups to reach the project's ending.

Planning the Project

The planning process group in project management has the most processes of all the project management process groups. There are, as you can see in Figure 11-2, 21 processes in planning. The primary goal of planning is to create a plan that provides structure for the project and communicates the intents of the project. The project plan serves as a guide for the execution process group.

Project planning moves through the same nine knowledge areas as a program, but the focus is, of course, on projects instead of programs:

- Project integration management

- Project scope management

- Project time management

- Project cost management

- Project quality management

- Project human resources management

- Project communications management

- Project risk management

- Project procurement management

The project management plan is actually a compilation of several subsidiary plans that direct the activities in each knowledge area. Each of these knowledge areas has at least one plan, and a couple of knowledge areas have two plans. The quality knowledge area has two plans, the quality management plan and the process improvement plan. Risk management may have two plans as well: the risk management plan and the risk response plan.

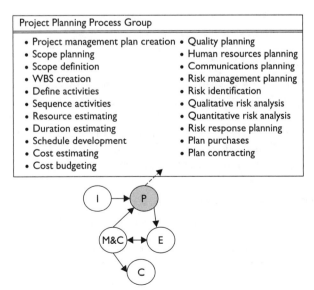

Figure 11-2
Planning is the largest process group, with 21 processes.

Project Planning Process Group

- Project management plan creation
- Scope planning
- Scope definition
- WBS creation
- Define activities
- Sequence activities
- Resource estimating
- Duration estimating
- Schedule development
- Cost estimating
- Cost budgeting
- Quality planning
- Human resources planning
- Communications planning
- Risk management planning
- Risk identification
- Qualitative risk analysis
- Quantitative risk analysis
- Risk response planning
- Plan purchases
- Plan contracting

Planning the Project Scope

When it comes to planning, the scope management knowledge area has three processes that contribute to scope management. Whenever there is a change to the project scope, the project scope is updated to reflect the approved change. This is just one quick example of how planning is an iterative process that allows planning activities to happen when and as they are needed.

Project scope planning is a process to plan how the project scope will be defined, how the WBS will be created, and then how the project scope will be controlled. The project scope is all of the required work, and only the required work, to complete the project objectives. Work, in this instance, defines work as the actual deliverables the project will be creating for the program rather than the labor to create the deliverables. Scope planning actually defines how the project manager, the project team, and the key stakeholders will define and then control the project scope. This process creates the scope management plan.

The second scope planning process is the actual definition of the project scope. Based on the preliminary project scope statement and rounds of progressive elaboration, the project scope statement may be created and defined for the project. The scope definition process creates the project's scope statement. The project sponsor, the program manager, the project manager, and often the program customers will sign off on the document. The creation and agreement of the completeness of the project scope is paramount, or the project may undergo risks, changes, and frustration on the part of the project team.

The final scope planning process is the project work breakdown structure (WBS) creation. Similar to the PWBS, the project WBS is a visual decomposition of the project scope. It illustrates all of the deliverables down to the work packages within the project scope. The WBS is needed in order to complete five other project processes:

- Cost estimating
- Cost budgeting
- Resource planning
- Risk management planning
- Activity definition

You'll need the WBS in order to do these processes, so you can see, it's a major cornerstone of project management. There is one caveat to the preceding list: cost estimating needs the WBS if the project manager wants to create the definitive cost estimate. The definitive cost estimate is the most accurate estimating approach and requires the WBS input. You could, technically, create a cost estimate without the WBS—it just wouldn't be as accurate. Fascinating, I know.

Planning for Project Time

There are five time management planning processes:

- **Defining the project activities** The project manager needs the WBS to determine what the activities are to create the things the WBS promises.

- **Sequencing the activities**   Once the project manager has created the activity list, it's time to put the activities in the order in which they should happen.

- **Resource estimating**   The activities have been defined, so it's now time to estimate the resources needed to complete the activities. While the heart of this process is dealing with the labor needed to complete the work, don't forget that some resources are just people. Resources dealing with time may also relate to the equipment and materials you'll need to procure in order to complete the project activities.

- **Duration estimating**   Once you know what activities the project requires, you've sequenced the activities, and you've determined the required resources, you can now calculate the estimated duration of how long it'll take to complete each activity.

- **Developing the schedule**   This final time management planning process deals with creating the project network diagrams, determining the available float on activities within the project, and attempting to massage the schedule for the betterment of the project. The project manager may reorder the network diagram, add labor, add and remove constraints, and adjust the schedule to try to finish the project in the best amount of time the project has.

These five planning processes can be revisited over and over as needed throughout the project. Usually, these processes are revisited when there are changes to the project scope. Changes to the project scope will usually cause the activity list to change, which in turn causes the network sequencing and project network diagrams to change, and can cause even the project's critical path to change.

Planning for the Project Costs

There are just two planning processes for the project cost management knowledge area. The first process is cost estimating. The cost estimating process attempts to predict how much the project will likely cost to reach the conclusion. There are three flavors of cost estimating:

- **Rough order of magnitude**   This project cost estimate approach is very broad and unreliable. It's usually created with the preliminary project scope statement and has a range of variance of –25% to +75% for the project completion. It's wild.

- **Budget estimate**   This project cost estimate is somewhat reliable, as it's usually created once the project scope statement is approved. The budget estimate has a range of variance of –10% to +25% for the project completion.

- **Definitive estimate**   This project cost estimate is the most reliable, but it takes the longest to complete, because you'll need the project's WBS created. The approach is also called bottom-up estimating, because you're starting at the bottom of the WBS and working your way to the top. The range of variance for the definitive estimate is –5% to +10% for the project completion.

PART III

As the project moves into execution, you'll compare the actual costs of the project work to the actual costs to deliver the project work. This is where cost budgeting begins. Cost budgeting is the actual costs to create the individual work packages as defined in the WBS. This process creates the project's cost baseline.

Planning for Project Quality

Planning for project quality involves determining first what quality means to the program. This isn't an esoteric exercise. Quality is a conformance to the requirements and a fitness for use. The scope statement defines what the requirements are for the project—that part's easy. You can quickly deduce that to have quality in the project, you'll need to simply adhere to the scope. While that's true, there's the second part of the quality definition: fitness for use.

Imagine a project to create a brick wall as part of your program. The project calls for the exact type of bricks to be used, the dimensions of the wall, and all the other specs related to the brick wall. The project team can create the wall to the exact specs of the requirements, but if the mortar between the bricks is splattered around the pavement and onto the bricks, and it bulges in and out of the wall—that's not fit for use. There are implied needs that go along with the project requirements.

Quality planning defines the conformance to requirements and captures the spirit and intent of the deliverable. Quality planning also defines the quality assurance and quality control processes the project will adhere to. Quality planning creates the quality management plan and the scope management plan.

Creating the Staffing Management Plan

When it comes to human resources planning in a project, most of the activities will defer to the constraints created by the program manager and the enterprise environmental factors established by the organization as a whole. Human resources planning creates the staffing management plan, which communicates several things:

- Resource requirements to complete the project work
- Project management activities the project team will participate in, such as quality assurance, risk management, and procurement
- Roles and responsibilities for the project
- When project team members are brought onto and released from the project team

This process will rely largely on the enterprise environmental factors to guide decisions within the project. Considerations are given for the interfaces the project team will interact with, union-based agreements, and the organizational structure where the project is being held.

NOTE Unions are not constraints—they are stakeholders. The collective bargaining agreement, however, may have constraints on the project.

Planning for Project Communications

It's been said that 90 percent of project manager's time is spent communicating. When you think about all the project team members, managers, customers, and other stakeholders the project manager must speak with, it's easy to believe this wild quote. As a rule, the larger the project, the more planning you'll have to provide in communications. Just as communications are a key activity in managing a program, it's not much different in a project.

Project communications planning creates the communications management plan. This subsidiary plan answers some familiar questions:

- Who needs what information?
- When is the information needed?
- What is the modality in which the communication is expected?

The plan will be updated as conditions change within the project—such as new projects within the program, newly identified stakeholders, or even the requested frequency of communications. The program manager may direct the project manager to communicate information about certain conditions within the project, such as earned value management variables.

Preparing for Project Risks

There are five processes in the risk management planning process. Each of the risk planning events is iterative, as risk management does not end until the project moves into its closing phase. A risk is an uncertain event or condition that can have a negative or positive effect on the project. That's right—not all risks are bad; it's their impact and probability you're most concerned with.

Here's the order and description of these five risk management planning activities:

- **Risk management planning**   This risk management process creates the risk management plan. The risk management plan defines how the project manager and the project team will complete the remainder of the risk management tasks within the project.

- **Risk identification**   Throughout the project risks must be identified. Risk identification is the first process to address specific project risks by means of brainstorming, testing, simulations, and stakeholder analysis.

- **Qualitative risk analysis**   This is a high-level, subjective analysis of the risk events. The goal is to "qualify" risks for additional, in-depth analysis in quantitative analysis.

- **Quantitative risk analysis**   This in-depth risk analysis quantifies the identified risks through testing, simulations, and studies. Quantitative analysis seeks to find a true risk probability, impact, and risk exposure. This process helps create the contingency reserve for the project.

- **Risk response planning**   The project management process addresses the risks with one of seven potential risk responses: acceptance, avoidance, transference, mitigation, enhancing, exploiting, and sharing. These are the same risk responses available for a program.

All of these process outcomes are documented in the risk register for each project within the program. The risk register can be linked to other projects within the program through a risk database. This allows the program management team to look for trends, multiple risk responses, and opportunities to enhance and exploit positive risks within the program.

Preparing for Project Procurement

There are just two procurement processes in the planning process group. The first is to plan what the project needs to procure. This process should be tied back to the program's budget for each project. The demand to procure materials and resources should be documented via this process, as should the timing when the materials and resources should be purchased. This allows the program to manage cash flow and anticipate purchases across multiple projects.

Whenever a project moves through the procurement processes, the contracts that are to be used should be determined at the program level. With each contract type the buyer or the seller carries the majority of the risk. Project managers and the program manager should be familiar with the following contract types:

- **Cost Plus Fixed Fee** This contract represents the actual costs plus a profit margin for the seller. It's considered risky for the buyer, because any wasted materials are paid for by the buyer, not the vendor.

- **Cost Plus Percentage of Cost** This is often called the most dangerous contract type, because costs can quickly skyrocket. The buyer pays for the materials and a percentage of the cost of the materials. If the vendor wastes materials, the buyer has to buy new materials and pay another percentage of the costs of the new materials. Not so hot.

- **Cost Plus Incentive Fee** Actual costs plus profit margin for seller—and an incentive to finish the work early. Cost overruns represent risk to the buyer.

- **Fixed-Price** Agreed price for contracted product. This contract can include incentives for the seller. The seller assumes risk, because if they waste materials or labor, they, not the buyer, have to absorb the cost overruns.

- **Lump-Sum** This is the same thing as a fixed-price contract, just a different name. The buyer and the seller create an agreed price for contracted product. This contract may also include incentives for the seller.

- **Firm-Fixed-Price** Very similar to fixed-price and lump-sum contracts, as there's an agreed price for contracted product. This one is usually used for materials, such as two tons of pea gravel or five laptop computers.

- **Fixed-Price Incentive Fee** Agreed price for contracted product. There are many flavors of this contract type, but most have bonuses for the vendor tied to completion dates for the project.

- **Time and Materials** This simple contract has a price assigned for the time and materials provided by the seller. Time and materials contracts without "not-to-exceed" clauses can lead to cost overruns.

- **Unit-Price** This contract uses a simple parametric approach. Price is assigned for a measurable unit of product or time. An example of this contract is $178 per software license.

Contract and selection may happen at the project level, but probably most will be influenced by the program's influence over the projects. The program's governance and procurement practices will likely override the project manager's participation in procurement, but not always. In some programs the project manager may be solely responsible for the budget and procurement approaches at the project level.

Executing the Project

Planning cannot go on forever. At some point the projects within the program have to get down to business and start doing the work that'll create their project scopes. The execution of the project plans, the fulfillment of the project scopes, and the assurance that the projects are completing their scopes as planned will result in the deliverables the program has promised to its customers.

Project execution has seven processes, as seen in Figure 11-3. Project execution succeeds project planning and is balanced with the monitoring and controlling processes. As events such as risks, issues, and changes happen within the project, additional planning will likely be required. When the project shifts back to planning, the project team should be involved to anticipate the new work and the new execution that may come from the planning processes.

Working the Plans

I'm sure you've heard the old cliché that you need to plan your work and then work your plans. There's a reason clichés like these hang around for so long—they're true. It's no different in project management: the plan is created and now the plan has to be executed. This is working the project plan. It really is about getting stuff done.

Figure 11-3
There are seven project executing processes.

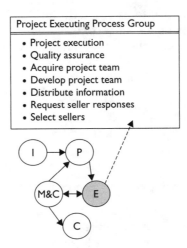

Project Executing Process Group

- Project execution
- Quality assurance
- Acquire project team
- Develop project team
- Distribute information
- Request seller responses
- Select sellers

This process relies on the project management plan and approval of changes to the project plan. Approved corrective and preventive actions are fleshed into the project, as are approved change requests to the project scope. The project team may not always be happy about these project approvals—but too bad! That's not to say the project manager is a brute crashing work down on project team members, but rather this is what the project team should do—and should expect within a program. Program changes are going to happen, and the project team should expect the changes. The key is to communicate the change control processes and expectations with the project manager, and she should do the same with her project team.

Managing Quality Assurance

The quality management plan from the project's planning process group assures that quality is planned into the project. The execution of the project according to plan and according to scope is the best effort to ensure that quality is created as part of the project deliverables. Within the program and perhaps within the performing organization there may be a quality assurance program to guide the quality assurance within the project. Quality assurance (QA) uses four activities within projects:

- **Quality planning** The same activities that were used to plan quality into the project can be used to execute quality as part of the project.

- **Quality audits** A quality audit is a review of the project to confirm that the project is participating and adhering to the organization's quality assurance program. Quality audits confirm that the project is being managed according to the QA rules of the organization and takes steps to bring the project back into alignment with the QA policies if the project is out of bounds.

- **Process analysis** The quality planning process created the process improvement plan. QA executes that plan by inspecting the project's processes and aims to make the project's processes run smoother, better, and faster to rid the project of non–value added activities.

- **Quality control tools and techniques** Some of the same inspection-driven tools used in the quality control can be used in QA. This is one of those weird PMI-isms where there's an overlap between process groups. Don't sweat it too much; quality control tools are used to inspect the project's execution. I'll talk more about QC in just a bit.

The results of these four QA activities can lead to new change requests, recommendations for corrective actions, and records for the project archives. QA happens throughout the project, not just once and then forgotten. The big message of QA is to do the work right the first time—it's cost effective and saves time.

Managing the Project Team

Before a project manager can manage the project team, he has to get one. That's why the first executing process for human resource management is to acquire the project team. The project manager may, or more likely may not, have any control over what resources are assigned to the project team. Preassigned project teams are the norm for most organizations I've consulted with, but there are some lucky project managers who get to cherry-pick and build their teams.

In a matrix-structured environment, the project manager may negotiate with other project managers and even functional managers to trade and bargain resources onto the project team. In some instances the project manager may need to work with the procurement processes to contract labor onto the project team.

It's the norm these days to work with virtual teams through web-based and collaborative software. Virtual teams allow programs to take advantage of resources around the world, save on travel, and allow employees to work from home. Virtual teams do, however, create some challenges. Planning for language barriers, time zone differences, and the challenges of communications needs to be developed.

The second human resources executing process is team development. Team development is more than taking the gang out for pizza. Team development is a facilitated approach to create bonds and synergies within the project. Team development should happen with all of the project team members, not just a handful. This is another challenge for those pesky virtual team members.

Distribute Project Information

The only executing process that deals with communications management is to distribute project information. The project manager will do this by following the directions of the communications management plan and acting as conditions within the project warrant. Formal and informal communication methods are called upon to communicate the proper information to the right stakeholders. It's easy to talk about, but tough to do.

Information distribution is also the project execution process that manages lessons learned documentation within a project. Lessons learned activities do not happen only at the end of a project, but throughout the project as lessons are learned. The documentation from lessons learned, information gathering, and other project management communications all becomes part of the project's contribution to organizational process assets updates.

Hiring Project Sellers

I hope by now you don't find it surprising that sellers are not selected in planning but in execution. There are two executing procurement processes; the first is the request seller responses. This is where the project manager issues a statement of work (SOW) and one of the following documents to the sellers:

- **Request for proposal (RFP)** This document asks the sellers to create an offer, ideas, and suggestions to accomplish the work outlined in the statement of work. An RFP is also looking for the seller to provide a price to create the things outlined in the statement of work.

- **Invitation for bid (IFB)** This document is asks the sellers to provide a cost for the items outlined in the SOW.

- **Request for quote (RFQ)** This procurement document is the same thing as a bid, just under a different name. It is asking the vendor to provide a price only.

Drawing on the response from the sellers, the project management team can evaluate the bids, quotes, and proposals to choose the best vendor for the project. An intermediary step, the bidders' conference, allows the bidders to query the project manager about the SOW. The project manager will update and redistribute the SOW if needed. Once the negotiations have been completed and a seller is selected, a contract is drawn up for both parties in the agreement.

Monitoring and Controlling the Project

While most project managers are certain their project team members are out working away and completing the project according to scope, there can't be surprises as to the team's and project's performance. The monitoring and controlling processes work in tandem with the project executing processes to keep the project on track, on budget, and finishing on schedule.

There are 12 processes in the monitoring and controlling process group (see Figure 11-4). Most of these 12 processes rely on work to be executed based on the corresponding project plan. The basic goal of these processes is to ensure that the project is completed according to plan—and to save money from having to do the work twice.

Project managers and the project team members both participate in these processes. The project manager oversees and directs these processes, while the project team members operate within the confines of the project to ensure that their work results meet expectations. When the project goes astray, these processes aim to nudge things back in alignment or to send the project back to planning.

Monitoring the Project

Two project processes are the engine of the monitoring and controlling process group. The first, and perhaps the most obvious, is the monitor and control project work process. When the project team members complete their work, they'll create deliverables for the project and for the program. These deliverables must be in alignment with the project plan or the deliverables are a big waste of time and money.

Figure 11-4
There are 12 monitoring and controlling project processes.

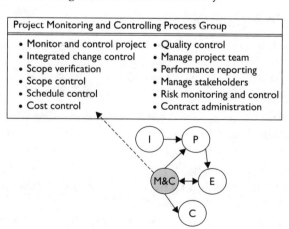

Project Monitoring and Controlling Process Group

- Monitor and control project
- Integrated change control
- Scope verification
- Scope control
- Schedule control
- Cost control
- Quality control
- Manage project team
- Performance reporting
- Manage stakeholders
- Risk monitoring and control
- Contract administration

The second process is the management of the integrated change control. This process examines all the impacts of a change for a project. Consider a change in the project scope. The change must be examined to see what its effect on all of the knowledge areas may be:

- **Cost** The scope change may incur new costs.
- **Schedule** Scope changes may require more time to deliver.
- **Quality** The quality attributes of the change must be examined.
- **Human resources** The change may require additional labor or specialized labor to implement.
- **Communications management** The change will need to be communicated throughout the project and possibly the program.
- **Risk management** The change may introduce new risks for the project.
- **Procurement management** The change may introduce new contracts or changes to vendors' contracts.

Project integration management is used whenever there is a change to time, costs, scope, or contracts, and it always examines all of the project knowledge areas.

Monitoring the Project Scope

There are two processes dealing with the project scope. The first I'll address is the most accessible: scope control. The project manager wants the project team to do their work according to design. Little bells and whistles are nice to have, but if the project scope doesn't call for these little doodads, these extras are known as scope creep. Scope creep is anything that's added to the project scope without following the documented scope change control system.

 NOTE Scope creep is also known as project poison.

The scope control process is also concerned with completing the project scope as it was designed. This process is somewhat linked to quality control as quality is the conformance to project requirements. Scope control is directly tied to the scope change control system and the project's integrated change control process. When changes happen to the scope, the project configuration management system is invoked. Configuration management is the documentation and control of the features and functions of the project scope.

The second process in this knowledge area is scope verification. This is an easy one. When the project team builds something, the project's customer inspects the work and signs off on the work, allowing the project to move forward. Scope verification is all about getting the project customer to accept the work so that the project may move forward.

Controlling the Project Schedule and Costs

These two processes are done throughout the project to ensure that the project is completed as closely to the designed project schedule and to the project costs as planned. Controlling the project schedule relies on progress reporting and then project reactions to the news the progress reports share. When schedule variances, schedule slippage, or changes to the project schedule haunt the project, the project manager will apply corrective actions to the project to address the schedule.

Controlling the project costs is very similar. The project manager will rely on performance measurements to see how the project's doing—and where the project is very likely to end. Performance reports, for your exam, are most likely to come about in the form of earned value management. Specific to time and cost is the schedule variance and cost variance and the cost performance index and the schedule performance index.

Managing the Project Team

It's up to the project manager to manage the project team, though the program manager may offer guidance and take over some human resource matters that have to be escalated to the program level. The management of the project team should be documented in the staffing management plan—though general management skills are called upon as conditions within the project demand.

Managing the project team relies on good old-fashioned observations and conversations with the project team. The project manager has to see how the team is performing, how the project team members interact with one another, and where issues may be lying in wait. The project manager can use conflict management techniques to help the team resolve their differences and keep the project moving forward.

One tool for team management is project performance appraisals. The project manager should follow the guidelines from the program level or the performing organization for creating team member reviews. Often when a project team member realizes that her project performance is directly tied to her yearly performance reviews wonderful things can happen.

Controlling Communications

As communication is core to the program, it's also core to the constituent projects within the program. Monitoring and controlling offers two communication processes that'll balance the project execution. The first—and this shouldn't be a surprise—is performance reporting. Considering earned value management, project completion, and issues within the project, the project manager communicates how well the project is doing. The performance reporting can highlight key areas, such as cost, schedule, or risks. The program manager and the project managers should establish a regular schedule for these performance reports.

The second process is a bit, well, soupier: managing the project stakeholders. Stakeholders include anyone that has a vested interest in the outcome of the project. Key stakeholders are the project team members, the project manager, the program manager, and project and program customers. These stakeholders will be the people the project manager is most interested in managing.

Stakeholder management means talking and communicating with stakeholders. The project manager needs to stay in contact with the stakeholders and address their perceptions, threats, and worries by communicating both good and bad news. When issues pop up in the program, these should be recorded in the issues log and addressed by a given deadline. Issue management is linked to stakeholder management because stakeholders may create or identify issues within the project.

Monitoring Project Risks

The monitoring and controlling of project risks are important, ongoing activities within each project. The most reliable tool for this process is risk reassessment. The program and the project manager are constantly on the lookout for new risks. New risks are sent back to planning for analysis and response planning. Risk reassessment also considers risks that have been identified but may be stashed away on the low-level watch lists in the risk register.

Through status meetings the project team is invited to share any new risks that have been identified and to consider the measured likelihood and impact of risks. The project manager can also use status meetings to discuss technical performance measurements and how these measurements can introduce risks into the project.

As risks happen within a project, their cost impact is subtracted from the project's cost reserve. As events happen, however, the contingency reserve needs to be reviewed to consider the amount of funds available to balance the risk exposure for the remainder of the project. Too few funds in the contingency reserve can wreck the project's ability to finish on time and on budget—and that's a risk.

Performing Contract Administration

The final monitoring and controlling process is to make certain those pesky project vendors are living up to the terms of the contract. The buyer, typically the project manager, will review the work and deliverables the vendors provide for the project to ensure that it's up to the terms of the contract. The project manager may rely on expert judgment, such as that of the project team, to measure the completeness of the vendors' work.

Vendors like to get paid for their work, so part of this process is for the project manager and the performing organization to live up to their end of the bargain as well. When a vendor submits an invoice for work performed, the project manager confirms the work is complete and then approves the invoice for payment as directed by the terms of the contract.

Sometimes, however, the work won't be performed according to terms. If the vendor and the buyer disagree, this is a claim. Claims administration tries to settle the differences between the two parties—especially if the claim is preventing the project from moving forward. The contract must have stipulations about disagreements for the claims and how the claims may be escalated through the program all the way to the court system if needed.

All documentation regarding the project contract, the communications between the seller and buyer, and other supporting detail goes into the records management system. The contents of the record management system will be folded into the program's contribution to the organizational process assets once the program is closed.

Closing the Project

There are just two straightforward processes for the project's closing process group, as you can see in Figure 11-5. The first process wraps up the project—it's the close project process. Guess what this one does. While it's simple and direct, there are significant creations from the process.

The major component of the close project process is the administrative closure procedures. Administrative closure is the formal documentation and sign-off from the stakeholders that the project is complete. This process also readies the project deliverable for the program to begin using its deliverables.

All of the documentation of the project is archived as part of the organizational process assets created by the program. This includes the formal acceptance documentation, project files, closure documentation, and any other relevant historical information.

The second closing process is the contract closure process. This procurement activity is done throughout the project, not just at the end of the project life cycle. When a project's vendor has completed their work according to the terms of the contract or when a contract is terminated, this process is invoked. A procurement audit ensures that the buyer and seller both completed their obligations for the project, and the contract is closed according to terms.

Figure 11-5
There are just two closing processes.

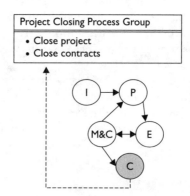

Project Closing Process Group
- Close project
- Close contracts

Chapter Summary

Programs are full of projects. Projects are the gears for the program that will create the deliverable and benefits for the organization. The project managers within the projects need to see the big picture of how their projects help the program reach its goals and how the projects are linked to one another. The 44 processes discussed in this chapter make up the five process groups for every project within a program.

All projects begin with the initiation process group. I think the most important thing from this process group is the project charter, as it authorizes the project to exist. The charter names the project manager and assigns power to the project manager to manage the resources to complete the project objectives. You technically don't have a project without also having a project charter.

The fattest process group is the planning process group. This iterative process group has 21 processes and touches each of the nine knowledge areas. The whole point of planning is to create a plan. The point of having a plan is to communicate what the project manager's intentions are for the project. Every knowledge area has at least one project plan except for quality—it's special and gets two plans (the quality management plan and the process improvement plan).

The executing process group is where all of the project work gets done. Its seven processes consume the most project time and the most project cash. Project execution is the largest process group, though quality assurance can be time-consuming as well. The two tricky processes from the executing group deals with procurement. Remember, requesting seller responses and selecting the sellers happens during project execution—not planning.

Parallel with the project execution process group is the monitoring and controlling process group. There are 12 processes in this group, and all of them keep checks on the project work to ensure the project is executed according to project plan. When problems, issues, and risks arise in the project, it'll be the monitoring and controlling processes that'll send them back to planning.

Finally, your favorite process group is closing; it's my favorite too. Closing has but two processes: close project and close contract. Closing the project involves someone, probably the program manager, signing off on the project work, closing the project, and releasing the resources. Contract closure involves ensuring that all of details of the contract have been met and closing the contract according to the contract terms.

Key Terms

Administrative closure The formal documentation and sign-off from the stakeholders that the project is complete. This process also readies the project deliverable for the program to begin using its deliverables.

Budget estimate This project cost estimate is somewhat reliable, as it's usually created once the project scope statement is approved. The budget estimate has a range of variance of −10% to +25% for the project completion.

Closing process group This process group has two processes that close the project and close out project contracts.

Collective bargaining agreement   A constraint the project and the program must follow when it works with union stakeholders.

Constituent project   A temporary undertaking to create a unique product or service for the program in which the project resides

Definitive estimate   Also called bottom-up estimating, because you're starting at the bottom of the WBS and working your way to the top. The range of variance for the definitive estimate is –5% to +10% for the project completion.

Execution process group   This process group has seven processes and completes the work defined in the project plans.

Initiating process group   This group hosts two project processes and begins the project management life cycle.

Invitation for bid (IFB)   This document is asking the sellers to provide a cost for the items outlined in the SOW.

Milestone   A milestone is a timeless event that shows progress within the project.

Milestone schedule   The milestone schedule offers the dates when the project is expected to reach the identified milestones.

Monitoring and controlling process group   This process group has 12 processes and seeks to maintain the integrity of the project's baselines, quality, and overall performance.

Planning process group   This process group has 21 project processes, documents the intent of the project, and creates plans to manage each of the nine knowledge areas.

Preliminary project scope statement   An initial foundation for the direction the project will take, this statement offers some direction for the planning process group.

Project communications management   This knowledge area creates the communications management plan, oversees information distribution, ensures that project performance is reported, and is where the stakeholder management process resides.

Project cost management   This knowledge area is concerned with estimating the project costs, budgeting the project costs, and then controlling the project expenses.

Project human resource management   This knowledge area creates the staffing management plan that defines how the team will be acquired and developed and what approaches the project manager will take to manage the project team.

Project integration management   This knowledge area coordinates how each process group and project knowledge area works with the others.

Project management life cycle   The progression of a project through its five process groups: initiating, planning, executing, monitoring and controlling, and closing.

Project procurement management   This knowledge area creates the procurement management plan to define what needs to be procured, how sellers will be selected, how the project manager will perform contract administration, and how the contracts will be closed.

Project quality management There are three quality processes in this knowledge area: quality planning, quality assurance, and quality control.

Project risk management This knowledge area creates the risk management plan and oversees risk identification, qualitative and quantitative analysis, risk response planning, and the ongoing efforts of risk monitoring and control.

Project scope management This knowledge area defines how the project scope will be planned, the WBS created, the scope work verified, and overall control achieved for the project scope.

Project time management This knowledge area begins with activity definition, schedule estimates, and scheduling, and then moves on to controlling the project schedule.

Request for proposal (RFP) This document asks the sellers to create an offer, ideas, and suggestions to accomplish the work outlined in the statement of work. An RFP is also looking for the seller to provide a price to create the things outlined in the statement of work.

Request for quote (RFQ) This procurement document is the same thing as a bid, just going by a different name. It is asking the vendor to provide a price only.

Risk register A project's log of risk events: their nature, status, and potential responses.

Rough order of magnitude This project cost estimate approach is very broad and unreliable. It's usually created with the preliminary project scope statement and has a range of variance of −25% to +75% for the project completion.

Scope creep Small, undocumented changes added to the project scope; this is also known as project poison.

Questions

1. Which process group has the most project processes?

    A. Initiating

    B. Planning

    C. Executing

    D. Closing

2. What project document officially names the project manager in a project that exists within a program?

    A. Program scope statement

    B. Program charter

    C. Project charter

    D. Project scope statement

3. What project document defines how the project will be executed?

   A. Project management plan

   B. Project scope management plan

   C. Work breakdown structure

   D. Project execution plan

4. You are the program manager for your organization. You have 12 projects within your program that all work together to contribute to the deliverables of the program. Your program has just approved a change request that will affect the project scope of one of the constituent projects. What project process should the project manager carry out to inspect the impact of the change on her project?

   A. She should use the scope management process.

   B. She should use the risk monitoring and control process.

   C. She should use the contract administration process.

   D. She should use the integrated change control process.

5. A project has recently completed the project scope and is ready to close. What closing activity ensures that the project work is completed and ready to close?

   A. Procurement audit

   B. Scope verification

   C. Administrative closure

   D. Quality control

6. Which project knowledge area is responsible for managing the project team?

   A. Project human resource management

   B. Project scope management

   C. Project communications management

   D. Project integration management

7. Which project process group is responsible for creating the project's risk contingency reserve?

   A. Planning

   B. Executing

   C. Monitoring and controlling

   D. Project risk management

8. Which project management process is responsible for finding mistakes before the customer does?

   A. Quality assurance

   B. Quality control

C. Quality planning

D. Scope verification

9. A project within your program has identified several risks. What project management process will help the project management team build a risk contingency reserve?

   A. Qualitative risk analysis

   B. Quantitative risk analysis

   C. Risk response planning

   D. Cost estimating

10. Todd, a software developer for the NHG Project within your program, has been adding fields, buttons, and other extras for customers of the project. The customers, however, have been approaching Todd directly and asking him to make the changes without following the prescribed project change control system. These changes are known as what?

    A. Value-added changes

    B. Scope creep

    C. Errors and omissions

    D. Stakeholder management

11. Marcy has created a request for quote for a group of sellers. What thing does Marcy expect back from the sellers?

    A. Bid

    B. Price

    C. Proposal

    D. Statement of work

12. What procurement activity allows sellers to query a statement of work for clarity?

    A. Scope reassessment

    B. Claims management

    C. Bidders' conference

    D. SOW update

13. What project management knowledge area gets two plans?

    A. Project scope management

    B. Project procurement management

    C. Project integration management

    D. Project quality management

14. You are the program manager for your organization. One of your project managers is confused about performance reporting and doesn't understand your approach. You want the project manager to report on the cost and schedule variances and overall health. What management approach should you explain to the project manager?

   A. Quality management

   B. Earned value management

   C. Project integration management

   D. Total quality management

15. A project manager has hired an electrician to complete part of the project work, because the electrical work is too dangerous. This is what type of risk response?

   A. Mitigation

   B. Sharing

   C. Avoidance

   D. Transference

16. How many project management processes are there in the project management life cycle?

   A. 44

   B. 21

   C. 9

   D. 5

17. Which project management process is responsible for creating the WBS?

   A. WBS creation

   B. Scope definition

   C. Scope planning

   D. Project integration management

18. What project management plan will define the reports the project stakeholders will need throughout the project?

   A. Project management plan

   B. Staffing management plan

   C. Communications management plan

   D. Schedule management plan

19. A seller and a project manager are in disagreement about a deliverable the seller has created for the project. This disagreement is known as what?

   A. Issue

   B. Risk

    C. Claim

    D. Stakeholder management

20. All of the following are project planning processes except for which one?

    A. Cost estimating

    B. Selecting sellers

    C. Schedule development

    D. Quantitative risk analysis

Questions and Answers

1. Which process group has the most project processes?

    A. Initiating

    B. Planning

    C. Executing

    D. Closing

    B. The planning process group has 21 project processes. Initiating has two processes, executing has seven processes, and closing has but two processes, so Choices A, C, and D are incorrect.

2. What project document officially names the project manager in a project that exists within a program?

    A. Program scope statement

    B. Program charter

    C. Project charter

    D. Project scope statement

    C. The project charter officially names the project manager. The program scope statement does not name the project manager, but rather the program objectives, so Choice A is wrong. B, the program charter, is also incorrect, as this document names the program managers and not the individual project managers. D, the project scope statement, defines the work the project will accomplish.

3. What project document defines how the project will be executed?

    A. Project management plan

    B. Project scope management plan

    C. Work breakdown structure

    D. Project execution plan

    A. The project management plan defines all of the work and the management of the project. Choice B defines how the project scope will be managed. Choice C defines the WBS, which is a visual representation of the project scope. Choice D, the project execution plan, is not a valid project management term.

4. You are the program manager for your organization. You have 12 projects within your program that all work together to contribute to the deliverables of the program. Your program has just approved a change request that will affect the project scope of one of the constituent projects. What project process should the project manager carry out to inspect the impact of the change on her project?

   A. She should use the scope management process.

   B. She should use the risk monitoring and control process.

   C. She should use the contract administration process.

   D. She should use the integrated change control process.

   D. When a scope change occurs, or technically when any change to scope, time, cost, or contracts occurs, the integrated change control process is used to determine the impact of the change on all of the project knowledge areas. Choice A is incorrect, as there is not a scope management process. Choice B is incorrect, as this only addresses the risks the new scope may introduce and not all of the project knowledge areas. Choice C is also incorrect, as this only addresses changes to the project contracts; the question does not indicate that changes to the project contracts have occurred.

5. A project has recently completed the project scope and is ready to close. What closing activity ensures that the project work is completed and ready to close?

   A. Procurement audit

   B. Scope verification

   C. Administrative closure

   D. Quality control

   C. Administrative closure is part of the closing process to ensure the project is completely finished and ready to be transferred into the program deliverables or operations. A, procurement audit, happens as part of contract closure. B, scope verification, is a monitoring and controlling process that works with the customer to inspect the project scope deliverables. D, quality control, is also a monitoring and controlling process that inspects the project work.

6. Which project knowledge area is responsible for managing the project team?

   A. Project human resource management

   B. Project scope management

   C. Project communications management

   D. Project integration management

   A. Project human resources management hosts the monitoring and controlling process of managing the project stakeholders. Choices B, C, and D are knowledge areas that do not include stakeholder management, so these choices are wrong.

7. Which project process group is responsible for creating the project's risk contingency reserve?

    A. Planning

    B. Executing

    C. Monitoring and controlling

    D. Project risk management

    A. The project's risk contingency reserve is part of the risk management planning processes. Choices B and C are two processes groups that do not include risk management planning, so these choices are incorrect. Choice D, project risk management, is a knowledge area, not a process group; the question asks which process group hosts the risk processes.

8. Which project management process is responsible for finding mistakes before the customer does?

    A. Quality assurance

    B. Quality control

    C. Quality planning

    D. Scope verification

    B. Quality control is an inspection-driven process that aims to identify mistakes in the project deliverables prior to scope verification. Choice A, quality assurance, is incorrect because QA is a prevention-driven process, not an inspection-driven activity. C, quality planning, is an attempt to plan quality into the project so that the work is done properly and precedes quality control. D, scope verification, is the customer inspection of the project work and succeeds quality control, so this choice is incorrect.

9. A project within your program has identified several risks. What project management process will help the project management team build a risk contingency reserve?

    A. Qualitative risk analysis

    B. Quantitative risk analysis

    C. Risk response planning

    D. Cost estimating

    B. Quantitative risk analysis examines the true probability and impact of project risks and helps create the project's risk contingency reserve. A, qualitative risk analysis, is a subjective, fast risk assessment and doesn't contribute to the contingency reserve creation. Choice C defines the best responses to project risks, so this choice is incorrect. Choice D, cost estimating, is not related to the risk contingency reserve but to the costs of the project's resources.

10. Todd, a software developer for the NHG Project within your program, has been adding fields, buttons, and other extras for customers of the project. The customers, however, have been approaching Todd directly and asking him to make the changes without following the prescribed project change control system. These changes are known as what?

    A. Value-added changes

    B. Scope creep

    C. Errors and omissions

    D. Stakeholder management

    B. Undocumented, small changes to the project scope are known as scope creep. Choices A and D are reasons why a change request may be created, but no change request has been created in this scenario. Choice D is incorrect, as this is an example of ineffective change control rather than stakeholder management.

11. Marcy has created a request for quote for a group of sellers. What thing does Marcy expect back from the sellers?

    A. Bid

    B. Price

    C. Proposal

    D. Statement of work

    B. Marcy is asking for the sellers to provide only a price for their work. While choice A is tempting, it is technically incorrect as a bid, which is a price for the work. C is a response to an invitation for bids, not a request for quote. Proposals are in-depth explanations and ideas of how the seller can complete the contracted work. D, the statement of work, does not come from the seller, but from the buyer.

12. What procurement activity allows sellers to query a statement of work for clarity?

    A. Scope reassessment

    B. Claims management

    C. Bidders conference

    D. SOW update

    C. A bidders conference is a meeting where all of the project bidders can come and ask questions about the statement of work. Choices A, B, and C do not provide an opportunity for bidders to ask questions.

13. What project management knowledge area gets two plans?

    A. Project scope management

    B. Project procurement management

    C. Project integration management

    D. Project quality management

D. Only the project quality management knowledge area provides at least two plans. Choices A, B, and C create the scope management plan, the procurement management plan, and the project plan respectively.

14. You are the program manager for your organization. One of your project managers is confused about performance reporting and doesn't understand your approach. You want the project manager to report on the cost and schedule variances and overall health. What management approach should you explain to the project manager?

   A. Quality management

   B. Earned value management

   C. Project integration management

   D. Total quality management

   B. The project manager should rely on earned value management; specifically the cost and schedule variance formulas and the cost and schedule performance index formulas. The other management approaches don't provide cost and schedule performance specifics, so these choices are incorrect.

15. A project manager has hired an electrician to complete part of the project work, because the electrical work is too dangerous. This is what type of risk response?

   A. Mitigation

   B. Sharing

   C. Avoidance

   D. Transference

   D. This is an example of transference, because the project transfers the risk to a third party. Mitigation is a risk response that reduces or eliminates the probability and/or impact of a risk event. Sharing is when two or more parties share a positive risk. Avoidance is an action to work around a risk within a project or program.

16. How many project management processes are there in the project management life cycle?

   A. 44

   B. 21

   C. 9

   D. 5

   A. There are 44 project management processes. B, 21, is the number of processes in the planning process group. There are nine knowledge areas and five process groups in project management.

17. Which project management process is responsible for creating the WBS?

    A. WBS creation

    B. Scope definition

    C. Scope planning

    D. Project integration management

    A. This isn't a trick question, just a tricky one. The project management process WBS creation creates the WBS. The other choices are wrong.

18. What project management plan will define the reports the project stakeholders will need throughout the project?

    A. Project management plan

    B. Staffing management plan

    C. Communications management plan

    D. Schedule management plan

    C. The communications management plan defines how all project communications will be managed throughout the project. A, the project management plan, defines how the project will be managed. The staffing management plan defines how team members will be brought onto the project, managed, and then released from the project. D, the schedule management plan, defines how the project schedule will be planned and controlled.

19. A seller and a project manager are in disagreement about a deliverable the seller has created for the project. This disagreement is known as what?

    A. Issue

    B. Risk

    C. Claim

    D. Stakeholder management

    C. This question describes a claim between the seller and the buyer. The other choices do not answer the question, so these are incorrect choices.

20. All of the following are project planning processes except for which one?

    A. Cost estimating

    B. Selecting sellers

    C. Schedule development

    D. Quantitative risk analysis

    B. Selecting the project sellers is an execution process. Choice A, C, and D are all planning process, so these choices are incorrect.

PART IV

Appendixes

Understanding the Code of Ethics and Professional Conduct

In this appendix, you will
- Explore the PMI Code of Ethics and Professional Conduct
- Learn the structure of the Code
- Learn about the Code's stance on fairness and honesty

In 1981 PMI created the "Ethics, Standards, and Accreditation Group" to create a code of ethics for the project management profession. This group then created the Ethics Standard for the Project Management Professional. This document, in 1998, became the early version of a new member Code of Ethics. The Code of Ethics was a code that all PMI members, certified as project managers or not, agreed to abide by in their professional practices as part of their membership in PMI. Then, in January 1999, the Ethics, Standards, and Accreditation Group approved a process for ethics complaints to be filed, reviewed, and then acted on if the complaint proved valid.

As I'm certain you know, the global economy has changed, and the business world has been rocked by the demise of billion-dollar companies going bankrupt, shady loans and practices have taken their toll, and millions have experienced the world-wide competition for jobs. Part of all this chaos is the realization that ethics and moral standards vary among countries, companies, and cultures. The once-simple PMI Code of Conduct, most recently a one-page document with broad definitions and approaches, has become outdated.

PMI also considered the boom in their membership population. PMI has grown from just a few hundred U.S.-based members to several hundred thousand members worldwide. The goal of the Code of Conduct, from its inception, was to create a moral guideline for project managers of all industries to subscribe to a common belief in fairness and honesty, and to be held to a higher level of expectations than project managers who were not members of PMI.

The realization that the PMI Code of Conduct was outdated prompted PMI to create a new governing body, the Ethics Standard Review Committee, to examine the project management code of ethics. Part of this committee's task was to develop a global approach to reviewing the now-defunct Code of Conduct, considering the ethical considerations of the global market, and realizing a desire to create a more exact and detailed description of what the ethics and character of a PMI member should be.

In October 2006 the new six-page PMI Code of Ethics and Professional Conduct was released. This code is for all PMI members and professionals—not just the PMPs. The document is arranged by chapters and sections. The PgMP exam does not include test questions on this document, but you'll have to agree to abide by the code as part of your exam application. In this appendix, I'm going to break down the document in a slightly less formal, and much less official, approach. I hope you like it.

Chapter One: Vision and Applicability

The vision of the code is, no doubt, that the project management and program management community will adhere to the code in its day-to-day operations and its members' lives as representatives of PMI. The code is needed because project and program managers are often in situations where their ethics could be jeopardized.

Exploring the Code's Vision and Purpose

PMI wants the project management community to do what's "right and honorable." I'm sure we all want those same values for ourselves and other project managers. PMI expands that vision, however, to extend beyond your role as a project manager; the code wants adherence in all areas of our lives: "at work, at home, and in service to our profession."

The real purpose of the code is reputation. From PMI's point of view, the code and our agreement to adhere to the code will raise the perception of the ethical values project and program managers agree to—and are expected to abide by—as members and participants in PMI programs. The code is also a motivation to become a better management practitioner. By establishing a globally accepted standard for our ethics and behavior, the code should raise our credibility, reputation, and collective behavior to new standards, at least in theory.

Participating in the Code

In the past PMPs were expected to adhere to the PMP Code of Conduct. CAPMs were expected to adhere to the CAPM Code of Conduct. And members of PMI that were credentialed as PMPs or CAPMs were also held to a separate ethical standard. It made more sense, of course, to create a blanket code of ethics for all members and certified candidates. So basically, everyone that's a PMI member, a CAPM, a PMP, or a PMI-certified Program Manager Professional (PgMP) as you hope to be, will have to agree to participate in this PMI Code of Ethics and Professional Conduct.

NOTE   Kudos to PMI on this decision! A simple solution is usually the best solution. I'm personally thrilled with this new code, its detailed descriptions, and its application to all PMI participants.

Learning the Code Details

The code includes four values that PMI has deemed core to the ethics and standards for project managers:

- Responsibility
- Respect
- Fairness
- Honesty

These four values make up the final four chapters of the Code of Ethics and Professional Conduct. Within each of these values there are aspirational standards and mandatory standards. Basically, there are some characteristics of these values that we as project managers should aspire to and there are other facets of these values that we must adhere to.

The code provides some comments and examples for clarification. You'll also find a glossary of terms in the code—something prior versions of this code hadn't provided. I'll list those terms at the end of this appendix.

Chapter Two: Responsibility as a Program Manager

The second chapter of the PMI Code of Ethics and Professional Conduct focuses on responsibility. As a program manager, you already have a level of responsibility in terms of the organizational structure you operate in (from functional to projectized). You also have responsibility for the project managers within your program and to the stakeholders the program represents.

What Is Responsibility?

According to the Code of Ethics and Professional Conduct, responsibility is our duty to take ownership for the decisions we make—or fail to make. It's also our duty to take ownership of our actions—or lack of actions. And finally, it's our duty to take ownership of the results of those decision and actions.

NOTE   That's my favorite section of the entire Code of Ethics and Professional Conduct. I may be on my soapbox here, but I tire of project and program managers that won't own their decisions or failures.

Aspiring to Responsibility Expectations

Program managers need to aspire to responsibility. Here are the details of the responsibility aspirations for this section of the Code of Ethics and Professional Conduct:

- Make good decisions that are in the best interests of society, public safety, and the environment.
- Accept only assignments that mesh with our background, experience, skills, and qualifications.
- Deliver on promises.
- Take ownership of errors and omissions and be accountable for them, and make quick and accurate corrections. Should a program manager discover errors and omissions caused by others, she must communicate with the appropriate people as soon as she discovers the errors.
- Protect proprietary and confidential information. Privacy is paramount.
- Uphold the Code of Ethics and Professional Conduct and hold others accountable to it as well.

Remember, these are aspirations of the responsibility portion of the Code of Ethics and Professional Conduct. There are going to be tough instances, ethical dilemmas, and scenarios that will call these aspirations into question.

Adhering to Mandatory Standards

There are regulations, laws, contracts, and other mandatory requirements that project and program managers have to abide by in projects and programs. This section acknowledges those requirements. The Code of Ethics and Professional Conduct makes these points:

- Project and program managers have a mandatory responsibility to adhere to regulatory requirements and laws.
- Project and program managers adhering to this code have a mandatory responsibility to report unethical or illegal conduct to management and those affected by the conduct.
- Project and program managers are required to bring valid, fact-driven violations of the Code of Ethics and Professional Conduct to PMI for resolution.
- Disciplinary action should commence for project and program managers that seek to retaliate against a person raising ethics violations concerns.

Project and program managers must adhere to these points and agree to participate in them in their roles in the program and project management communities.

Chapter Three: Adhering to the Respect Value

Respect in the PMI Code of Ethics and Professional Conduct centers not only on the respect we may deserve as managers, but the respect that others are due through their work and contributions to our projects and programs. Respect in project and program management also includes our respect for the environment we operate within.

According to PMI, respect among individuals and toward the environment promotes trust and confidence.

Aspiring to Respect

There are four aspiration standards for respect:

- Learn about the norms and customs of others and avoid behavior that others may find disrespectful.
- Listen to others and seek to understand their points of view and opinions.
- Don't avoid people that you have conflicts or disagreement with; you should approach them in an attempt to resolve differences.
- Always conduct yourself professionally even when those you deal with do not.

According to PMI, respect among individuals and toward the environment promotes trust and confidence. It's admirable.

Adhering to the Mandatory Values of Respect

As a program manager, you should demand four things regarding respect and values. Here's what the Code of Ethics and Professional Conduct details:

- Negotiations are always in good faith.
- Don't influence decisions for personal gain at the expense of others.
- Don't behave in an abusive manner toward others.
- Respect the property rights of others.

These four values are mandatory for PMI participants. Obviously the program manager is to "take the high road" in dealings with clients and stakeholders.

Chapter Four: Adhering to the Fairness Value

Fairness, according to the PMI Code, is the duty to make decisions and act impartially and objectively. Our behavior, as program managers, is to be void of competing self-interests, prejudice, and favoritism. Sounds wonderfully complex, doesn't it?

Aspiring to Fairness

According to the Code of Ethics and Professional Conduct, there are four things that you are to aspire to in the realm of fairness:

- Demonstrate transparency in your decision-making.
- Constantly reexamine your impartiality and objectivity and take corrective actions when appropriate.
- Provide equal access to information to those who are authorized to have that information.
- Make opportunities equally available to all qualified candidates.

These are some lofty aspirations that you are to have as a project or program manager. The goal, no doubt, is to strive toward these characteristics in our day-to-day lives.

Adhering to the Mandatory Standards on Fairness

There are five values that PMI participants must adhere to in regard to fairness. Two of the standards apply to conflict of interest scenarios, while the remaining three requirements center on favoritism and discrimination. As project and program managers, we are to

- Fully disclose any real or potential conflict of interests.
- Refrain from participating in any decision where a real or potential conflict of interest exists until you've disclosed the situation, have an approved mitigation plan, and have the consent of the program stakeholders to proceed.
- Don't hire or fire, reward or punish, or award or deny contracts out of personal considerations such as favoritism, nepotism, or bribery.
- Don't discriminate against others on things such as race, gender, age, religion, disability, nationality, or sexual orientation.
- Always apply the rules of the organization (the organization being our employer, PMI, or any other performing organization) without favoritism or prejudice.

I think it's safe to say, in regard to these requirements, if you follow the rules of your employer, the laws of your country, and the calling voice of your conscience, you'll be all right.

Chapter Five: Adhering to Honesty

Honesty is being truthful in our conversations and in our actions. This means that as a manager you don't over-promise, give dates that you know are bad, or sandbag your budgets and deliverables. You do what you say, and you say what's truthful. Like the other values in the Code of Ethics and Professional Conduct, honesty has both aspirational and mandatory standards.

Aspiring to Honesty

According to the Code of Ethics and Professional Conduct, there are five traits of honesty that you should aspire to:

- Seek to understand the truth.
- Be truthful in communications and conduct.
- Provide accurate and timely information.
- Provide commitments and promises in good faith.
- Strive to create an environment where others feel safe to tell the truth.

These five aspirations, I think, are noble. As a manager, you are often in a rapid-paced mode, out to get the work done and allot time to get the work done. These five aspirations cause you to pause and reflect on what's honest and truthful in your communications to project team members and stakeholders.

Adhering to the Honesty Requirements

There are just two mandatory standards for honesty in the Code of Ethics and Professional Conduct:

- Do not engage in or condone behavior that is designed to mislead others; this includes, but isn't limited to
  - Creating misleading statements
  - Creating false statements
  - Stating half-truths
  - Providing information out of context
  - Withholding information that if known would demonstrate our statements to be false
- Do not engage in dishonest behavior with the intention of personal gain at the expense of others.

Basically, as a project or program manager, you don't lie. You are required, according to the code, to tell the truth regardless of the impact it may have on yourself, your program management team, or your programs and projects. How many program managers do you know that are living by this requirement already?

Key Terms

Abusive manner   Treating others with conduct that may result in harm, fear, humiliation, manipulation, or exploitation. For example, berating a project team member because she's taken longer than expected to complete a project assignment may be considered humiliation.

Conflict of interest   A situation where a project manager may have two competing duties of loyalty. For example, purchasing software from a relative may benefit the relative but may do harm to the performing organization.

Duty of loyalty   A program manager's responsibility to be loyal to another person, an organization, or a vendor. For example, a program manager has a duty of loyalty to promote the best interests of an employer rather than the best interests of a vendor.

PMI Member   Anyone, certified as a project manager or not, that has joined the Project Management Institute.

Practitioner   A person that is serving in the capacity of a project manager or contributing to the management of a project, portfolio of projects, or program. For example, a program manager is considered to be a project practitioner under this definition.

Program and Project Documents

Acceptance report A report that finalizes the deliverables of a program's project, the program, and deliverables the program generates; also linked to procurement management and the acceptance of the things the seller has created for the program.

Assumptions Documented facets of the program that are believed to be true but have not been proven to be true.

Authorization to test letter A letter from PMI to the PgMP candidate with the Prometric Testing Center information, instructions for scheduling an examination, and approval of the PgMP candidate's application for certification.

Basis of estimates The documentation, simulations, and technical files that have been used to create the time and cost estimates for the program.

Benefits management plan Defines the purpose, creation, and management of the benefits the program will create.

Benefits realization plan Defines the program's expected benefits; created during the early stages of the program and defines program success factors for the program manager and its stakeholders.

Certificate of program completion This document details the deliverables of the program, its projects, and the success or failure of the program's objectives.

Change request status information The requestor of a change may also issue this request to determine the status of her change request as it moves through the change request process and queue.

Communications management plan Identifies the program stakeholders, provides the information they'll need to participate in the program, and defines the expected modality of the communication.

Communications technology requirements plan This is an output of the communications management planning and defines the technology the program may need to effectively communicate. This plan considers telecommunications, e-mail, and collaborative software, and it looks for new technology that may supersede or improve current program technologies.

Constraints Documented facets of the program that limit the program's options; time, cost, and scope are the most common constraints.

Contract A legally binding agreement between two or more parties.

Contract completion certificate An official designation that the contract has been completed by the seller for the organization.

Contract statement of work Defines the work and general agreement for a performing organization that completes programs for other entities; the contract statement of work generally precedes the contract.

Contract termination documentation Should a contract be terminated for any purpose, this document defines why the contract was canceled and the outcome of the relationship between the buyer and the seller.

Contracts management plan Defines the details of the contracts that will be utilized.

Cost management plan Defines how costs will be estimated, budgeted, and controlled in the program.

Definitive estimate The most accurate estimate type but also the longest to create, because you must have the PWBS created to account for the costs of each program package. The range of variance for this estimate type is –5% to +10% of the predicted costs.

Earned value scorecard A quick report on the program's health using earned value management's most common performance formulas.

Equipment reclamation requests The performing organization may assign equipment to the program for a specified duration. When the program is done with the equipment, the organization may reclaim the equipment for use elsewhere.

Feasibility study The pre-program research that helps the performing organization to determine the likelihood that a program will reach certain objectives such as time, cost, scope, and quality.

***Guide to the Project Management Body of Knowledge* (PMBOK)** A PMI publication that defines the generally accepted practices of project management.

High-level program plan Defines the mission, values, and vision of the program and how the program intends to support the organization by its benefits and deliverables.

Historical information Organizational process assets from previous projects and programs that can assist the program management team in making decisions about the current program.

Inspection reports An output of quality control that reports on the findings of program work inspection activities.

Interface management plan Defines these relationships within, and beyond, the organization, including departments, lines of business, and other open programs.

Invitation for bid (IFB) This document asks the sellers to provide a cost for the items outlined in the SOW.

Issues register A database of issues within the program and their current statuses.

Lease termination requests When a program no longer needs to lease equipment, facilities, or other resources, a termination request is generated to cancel the lease agreement; terms of the agreement may affect the ability to cancel the lease.

Lessons learned Documentation of what was learned about the program's weaknesses, failures, and opportunities to improve overall performance.

Organizational strategic plan Defines the means of achieving organizational goals and objectives; the program must fit within the organizational strategic plan.

Performance reports Regularly scheduled communication on the overall health of the project.

Personnel records The history of how the program and project participants performed on their assignments and duties in the program; these records also document new skills learned and technical experiences on the program.

Preliminary program scope statement The initial program scope statement, which includes the high-level objectives for the program.

Preliminary project scope statement An initial foundation for the direction the project will take; offers some direction for the planning process group.

Process asset library An organization's program- and project-related plans on managing processes, policies, procedures, and internal and related industry guidelines that may help the program management team manage the current program.

Procurement management plan Defines the program's procurement management process: the procurement process, bidder selection, and vendor management.

Product description Details the products and/or services the program will create.

Program archives   All of the documentation on the program, contracts, communications, supporting detail, and program projects are archived and become part of organizational process assets.

Program benefits statement   This document defines all of the good that will come out of the program. It defines the benefits the organization can expect as a result of completing the program and helps the program manager adhere to the benefits management theme of the program.

Program business case   Defines how the program may fit into the organization's strategic plan, and it defines the need for the program to be initiated and to exist in the organization.

Program change requests   Documented requests to change the program scope.

Program charter   Identifies the program manager and grants the program manager the authority to manage all aspects of the program.

Program communications management plan   Defines the communication demands and expectations for the program stakeholders.

Program management plan   Documents and communicates how the program will create the benefits, outlines the actions to realize the benefits, and serves as the baseline for tracking benefits realization. It is the consolidation of the outputs of the other planning processes.

Program scope statement   Defines all of the work the program will and will not do as part of the work. The program scope statement becomes the basis for all future program decisions and is controlled through scope control and the scope change control system.

Program setup phase roadmap   A document that defines the goals of the program and those most likely to reach the program objectives. Defines the goals, costs, time frame, dependencies, assumptions, and constraints, as well as how the program will be managed.

Program statement   The program scope defines all of the required work—and only the required work—in order to satisfy the program's objectives; serves as the baseline for all future program decisions.

Program team directory   A document that defines all of the contact information, roles, and responsibilities for all of the program team members.

Program termination requests   If a program is not performing well or there are conditions outside of the program's control, such as a law or condition, the program may be terminated.

Program work breakdown structure (PWBS)   A hierarchical decomposition of the program scope. It decomposes the program scope statement into the individual deliverables, called program packages, that the program promises to deliver.

Program-specific qualified vendor list   The program may use its own set of qualified vendors that the project managers and the program management team will buy from.

Project business case   Each project within the program demands a business case that defines the project's scope, cost, schedule, and technical aspects, along with any regulatory requirements the project may have.

Project calendar   Defines when the project work is expected to take place.

Project charter   The document that authorizes the project to exist within the program. This document also identifies the project manager and his level of authority in the project. The project charter is signed by the project sponsor.

Quality improvement plan   A program subsidiary plan that defines how the program may improve its performance, remove non–value adding activities, and improve overall program efficiency and performance.

Quality management plan   Defines how the quality objectives will be met within the project, including the adherence to quality assurance (QA) programs, quality control at the project level, and the expected reactions when quality inspections are lower than what was expected.

RACI chart   A matrix using the actions of Responsible, Accountable, Consult, and Inform to designate the action required by the role.

Rejected change requests   Program change requests that are denied approval are cataloged for future reference.

Request for information (RFI)   You need more information about a vendor's services or products, so you ask for more information. This can be anything from a brochure or a catalog to a white paper or references about the seller.

Request for proposal (RFP)   This document asks the vendor to create a proposal for your program. An RFP takes your basic vision and allows the vendor to run with it, designing a solution with a lot of features and solutions you may not have thought of. The creation of a web site is a good example. RFPs are a lot of work for vendors.

Request for quote (RFQ)   You want a price for whatever the seller can provide. You don't need any dream solutions or ideas   just tell me how much. For example, I need a quote for three tons of pea gravel.

Resource calendar   Shows the availability of program resources.

Resource histogram   A bar chart that visualizes the utilization of program resources.

Resource management plan   Defines how resources will be obtained, managed, and allocated throughout the program. This plan also defines how the resources will be tracked across the program's projects to ensure that resources are not over-allocated and are being used as efficiently as possible.

PART IV

Resource pool description   Defines the available people, skills, materials, facilities, equipment, and other resources within the organization that the program may use.

Responsibility assignment matrix   A generic matrix that lists the individuals that will be working on the program and aligns them with all of the responsibilities that have to be done.

Risk response plan   Addresses the responses to the identified risk events. The risk response plan defines how the risk owner should react if the risk event passes the risk threshold and the event comes into play.

Role and responsibility chart   A matrix to demonstrate which role is responsible for what.

Rough order of magnitude   This project cost estimate approach is very broad and unreliable. It's usually created with the preliminary project scope statement and has a range of variance of –25% to +75% for the project completion.

Schedule management plan   Defines, well, the schedule. It also defines how changes to the schedule may be allowed, fleshed into the program, and then executed.

Scope management plan   Defines the program scope and how the program scope will be controlled. The plan defines the program management scope change control system and the process program change requests must follow to be incorporated into the program plan.

Staffing management plan   Defines the needed resources for the program and how the program will obtain those resources. This program plan also defines how the staff may be brought onto and released from the program.

Staffing pool description   Depicts the talent, competencies, interest, availability, and cost of the resources that may be able to participate on the program management team.

Stakeholder analysis chart   This chart can capture each stakeholder and her position and influence on decisions and outcomes of the project.

Stakeholder management plan   A plan that defines how the program manager will manage the program stakeholders through communications, involvement, and marketing of the program, along with how he will address perceived stakeholder threats and concerns regarding the program.

Statement of work (SOW)   Defines all of the details of the program and is sent to the prospective vendors from the client. The SOW allows the vendors to understand the request of the client and to create a quote, bid, or proposal based on the SOW.

Status reports   Regular communication on the program's status on performance, cost, schedule, scope, quality, and other facets of the program.

Supporting detail   Any documentation that has influenced decisions within the program; supporting detail should be archived as part of the program records.

The Standard for Program Management   A PMI publication that defines the generally accepted practices of program management.

Training plan   The program management team and the project team members may need to be trained on the new technologies, program approach, and materials used within the program; this plan defines the training needs and the approach the program will take to satisfy the training demands.

Training records   Linked to the personnel records, these documents show the classes, training, and education brought about by participating in the program.

Transition agreement   Defines the terms of the organization accepting the benefits of the program and moving them into operations. Defines the support and acceptance of the deliverables and the responsible party for maintaining the deliverables.

Transition plan   Defines how the benefits and deliverables will be transferred from the program into the organization. May also define the life cycle cost of the deliverables, how the deliverables and benefits will be supported post-program, and transition agreement terms.

Utilization reports   Communication on how specific resources (people and equipment) are being used within the program.

Variance reports   Details any schedule or cost variances, why each variance has occurred, and what the program intends to do to address the variances.

PgMP Exam Passing Advice

I know you don't want to prolong the misery of preparing to pass your PgMP exam any longer than necessary. Learning a topic is hard work—studying to pass an exam can be even harder: there's the pressure from your colleagues, your boss, your lover, and that fat guy down the hall who likes to moan about everything you do. My goal for you is to pass your PgMP certification exam on this first attempt and then to get on with your life. I'm sure that's your goal as well.

The point of this appendix is to capture all of the exam-critical info in one juicy spot as a quick summation of what you must know in order to pass the exam. I'm not saying that knowing only this appendix will guarantee a pass on the exam. I am saying, however, that not knowing this appendix will likely guarantee a fail on the exam. This appendix will also give you some strategies and tips for passing the exam beyond just program management content.

Preparing to Pass the Exam

If you want to just take the PgMP exam, assuming that you qualify, you don't really have to study at all. Just complete the application, get approved, and drop some cash. And then show up and take it. Preparing to pass, however, is totally different. Anyone can take an exam, but not everyone can pass an exam. The key is to enter the test-taking arena with a positive and powerful mind set that you mean business—and the business is to pass the exam on the first attempt.

What to Do First

The first thing you want to do is schedule your exam. That's right—pick a date in the not-so-distant future and treat the date as a deadline. If you haven't scheduled your exam yet, get to work on the application. The application process to get to the exam itself can take some time, so let PMI do their processing while you do your preparing. If you prepare for the exam and then submit the application, you're only delaying your certification and prolonging your misery.

Once your application is approved by PMI, then you'll need to schedule the exam through Prometric. Even if you don't believe you're quite ready, choose a date a few weeks out and schedule the exam pass date. This is your goal, your deadline, the pinnacle of your PgMP efforts. I generally advise people to not take too long to pass their exam. All these facts, figures, and formulas have a funny way of oozing out of your head if you take too long to get to the exam room.

You're probably wondering how long you should study before you schedule the exam. I don't want you to do anything foolish and schedule an immediate exam if you're not ready for it. Considering the end-of-chapter exams in this book and the two exams available on the CD-ROM, you should have a pretty good idea of where you stand as an exam candidate. When I teach my exam prep courses based on the exams in this book or my *PMP Study Guide*, I set the goal in class of an 80 percent success rate on practice questions. It's much higher than the PMI requirements, but I feel that if someone can score an 80 on my goofy questions, they should be in alignment to pass PMI's goofy exam.

Take some time and look over your end-of-chapter exam scores from this book. You should have a quick SWOT analysis of your exams. And you know that SWOT is your strengths, weaknesses, opportunities, and threats. Most people, I've learned, do very well on questions that are bunched together by topic—like the chapter exams you've completed. However, it's tougher to recall the information when the question topics are all scrambled as they are on the CD—and on the PgMP examination.

What to Do Second

Once you've scheduled your exam and you're on your way to passing, you've got to look at your energy level. In my opinion (and based on my experience), if you're eating junk food, drinking barrels of scotch, and smoking stinky cigars, you're probably not going to feel all that great for studying efforts. I'm no doctor, but you and I know what'll make you feel well, rested, and sharper for your exam efforts:

- Get some moderate exercise. Find time to go for a jog, lift weights, take a swim, or do whatever workout routine works best for you.

- Eat smart and healthy. If you eat healthy food, you'll feel good—and feel better about yourself. Be certain to drink plenty of water, and don't overdo the caffeine.

- Get your sleep. A well-rested brain is a sharp brain. You don't want to sit for your exam feeling tired, sluggish, and worn-out.

- Time your study sessions. Don't overdo your study sessions—long crash study sessions aren't that profitable. In addition, try to study at the same time every day at the time your exam is scheduled.

Make Your PgMP Cheat Sheet

I think a big chunk of being able to pass the PgMP exam is to get over test anxiety. Most professionals that I meet haven't take an exam in years and years. This only magnifies the test anxiety and makes it tougher to remember all the facts and formulas. Here's your secret weapon: a page of notes. If you could take one page of notes into the exam, what information would you like on this one-page document? Of course you absolutely cannot take any notes or reference materials into the exam area. However, if you can create and memorize one sheet of notes, you absolutely may recreate this once you're seated in the exam area.

I highly recommend that you create your own "cheat sheet" of notes, formulas, and whatever PgMP exam tips you want to see at a glance. Practice creating a reference sheet so that you can immediately, and legally, recreate this document once your exam has begun. You'll be supplied with several sheets of blank paper and a couple of pencils. Once your exam process begins, recreate your reference sheet. The following are key pieces of information you'd be wise to include on your reference sheet (you'll find all of this key information in this appendix):

- Activities within each process group
- Estimating formulas
- Communication formulas
- Earned value management formulas
- Management theories

Testing Tips

The questions on the PgMP exam are fairly direct but can be verbose and may offer a few red herrings. For example, you may face questions that state, "All of the following are correct options expect for which one?" The question wants you to find the incorrect option, or the option that would not be appropriate for the scenario described. Be sure to understand what the question is asking for. It's easy to focus on the scenario presented in a question and then see a suitable option for that scenario in the answer. The trouble is, if the question is asking you to identify an option that is not suitable, then you just missed the question. Carefully read the question to understand what is expected for an answer.

Here's a tip that can work with many of the questions: identify what the question wants for an answer and then look for an option that doesn't belong with the other possible answers. In other words, find the answer that doesn't fit with the other three options. Find the "odd man out." Here's an example: EVM is used during the
_____.

- **A.** Controlling phase
- **B.** Executing phase
- **C.** Closing phase
- **D.** Entire project

Notice how options A, B, and C are exclusive? If you choose A, the controlling phase, it implies that EVM is not used anywhere else in the project. The odd man out then is D, the entire project; it's considered the "odd" choice because it, by itself, is not an actual process group. Of course, this tip won't work with every question—but it's handy to keep in mind.

For some answer choices, it may seem that two of the four options are both possible correct answers. However, because you may choose only one answer, you must discern which answer is the best choice. Within the question, there will usually be some hint describing the progress of the program, the requirements of the stakeholders, or some other clue that can help you determine which answer is the best for the question.

Answer Every Question—Once

The PgMP exam has 170 questions—of which 150 are "real questions"—you don't have to answer every question correctly, just enough to pass. In other words, don't waste three of your four hours laboring over one question—difficult questions and easy questions are worth the same amount in your exam. And you know, I'm sure, that you never leave any question blank—even if you don't know the answer to the question. A blank question is the same as a wrong answer. As you move through the exam and you find questions that stump you, use the "mark question" option in the exam software, choose an answer you suspect may be correct, and then move on. When you have answered all of the questions, you are given the option to review your marked answers.

Some questions in the exam may prompt your memory to come up with answers to questions you have marked for review. However, resist the temptation to review those questions you've already answered with confidence and haven't marked. More often than not, your first instinct is the correct choice. When you completed the exams at the end of each chapter, did you change correct answers to wrong answers? If you did in practice, you'll do it on the actual exam.

You'll have four hours to complete the PgMP examination. You do not get any extra credit for getting done early—use as much of the time as you need. There probably won't be any real reason to rush through the exam—four hours should be plenty of time to answer 170 questions. I like to say that it's like when I play golf; I take a lot of swings to get my money's worth on the golf course. For your exam, get your money's worth and take your time. Slow down. Be methodical. Think about what the question is asking and not about what the question is implying.

Use the Process of Elimination

When you're stumped on a question, use the process of elimination. For each question, there'll be four choices. On your scratch paper, write down "ABCD." If you can safely rule out "A," cross it out of the "ABCD" you've written on your paper. Now focus on which of the other answers won't work. If you determine that "C" won't work, cross it off your list. Now you've got a fifty-fifty chance of finding the correct choice.

If you cannot determine which answer is best, "B" or "D" in this instance, here's the best approach:

1. Choose an answer in the exam (no blank answers, remember?).

2. Mark the question in the exam software for later review.

3. Circle the "ABCD" on your scratch paper, jot any relevant notes, and then record the question number next to the notes.

4. During the review, or from a later question, you may realize which choice is the better of the two answers. Return to the question and confirm that the best answer is selected.

Everything You Must Know

As promised, this section covers all of the information you must know going into the exam. It's highly recommended that you create a method to recall this information. Here goes.

Working Smart to Pass

The 170 exam questions are chunked into the following domains and percentages of the PgMP exam:

Domain	Processes/Activities	Percentage	Approximate Number of Questions
Defining the program	11	14%	24
Initiating the program	3	12%	20
Planning the program	11	20%	34
Executing the program	7	25%	42
Controlling the program	11	21%	36
Closing the program	3	8%	14

This information is right from PMI. In the preceding table take a look at initiating and closing the program. These process groups have the smallest number of processes but loads of exam questions linked to them. So ideally, you'd be better off knowing these six processes incredibly well, as they equate to 34 questions on your exam. Next, the Executing process group has only seven processes, but you'll have 42 questions related to executing the program plans. See the logic? While it's tempting to spend the bulk of your study time on planning and controlling, there are more things to know and less questions per process. Work smart, not hard. See Table C-1 for a recap of all the program management processes.

Knowledge Areas	Process Groups				
	Initiating (3)	Planning (11)	Executing (7)	Monitoring and Controlling (11)	Closing (3)
Program Integration Management	Initiating the program Authorizing projects	Developing the program management plan	Directing and managing program execution	Integrated change control Resource control Monitoring and controlling program work Issue management and control	Closing the program Component closure
Program Scope Management		Scope definition PWBS creation		Scope control	
Program Time Management		Developing the schedule		Schedule Control	
Program Cost Management		Cost estimating and budgeting		Controlling costs	
Program Quality Management		Quality planning	Quality assurance	Quality control	
Program Human Resources Management	Initiating the team	HR planning	Acquiring the team Developing the team		
Program Communications Management		Communication planning	Distributing information	Communications control Performance reporting	
Program Risk Management		Risk management planning and analysis		Risk monitoring and control	
Program Procurement Management		Planning program purchases and acquisitions Planning contracting	Requesting seller responses Selecting sellers	Program contract administration	Contract closure

Table C-1 Program Management Processes

Quick PgMP Facts

This section has some quick facts you should know at a glance. Hold on, this moves pretty fast.

Organizational Structures

Organizational structures are relevant to the program manager's authority. A program manager has authority from weakest to highest in the following order:

- Functional
- Weak matrix
- Balanced matrix
- Strong matrix
- Projectized

Program Time Facts

Time can be a project constraint. Effective time management is the scheduling and sequencing of activities in the best order to ensure that the project completes successfully and in a reasonable amount of time. These are some key terms for time management:

- **Lag** Waiting between activities
- **Lead** Activities come closer together and even overlap
- **Free float** The amount of time an activity can be delayed without delaying the next scheduled activity's start date
- **Total float** The amount of time an activity can be delayed without delaying the project's finish date
- **Float** Sometimes called *slack*—a perfectly acceptable synonym
- **Duration** May be abbreviated as "du." For example, du = 8d means the duration is 8 days

There are three types of dependencies between activities:

- **Mandatory** This hard logic requires a specific sequence between activities.
- **Discretionary** This soft logic prefers a sequence between activities.
- **External** Due to conditions outside of the project, such as those created by vendors, the sequence must happen in a given order.

Program Cost Facts

There are several methods of providing estimates:

- **Bottom-up** Costs start at zero and each component in the PWBS is estimated for costs, and then the "grand total" is calculated. This is the longest method to complete, but it provides the most accurate estimate.

- **Analogous** Costs are based on a similar program. This is a form of expert judgment, but it is also a top-down estimating approach, so it less accurate than a bottom-up estimate.
- **Parametric Modeling** Price is based on cost per unit; examples include cost per metric ton, cost per yard, and cost per hour.

There are four types of costs attributed to a program:

- **Variable costs** The costs are dependent on other variables. For example, the cost of a food-catered event depends on how many people register to attend the event.
- **Fixed costs** The cost remains constant throughout the project. For example, a rented piece of equipment has the same fee each month even if it is used more in some months than others.
- **Direct costs** The cost is directly attributed to an individual project and cannot be shared with other projects. For example, airfare to attend project meetings, hotel expenses, and leased equipment that is used only on the current project.
- **Indirect costs** These are the costs of doing business; examples include rent, phone, and utilities.

Earned Value Management Formulas

The following table shows the EVM formulas you should know for the exam:

Name	Formula	Sample Mnemonic Device
Variance	VAR = BAC − AC	Victor
Earned Value	EV = % complete × BAC	Eats
Cost Variance	CV = EV − AC	Carl's
Schedule Variance	SV = EV − PV	Sugar
Cost Performance Index	CPI = EV/AC	Corn
Schedule Performance Index	SPI = EV/PV	S (These three spell "SEE")
Estimate at Completion	EAC = BAC/CPI	E
Estimate to Complete based on atypical variances	ETC = BAC − EV	E
Estimate to Complete based on typical variances	ETC = (BAC − EV)/CPI	Edgy
Variance at Completion	VAC = BAC − EAC	Victor

Quality Management Facts

The cost of quality is the money spent investing in training; in meeting requirements for safety and other laws and regulations; and in taking steps to ensure quality acceptance. The cost of nonconformance is the cost associated with rework, downtime, lost sales, and waste of materials.

Some common quality management charts and methods include the following:

- *Ishikawa diagrams* (also called *fishbone diagrams*) are used to find cause-and-effect relationships that contribute to a problem.

- *Flow charts* show the relationship between components and the flow of a process through a system.

- *Pareto diagrams* identify project problems and their frequencies. These are based on the 80/20 Rule: 80 percent of project problems stem from 20 percent of the work.

- *Control charts* plot out the result of samplings to determine if projects are "in control" or "out of control."

- *Kaizen technologies* comprise approaches to make small improvements in an effort to reduce costs and achieve consistency.

- *Just-in-time* ordering reduces the cost of inventory but requires additional quality, because materials would not be readily available if mistakes occur.

Human Resource Theories and Philosophy

You should be somewhat familiar with these common human resource management theories for your PgMP examination.

- **Maslow's Hierarchy of Needs**   There are five layers of needs for all humans: physiological, safety, social needs (such as love and friendship), self-esteem, and the crowning jewel, self-actualization.

- **Herzberg's Theory of Motivation**   There are two catalysts for workers: hygiene agents and motivating agents.

  - **Hygiene agents**   These do nothing to motivate, but their absence demotivates workers. Hygiene agents are the expectations all workers have: job security, a paycheck, clean and safe working conditions, a sense of belonging, civil working relationships, and other basic attributes associated with employment.

  - **Motivating agents**   These are the elements that motivate people to excel. They include responsibility, appreciation of work, recognition, opportunity to excel, education, and other opportunities associated with work other than just financial rewards.

- **McGregory's Theory of X and Y**   This theory states "X" people are lazy, don't want to work, and need to be micromanaged. "Y" people are self-led, motivated, and can accomplish things on their own.

- **Ouchi's Theory Z**   This theory holds that the workers are motivated by a sense of commitment, opportunity, and advancement. Workers will work if they are challenged and motivated. Think participative management.

- **Expectancy Theory**   People will behave in accordance with what they expect as a result of their behavior. In other words, people will work in relation to the expected reward of the work.

Communication Facts

Communicating is the most important skill for the program manager. With that in mind, here are some key facts on communications:

- Communication channels formula: $N(N - 1)/2$. N represents the number of stakeholders. For example, if you have 10 stakeholders, the formula would read $10(10 - 1)/2$ for 45 communication channels. Pay special attention to questions wanting to know how many additional communication channels you have, given added stakeholders. For example, if you have 25 stakeholders on your program and have recently added 5 team members, how many additional communication channels do you now have? You'll have to calculate the original number of communication channels, $25(25 - 1)/2 = 300$; then calculate the new number with the added team members, $30(30 - 1)/2 = 435$; and finally, subtract the difference between the two: $435 - 300 = 135$, the number of additional communication channels.

- 55 percent of communication is nonverbal.

- Effective listening is the ability to watch the speaker's body language, interpret paralingual clues, and decipher facial expressions. Following the message, effective listening has the listener asking questions to achieve clarity and offering feedback.

- Active listening requires receivers of the message to offer clues, such as nodding the head to indicate they are listening. It also requires receivers to repeat the message, ask questions, and continue the discussion if clarification is needed.

- Communication can be hindered by trendy phrases, jargon, and extremely pessimistic comments. In addition, other communication barriers include noise, hostility, cultural differences, and technical interruptions.

Risk Management Facts

Risks are uncertain events that can have positive or negative effects on the program and the projects within the program. Most risks are seen as threats to the program success—but not all risks are bad. For example, there is a 20 percent probability that a constituent project will realize a discount in shipping, which will save the project $15,000. If this risk happens, the project will save money; if the risk doesn't happen, the project will have to spend the $15,000. Risks should be identified as early as possible in the planning process. A person's willingness to accept risk is the Utility Function (also called the Utility Theory). The Delphi Technique can be used to build consensus on project risks.

There are two broad types of risks:

- **Business risk** The loss of time and finances (where a downside and an upside exist).

- **Pure risk** The loss of life, injury, and theft (where only a downside exists).

Risks can be responded to in one of the following ways:

- **Avoidance** Avoid the risk by planning a different technique to remove the risk from the program or project.

- **Mitigation** Time and/or monies may be invested to reduce the probability or impact of the risk.

- **Acceptance** The risk's probability or impact may be small enough that the risk can be accepted. Acceptance can also be used for external risks, such as pending law, regulation, or weather.

- **Transference** The risk is not eliminated, but the responsibility and ownership of the risk is transferred to another party (for example, through insurance).

- **Exploitation** The organization wants to ensure that the identified risk does happen to realize the positive impact associated with the risk event.

- **Sharing** Sharing is nice. When sharing, the risk ownership is transferred to the organization that can most capitalize on the risk opportunity.

- **Enhancement** To enhance a risk is to attempt to improve its probability and/or its impacts to realize the most gains from the identified risk. You're trying to make the positive risk happen.

- **Contingency funds** Monies reserved for risk events.

- **Secondary risks** Risks that comes into a project as a direct result of another risk response.

- **Risk triggers** Conditions, events, or warning signs of a risk event that causes a risk reaction.

- **Residual risks** Risks that reside after a risk response. These are usually small and are accepted by the project team.

Procurement Facts

A contract statement of work (SOW) is provided to the potential sellers so that they can create accurate bids, quotes, and proposals for the buyer. A bidders' conference may be held so that sellers can query the buyer on the product or service to be procured.

A contract is a formal agreement, preferably written, between a buyer and a seller. On the PgMP exam, procurement questions are usually from the buyer's point of view. All requirements for the seller should be clearly written in the contract. Requirements of both parties must be met, or legal proceedings may follow. Contract types include the following:

- Cost-reimbursable contracts require the buyer to assume the risk of cost overruns.

- Fixed-price contracts require the seller to assume the risk of cost overruns.

- Time-and-material contracts are good for smaller assignments but can impose cost overrun risks to the buyer if the contract between the buyer and the seller does not include a "not to exceed clause." This clause, commonly called an NTE clause, puts a cap on the maximum amount for the contract time and materials.

- A purchase order is a unilateral form of contract.

A letter of intent is not a contract but shows the intent of the buyer to purchase from a specific seller.

About the CD-ROM

The CD-ROM that comes with *PgMP Program Management Professional All-in-One Exam Guide* includes:

- **Live video training** Flash video/audio files with "live" video training on project management, presented by Joseph Phillips. The Flash player must be installed on your computer to play this file. It is available from **www.adobe. com/products/flashplayer/**. See the following sections for more instructions.

- **Practice questions** Total Seminars' Total Tester Software, with 300 practice questions covering all of the PgMP domains. This testing engine features Practice and Final modes of testing.

The CD-ROM is set up with an autorun function. If your computer does not have autorun turned on, browse the CD-ROM and double-click the launcher.exe file to access the software menu page. From the software menu page, you can launch the installation wizard (to install the Total Tester) or run the video training Flash files using the links provided.

Running the Project Seminars Video Samples

Once you have started the CD menu (either through autorun or by double-clicking the file on the CD-ROM), you may click the individual links to start the Flash Video files.

The following are the minimum system requirements for the video samples:

- Windows 98, 800 MHz Pentium II, 24X CD-ROM drive, 64MB RAM, 800×600 monitor, millions of colors, QuickTime 5, Microsoft Internet Explorer 5 or Netscape Navigator 4.5, and speakers or headphones

- Macintosh OS 9.2.1, 450 MHz G3, 24X CD-ROM drive, 64MB RAM, 800×600 monitor, millions of colors, QuickTime 5, Microsoft Internet Explorer 5 or Netscape Navigator 4.5, and speakers or headphones

The following are the recommended system requirements for the video samples:

- Windows 2000, 2 GHz Pentium IV, 48X CD-ROM drive, 128MB RAM, 1024×768 monitor, millions of colors, QuickTime 6, Microsoft Internet Explorer 5.5 or Netscape Navigator 4.7, and speakers or headphones
- Macintosh OS 10.1, 800 MHz G4, 48X CD-ROM drive, 128MB RAM, 1024×768 monitor, millions of colors, QuickTime 6, Microsoft Internet Explorer 5.5 or Netscape Navigator 4.7, and speakers or headphones

Troubleshooting

This software runs inside of your Internet browser. You must have its preferences set for correct playback of Flash files. The Flashplayer installer (free download from **www. adobe.com/products/flashplayer/**) may not change all of your file helpers properly.

After installing Flash, if the video takes a very long time to load or doesn't load at all, verify that your browser associates the file type .swf with the Flash Player plug-in. To verify this, do the following:

- If using Internet Explorer for Windows, go to Tools | Internet Options | Advanced | Multimedia or Control Panels | FlashPlayer.
- If using Internet Explorer for Macintosh, go to Preferences | Receiving Files | Helpers.

Technical Support

For technical support for the video training samples from Joseph Phillips, please e-mail support@projectseminars.com.

Installing Total Seminars' Test Software

Click the Install Test Software button on the wizard, and the installation will proceed automatically.

Once you've completed installation, you can open the test program by selecting Start | Programs | Total Seminars and then click on the CAPM or PMP test suites. You can also start the program with the shortcut the installation places on your desktop.

Navigation

The program enables you to take each of the six tests in either Practice or Final mode. An Adaptive mode exam, which uses a large pool of questions, is also included. Begin by selecting a testing mode and specific test from the menu bar.

Practice Mode

In Practice mode, the test includes an assistance window. This gives you access to several features: Hint (helps you figure out the correct answer), Reference (where in the book to learn more), Check (is your selection correct?), and Explanation (a short note explaining the correct answer). This is a good way to study and review. Answer each question, check to see if you answered correctly, review the explanation, and refer to the book for more detailed coverage. At the end of the test, you are graded by topic and can review missed questions.

Final Mode

Final mode enables you to test yourself without the ability to see the correct answers. This is a better way to see how well you understand the material. Upon completion, you receive a final grade by topic, and you can look over the questions you missed.

Minimum System Requirements for Total Seminars' Software

The minimum system requirements for Total Seminars' software include:

- Pentium 200 MHz
- 4X or faster speed CD-ROM
- 16MB of RAM
- 30MB available hard disk space
- 800×600 resolution at 256 colors
- Windows 9x/2000/XP operating system

Technical Support

For technical support of the Total Tester practice test application, please go to **www .totalsem.com**. For information on errata for this book, please go to **www.mcprofessional.com** and click the "errata" link. Locate the title of the book for more information. For other technical support issues, please e-mail **customer.service@mcgraw-hill.com**. For customers outside the 50 United States, e-mail **international_cs@mcgraw-hill.com**.

PART IV

Glossary of Key Terms

acceptance   This response is acceptable for both positive and negative risk events.

acknowledgment   A receipt of the message, but not necessarily agreement with the message.

administrative closure   The formal documentation and sign-off from the stakeholders that the project is complete. This process also readies the project deliverable for the program so that the program may begin using the project's deliverables and benefits.

application audit   A review of the accuracy of the reported education and program management experience the PgMP applicant has reported to PMI.

authorization to test letter   A letter from PMI to the PgMP candidate with the Prometric testing center information, instructions for scheduling an examination, and approval of the PgMP candidate's application for certification.

authorize projects process   The initiating process that allows the project manager to authorize component projects within the program. This process may be done at any time during the program expect during the closing phase of the program.

avoidance   Any actions that you take to avoid a risk event.

barrier   Anything that prevents communication is a barrier.

benefit measurement methods   Approaches to measure, compare, and contrast the expected benefits of projects that may be chartered and included in a program.

benefits analysis   A program setup process that derives and prioritizes program benefit components and establishes benefit metrics.

benefits management   The sum of the planning, tools, techniques, and overall management of the activities that define, create, maximize, and sustain the benefits created by the program.

benefits management plan   Defines the definition, creation, and management of the benefits the program will create.

benefits planning   A program management and technical infrastructure phase process that creates a benefits realization plan, establishes benefits monitoring, and maps the expected benefits into the program plan.

benefits realization   A process found in the delivering the incremental benefits program phase. This process includes the monitoring of the program components, the maintenance of the benefits register, and the reporting of the benefits as they come into program fruition.

benefits realization plan   Defines the program's expected benefits; created during the early stages of program, it defines program success factors for the program manager and its stakeholders.

benefits transition   A program closure process that consolidates the benefits the program has created and then transfers the realized benefits into ongoing operations.

budget estimate   Usually created when the scope statement has been fully developed and approved. Sometimes called a top-down estimate, because its cost may be based on similar programs to predict what the current program is likely to cost. The range of variance on this estimate type is –10% to +25% of the predicted costs.

business risks   These risk events can have a positive or negative effect on the program, depending on their outcome.

certificate of program completion   This document details the deliverables of the program, its projects, and the success or failure of the program's objectives.

change management system   The change control processes and the change control process interactions with program stakeholders.

close program process   The formal acceptance of the program's outcome.

closing process group   The final program management process group that officially closes the program's component projects, releases the organizational resources, and also closes the program contracts.

closing the program   A program management process group that uses select processes, inputs, tools, and techniques to create outputs that lead to the closure of the entire program, program projects, or portions of the program as needed.

closing the program phase   The program moves through its closure and documentation of its successes and failures.

closure report   The final report on the program's health and completion.

collective bargaining agreement   A constraint the project and program must follow when it works with union stakeholders.

communication channels formula $N(N - 1)/2$, where N represents the number of stakeholders; the result of the equation reveals the number of communication channels in a program.

communications control   A monitoring and controlling process to manage program communication among the program stakeholders.

communications management plan   Identifies the program stakeholders, provides the information they'll need to participate in the program, and defines the expected modality of the communication.

component closure   The program process to close a project within a program or to close a non-project activity within the program.

constituent project   A temporary undertaking to create a unique product or service for the program in which the project resides.

constrained optimization   A project selection method that uses mathematical models to determine the best, worst, and/or most likely outcome of proposed project.

consumer and environmental groups   These entities can also be considered stakeholders if their interests are affected, or perceived to be affected, by the outcome of your program.

continuing certification requirements   PgMPs are required to earn 60 professional development units (PDUs) per three-year certification cycle.

contract   A legally binding agreement between two or more parties.

contract statement of work   Describes the requirements for acceptance, quality expectations, delivery requirements, scheduling demands, and characteristics of the program you want the vendor to adhere to.

contract termination documentation   The formal documentation of why a contract has been terminated before it was originally scheduled to end.

contracts management plan   Defines the details of the contracts that will be utilized.

controlling the program   A program management process group that uses select processes, inputs, tools, and techniques to create outputs to monitor and control varying aspects of the program and its constituent components.

corrective action   Any effort to rectify problems or issues that are taking the program (or project) off of its scope.

cost budgeting   The process of creating budgets for the entire program, including the constituent projects, non-project activities that are still required to complete the program, and considerations for budget constraints.

cost control   A monitoring and controlling process to monitor, control, approve, decline, and respond to changes to the program costs.

cost estimating   The process of aggregating the costs of the program to determine how much the program should cost.

cost management plan   Defines how the program's cost will be defined, committed, and maintained.

cost of quality   The amount of funds the program will need to spend in order to achieve the expected level of quality.

Cost Plus Fixed Fee   A contract that defines the actual costs plus a fixed profit margin for the seller.

Cost Plus Incentive Fee   A contract that defines the actual costs plus profit margin for a seller for reaching a predefined goal, such as completing the work early or coming in under budget.

Cost Plus Percentage of Cost   A contract that defines the actual costs plus a percentage profit margin for the seller.

crashing   Labor is added to the project work in an attempt to complete the project work faster; often adds costs to the program.

customer   The entity that gets the benefits the program creates.

decoder The device that decodes the message into a usable format in the communication model; think of a receiver's fax machine.

defect repair An example of corrective action.

defect repair validation Confirming that the defect has been repaired and that the result is in alignment with the program scope.

defining the program A program management process that uses select processes, inputs, tools, and techniques to create outputs to define the goals, vision, and business objectives of the entire program.

definitive estimate The most accurate estimate type but also the longest to create, because you must have the PWBS created to account for the costs of each program package. The range of variance for this estimate type is –5% to +10% of the predicted costs.

delivering the incremental benefits phase The program's projects are initiated and the project managers and their project teams go about creating the incremental benefits for the goal of the program.

Delphi Technique A tool that uses rounds of anonymous surveys to build a consensus on issues, risks, and objectives within a program.

discretionary dependencies The program activities don't have to happen in a particular, set order. Discretionary dependencies are also known as soft logic.

effort-driven activities The more effort that is applied, the less time the activity may take to complete.

encoder The thing that encodes the message to be delivered; think of fax machines, languages, or e-mail systems.

enhance A positive risk response for a risk you'd like to have happen. Consider vendor discounts, a favorable window for weather conditions, or beating a deadline.

enterprise environmental factors The policies, procedures, regulations, culture, and conditions that affect the way a program is managed within a performing organization.

establishing a program management and technical infrastructure phase The "bones" of the program are created. The infrastructure defines how the program and its projects will operate.

evaluation criteria The rules, qualifications, screening systems, and determinations that help determine which vendor you'll choose to provide the goods and services for your program.

PART IV

executing process group   The collection of the program management execution processes that put the decisions made in the program management planning process group into action.

executing the program   A program management process group that uses select processes, inputs, tools, and techniques to create outputs that lead to the execution of the entire program, program projects, or portions of the program as needed.

exploit   A positive risk response used when a probable risk event is exploited to realize as many gains from the event as possible.

fast tracking   This approach allows complete phases of a program or a project to overlap; often adds program risk.

feasibility study   The pre-program research that helps the performing organization to determine the likelihood of a program reaching certain objectives such as time, cost, scope, and quality.

Firm-Fixed-Price   A contract that defines the agreed price for a contracted product. There is no incentive or bonus offered with this contract.

Fixed Price Incentive Fee   A contract that defines the agreed price for contracted product; can include incentives for the seller.

Fixed Price   A contract that defines the agreed price for contracted product; can include incentives for the seller.

future value of money (FV)   Calculates how much a present amount of money may be worth at some point off in the future. The formula is: Future Value = Present Value $(1 + \text{interest rate})^n$, where n is the number of time periods.

government regulatory agency   The program manager identifies and manages this stakeholder according to which country the program work is occurring in, the discipline the program entails, and any new policies or laws that may affect the program work.

Guide to the Project Management Body of Knowledge (PMBOK)   A PMI publication that defines the generally accepted practices of project management.

Herzberg's Motivation-Hygiene Theory   Hygiene factors are expected and do not promote performance, but their absence can demotivate employees. Motivating agents are factors that promote performance.

initiate team process   An initiating process group process that allows the program team to be assembled, duties assigned, and the program work to begin.

initiating process group The result of an organizational strategic decision to launch the program, initiate component projects, and identify the program management team.

initiating the program A program management process group that uses select processes, inputs, tools, and techniques to create outputs that lead to the initiation of the entire program.

integrated change control A process to approve and decline program changes by examining all of the areas the change may affect in the program. These areas include scope, time, cost, quality, human resources, communications, risk, and procurement.

interface management plan Defines these relationships inside and outside of the organization, including departments, lines of business, and other open programs.

interface planning This planning process identifies and documents all the relationships within the program, external to the program, and between programs within an organizational portfolio.

invitation for bid (IFB) This document asks the sellers to provide a cost for the items outlined in the SOW.

issue A topic that needs direction and determination to reach a resolution. Issue resolution can go in several different directions, and usually there's some turmoil and opposing views on each side of the proposed outcome of the issue.

issue management and control A monitoring and controlling process to facilitate the documentation, management, and resolution of program issues.

issue owner The person that is responsible for reaching a decision on an issue.

knowledge area A portion of the program management focusing on a specific topic; there are nine program management knowledge areas (program integration management, scope management, time management, cost management, quality management, human resource management, communications management, risk management, and procurement management).

Law of Diminishing Returns The limitation of adding labor to reduce the amount of time the work takes to complete; the work itself, the yield, and the profit versus labor constraints restrict the ability to exponentially add labor to reduce the amount of time allotted to the work.

lessons learned Documentation of what was learned about the program's weaknesses, failures, and opportunities to improve overall performance.

Lump-Sum   A contract that defines the agreed price for contracted product; can include incentives for the seller.

mandatory dependencies   The program activities must happen in this particular order; there's no other way of scheduling the program work. A mandatory dependency is also known as hard logic.

Maslow's Hierarchy of Needs   Five needs that humans require: physiological, safety, social, esteem, and self-actualization.

McGregor's X and Y   X management sees the employees as lazy, untrustworthy, and generally incompetent. Y management sees the employees as motivated, competent, and able to self-lead.

medium   The intermediary network between senders and receivers in the communication model; think of the phone lines between fax machines.

milestone   A milestone is a timeless event that shows progress within the project.

milestone schedule   Milestone schedule offers the dates when the project is expected to reach the identified milestones.

mitigation   This risk response is an attempt to reduce the probability and/or impact of a risk.

monitoring and controlling process group   The program management processes used to manage changes to the program scope, control the project work, and address all levels of change, consistency, and expectations in all facets of the program.

Multi-Rater Assessment (MRA)   An assessment by 12 colleagues of the PgMP candidate. Raters consist of one supervisor, four peers, four direct reports, and three professional references. Raters will assess the PgMP candidate's ability to lead programs.

negative stakeholder   A stakeholder that does not want your program to exist or to reach its objectives.

net present value (NPV)   A formula that considers the present value of each predicted return on investment for a program that may have tiered deliverables and intermediate returns on the program's investment over a series of years.

noise   Any element that may disrupt or distort the communication between the sender and the receiver.

operations   The normal, ongoing, day-to-day functions of an organization.

organizational process assets The collection of tools, templates, software, and other assets that an organization has to benefit the completion of programs and projects.

Ouchi's Theory Z The Japanese Management theory. Organizations can thrive as the management of Japanese businesses did with familial environments, participative management, and life-long employment.

parametric modeling A parameter is used to calculate costs, such as cost per metric ton, cost per server license, or even cost per hour. Also called a parametric estimate.

Parkinson's Law A law that states that work will expand to fill the amount of time allotted to it.

perform quality control A monitoring and controlling process to manage the program quality; it is an inspection-driven process to keep mistakes from reaching the program customers.

performance reporting A monitoring and controlling process that works in tandem with the communications control process to report on the health of the program in all areas.

performing organization The entity that the program works within.

PgMP multiple-choice assessment exam A 170-question examination on the skills and concepts of program management. The exam is administered through a Prometric testing center and lasts four hours.

phase gate review The review of the program's adherence to the performing organization's strategic objectives, analysis of any immediate ROI, review of program risks and threats, and a confirmation that the program manager and the program management team are adhering to the established rules and policies of the program. Phase gate reviews happen at the end of a program phase.

planning process group The collection of iterative planning processes that guide the program manager and stakeholders through the decision-making activities for the program's direction.

planning the program A program management process group that uses select processes, inputs, tools, and techniques to create outputs that lead to the effective planning of the entire program.

PMI Credential Associate A PMI representative that may contact the PgMP applicant to discuss the candidate's failure to meet the requirements of the PgMP certification process. The PMI Credential Associate and the PgMP applicant may discuss what additional information is needed on the application for the certification process to continue.

portfolio   A collection of programs, projects, and even ongoing operations that all have a common purpose: to reach some business objectives.

positive stakeholder   A stakeholder that is in favor of your program existing and accomplishing its objectives.

preliminary program scope statement   The initial program scope statement, which includes the high-level objectives for the program.

preliminary project scope statement   An initial foundation for the direction the project will take, which offers some direction for the planning process group.

pre-program setup phase   The program concept is shared, and there's an organizational rally cry for program support and stakeholder buy-in.

present value of money (PV)   Determines how much a future amount of money is worth today. The formula is: Present Value = Future Value/$(1 + \text{interest rate})^n$, where n represents the time periods.

preventive action   An action to prevent a mistake from entering the program.

procurement management plan   Defines the program's procurement management process: the procurement process, bidder selection, and vendor management.

Professional Development Unit (PDU)   One hour of PMI-approved continuing education, knowledge base contribution, or program management volunteer work typically equates to one PDU. Always check with PMI's policies on how many PDUs volunteer activities, article creation, and PMI-chapter events actually create. Each PgMP is required to earn 60 PDUs per three-year certification cycle.

program   A program is a collection of projects managed in a controlled, balanced effort to realize benefits not available by managing each project independently. Programs are composed of projects that work in tandem to create a consolidated deliverable that aligns with the strategic vision of the performing organization.

program archives   All of the documentation on the program, contracts, communications, supporting detail, and the program's projects are archived and become part of organizational process assets.

program benefits identification   A pre-program setup phase activity that identifies the expected benefits the program is to create for the performing organization.

program benefits statement This document defines all of the good that will come out of the program. It defines the benefits the organization can expect as a result of completing the program and helps the program manager adhere to the benefits management theme of the program.

program business case Defines how the program may fit into the organization's strategic plan, and it defines the need for the program to be initiated and to exist in the organization.

program change requests Documented requests to change the program scope.

program charter Identifies the program manager and grants the program manager the authority to manage all aspects of the program.

program communications management The program management knowledge area responsible for communications planning, information distribution, communications control, and performance reporting.

program communications management plan Defines the communication demands and expectations for the program stakeholders.

program contract administration A monitoring and controlling process to ensure that the buyers and sellers are both following the terms of the program contracts.

program cost management The program management knowledge area that facilitates the cost estimating and budget for the program and provides for cost control.

program customer The recipient of the program deliverables.

program director The executive owner of the program; this is the person to whom the program manager reports.

program governance Program governance is the enforcement of the rules and procedures of an organization to ensure that they are followed for the program's planning, executing, monitoring and controlling, and closing a program phases. It the assurance that all program procedures are followed as planned and expected by the organization, the project managers, and you, the program manager.

program governance board A group that ensures that the program goals are being achieved, risks are being anticipated and planned for, and the board provides support for program issue resolution.

program human resource management The program management knowledge area that allows the program team to be initiated and acquired and the human resources for the program to be planned. This is also the knowledge area that hosts team development.

program initiating process group   The first of five process groups, which authorizes the program, authorizes the component projects, and initiates the program management team.

program integration management   The program management knowledge area that provides processes for initiating the program, developing the program plan, executing the plans, providing program control, and closing the program and its components.

program interface   An entity or person that the program has to interact with.

program life cycle   The series of phases within a program used to govern the program, manage the program benefits, coordinate the component projects, and collectively manage risks and issues within the program.

program management office (PMO)   The centralized organization that defines and manages the program governance procedures, establishes program processes, and provides program templates and forms.

program management plan   Documents and communicates how the program will create the benefits, describes the actions to realize the benefits, and serves as the baseline for tracking benefits realization.

program management processes   The processes that compose the program management activities to complete the program life cycle.

Program Management Professional (PgMP)   A PMI-certified program manager who has exhibited program management experience, attained sufficient education, passed a multiple-choice examination, earned a Multi-Rater Assessment, and is in good standing with PMI.

program management review panel   A collection of PMI-sponsored program managers that will review program management applicants to determine if an applicant should be approved, audited, or declined access to the certification process.

program manager   The person that is responsible for the management of a program.

program office   Supports the program by handling the administrative functions of the program at one central locale.

program packages   The smallest item in the program work breakdown structure.

program preferred vendor list   A list of prescreened and qualified vendors from which a program manager is allowed to procure program resources.

program procurement management   The program management knowledge area that facilitates the planning of purchasing, contracting, working with sellers, performing contract administration, and control closure.

program quality management   The program management knowledge area that hosts the quality planning–, quality assurance–, and quality control–related processes.

program resource   A human resource, equipment, materials, or facilities that contribute to the program work.

program risk management   The knowledge area responsible for risk management planning and analysis while also supporting risk monitoring and control.

program scope management   The program management knowledge area that is responsible for defining the program scope, creating the program work breakdown structure (PWBS), and controlling the program scope.

program setup phase   The program is chartered, and the program manager is officially assigned.

program sponsor   The champion of the program; this can be an individual, customer, or line of business within the performing organization. The sponsor, whoever it may be for a program, is responsible for providing the resources to deliver the expected benefits of the program.

program scope statement   The program scope defines all of the required work—and only the required work—in order to satisfy the program's objectives; serves as the baseline for all future program decisions.

program team directory   A document that defines all of the contact information, roles, and responsibilities for all of the program team members.

program team members   Assist the program manager to get the program work done by helping her to communicate with stakeholders, in addition to executing and completing program processes.

program termination   The program is canceled due to poor performance, changes in technology, organizational demands, cash flow, marketplace considerations, or any number of reasons.

program termination requests   If a program is not performing well or there are conditions outside of the program's control, such as a law or a regulation, the program may be terminated.

PART IV

program time management The program management knowledge area responsible for creating and controlling the program schedule.

program work breakdown structure (PWBS) A hierarchical decomposition of the program scope. It decomposes the program scope statement into the individual deliverables, called program packages, the program promises to deliver.

project business case A document that defines how the component project will support the program scope.

project calendar Defines when the project work is expected to take place.

project charter The document that authorizes the project to exist within the program. This document also identifies the project manager and his level of authority in the project. The project charter is signed by the project sponsor.

project closure Project activities that close out the project to support the goals of the program.

project communications management This knowledge area creates the communications management plan, oversees information distribution, and ensures that project performance is reported; this is where the stakeholder management process resides.

project cost management This knowledge area is concerned with estimating the project costs, budgeting the project costs, and controlling the project expenses.

project human resource management This knowledge area creates the staffing management plan, which defines how the team will be acquired and developed and what approaches the project manager will take to manage the project team.

project integration management This knowledge area coordinates how all the process groups and project knowledge areas work with one another.

project life cycle The unique project phases that compose a project.

Project Management Institute (PMI) A global advocate for the profession of project management. PMI is the certifying body for the Certified Associate in Project Management (CAPM), Project Management Professional (PMP), and Program Management Professional (PgMP) certifications. The not-for-profit organization was founded in 1969 and is based in Newton Square, Pennsylvania.

project management life cycle The universal project phases of initiating, planning, executing, monitoring and controlling, and closing.

Project Management Professional (PMP) A project manager who has exhibited educational and project management experience and has passed a 200-question project management assessment exam.

project managers   The managers of the projects that make up the program.

project procurement management   This knowledge area creates the procurement management plan to define what needs to be procured, how sellers will be selected, how the project manager will perform contract administration, and how the contracts will be closed.

project quality management   There are three quality processes in this knowledge area: quality planning, quality assurance, and quality control.

project risk management   This knowledge area creates the risk management plan and oversees risk identification, qualitative and quantitative analysis, risk response planning, and the ongoing efforts of risk monitoring and control.

project scope management   This knowledge area defines how the project scope will be planned, the WBS created, and the scope work verified; it establishes overall control for the project scope.

project team members   These are the people on the program's project teams, the experts who do the project work.

project time management   This knowledge area begins with activity definition, schedule estimates, and scheduling, and then moves onto controlling the project schedule.

Prometric Testing Center   A professionally monitored and proctored examination facility where PMI, and other organizations, require their certification candidates to take their assessment examinations.

pure risks   These risks events have only a negative effect on the program.

quality   The conformance to requirements and a fitness for use.

quality assurance (QA)   A management-driven process to prevent mistakes from entering the program's products, deliverables, and benefits.

quality control (QC)   An inspection-driven process to confirm that quality exists within the program's deliverables and to keep mistakes out of the customer's hands.

quality management plan   Defines how the quality objectives will be met within the project, including the adherence to quality assurance (QA) programs, quality control at the project level, and the expected reactions when quality inspections are less successful than expected.

RACI chart   A matrix using the actions of Responsible, Accountable, Consult, and Inform to designate the action required by the role.

receiver   The receiver of a message in the communication model.

request for information (RFI)   You need more information about a vendor's services or products, so you ask for more information. This can be anything from a brochure or a catalog to a white paper or references about the seller.

request for proposal (RFP)   This document asks the vendor to create a proposal for your program. An RFP takes your basic vision and allows the vendor to run with it, designing a solution with a lot of features and solutions you may not have thought of. The creation of a web site is a good example. RFPs are a lot of work for vendors.

request for quote (RFQ)   You want a price for whatever the seller can provide. You don't need any dream solutions or ideas—just tell me how much. For example, I need a quote for three tons of pea gravel.

resource calendar   Shows the availability of program resources.

resource control   A monitoring and controlling process to control the utilization of all program resources, including human resources, materials, facilities, and equipment.

resource histogram   A bar chart that visualizes the utilization of program resources.

resource leveling   The compression of the amount of time a resource may be utilized during a given time period; often extends the program schedule.

resource management plan   Defines how resources will be obtained, managed, and allocated throughout the program. This plan also defines how the resources will be tracked across the program's projects to ensure that resources are not over-allocated and are being used as efficiently as possible.

resource planning   This iterative planning process defines all of the people, materials, equipment, facilities, and other program resources needed to satisfy the program scope. Resource planning also defines how the identified resources can best be used across the program for maximum return on program investment.

resource reallocation   The reassignment of project resources once a project has been closed.

resources   The people, materials, facilities, and equipment the program requires to be successful.

responsibility assignment matrix   A generic matrix that lists the individuals that will be working on the program and all of the responsibilities that have to be undertaken.

risk   An uncertain event or condition that may have a positive or negative effect on the program.

risk monitoring and control   A monitoring and controlling process to ensure that new risks are being identified, existing risks are being monitored, and the planned responses for risk events are monitored for their effectiveness.

risk owner   The program team member closest to the risk event with the authority to respond to the risk event as planned.

risk register   The collection and documentation for risks within the program, the risk characteristics, status, probability, and impact, along with potential risk responses.

risk response plan   Addresses the responses to the identified risk events. The risk response plan defines how the risk owner should react if the risk event passes the risk threshold and the event comes into play.

role and responsibility chart   A matrix to demonstrate which role is responsible for what.

rough order of magnitude   This project cost estimate approach is very broad and unreliable. It's usually created with the preliminary project scope statement and has a range of variance of –25% to +75% for the project completion.

schedule control   A monitoring and controlling process to manage and react to changes of the program schedule.

schedule management plan   Defines, well, the schedule. It also defines how changes to the schedule may be allowed, fleshed into the program, and then executed.

scope control   A monitoring and controlling process to control, approve, and decline changes to the program scope.

scope creep   Small undocumented changes added to the project scope; this is also known as project poison.

scope management plan   Defines the program scope and how the program scope will be controlled. The plan defines the program management scope change control system and the process program change requests must follow to be incorporated into the program plan.

PART IV

sender   The person or entity sending the communication.

share   A positive risk response for two or more entities to realize the benefits of a risk they couldn't seize individually.

staffing management plan   Defines the needed resources for the program and how the program will obtain those resources. This program plan also defines how the staff may be brought into and released from the program.

staffing pool description   Depicts the talent, competencies, interest, availability, and cost of the resources that may be able to participate on the program management team.

stakeholder analysis chart   This chart can capture each stakeholder and their position and influence on decisions and outcomes of the project.

stakeholder management   A stakeholder is any person, group, or entity that may be affected positively or negatively by the outcome of the program. Technically this may include passive stakeholders that are interested in your program but aren't directly affected by its outcome. Stakeholder management is the balance of stakeholder identification, communication, leadership, trade-offs, competing objectives, and prioritization of needs and demands.

stakeholder management plan   A plan the defines how the program manager will manage the program stakeholders through communications, involvement, marketing of the program, and strategies to address perceived stakeholder threats and concerns regarding the program.

statement of work (SOW)   Defines all of the details of the program and is sent to the prospective vendors from the client. The SOW allows the vendors to understand the request of the client and to create a quote, bid, or proposal based on the SOW.

team development   Developing the program team so that their competency levels are in alignment with the responsibilities they have been tasked with in the program.

The Standard for Program Management   A PMI publication that defines the generally accepted practices of project management.

Time and Materials   A contract that defines how the vendor will bill the client for the time spent on the program and for the materials; must have a not-to-exceed clause.

transference   This risk response is usually based on a contractual relationship with a vendor.

transition planning   This process (thankfully) aims to define how the program's deliverables will be transferred from the program ownership to the organizational operations.

trigger   A warning sign or condition that a risk event is pending.

utility   A way in which something is useful. It allows program managers to quantify the usefulness of different attributes of a program and its projects.

INDEX